THE RISE OF ROMANTICISM

BRIAN HEPWORTH

The Rise of Romanticism
~ essential texts ~

Carcanet · Manchester

Copyright © Brian Hepworth 1978

SBN 85635 112 1

All Rights Reserved

First published in 1978 by
Carcanet New Press Limited
330 Corn Exchange Buildings
Manchester M4 3BG

The Publisher acknowledges the financial assistance
of the Arts Council of Great Britain.

Printed in Great Britain by
Billings, Guildford

CONTENTS

PREFACE

This collection is the outcome of a conviction born of some twenty years of reading and teaching that the eighteenth century and Romanticism contain a more convincing continuity than contrast and that the connection between the rise of 'creative imagination' and the major concerns of English philosophy in its greatest period is more intimate than has been recognized, at least since the days of R. G. Collingwood.

I wish to thank especially my post-graduate students for their generous interest in 'the rise of Romanticism' during the past decade and the helpers who have suffered the mechanics of compilation, especially Shirley Wiley and Brenda Rosen who did the typing.

Brian Hepworth
Toronto, June 30, 1976

INTRODUCTION

The Disappearance of the Unseen

Roots of Romanticism may be located in the work of the not always major or even highly-regarded enquirers of The Royal Society in the late seventeenth and early eighteenth centuries. Partial founder of the Society and Cromwell's brother-in-law, John Wilkins, was the author of the *Discovery of a World in the Moon* and a postscript on means of getting there. In 1668 he published his *Essay Towards a Real Character and a Philosophical Language*. John Wallis, who broke the Royalist code at Carisbrooke Castle, wrote the *Arithmetica infinitorum* (1655), which prompted Newton, it is said, to the binomial theorem, and as an appendage to his *Grammatica linguae Anglicanae* (1653) the *De loquela*, an enquiry into the physical roots of English sounds which was used in treating deaf mutes. Sufficient glory might have accrued to George Hickes through his niece, who edited the *Anglo-Saxon Homily on the Nativity* in 1709, and produced in 1715 her *Rudiments of Grammar for the English-Saxon Tongue* but Elizabeth Elstob followed a family tradition. Hickes's own Anglo-Saxon and Moeso-Gothic grammar had appeared in 1689, and his *Linguarum veterum septentrionalium thesaurus* or *Thesaurus of the Ancient Northern Languages* between 1703 and 1705. The journals of Thomas Hearne, the under-librarian at the Bodleian Library until 1716, are more amusing but less constructive than his work as antiquarian and editor of texts such as *The Battle of Maldon* without which it is doubtful that the poetry of for example Thomas Warton the Elder would have been written. Among the Society's correspondents was Edward Pococke, chaplain to the 'Turkey Merchants' at Aleppo, first Professor of Arabic at Oxford, and substantial donor of the Bodleian's original Arabic collection. His *Specimen historiae Arabum* (1649) was one of the first two books set from the University press's Arabic fount. His emendation, perhaps after sleepless nights in Aleppo, of 'wailing like the dragons' (Micah, 1:8) to 'howling like the jackals' nicely pinpoints the effect on mythology of on-the-spot enquiry. The source of the contemporaneity science gave to the Old Testament, a novelty extensively effective in the poetry of Young, Smart and Blake, may be seen also in the work of Dr Richard Mead (1673-1754), largest collector of curiosities of the era. At one time Vice-President of the Royal Society, he diagnosed successfully the complaints not only of Pope and Young, but in his *Medica sacra* (1749) those of Hezekiah, Jehoram, Saul, Nebuchadnezzar and Job as, respectively, an abscess, dysentery, melancholia, hypochondria and elephantiasis.

Pope and Swift were accurate in prophesying Augustan doom. Not until the *Poetical Sketches* of Blake in the second half of the century did Northern and oriental verse rival in quality the classical imitation of Pope but the spring from which this shift derived was flowing before the turn of the century. Indeed, the major tributaries which converged in Romanticism, the notion of a 'real' language of men, the focus on the barbaric Goths, on Anglo-Saxon and the Middle Ages, the curious reliance which Swift found threatening, on the physics of motion, which even-handedly sought solutions to cosmic travel and the mechanics of sound, the scrutiny through the naturalists' glass of the primitive orient in the Old Testament, the apprehension of infinity by the mind of man unaided by religion, may all be discerned.

More convincing than the subject matter, however, is the attitude of the *virtuosi*. It was not atypical for one man to take on a treatise in mathematics, a study of the musculature of speech and an historical grammar of the vernacular. One senses here the *hubris* of Swift's 'Moderns' who took seriously to heart the Baconian injunction that the whole of Nature be comprehended anew. Something faintly ridiculous adheres to Romanticism at its height. In its earliest stirrings this quality was less faint. Like Cromwell, under whom the curriculums of the two universities were significantly 'modernized' and whose spirit informs the succeeding era, the *virtuoso* found no subject too awful for his solitary authority. The indispensable element in European classicism had been an awareness of context. The paintings of Canaletto, Guardi, or Claude Lorraine, the Alexander Pope of painters, remind us that men knew a single particular in art or life by means of other works, other minds, other moments in the same work or life, other places, other eras, and, not least, other worlds. The Romantic was to voyage absorbed by the infinite dimensions of a single moment, as Wordsworth wrote of Newton, 'through strange seas of thought, alone'.

In the late seventeenth and early eighteenth centuries the New Philosophy of the scientific revolution effected a change in men's sense of reality so great that it might lay claim as the most significant cultural event in the history of the West. In Milton and Dryden, to take two major writers of the late seventeenth century, and less intensely but crucially in Swift and Pope, assumptions persisted fundamentally unchanged since the Middle Ages. The artist instructed the reader, if pleasurably, in the moral structure of the cosmos, as Johnson, sole classical survivor into the mid-century, said of Shakespeare, holding up a mirror to Nature. The 'Neo-classical' thinker assumed the reality of an external cosmos as easily as the most thoughtless uninstructed reader today. He assumed also the con-comitant of the finite outlook, that the dimensions apparently separating objects external to himself — in time and space — coincided with the groundplan of moral value in the design of Providence. One need ponder the abstractions only of, for example, *The Vanity of Human Wishes*, to conclude that for Johnson reality was a control over concepts of space. Indeed, we might hazard, morality was space. Men lived in a fallen world of extension and duration, and the supernatural was *supra* and im-measurable, the opposite, if such might be imaged, of all they could know here below. The most perfect art of this kind, for example Pope's

Pastorals, was a complex structure of temporal-spatial images which only in its perfection suggests eternity. Himself objectively aware of time, man lived, as it were, like the mirror, in opposition to Nature rather than within her unthinking processes. Clearly, the intelligence within the *Pastorals* is the experiencer of process as day succeeds to day, season to season, and hour to hour, but in a pyramidic perspective, since he is also the external observer of his own processes, comparing, contrasting, bearing always in view the dimension of other emotions and other moments while immersed in one. His own reality thus is also an object localized in a context of time and space. He is self-divided, the quintessence if not of classical, certainly of New-classical man. Blake's self-dividing Urizen (see pp. 298-305) images every unhappy facet of this perceptive position. The painters alluded to above show how precisely the simile of seeing fitted this attitude to spirit; but the simile of seeing, a simile which is as old as classical epic, is as essential in the world of Pope and Johnson. With the coming of Romanticism, and beginning with the undermining influence of the lens, both in microscope and telescope, seeing as the iconography of mental processes gave way to hearing, touching and feeling, or simply apprehending mass as it were through a synaesthesia of all the senses just as the simile gave way to the metaphor, reason to imagination, and the primacy of the image of the sun to that of the moon.

Above all, the English classical writers of whom we speak were mediaeval most in their assumption of hierarchy, and it is in the total dissolution of the scale of superiority that the most fundamental change occurred in the eighteenth century. In Pope and Johnson as in Chaucer, and, with a different reason, in many unsophisticated people today, the spatial sense extended not only laterally but vertically. Images associated with the sun, illumination, goldenness, sequence, since after all, the sun is the great chronometer in the sky, seemed 'good' while pain, blackness, ugliness, and irrationality were associated with the opposite pole, deep below the earth, perhaps, and taken to be 'bad'. In Swift's *A Tale of a Tub* reason is elevated by the central core of images of small animals, excrement, reduction, while Pope's *Dunciad* opposes to a similar excremental vision the epic achievement of classicism seen as sunlit illumination. The end of the seventeenth century saw a significant disappearance of the unseen. Once the uppermost rung in the ladder of ascension began to disappear, and this assumption of opposing *locae* was challenged, as it was in the satirists' lifetime for example by Shaftesbury (see pp. 80-88), form, judgment, and reason flew out of the literary window and formlessness, feeling, and the inability to differentiate between pleasure and pain, good and evil, the sublime and the terrifying, entered. The most significant title in the entire eighteenth − and early nineteenth − century, *The Marriage of Heaven and Hell*, marks the completion in Blake (see pp. 292-298) of a movement which may be traced, in the following pages, from the last years of the seventeenth century.

The Abolition of Space

With John Locke the lens of Galileo turned inwards and the great century of English epistemology, which was simultaneous with the rise of Romanticism, began. It is worth pausing to consider the boldness, characteristic of the era, of setting out to describe not the objects but the means of knowledge. This subjectivism was to become of the very essence of Romanticism, yet the contribution of Locke to the crucial disappearance of the unseen must be attributed more to the example he set for Berkeley, Hume and Hartley (see pp. 62, 114 and 219) his fellow epistemologists, than to his unaided precept. Taking the Coleridgean description of creative imagination as our touchstone of Romanticism (see pp. 339, 350), we discover a number of concepts in Locke to be at least contiguous. Locke's *Essay Concerning Human Understanding* denies innate ideas and outlines the means of knowing mechanically as if all knowledge might be identified with the capacity to know. However, it is possible to argue for Locke an innate power or creativity in the human brain which prepares the mind's ground for ideas, and through something akin to a motion provides the means by which single, simple ideas form into complex notions. Hartleyan associationism is not entirely without precedent half a century earlier. Hence, there seems to be some area of greyness or uncertainty between the idea or sensation in the mind and the reality of the object which, uncritically, we might have said 'caused' it, a doubt which suggests the weakening of the certainty of externality, in Berkeley's terms 'outness', and which puts one in mind of the achievement of Gray's *Elegy*. Further, we might point to the *Essay*'s delicacy with the *supra*-natural. Locke does not say that angels do not exist, but he does say (*Essay* II, xxiii, 35) that our image of God is an abstraction constructed from simple ideas of sensation. The characteristic Romantic dismantling of the image of hierarchy is, thus, central in this most crucial of eighteenth-century philosophers.

There are, however, several obstacles to Locke's claim to be the first Romantic philosopher. General ideas, we note, rank other ideas in formations we might see as hieratic blocks of knowledge, in which, as in Johnson, and Pope, value and mental space are identical. For Locke, further, the association of ideas, in spite of the distant anticipation of Hartley, is causal rather than timeless and creative. Moreover, the sense of the 'progress' of the mind in building its knowledge is indispensable in Locke. We move from simple ideas in our earliest infancy to more complex, general constructions later. Time, incestuous cousin to space, however much allied to motion, appears to be a fundamental binding force in the Lockian edifice, and the rise of Romanticism cannot be divorced from the undermining of the traditional importance of time in Western thought.

Comprehensive Romantic perception begins with George Berkeley (see pp. 62-79). Students of Romanticism should seldom overlook the opportunity to recall that whilst Coleridge named one son 'Hartley', the other he called 'Berkeley'. In Berkeley's theories of perception it is difficult to disengage one indispensable facet, but if pressed, one might securely conclude that the achievement most crucial for literary history was the abolition of the objective certainty of space or 'outness' In the history of ideas several thinkers seem to hover frequently around the same change, expressing as it were, an insight of the psyche of the age. Some doubt might be discovered in Locke about the absoluteness of externality. In geologizing Eden Thomas Burnet (see pp. 20-36) weakened the roots of allegory, suggesting the complete presence of truth in the evidence of the senses before us. Berkeley, however, was a subtle genius any one of whose ideas penetrates to a core and begins a chain reaction. A close second is the doubt which his philosophy casts on the importance of past-ness or memory in knowledge. The mind appears in Berkeley to deal always with a kind of timeless creativity, which it is difficult to divorce entirely from the construction of its own futurity, a notion which in various guises, such as the primacy of prophecy throughout the Romantic era and the rise of the notion of 'creative' autonomous imagination, sits at the very heart of the matrix of Romantic theories.

Berkeley's *A New Theory of Vision* (1709) a title which in itself images doubt about the entire epic and classical tradition in which seeing (over a perspective of time and space) was the fundamental simile for spiritual progress, noted that men judge the size of objects 'external' to themselves and hence their distance, from what we might assume to be an instan-taneous tension in the fibre of the eye (see pp. 64-69). Since internal bodily sensation was the source of our ideas of distance, true externality we had to deduce was, at best doubtful. A whole generation of poets in the mid-eighteenth century were to agree that 'feeling' rather than reason was the source of true knowledge about the world, and were, similarly to dwell on the subjectivity of space, and time. It is, incidentally we note, interesting that Burke's 'Sublime' rests also on a basis of the tensions of bodily fibres (see pp. 195-206). The dubiousness of space continued close to the centre of Berkeley's concerns. In *De Motu* or *Concerning Motion* a work which attacked the related notion that motion was inherent in bodies, he wrote,

> Many are far from considering absolute space as a non-entity, that they think it the only thing, except God, which cannot be annihilated; and maintain that it necessarily exists by its own nature, and is eternal and uncreated, and consequently participates in the divine attributes... let us diligently inquire whether we can form any idea of that pure, real, absolute space, which would continue to exist after the an-nihilation of all body. Examining such an idea accurately, I find it to be the most perfect idea of nothing, if it can be called an idea.   (54)

In *Siris*, his treatise on tar-water, a topic which characteristically gives rise to creative association and broader concerns, he noted 'concerning absolute space, that phantom of the mechanic geometrical philosophers, it may suffice to observe, that it is neither perceived by any sense, nor proved by any reason.' (271)

It is to be observed that the concept of 'the Sublime' which finds its true eighteenth-century expression in Burnet, Addison, and Burke, is an experience of as it were, self-induced, non-rational and subjective spatial elevation. It is, as has been observed, not far from Berkeley on space, to the twin concepts central to Romanticism of 'creative imagination' and of the poet as prophet. If the human perception was not, as had been assumed, 'of' an external, hieratic structure, and time and space, the twin scaffolds of that structure were mere single ideas in the creating mind, then all objects of perception might be imagined to press as it were, regardless of time as of space, continually on the gates of consciousness waiting to be created into art. Instead of being the passive observer or reflector, man might be a godlike and indispensable energy in a continuing, ongoing Creation, participation in which could be construed (as Ezekiel observed to Blake, see p. 296) as true knowledge. The prevalence of apparently Berkeleyan concepts in literature is early and continuous. In Shaftesbury's *Characteristics* (see pp. 81-88) the mind of the voyager, already an archetypal Romantic image, released from the bonds of time and space wanders, in a simulacrum of divinity, without judgment, everywhere throughout the cosmos. The primitive incoherence of Young, which charmed readers for more than a century, the poetic equivalent of the sentimental novel, already seems characteristically to avoid sequence as a species of cognition, in his *Last Day* (1713) where 'Time, and Place/Matter and Form, Fortune, Life and Grace, / Wait humbly at the footstool of their God', which equally without space seems remarkably similar to the footstool of Queen Anne. The nearness of even the furthest concepts is as central to the art of Young as it is distant from Pope. The contrast between the two major theodicies of the eighteenth century, Pope's *Essay on Man* (1734) and Young's *Night Thoughts* (1742–45) is that between the pre-Berkeleyan and post-Berkeleyan *mode*. Like his *Elegy*, Gray's *Progress of Poesy* moves fundamentally around the dismantling of spatial certainties, as does Collins's *Ode on the Poetical Character* (see pp. 189-194 and 186-188) while for Blake 'the Sea of Time and Space' is the constant if creative opposition to Imagination. Like Berkeley, Hume and Hartley are centrally concerned with the nature of spatial reality, while the major poems of the recognized great Romantics, *The Ancient Mariner*, for example or *The Excursion*, create ambiguous spatial images, in which the creative imagination first travels around the world or across the Lake District and then moves to an infinite awareness of the relativity of its experience. Keats's reminder to his brother (see p. 81) that there is no time and space, fittingly sent from the Lake District, underlines the centrality of century-old theories of perception in his own great poetry.

The Shapes of Time

'Choose a firm cloud before it fall, and in it / Catch, ere she change, the

Cynthia of this minute', Pope writes in the climax to his portrait of
'Arcadia's Countess' in *Epistle II* (lines 19–20). The comparison of an
insecure woman and the moon could not have a more prestigious lineage.
In the sixth book of the *Aeneid* the hero is accosted in the forests of the
Underworld by his Carthaginian *inamorata* floating, as it were, from the
shelter of tree trunk to tree trunk, the suicide's wound on her bosom, in
Dryden's lines

> Obscure in shades, and with a doubtful view,
> (Doubtful as he who sees through dusky night,
> Or thinks he sees the moon's uncertain light;)   (*Aeneis*, vi. 613–15)

These passages point, of course, to the use of the image of seeing referred
to above. A number of other assumptions shared by the first-century
epic writer and the eighteenth-century satirist include a parallel between
passion and the fate of cities, the connotations of 'lunar', the disapproval
of change, the necessity of rationality even in love, the notion of the
artist as arbiter. An exhaustive questioning about Pope's verse at this
point in his poem, however, suggests that there is something more at
work. One critic has called Pope's poetry 'the poetry of allusion'. We
might be forgiven for concluding that this phrase suggests poetry that
alludes, but it means something more. It points to a unique kind of
poetry which works almost exclusively *by alluding*. Like the spider
which launches threads unanchored into the air and edges along them,
the Augustan poet structures an edifice of pastness 'back' as it were to
Dido. The lunatic short span of the Countess indeed is judged by light
of the reach of the poet just as Dido's failure to create Carthage is
revealed completely by comparison with Virgil's successful epic. Pope
suggests a poet two thousand miles away in space and seventeen hundred
years in time. Correspondingly his own images are impressed with the
context of these measures of extension and duration. We should, of
course, be wary of accepting Pope's view of Virgil as a poet of reason.
He was able to serve equally well the next generation of poets as a model
of sentiment. As with Homer, Pope created the author of the *Aeneid* in his
own image.

The instance goes far to suggest the subtleties of 'imitation' in which,
as for example in Lowell's version of *Ou sont les neiges d'antan?*, one feels
that, in spite of the distancing image of time, at heart, the picture of
reality of Villon's Middle Ages and Lowell's twentieth century at any
two given points is significantly the same. This cognitive assumption, and
it is a bold one, is at the heart of Pope's '*Neo*-classicism'. Like the main
street of Pompeii and that of the tourist's home town juxtaposed, the
view to be found in the ancient scene, stratum for significant stratum,
seems to duplicate that of the modern view. The attitude is, of course,
as highly creative as it is without foundation in reality. No one knows, as
Fellini's *Satyricon* has recently demonstrated, what the state of mind at
any moment was in Rome. We may not even have the terms available to
help us to such knowledge. Pope creates the past to which he alludes even

as he alludes to it, imposing a structure of generality as he goes, on poets who might well be discovered, as Blackwell and his successors (see pp. 107-113) discovered of Homer, to be the product only of their time and country. We might well conclude, that Pope's major achievement was the moulding of time.

The lens persuaded men to another view. We might conclude finally as apparently Swift did that the enormous change in the imaging of time which divides English classicism from Romanticism should be traced to Copernicus and Galileo. Whatever the resting place of that thought, it is to the science of the seventeenth and early eighteenth century that Romanticism may be traced, for science and the lens made men keenly aware of the detail without context. Happily in his *Essay on Pope's Odyssey* in which he invented a term for many of the major poems of the next century (see pp. 100-106) Joseph Spence observed that in poetry and history where there are no particulars there exists a falsehood (see p. 104). Without Spence it is doubtful that Warton's *Essay on Pope* would have had the shape it now has (see pp. 168-182), and it is in Warton's preference for Thomson's *Nature* over Pope's that we may see the radical preference for the unique moment out of time which is at the root of the mid-eighteenth-century revolution in taste (see pp. 178-81). In passing, it is useful and entertaining to observe that the more men collected its materials, for example in the recently founded British Museum, the less the past remained neatly in sequential corridors. For writers and *dilettanti* alike, as the philosophers and enthusiasts of the Gothic witnessed, time became but another sensation or *frisson* in the contemporary mind. For Blake who could find infinity (as indeed could Hume) in a grain of sand, to generalize was to be an idiot. In Blake 'minute particulars' like the 'spots of time' in Wordsworth's *Prelude* are gateways to infinity not beads on a finite thread assumed to be, in the future as in the past, 'ever' the same. Young told his readers to *be* Homer, primitive originals in their own right (see pp. 144-148). Lowth, who prized his ancient hand-mirror from recently excavated Herculaneum, told his listeners to practise what Keats would call 'negative capability', thinking, feeling, imaging exactly as had the Ancient Hebrews. Significantly it was to comparative astronomy that he turned for his example (see p. 153). His students should continually change their *locale*, clearly in the process weakening their sense of who and where they were. The relativity of the reader's identity is clearly spelled out in the new 'primitive' poetry as is the subjectivity of the experience of time.

It was on a basis of feeling that the past became a malleable entity whose shape changed during the course of a poem. It is interesting to observe in this regard that frequently, the most successful practitioners of the new poetry, for example Collins, Smart, Blake, Wordsworth and Coleridge, had experienced personal instability. We might observe too, with psychological hindsight, that the majority of them were interested both in the supposed first ages of man at large *and* in the ever-present reality of childhood experience. The *angst* derived from the displacement of time – and place – within the poetry of the mid-eighteenth century and the related conviction of insecurity and motion in the *persona* of poet *and* reader during the process of the poem are the great achievements of the so-called 'pre-Romantics' and join them too firmly to their 'Romantic' successors for any severance on grounds of 'feeling' and 'imagination'. The important aspect of Gray's *Elegy* as it is of Young's *Night Thoughts* is the creation of an image of prophecy, and it is this which unites these pioneering works firmly to *Frost at Midnight* and *Hyperion.* From being a perceived structure, apparently one with 'reason', stretching back to classical eras, time and space, in the form of individual memory the very means of knowing, became the clay in the hands of feeling. The poet and reader, unlike Pope, shared not a firm sense of who they were but an obscure, hence, 'sublime' conviction of a disruptive futurity.

The concept of the moment of perception which is so totally distinct from every other that it demands a new reach of the imagination in the invention of unknown terms is the central concern of Romanticism. Needless to say, no doubt, such a moment might be found in a soliloquy of Job, a mediaeval life for example of William of Wykeham, or on a canvas by Keats' friend Haydon. This new view of time appears to be related to the growth in the variety of the past mentioned above which paralleled the development of the creative imagination. How different the treatment of such moments is in classical and Romantic poetry may be seen, for example, in the contrast between Dryden's *Alexander's Feast* and Shelley's *Ozymandias.* We might trace the kind of history we still trust today, not mythic like Spenser's, but an ever-growing collection of ever-more minute particulars, to this era. It is no coincidence that the most successful poems of the creative imagination, *Kubla Khan, Christabel, The Ancient Mariner, The Excursion, The Eve of St Agnes*, are laden with images of the recently invented past. The new moment of perception of a particular in time isolated and surrealistically distorted against the backdrop of infinity was the most exciting experience art, perhaps like life, had to offer.

Time, Space, Simile and Metaphor
It has frequently been observed that as 1800 'approaches' and the London of Dryden and Pope is replaced as a *locale* of poetry by Wordsworth's Lake District, the metaphor becomes increasingly prominent. It is the theme of these pages that the shift from simile is fundamentally related to the change in the imaging of time and space to which we have referred, and especially to changes in the association of ideas, first from Locke to Berkeley, then to their associative successors, especially Hartley, Wordsworth and Coleridge.

One cannot carve the heads of the Caesars on a nutshell or sum up mediaeval and Renaissance aesthetics in a line. However, at various times men were concerned in poetry as in literature at large to give a picture of the divinely organized cosmos. During the eighteenth century, as perhaps not even in modern times, poets were concerned to present in their verse an image of the mind in the processes of cognition, even encompassing within a poem changes in response to new knowledge in the poem. A brief consideration of Thomson, Young, Gray, Collins, Blake, and the 'major' Romantics, indicates that the preoccupation of all of these writers was the nature of the imaging of time in the understanding. The permanent achievement of the age's aesthetics, for example 'the serpentine line' (see pp. 280-287) was related to the perceived ambiguity of time in process, the ambivalence of simultaneous stasis and motion. A brief glance through the major works of Locke, Berkeley, Hume and Hartley, indicates also that this is precisely the concern of England's and Scotland's finest minds in the greatest era of British epistemology. At a different level of achievement one observes Ireland's Edmund Burke, no less essentially involved with time in aesthetics in his *Sublime and Beautiful* (see pp. 195-206). Perhaps even more fascinating than the parallel concerns of poet and philosopher, is the observation that from the beginning of the century the eighteenth-century philosopher's imaging of the mind's iconography of time led him immediately into areas of the greatest importance for literature of contrast and comparison. Indeed, the thinking of the age appears to hover around the insight that knowledge itself is a matter of simultaneous categorizing, and differentiation, or separation and synthesizing. In Book II, Chapter 15 of the *Essay Concerning Human Understanding* Locke writes, '*the mind, having got the idea of any length of duration, can double, multiply, and enlarge it.*' Having observed the passing of several segments of light and darkness which he learns to know as days and nights and later accumulates into weeks and months, like a prism projecting onto a screen, a child then may double his experience of segmentation into centuries and decades, millennia and aeons. Lockian man, like Blake's detested Urizen (or the less realized infant prisoner of Wordsworth's *Immortality Ode*), practises a fundamental folding or overlaying of one second on another, one day, centuries, and so forth. His concept of reality is of one unit of extension held next to a supposed 'similar' if longer measurement. Not only does this image of time condemn man to fallen, finite, existence, it is paralleled in imaginative literature by a modelling on a supposed reliable classical era whose aeons may be seen at this remove as extensions of individual memory, and in which the simile, especially in its Homeric or epic form, is a major technique. The 'Lockian' assumption about time, and of course space, lies close to the core of Pope's art, perhaps most apparently in the *Pastorals* where the shape of a day simultaneously overlays in the internal structure of the poems, the shapes of the year's seasons, of human lives from love to death, and extensive centuries imaged as stretching back (a major feat on a piece of paper measuring inches) to first Spenser, then Virgil and Theocritus.

The erection of structures seems close also to Locke's notion of space. In the same chapter of the *Essay* he observes 'the *mind* having got the idea of the length of any part of *expansion*, let it be a span or a pace or what length you will, can as has been said, repeat the idea and so, adding it to the former, enlarge its idea of length . . .'. Here, close to the core of reality of the early eighteenth century, is a clue to why our ancestors imaged the positions on the globe of other countries as they did, just as Locke's crystallization of time suggests their sense of where other centuries 'were'. Blake's ironic use of compass points, like his encapsulation of the spaces for instance across the Atlantic in *America, A Prophecy* (as with our Vietnam experience, the 'reason' for imaginative dissociation) answers Locke centrally. In the 'oriental' revolution which followed the first decades of the century, Jerusalem became England, pagodas rose at Kew, and tigers burnt bright in Lambeth. For Locke apparently the conviction uppermost in Hume's sense of 'necessary relation' (see pp. 118-121) that the mind makes time and space seem significant, but that it is, for all we are able to know, misleading, does not enter the question. This, says Locke, is an experimental description of how the mind works at its fundamental level, and, apart from the poetic effect of the complete embodiment of these processes in Locke's writing, we find little to suggest that time and space thus managed and extended, contrasted and compared, are not the acceptable basic tools, like simile in creative literature, of whatever truth there is. In Locke's account of the relations, or associations, of space as well as time, we may find the most explicit account of the negative half of the dialectic which is Blake, his 'Sea of Time and Space'. For Blake, of course, such imaging of time and space was an enormous delusion, turning man away from his proper infinite hence imaginative creation.

But even in Locke, who tantalizingly seems from the heart of his finiteness to move perilously close to central Romantic positions, we find a suggestion related to the very core of the dawning awareness of the inadequacy as poetry of memory-bound imaging. 'Duration . . . ' Locke writes again in Chapter 15 of Book II of the *Essay* 'is the idea we have of perishing distance'. It is difficult to imagine a more poetic and metaphorical suggestion. It is the dimming memory of our parents' house as we journeyed away from it and as perhaps it still fades in our middle-aged memory which gives us our notion of time's prolongation. In parenthesis, we might observe the interesting thought which frequently surfaces during the next hundred years (for example in Collins' *Ode to Evening*) that the 'objects' of perception are in their own motion as we perceive them with our changing faculties, and that human perception is best imaged as a movement pursuing a movement. The relative plasticity of time here, almost, but not quite as explicit as Coleridge's intermingling of time and space (see pp. 333-50) suggests that man structures time and space from similar basic common imaging material which is drawn from neither time nor space. We are here close to the modern notion that, as some sociologists emphasize, man is a creature whose function is to build structures of different kinds as it were out of instinct or airy nothings, an activity related to the distancing or ceremony of any society, for example the decorum of the servant or porter in an eighteenth-century town house. A momentary comparison of the equilibrium with which an eighteenth-century nabob sailed for months with his card table and port from Bristol to his Calcutta factory to the fantasy of a Mid-Western matron flying today in ten hours from Chicago to the Taj Mahal, suggests the weight of spatial and temporal considerations in any day and culture.

The preoccupation of the practising poet was the constant puzzle of the eighteenth-century philosopher. How, both wondered, given a single, simple sensation, 'idea' or image, does the mind link it effectively to the next one? To get this right, was clearly to write successful, moving poetry. For Locke, clearly, the association of ideas was related to the distinctions of judgment, or an activity very like that of\the simile. 'The *nature . . . of relation* consists in the referring or comparing two things one to another, from which comparison one or both comes to be denominated,' he writes in Chapter 25 of Book II. Among relations of ideas 'cause and effect', to which a whole chapter is devoted in the *Essay*, is high on the list. It is, of course, at this point that Berkeley especially (see pp. 77-79) parts company with his esteemed predecessor, and in this parting we may well discern a major distinction between the poetry of reason and that of emotion or feeling. Following close on cause and effect among 'other relations' listed, we find 'time' and 'place'. At the basis of association in Locke, however, we will always find a ground of temporality, just as in Berkeley and his successors, we will find a ground of the infinite. For Locke, unlike Berkeley, externality exists, and ideas have objective attributes from which arises association. In Chapter 33 of Book II, 'The Association of Ideas' Locke finds, revealingly, 'some of our ideas have a natural correspondence and connexion one with another; it is the office and excellency of our reason to trace these'. Nature, is, apparently, external to perception, finite, and with its own, irreducible characteristics, including relation. Tellingly, we find that even when Locke is at pains to explain aberrations or wrong associations, in a manner leading straight into Addison's discussion of 'the fairy way of writing' (see pp. 97-99), he assumes, apparently automatically, a temporal association. 'The ideas of goblins and sprites have really no more to do with darkness than light,' he writes (see pp. 45-46) 'yet let but a foolish maid inculcate these often on the mind of a child and raise them there together, possibly he shall never be able to separate them again so long as he lives, but darkness shall ever afterwards bring with it those frightful *ideas*, and they shall be so joined that he can no more bear the one than the other.' It is evident that what will be brought back most fundamentally when either of these ideas recalls the other, is a complete segment of associated time, two seconds together being the very ground of the mental association.* This

---

*Coleridge specifically denounces this associative principle in the *Biographia Literaria*. See pp. 344-349.

is the very epistemology of memory; and it is against this undeniable aspect of Locke — and Pope — that the coming century's revolution was waged, and finally consolidated by Coleridge.

One of the most frequently recurring images in eighteenth-century poetry is the personified abstraction. 'See Sin in state . . . ' writes Pope characteristically in *Epistle II*, and again, 'if Folly grows romantic . . . I must paint it.' The 'tribes of mind' circulate harmoniously on the day of creation in Collins's *Ode on the Poetical Character* whilst all of Blake's limitless characters, like Ezekiel's God and four 'zoas', might be seen as species of personifications. The major concern of poetry was, again, a major consideration of philosophy. Locke's 'system', so profoundly concerned with association, gives enormous importance to the creating of the abstraction. The method by which individual instances of warmth, pain, affection in childhood coalesce into the brain's creation of Passion, Hate, Love, 'abstracted' or 'removed from' the experience which gave them birth, was at the heart of Locke's notion of ranking and generalization, which might be construed as knowledge itself. If the poet could give back the picture of the mind itself in the act of such creation, then how unnerving and effective such art would be! The problem of abstraction in eighteenth-century poetry is mentioned frequently in the following pages. However, it is perhaps important here to point to the persuasive argument that abstractions for example in both Locke and Pope give an impression — as in Ezekiel for example they do not — of finiteness. Individual simple ideas or sensations move into larger 'abstracted' units through a movement which takes place 'over' a period of a child's developing. 'Abstraction' or 'taking from' could be only imaged as a spatial movement. Pope's abstractions like 'Sin' or 'Folly', the triumphs of *Epistle II*, clearly are abstracted *from* something. There has been as it were, a cause for their effect, a before and an after. In the reading of the poem, there is likely to be a peripheral assumption that there has been a significant and rational movement in patterns of imaging. It is precisely this sense of finite progress which seems to be at the basis of Berkeley's dislike of the notion of abstractions. After Berkeley, as for example in Addison (see pp. 90-91), they tend to be 'sublime' and infinite.

With the weakening of the trust in space and time and what we might call 'the spaces of time' during the eighteenth century some other sense of association arose. We observe here, of course, as well as elsewhere, that poets are not philosophers, and do not necessarily reproduce exactly the finest epistemological insights of their age. Nevertheless a new movement in the progress of ideas in the poetry of the period of 'feeling' paralleled a gradual change in assumptions about association. The heart of Berkeley's philosophy would appear to be the removal of the inevitability of temporal—or spatial—sequence from the iconography of thought. Two ideas might be imagined to exist not separated by some duration (or extension) but as occurring simultaneously in a mind, as it were attuned, as the theorists of 'the Sublime' insisted, to infinity. At the most subtle, musical level, in the development of English verse in the eighteenth century 'from classical to Romantic' lies the abandonment of a sense of comprehensive progress for a sense of cumulative action of the verse significantly contrary to the movement of reading *down* the page. The spatial-temporal revolution of Berkeley was paralleled by a similar activity in the theory of verse. For example, of endless significance in an appreciation of the mechanics of Romantic verse, is one of Robert Lowth's crucial awarenesses about the poetic technique of the Hebrews (the major 'oriental' writers for the eighteenth century). In his lectures on *The Sacred Poetry of the Hebrews* he insisted that the touchstone of the highest sublimity was the 'lowest' imagery. Having pointed in the celebrated chapter sixteen to the comparisons of God to 'the roaring of a lion, the clamour of rustic labourers, and the rage of wild beasts' (see pp. 159-160), he concluded his lecture, suitably titled 'The Sublimity of Sentiment',

> from ideas, which in themselves appear coarse, unsuitable, and totally unworthy of so great an object, the mind naturally recedes, and passes suddenly to the contemplation of the object itself, and of its inherent magnitude and importance.

Classicism, as is well known, had always pursued elevation. Johnson notoriously disliked *Macbeth*'s 'blanket of the dark' (see *Rambler*, No. 168) because of its vulgarity. Pope had obsessively accused the 'Moderns' of sinking in his *Peri Bathos*, the satirical counterpart of *Peri Hypsous* or 'On the Sublime'. It is clear that the injunction to court the 'lowest' images in order to achieve the 'highest' effect is the point at which we may see philosophy enter literature, for the phenomenon is no other than a spatial one, related to the century's abolition of hierarchy noted in our discussions of Shaftesbury, Blake, and others. Smart's praise of God is nowhere so evident as in his delineation of a favourite cat, Wordsworth's egotistical sublime was erected on a *substratum* of the ramblings of idiot boys and hedgerow philosophers, Byron's demonic *persona* is inextricably tied up with carriage and ferry timetables and the female attire of the Venetian *demi-monde*.

The eighteenth-century belief that the poet was a prophet was no mystical wish formation. The mind worked in freedom from time and space manufacturing an important kind of unique futurity as its everyday activity. Gray's *Bard* and *Elegy*, and *Progress of Poesy*, Collins's *Ode on the Poetical Character*, Young's *Night Thoughts* are all prophecies which base on emotion the imaging of futurity. The philosophers were in the process of arguing that the mind worked without fundamental recourse to verifiable time and space. Similarly, the great poets of 'the first ages', Ossian for Blair and Macpherson, the oriental prophets who visited Blake, Hurd's primitive Spenser, did not hold up, as Pope and Johnson demanded, a mirror to Nature. In the attempt not to mirror what was known, but to manufacture the unique, the prophet might well adopt, as the very metaphor of prophecy, comparisons similar to those which Lowth had identified. The secret was to destroy the temporal, spatial or temporal-spatial expectations of listeners or readers.

How this was done might be observed in one of Christopher Smart's best-known images. 'My cat Jeoffry' he writes in *Jubilate Agno* 'camels his back to bear the first notion of business' (*Christopher Smart*, ed. N. Callan, London, 1949, i. 314). The figure follows one of Lowth's — and Blair's — most explicit observations about the comparisons of imagination, as opposed to those of reason. Comparisons should be made between objects different in all but one characteristic. A chapter on English thought in the eighteenth century, which did not occur to Leslie Stephen, might be written on this comparison. Perhaps it is useful here, however, to merely touch on some points of interest. A cat, in the serpentine arching of its back, *is* amusingly similar to a camel floating its hump into air beneath the palm trees to continue its groaning way. Of course, Smart's genius lies partially in his manipulation of the kinetic distinction between the — as it were — motionless curve of the camel and the flowing undulation of Jeoffry. More central, however, is the temporal-spatial displacement of a comparison of a domestic London cat in 1760 and a camel, not easily observed before Regent's Park Zoo, and reminiscent of the *fauna* of the Bible. The camel to a mid-century reader was both two thousand miles away — in the Fertile Crescent — Arabia — and rather more than two thousand years away, in the images of Hebrew writers. Not only is the temporal scaffolding of the reader's reality displaced, so also is the sense of where the reader is. Without precedent, cat and camel hang in a memory-less, non-allusive void. As distinct from Pope's Virgilian allusion we note above, this poetry does not mirror Nature. The sense of what Berkeley termed 'outness' is therefore absent. The dissolving of the compartments of time and space carries with it the separation of emotions. In the metaphor there is an enjoyable sense, in which religious awe and amusement mix, of the poet's individual, divine, creativity, as if he were anew creating camel and cat within and only within his poem, by the act of imagination. Thus the *percipi* became the *esse* (see Berkeley's *The Principles of Human Knowledge*), the perceiving made the actual reality in the poetry of the mid-century. The common infinity of the two animals in the human perception is the major image. Perhaps more usefully than the lunar simile indicated above, the distinction between Smart and the classical simile might be suggested in the famous comparison of Dido's Carthage to a bee-hive (Dryden, *Aeneis*, i. 598-609) where the finite measurements of cells, streets and houses seem to complement each other and reinforce instead of disturb the reader's sense of where and who he is. Of course, Smart's transformation of the noun 'camel' to a verb, reinforces the celebratory image of eternal motion which lies close to the success of his poem.

Hugh Blair is to Northern original poetry what Lowth is to oriental. It is interesting to note that in his essay on Ossian (see p. 267) the Edinburgh Professor of Rhetoric selects a metaphor from Olaus Wormius which precisely illustrates the principle noted above. 'The whole ocean was one wound' works, of course, largely by the denial of spatial expectations and is, clearly, Gothic and 'sublime' to a breathtaking degree. Gray's realization of the effectiveness of such metaphors may be seen extensively used in *The Fatal Sisters* which has its source also in Scandinavian myth. Perhaps the most effective instance of these kinds of metaphors is Gray's comparison of the village dead in the local parish with the gems (of course subtly redolent of Ezekiel) of the deepest parts of the undiscovered ocean and the — oriental — flower blooming in the quasi-Biblical desert:

Full many a gem of purest ray serene,
The dark, unfathom'd caves of ocean bear.
Full many a flower is born to blush unseen,
And waste its sweetness on the desert air.   (*Elegy*, 53–6)

Sufficient is said in the following pages (see especially pp. 165, 183-185, 190, 289 and 352) about the central position of Ezekiel in the new poetry of the eighteenth century. It is clear that his image of the sky as 'a sapphire throne' (one of the most important images in the history of poetry) represents, as Gray notes in *The Progress of Poesy* (see p. 193), the bursting of the bounds of time and place. It is clear in Gray's adroit use of the image, in order to dissolve time and space within his *own* poem, and to join Ezekiel in a single-textured prophecy, that such images were at the heart of Gray's notion of poetry.

The importance of *Job* in thinking about primitivism during the eighteenth century was related to its place, in a five-thousand-year-old cosmos, as 'the most ancient poem in the world'. Archibald Mac-Leish is not the first to have seen the contemporary values of Job, and, if Richard Mead's diagnosis is correct, his bothersome elephantiasis. 'John Lizard's' account of *Job*, to which Blake's concept of the ancient poet seems peculiarly related, is a crucial landmark in the recognition of the sublime superiority of oriental over the greatest classical poets. We need not anticipate here the comments on the images most admired by 'John Lizard' (probably Edward Young) and again by Edmund Burke. At this point, perhaps it is necessary to point only to the surrealism inherent in 'Lizard's' remarkable comment that the poet of *Job* created his images as if they were 'in the eye of the Creator', itself a Daliesque concept. The temporal denial of such a notion is of course obvious, as is the connection between *Guardian* No. *86* and the later widely accepted notion that the poet was himself a 'Deus Creator'. The parallel spatial disruptions of the images chosen by 'Lizard' and Edmund Burke, especially 'Hast thou cloth'd his neck with thunder?' and 'Canst thou make him afraid as a grasshopper?' suggest a continuity of a technique running by way of Smart, Lowth and Gray, to the noonday of the Romantic movement. In Keats's *Hyperion: A Fragment*, a true 'orientatalism' (see p. 101), the major images work on the principles suggested above, with a fidelity which is perhaps a little disconcerting to those who wish to separate 'eighteenth-century' aesthetics from nineteenth-century. Of especial interest in the context of a poem in which the greatest mythic hierarchy of ancient times, the Titans, has collapsed, and with it, memory and all structure of time and place, is Keats' mastery of the prophetic mode, in which only a finer modulation separates him from a hundred years of epistemology and aesthetic theory. Thea speaks to the fallen Saturn, in lines in which the classical simile, imploding as it were even as one reads, transmutes into the sublimity of *Job* and Ezekiel, in the very creation of imagination from the husks of memory:

As when, upon a tranced summer-night,
Those green-robed senators of mighty woods,
Tall oaks, branch-charmed by the earnest stars
Dream, and so dream all night without a stir,
Save from one gradual solitary gust
Which comes upon the silence, and dies off,
As if the ebbing air had but one wave:
So came these words and went; and while in tears
She touched her fair large forehead to the ground,
Just where her falling hair might be outspread
A soft and silken mat for Saturn's feet. (*Hyperion: A Fragment* 72—82)

It is the beginning of the world, yet Keats cites 'senators'; hierarchy has fallen, but Thea bends 'to the ground'. We experience time and space, and their infinite dissolution.

The Forms of Obscurity

As important as the development of the 'sublime' metaphor is the change in the forms of verse. Coleridge's *Biographia Literaria* (see pp. 333-350), to which all the texts in this collection move, is centrally concerned with the association of ideas. Perhaps most significantly, the object of attack is Hartley's apparent condemnation of man — in Coleridge's eyes — to the forms of finite memory rather than those of the infinite imagination. The dichotomy between infinity and temporality colours also Coleridge's notion of true poetry of the imagination, the repetition in the finite mind of the creative act of God (see p. 350), on the one hand, and the poetry of Pope's Homer, 'thoughts *translated* into the language of poetry', (see p. 337) on the other. For this latter Coleridge coined the term 'conjunction-disjunctive'. The shift from the 'conjunction-disjunctive' of Pope to the new forms of the prophetic, parallels at the formal level the shift from simile to metaphor. At the end of a line, or couplet, in Pope, we may paraphrase, the mind 'gets it', totally and clearly. Having understood, it is ready to move on, building steps as it were which follow one on the other. During the eighteenth century one may follow a gradual shift from the complete formal progress of a poem through a beginning, middle and end, to a pattern in which the 'progress' as Gray terms it, of a poem (see pp. 191-194) is an accretion which builds up, in opposition to the forward march of the eye down the page, half-understood loyalties to groups of images coalescing in obscurity.

It is interesting to observe that the ambiguity of time (and space) as a subjective experience, a phenomenon which begins with the scientific revolution of the late seventeenth century, may be first observed in Thomas Burnet (see pp. 20-36). Burnet is concerned with disputing the allegorical, or 'other worldly' nature of the first writers, Ezekiel, Plato, *et al.* The breakdown of a reliable forward direction in the experience of verse is already noticeable in the poetry of Thomson and Young (both of whom embraced Burnet's cosmology and his 'Sublime') in the early part of the century. It becomes more apparent in Collins, for example in the *Ode to Evening*, whose syntax not only produces a sense of lyric suspension, but discourages the memory from containing until the main clauses, the varied allusions of the subordinates. The revisions of Gray's *Elegy* point to a kind of triptychal simultaneity reminiscent of Spenser. The academic theorists, simultaneously as it were, discovered that the sublime stasis of infinity was the distinguishing characteristic of oriental poetry (see Lowth, pp. 162-164) and of the ballad, that is the primitive poetry of Northern Europe. It is clear that a kind of parallelism (to use Lowth's term) haunts both Coleridge's *Christabel* (a northern 'romance') and his *Ancient Mariner* which partially owes its incandescence to the subtle Burnetian double vision of matter existing both in finiteness and in the infinity of 'the Mundane Egg' at the same *time* (see pp. 33-36).

The problem of the nature of the 'knowledge' which poetry offers and its relation to the formal advance of poetry (which might well occur in ostensibly 'free' verse) is of great importance in the twentieth-century understanding of the poetry of the past. The intolerance of even intelligent readers for obscurity partially explains the recurrent popularity of Pope and, indeed, the longer discourses of Wordsworth, which in some sense return to the perspicaciousness of Pope. The eighteenth-century 'Sublime' is essentially anti-rational. The mighty *frisson* which Burnet experienced before oceans and great mountains, was accompanied by the sleep of reason and the suspension of memory. Burke's *Sublime and Beautiful* tells us that what we do not know and cannot understand offers, by way of terror, the greatest art. The Gothic novel of Walpole and his imitators, apparently attacked, as had Collins, the limits of memory. The obscurity of Ossian, the mists, mountains, madmen, idiots, distant ages of the sentimental and Gothic, all these were a mighty celebration of the irrational. Vast obscurities were the aim of the mid-century Romantic, and the theorists of the period found obscurity everywhere. For Hurd, Spenser is an example of fairy imagination, for Collins, Milton was a Gothic dreamer, for Maurice Morgann, Shakespeare was a 'barbarian', a magus within Nature's secrets.

In reading the literature of the past, the mid-twentieth-century reader too often asks himself whether what he is reading is 'good'. Is there an acute, fine, rare perception? For reasons distinct from Pope's adulation of 'what oft was thought' the mid and late eighteenth century had abandoned this aim. Its greatest achievements lie in the approximation of mysteries of perception in which the 'meaning' of words is only a small, superficial even, image in a larger totality. Gray's *Elegy*, in some ways a crucial poem, tells us that we are all going to die, but we feel we are in the presence of truths like those of Beethoven's last quartets, or even Michelangelo's Sistine Chapel, because Gray is making, through form and the manipulation of time and space, a comment on the relation between the perception of his words and the rest of cognition which is framed in the movement of his verse. The whole brings from us an irrational and massive response far beyond mere agreement with 'what is being said'. Our own psyches offer their timelessness, in unformed, unrepeatable, cognitive patterns, joining with Gray's, in an awareness of the partial nature of verbalization in any account of reality. Gray parallels to a nicety the processes of cognition by which sensations − verbal or not − join the mass of memory and pastness, and are transformed into new, prophetic knowledge, by our creative forces. Words become only one image in a process, in which a sense of 'motion' is far and away foremost, and where the 'aboutness' of the poem, of prime importance in Pope, is the first and major casualty. In this achievement Gray is one with the greatest writers of his period. For words held in a critical aura of their own limitation, divided between their referential value in memory and a prophetic *nebula* of futurity is the common real achievement of Berkeley, Thomson, Young, Blake and Smart, to be handed on and exploited by Coleridge and Keats especially, and to a lesser extent by Wordsworth.

The book for which eighteenth-century and Romantic readers wait will deal with 'seven types' not of 'ambiguity' but 'obscurity'. At the most obvious levels, in formal shapes and the single metaphor, at a less obvious level, in the function of single words within the line, the mid-century Romantic avoided coherence and rationality, attempting to catch the true nature of everyday reality, in which *angst* and half-formed glories are the half-realized awarenesses only partially registered in minds which do not know whether to look back or forward, and continually do both.

THOMAS BURNET (1635?–1715)

Thomas Burnet, Master of the Charterhouse, is radically important as the father of the eighteenth-century 'Sublime'. Beginning a fashion which still influences vacations as well as literature, he discovered, as he outlines in the *Telluris theoria sacra* (1681-9), that when looking upon mountains or seascapes, his mind was filled to excess by an irrational stupor of awe and admiration.

Burnet theorized that the globe had once been perfectly smooth — 'the Mundane Egg' — and that at the Creation, five thousand years before, the inner sea and fire had cracked the shell producing the mountain ranges and the Flood whose waters still lay around us. Thrillingly 'we have still the broken materials of that first world, and walk upon its ruins'. Geology, not allegory, provides the key to scriptural truth. No mythic Eden or Golden Age predated the materials which our senses, rightly, fed on; we were directly heirs to God's creative perfection, and through the great objects of the finite world could perceive, unaided by religion, the infinite. Antedating the most famous alumnus of the Charterhouse in his time, who wrote an ode in Latin acknowledging the theory of his master, Burnet in effect popularized, before Addison's 'The Pleasures of the Imagination' (see pp. 92-99), the transference of religious responses to aesthetics, and offered man the image of a Creation in which he could identify the timeless factor of his own vision.

Eighteenth-century writers saw the prophets, especially Ezekiel, as original, primitive writers who corroborated contemporary theories of perception. Apparently viewing Moses, Ezekiel, and St John as corresponding members of the Royal Society, Burnet inaugurated more than a century of interest in their simultaneous 'sublimity' and originality. In the *Archaeologicae philosophicae* (1692) may be observed an image of light more poetically influential than that of Newton's *Optics*. The existence of 'the Mundane Egg', more elevated and sublime than our own globe, is attested to by the jewelled visions of the prophets, for example the 'sapphire throne' of Ezekiel, whose rays are not those of the sun but of eternal light. The line from Burnet to Young, Gray, Collins, and Wordsworth is direct.

Not only did Burnet's theory of the 'Sublime' shape Addison's and Burke's and his geological theory dictate that of Thomson and Young — who gives to Job Burnet's theory of Creation — his crystallization of the ambiguousness of man's native perception, which appeared to image the objects of time and place but at the same moment contained distinct shapes of eternity, spoke directly to the major Romantics a hundred years later. As Lowes has shown at length in *The Road to Xanadu*, Coleridge not only found *The Theory of the Earth* evidence that 'poetry of the highest kind may exist without metre' (*Biographia Literaria*, Chap. XIV) and drew the epigraph of *The Ancient Mariner* from the

Archaeologicae philosophicae, but discovered the images of these physico-theological works seminal at every level. Wordsworth found corroboration for the line 'Lost in unsearchable eternity' (*The Excursion*, iii, 112) in Burnet and confessed in his notes to the poem of 'corresponding sentiments, excited by objects of a similar nature'.

THE THEORY OF THE EARTH (1684)

from Book I, 'Concerning the Deluge'

'Tis now more than Five Thousand years since our World was made, and though it would be a great pleasure to the mind, to recollect and view at this distance those first Scenes of Nature: what the face of the Earth was when fresh and new, and how things differ'd from the state we now find them in, the speculation is so remote, that it seems to be hopeless, and beyond the reach of Humane Wit. We are almost the last Posterity of the the first Men, and faln into the dying Age of the World; by what footsteps, or by what guide, can we trace back our way to those first Ages, and the first order of things? And yet, methinks, it is reasonable to believe, that Divine Providence, which sees at once throughout all the Ages of the World, should not be willing to keep Mankind finally and fatally ignorant of that part of Nature, and of the Universe, which is properly their Task and Province to manage and understand. We are the Inhabitants of the Earth, the Lords and Masters of it; and we are endow'd with Reason and Understanding; doth it not then properly belong to us to examine and un-fold the works of God in this part of the Universe, which is faln to our lot, which is our heritage and habitation? And it will be found, it may be, upon a stricter Enquiry, that in the present form and constitution of the Earth, there are certain marks and Indications of its first State; with which if we compare those things that are recorded in Sacred History, concerning the first Chaos, Paradise, and an universal Deluge, we may discover, by the help of those Lights, what the Earth was in its first Original, and what Changes have since succeeded in it.

And though we shall give a full account of the Origin of the Earth in this Treatise, yet that which we have propos'd particularly for the Title and Subject of it, is to give an account of the primaeval PARADISE, and of the universal DELUGE: Those being the two most important things that are explain'd by the Theory we propose. And I must beg leave in treating of these two, to change the order, and treat first of the Deluge, and then of Paradise: For though the State of Paradise doth precede that of the Flood in Sacred History, and in the nature of the thing, yet the explication of both will be more sensible, and more effectual, if we begin with the Deluge; there being more Observations and Effects, and those better known to us, that may be refer'd to this, than to the other; and the Deluge being once truly explain'd, we shall from thence know the form and Quality of the Ante-diluvian Earth. Let us then proceed to the explication of that great and fatal Inundation, whose History is well known; and according to *Moses*, the best of Historians, in a few words is this –

Sixteen Hundred and odd years after the Earth was made, and inhabited, it was over-flow'd, and destroy'd in a Deluge of water. Not a Deluge that was National only, or over-run some particular Country or Region, as *Judea* or *Greece*, or any other, but it overspread the face of the whole Earth, from Pole to Pole, and from East to West, and that in such excess, that the Floods over-reacht the Tops of the highest Mountains; the Rains descending after an unusual manner, and the fountains of the *Great Deep* being broke open; so as a general destruction and devastation was brought upon the Earth, and all things in it, Mankind and other living Creatures; expecting only *Noah* and his family, who by a special Providence of God were preserv'd in a certain Ark, or Vessel made like a Ship, and such kinds of living Creatures as he took in to him. After these waters had rag'd for some time on the Earth, they began to lessen and shrink, and the great waves and fluctuations of this *Deep* or *Abysse*, being quieted by degrees, the waters retir'd into their Chanels and Caverns within the Earth; and the Mountains and Fields began to appear, and the whole habitable Earth in that form and shape wherein we now see it. Then the World began again, and from that little Remnant preserv'd in the Ark, the present race of Mankind, and of Animals, in the known parts of the Earth, were propagated. Thus perisht the old World, and the present arose from the ruines and remains of it.

*

All History, and all monuments of Antiquity of what kind soever, are but of a few thousand of years date; we have still the memory of the golden Age, of the first state of Nature, and how mortals liv'd then in innocency and simplicity. The invention of Arts, even those that are necessary or useful to humane life, hath been within the knowledge of Men: How imperfect was the Geography of the Ancients, how imperfect their knowledge of the Earth, how imperfect their Navigation! Can we imagine, if there had been Men from Everlasting, a Sea as now, and all materials for Shipping as much as we have, that men could have been so ignorant, both of the Land and of the Sea, as 'tis manifest they have been till of late Ages? They had very different fansies concerning the figure of the Earth! They knew no Land beyond our Continent, and that very imperfectly too; and the Torrid Zone they thought utterly uninhabitable. We think it strange, taking that short date of the World, which we give it, that Men should not have made more progress in the knowledge of these things; But how impossible is it then, if you suppose them to have been from Everlasting? They had the same wit and passions that we have, the same motives that we have, can we then imagine, that neither the ambition of Princes, nor Interest or gain in private persons, nor curiosity and the desire of Knowledge, nor the glory of discoveries, nor any other passion or consideration could ever move them in that endless time, to try their fortunes upon the Sea, and know something more of the World they inhabited? Though you should suppose them generally stupid, which there is no reason to do, yet in a course of infinite Generations, there would be some great Genio's, some extraordinary persons that would attempt things above the rest. We have done more within the compass of our little World, which we can but count, as to this, from the general Deluge, than those Eternal Men had done in their innumerable Ages foregoing.

*

There is another thing in Antiquity, relating to the form and construction of the Earth, which is very remarkable, and hath obtain'd throughout all learned Nations and Ages. And that is the comparison or resemblance of the Earth to an *Egg*. And this is not so much for its External Figure, though that be true too: as for the inward composition of it; consisting of several Orbs, one including another, and in that order, as to answer the several Elementary Regions of which the new-made Earth was constituted. For if we admit for the *Yolk* a Central fire (which, though very reasonable, we had no occasion to take notice of in our Theory of the Chaos) and suppose the Figure of the Earth *Oval*, and a little extended towards the Poles, as probably it was; those two bodies do very naturally represent one another; as in this Scheme, which represents the Interiour faces of both, a divided *Egg*, or Earth. [Here Burnet provides an illustration of the oviform earth with four layers in section.] Where, as the two inmost Regions A. B. represent the Yolk and the Membrane that lies next about it; so the Exteriour Region of the Earth (D) is as the Shell of the Egg, and the Abysse (C) under it as the White that lies under the Shell. And considering that this notion of the *Mundane Egg* or that the World was *Oviform*, hath been the sence and Language of all Antiquity, *Latins, Greeks, Persians, Egyptians*, and others, as we have shew'd elsewhere; I thought it worthy our notice in this place; seeing it receives such a clear and easie explication from that Origin and Fabrick we have given to the first Earth, and also reflects light upon the Theory it self, and confirms it to be no fiction: This notion, which is a kind of Epitome or Image of it, having been conserv'd in the most ancient Learning.

Thus much concerning the first Earth, its production and form; and concerning our Second Proposition relating to it: Which being prov'd by Reason, the laws of Nature, and the motions of the Chaos; then attested by Antiquity, both as to the matter and form of it; and confirm'd by Sacred Writers, we may take it now for a well establish'd truth, and proceed upon this supposition, *That the Ante-diluvian Earth was smooth and uniform, without Mountains or Sea*, to the explication of the universal Deluge.

*

I do not think it in the power of humane wit to determine how long this frame would stand, how many Years, or how many Ages; but one would soon imagine, that this kind of structure would not be perpetual, nor last indeed many thousands of Years, if one consider the effect that the heat of the Sun would have upon it, and the Waters under it; drying and parching the one, and rarifying the other into vapours. For we must consider, that the course of the Sun at that time, or the posture of the Earth to the Sun, was such, that there was no diversity or alternation of seasons in the Year, as there is now; by reason of which alternation, our Earth is kept in an equality of temper, the contrary seasons balancing one another; so as what moisture the heat of the Summer sucks out of the Earth, 'tis repaid in the Rains of the next Winter; and what chaps were made in it, are fill'd up again, and the Earth reduc'd to its former constitution. But if we should imagine a continual Summer, the Earth would proceed in driness still more and more, and the cracks would be wider and pierce deeper into the substance of it: And such a continual Summer there was, at least an equality of seasons in the Ante-diluvian Earth, as shall be prov'd in the following Book, concerning *Paradise*. In the mean time this being suppos'd, let us consider what effect it would have upon this Arch of the exterior Earth, and the Waters under it.

We cannot believe, but that the heat of the Sun, within the space of some hundreds of years, would have reduc'd this Earth to a considerable degree of driness in certain parts; and also have much rarifi'd and exhal'd the Waters under it: And considering the structure of that Globe, the exteriour crust, and the Waters lying round under it, both expos'd to the Sun, we may fitly compare it to an *Aeolipile*, or an hollow Sphere with Water in it, which the heat of the Fire rarifies and turns into Vapours and Wind. The Sun here is as the Fire, and the exteriour Earth is as the Shell of the *Aeolipile*, and the Abysse as the Water within it; now when the heat of the Sun had pierced through the Shell and reacht the Waters, it began to rarifie them, and raise them into Vapours; which rarefaction made them require more space and room than they needed before, while they lay close and quiet. And finding themselves pen'd in by the exteriour Earth, they press'd with violence against that Arch, to make it yield and give way to their dilatation and eruption. So we see all Vapours and Exhalations enclos'd within the Earth, and agitated there, strive to break out, and often shake the ground with their attempts to get loose.

*

'Tis incredible to what height sometimes great Stones and Cinders will be thrown, at the eruptions of fiery Mountains; and the pressure of a great mass of Earth falling into the Abysse, though it be a force of another kind, could not but impel the water with so much strength, as would carry it up to a great height in the Air; and to the top of any thing that lay in its way, any eminency, or high fragment whatsoever: And then rowling back again, it would sweep down with it whatsoever it rusht upon, Woods, Buildings, living Creatures, and carry them all headlong into the great gulf. Sometimes a mass of water would be quite struck off and separate from the rest, and tost through the Air like a flying River; but the common motion of the waves was to climb up the hills, or inclin'd fragments, and then return into the valleys and deeps again, with a perpetual fluctuation going and coming, ascending and descending, till the violence of them being spent by degrees, they settled at last in the places allotted for them; where *bounds are set that they cannot pass over, that they return not again to cover the Earth.* [Psalm 104: 6, 7, 8, 9.]

Neither is it to be wonder'd, that the great Tumult of the waters, and the extremity of the Deluge lasted for some months; for besides, that the first shock and commotion of the Abysse was extremely violent, from the general fall of the Earth, there were ever and anon some secondary ruines; or some parts of the great ruine, that were not well setled, broke again, and made new commotions: And 'twas a considerable time before the great fragments that fell, and their lesser dependencies could be so adjusted and fitted, as to rest in a firm and immoveable posture: For the props and stays whereby they lean'd one upon another, or upon the bottom of the Abysse, often fail'd, either by the incumbent weight, or the violent impulses of the water against them; and so renew'd, or continu'd the disorder and confusion of the Abysse. Besides, we are to observe, that these great fragments falling hollow, they inclos'd and bore down with them under their concave surface a great deal of Air; and while the water compass'd these fragments, and overflow'd them, the Air could not readily get out of those prisons, but by degrees, as the Earth and Water above would give way; so as this would also hinder the settlement of the Abysse, and the retiring of the Water into those Subterraneous Chanels, for some time. But at length, when this Air had found a vent, and left its place to the Water, and the ruines, both primary and secondary, were setled and fixt, then the Waters of the Abysse began to settle too, and the dry Land to appear; first the tops of the Mountains, then the high Grounds, then the Plains and the rest of the Earth. And this gradual subsidency of the Abysse (which *Moses* also hath particularly noted) and discovery of the several parts of the Earth, would also take up a considerable time.

Thus a new World appear'd, or the Earth put on its new form, and became divided into Sea and Land; and the Abysse, which from several Ages, even from the beginning of the World, had lain hid in the womb of the Earth, was brought to light and discover'd;* the greatest part of it constituting our present Ocean, and the rest filling the lower cavities of the Earth: Upon the Land appear'd the Mountains and the Hills, and the Islands in the Sea, and the Rocks upon the shore. And so the Divine Providence, having prepar'd Nature for so great a change, at one stroke

---

*The Abyss is the white of 'the Egg'. Ed.

dissolv'd the frame of the old World, and made us a new one out of its ruines, which we now inhabit since the Deluge. All which things being thus explain'd, deduc'd, and stated, we now add and pronounce our Third and last Proposition; *That the disruption of the Abysse, or dissolution of the primaeval Earth and its fall into the Abysse, was the cause of the Universal Deluge, and of the destruction of the old World.*

*

We have been in the hollows of the Earth, and the Chambers of the Deep, amongst the damps and steams of those lower Regions; let us now go air our selves on the tops of the Mountains, where we shall have a more free and large Horizon, and quite another face of things will present it self to our observation.

The greatest objects of Nature are, methinks, the most pleasing to behold; and next to the great Concave of the Heavens, and those boundless Regions where the Stars inhabit, there is nothing that I look upon with more pleasure than the wide Sea and the Mountains of the Earth. There is something august and stately in the Air of these things, that inspires the mind with great thoughts and passions; We do naturally, upon such occasions, think of God and his greatness: and whatsoever hath but the shadow and appearance of INFINITE, as all things have that are too big for our comprehension, they fill and overbear the mind with their Excess, and cast it into a pleasing kind of stupor and admiration.*

And yet these Mountains we are speaking of, to confess the truth, are nothing but great ruines; but such as show a certain magnificence in Nature; as from old Temples and broken Amphitheaters of the *Romans* we collect the greatness of that people. But the grandeur of a Nation is less sensible to those that never see the remains and monuments they have left, and those who never see the mountainous parts of the Earth, scarce ever reflect upon the causes of them, or what power in Nature could be sufficient to produce them. The truth is, the generality of people have not sence and curiosity enough to raise a question concerning these things, or concerning the Original of them. You may tell them that Mountains grow out of the Earth like Fuzz-balls, or that there are Monsters under ground that throw up Mountains as Moles do Mole-hills; they will scarce raise one objection against your doctrine; or if you would appear more Learned, tell them that the Earth is a great Animal, and these are Wens that grow upon its body. This would pass current for Philosophy; so much is the World drown'd in stupidity and sensual pleasures, and so little inquisitive into the works of God and Nature.

There is nothing doth more awaken our thoughts or excite our minds to enquire into the causes of such things, than the actual view of them;

---

*This paragraph defining the effect of 'the Sublime', is crucial. Cf. Addison's 'Sublime'. Ed.

as I have had experience my self when it was my fortune to cross the *Alps* and *Appennine* Mountains; for the sight of those wild, vast and indigested heaps of Stones and Earth, did so deeply strike my fancy, that I was not easie till I could give my self some tolerable account how that confusion came in Nature. 'Tis true, the height of Mountains compar'd with the Diameter of the Earth is not considerable, but the extent of them and the ground they stand upon, bears a considerable proportion to the surface of the Earth; and if from *Europe* we may take our measures for the rest, I easily believe, that the Mountains do at least take up the tenth part of the dry land. The Geographers are not very careful to describe or note in their Charts, the multitude or situation of Mountains; They mark the bounds of Countries, the site of Cities and Towns, and the course of Rivers, because these are things of chief use to civil affairs and commerce, and that they design to serve, and not Philosophy or Natural History. But *Cluverius* in his description of *Ancient Germany, Switzerland* and *Italy*, hath given Maps of those Countries more approaching to the natural face of them, and we have drawn (at the end of this Chapter) such a Map of either Hemisphere, without marking Countries or Towns, or any such artificial things; distinguishing only Land and Sea, Islands and Continents, Mountains and not Mountains; and 'tis very useful to imagine the Earth in this manner, and to look often upon such bare draughts as shew us Nature undrest; for then we are best able to judge what her true shapes and proportions are.

'Tis certain that we naturally imagine the surface of the Earth much more regular than it is; for unless we be in some Mountainous parts, there seldom occur any great inequalities within so much compass of ground as we can, at once, reach with our Eye; and to conceive the rest, we multiply the same *Idea*, and extend it to those parts of the Earth that we do not see; and so fancy the whole Globe much more smooth and uniform than it is. But suppose a man was carri'd asleep out of a Plain Country, amongst the *Alps*, and left there upon the top of one of the highest Mountains, when he wak'd and look'd about him, he would think himself in an inchanted Country, or carri'd into another World; Every thing would appear to him so different to what he had ever seen or imagin'd before. To see on every hand of him a multitude of vast bodies thrown together in confusion, as those Mountains are; Rocks standing naked round about him; and the hollow Valleys gaping under him; and at his feet it may be, an heap of frozen Snow in the midst of Summer. He would hear the thunder come from below, and see the black Clouds hanging beneath him; Upon such a prospect, it would not be easie to him to perswade himself that he was still upon the same Earth; but if he did, he would be convinc'd, at least, that there are some Regions of it strangely rude, and ruine-like, and very different from what he had ever thought of before. [Cf. Shaftesbury on the sublimity of mountains, p. 87.] But the inhabitants of these wild places are even with us; for those that live amongst the *Alps* and the great Mountains, think that all the rest of the

Earth is like their Country, all broken into Mountains, and Valleys, and Precipices; They never see other, and most people think of nothing but what they have seen at one time or another.

*

from Book II, 'Concerning Paradise'
All Antiquity speaks of the plenty of the Golden Age, and of their *Paradises*, whether Christian or Heathen. The fruits of the Earth at first were spontaneous, and the ground without being torn and tormented, satisfied the wants or desires of man. When Nature was fresh and full, all things flow'd from her more easily and more pure, like the first running of the Grape, or the Hony-comb; but now she must be prest and squeez'd, and her productions tast more of the Earth and of bitterness. The Ancient Poets have often pleas'd themselves in making descriptions of this happy state, and in admiring the riches and liberality of Nature at that time, but we need not transcribe their Poetry here, seeing this point is not, I think, contested by any. The second part of this Character, concerning the spontaneous Origin of living Creatures out of that first Earth, is not so unquestionable; and as to Man, *Moses* plainly implies that there was a particular action or ministery of Providence in the formation of his Body, but as to other Animals He seems to suppose that the Earth brought them forth as it did Herbs and Plants. (*Gen.* I.24 compar'd with the 11 Verse.) And the truth is, there is no such great difference betwixt Vegetable and and Animal Eggs, or betwixt the Seeds out of which Plants rise, and the Eggs out of which all Animals rise, but that we may conceive, the one as well as the other, in the first Earth: And as some warmth and influence from the Sun is requir'd for the Vegetation of Seeds, so that influence or impregnation which is necessary to make animal Eggs fruitful, was imputed by the Ancients to the *Aether*, or to an active and pure Element which had the same effect upon our great Mother the Earth, as the irradiation of the Male hath upon the Females Eggs.

Tum Pater omnipotens foecundis imbribus Aether
Conjugis in gremium laetae descendit.
[Lucretius, De rerum natura, i. 250-251.]
In fruitful show'rs of Aether Jove did glide
Into the bosom of his joyful Bride.

'Tis true, this opinion of the spontaneous Origin of Animals in the first Earth, hath lain under some *Odium*, because it was commonly reckon'd to be *Epicurus's* opinion peculiarly; and he extended it not only to all brute Creatures, but to Mankind also, whom he suppos'd to grow out of the Earth in great numbers, in several parts and Countries, like other Animals; which is a notion contrary to the Sacred writings; for they declare, that all Mankind, though diffus'd now through the several parts and Regions of the Earth, rise at first from one Head or single Man and Woman; which is a Conclusion of great importance, and that could not, I think, by the Light of Nature, have ever been discover'd. And this makes the *Epicurean* opinion the more improbable, for why should two rise only, if they sprung from the Earth? or how could they rise in their full growth and perfection, as *Adam* and *Eve* did? But as for the opinion of Animals rising out of the Earth at first, that was not at all peculiar to *Epicurus*; The *Stoicks* were of the same mind, and the *Pythagoreans*, and the *Aegyptians*, and, I think, all that suppos'd the Earth to rise from a Chaos. Neither do I know any harm in that opinion, if duly limited and stated; for what inconvenience is it, or what diminution of Providence, that there should be the principles of Life, as well as the principles of Vegetation, in the new Earth? And unless you suppose all the first Animals, as well as the first man, to have been made at one stroke, in their full growth and perfection, which we have neither reason nor authority sufficient to believe; if they were made young, little and weak, as they come now into the World, there seems to be no way for their production more proper, and decorous, than that they should spring from their great Mother the Earth. Lastly, considering the innumerable little Creatures that are upon the Earth, Insects and Creeping things: and that these were not created out of nothing, but form'd out of the ground: I think that an office most proper for Nature, that can set so many hands to work at once; and that hath hands fit for all those little operations or manufactures, how small soever, that would less become the dignity of Superiour Agents.

Thus much for the Preliminaries, or three general Characters of *Paradise*, which were common to it with the rest of the Primaeval Earth; and were the chief ingredients of the Golden Age, so much celebrated by the Ancients. I know there were several other differences betwixt that Earth and this, but these are the original; and such as are not necessary to be premis'd for the general Explication of *Paradise*, we reserve for another place. We may, in the mean time observe, how preposterously they go to work, that set themselves immediately to find out some pleasant place of the Earth to fix *Paradise* in, before they have consider'd, or laid any grounds, to explain the general conditions of it, wheresoever it was. These must be first known and determin'd, and we must take our aim and directions from these, how to proceed further in our enquiries after it; otherwise we sail without a Compass, or seek a Port and know not which way it lies. And as we should think him a very unskilful Pilot that sought a place in the new World, or *America*, that really was in the old; so they commit no less an error, that seek *Paradise* in the present Earth, as now constituted, which could only belong to the former, and to the state of the first World.

*

The third character to be explain'd, and the most extraordinary in appearance, is that of *Longaevity*. This sprung from the same root, in my opinion, with the other; though the connexion, it may be, is not so visible. We show'd in the foregoing Chapter, that no advantage of Diet, or of strong Constitutions, could have carried their lives, before the Flood, to that wonderful length, if they had been expos'd to the same changes of Air and of Seasons that our Bodies are: But taking a perpetual *Aequinox*, and fixing the Heavens, you fix the life of Man too; which was then not in such a rapid flux as it is now, but seem'd to stand still, as the Sun did once, without declension. There is no question but everything upon Earth, and especially the Animate World, would be much more permanent, if the general course of Nature was more steddy and uniform; A stability in the Heavens makes a stability in all things below; and that change and contrariety of qualities that we have in these Regions, is the fountain of corruption, and suffers nothing to be long in quiet: Either by intestine motions and fermentations excited within, or by outward impressions, Bodies are no sooner well constituted, but they are tending again to dissolution. The *Aether* in their little pores and chinks is unequally agitated, and differently mov'd at different times, and so is the Air in their greater, and the Vapours and Atmosphere round about them: All these shake and unsettle both the texture and continuity of Bodies. Whereas in a fixt state of Nature, where these principles have always the same constant and uniform motion, when they are once suited to the forms and compositions of Bodies, they give them no further disturbance; they enjoy a long and lasting peace without any commotions or violence, within or without.

We find our selves, sensible changes in our Bodies upon the turn of the Year, and the change of Seasons; new fermentations in the Bloud and resolutions of the Humours; which if they do not amount to diseases, at least they disturb Nature, and have a bad effect not only upon the fluid parts, but also upon the more solid; upon the Springs and Fibres in the Organs of the Body; to weaken them and unfit them by degrees for their respective functions. For though the change is not sensible immediately in these parts, yet after many repeated impressions every year, by unequal heat and cold, driness and moisture, contracting and relaxing the Fibres, their tone at length is in a great measure destroy'd, or brought to a manifest debility; and the great Springs failing, the lesser that depend upon them, fail in proportion, and all the symptoms of decay and old age follow. We see by daily experience, that Bodies are kept better in the same *medium*, as we call it, than if they often change their *medium*, as sometimes in Air, sometimes in Water, moisten'd and dri'd, heated and cool'd; these different states weaken the contexture of the parts: But our Bodies, in the present state of Nature, are put into an hundred different *mediums* in the course of a Year; sometimes we are steept in Water, or in a misty foggy Air for several days together, sometimes we are almost frozen with cold, then fainting with heat at another time of the Year; and the Winds are of a different nature, and the Air of a different weight and pressure, according to the Weather and the Seasons: These things would wear our Bodies, though they were built of Oak, and that in a very short time in comparison of what they would last, if they were always incompast with one and the same *medium*, under one and the same temper, as it was in the Primitive Earth.

The Ancients seem to have been sensible of this, and of the true causes of those long periods of life; for wheresoever they assign'd a great longaevity, as they did not only to their Golden Age, but also to their particular and topical *Paradises*, they also assign'd there a constant serenity and equality of the Heavens, and sometimes expresly a constant Aequinox; as might be made appear from their Authors. And some of our Christian Authors have gone farther, and connected these two together, as Cause and Effect; for they say that the Longaevity of the Ante-diluvian Patriarchs proceeded from a favourable Aspect and influence of the Heavens at that time; which *Aspect* of the Heavens being rightly interpreted, is the same thing that we call the Position of the Heavens, or the right situation of the Sun and the Earth, from whence came a perpetual Aequinox. And if we consider the present Earth, I know no place where they live longer than in that little Island of the *Bermudas*, where, according to the proportion of time they hold out there, after they are arriv'd from other parts, one may reasonably suppose, that the Natives would live two hundred Years. And there's nothing appears in that Island that should give long life above other places, but the extraordinary steddiness of the Weather, and of the temper of the Air throughout the whole Year, so as there is scarce any considerable difference of Seasons. *Second edition, 1691*

from *ARCHAEOLOGICAE PHILOSOPHICAE, Part I, or THE ANCIENT DOCTRINE CONCERNING THE ORIGINALS OF THINGS. Trans. 'Mr Foxton' (1729)*

This is the Sum and Substance of *Moses's* Account concerning Paradise, and the first State of Mankind; which, keeping always close to the Sense, I have explained in other Words, that we may more freely judge of the Thing it self; as if it were written by a modern Author. Now that there are in this Relation, some Things Parabolical, and, which will not bear a Construction altogether literal, there are few but do allow. Nay, some proceed farther, and will have even the whole Discourse to be artificially figurative, in order to explain things that were really true (*viz.*) the new and degenerate Condition of Mankind; as also the *Paradisiac*-State of Infant Nature, and its Degeneracy. For although in the Beginning of the Discourse, this state of Paradise seems confined only to one Region, which is called *Gan Eden*, yet afterwards, when the Curse of Barrenness comes out, the whole Earth is brought in for a share. *The Earth shall not for the future bring forth her increase of her own accord, nor any of her Fruits without Tillage and Husbandry: but hereafter*, saith the Lord, *with the sweat of thy brow shalt thou get those things that are necessary for Life and Sustenance.* [Genesis 3: 17–19.] Whence it is evident, that before this Alteration or Curse, the whole Earth yielded her Increase without Planting or Labour; for otherwise by this Curse, nothing had been made new, nothing had been changed in the Face of Nature. Besides, from another Thing it plainly appears, that one small Country, or some few Acres of Land, such as is a Garden, could not alone enjoy this Fertility, together with those other Privileges as well of Air as Soil; but that the whole inhabitable Globe did partake of them in the primitive State of Things. For suppose *Adam* had continued Innocent, how would there have been Room for his Posterity within the Inclosures of one Garden? Or admit you will have them all shut up there, like so many un-fledged Birds in a Nest, what must have been done with all those other vast Tracts of Earth? Should they have stood Empty, Desert, and without Inhabitants? Nature it self does not allow of that, neither is it becoming the Divine Wisdom. From all these Things, we may conclude what is very agreeable to Reason, (*viz.*) That *Moses* puts the Part for the Whole, and laid one Example before the Eyes of the People, instead of a greater Number; because it was more suitable to the Genius and Understanding of the Vulgar, to conceive a pleasant Garden or single Field, than that the whole Globe of the Earth should put on a new Face and new Nature entirely different from what we now enjoy. But let us proceed in the Road we have begun.

The aforesaid Relation consists of five or six Parts, whereof the first is, concerning the Birth and Formation of the *first* of Mankind. The second, the Description of the Garden of *Eden*. The third is, the History of the *two* Trees of *Life* and *Death*. The fourth treats of the *Serpent's* Conference with *Eve*. The fifth, about the Wrath of God, and his Curse, for eating the forbidden Fruit. Lastly, the sixth contains the Expulsion of these first of Mankind out of the Almighty's Garden, as also how God made them Coats of Skins, and placed Angels with flaming Swords at the Entrance of his Garden; together with other Things hereto belonging.

Great is the Force of Custom and a pre-conceived Opinion, over human Minds. Wherefore these short Observations or Accounts of the first Originals of Men and Things, which we receive from the Mouth of *Moses*, are embraced without the least Demur or Examination of them. But had we read the same Doctrine in another, for Example, in a *Greek* Philosopher, or in a Rabbinical or Mahometan Doctor, we should have stopped at every Period with our Mind full of Objections and Scruples. Now this Difference does not arise from the Nature of the Thing it self, or of the Matter in Hand, but from the great Opinion we have of the Faithfulness and Authority of the Writer, as being divinely inspired. All which we willingly acknowledge, neither do we on this Occasion doubt of our Author's Authority, but with what Intent it was that he wrote these Things, and what Kind of Style he has made use of, whether *Plebeian* or *Philosophical*; I say, *Plebeian*, and not Fabulous, although this last Word might have been used, did we speak of a profane Author. Now of Fables, some are pure Fictions; others are built upon some Foundation, but beautified with Additions and acquired Ornaments. Besides, there are some Relations that have Truth at the Bottom, but not in every particular Point of them; only as to the Substance of the Thing, and Drift of the Author.

*

As to the Temporal Rise of Mankind, I have ever held it most certain and undoubted; and that upwards of five Thousand Years, according to the Account given us by Sacred Chronology. But out of what Matter the first of Mankind, whether Male or Female was composed, is not so easily discovered, nor of so great Importance to know. If God had a mind to make a Woman start from one of *Adam*'s Ribs, it is true it seems to be a Matter not very proper; but however, out of any Wood, Stone, or other Being, God can make a Woman:

from *ARCHAEOLOGICAE PHILOSOPHICAE, Part II, or THE THEORY OF THE VISIBLE WORLD. Trans. 'Mr Foxton' (1729)*

We do not undertake this new Task, as though it were necessary for the Support of the above-mentioned *Theory*, which stands, firm on its own Foundation; but to remove every objection against Providence, and comply a little with their Obstinacy, who will not receive the Truth it self, unless delivered and recommended to them by their Ancestors.

To come therefore to the Matter in hand, the Conclusion to be now proved, is this. *That the World had Formerly a different Shape and Situation from what it has at Present.*

By the World here, I do not mean the immense University of Things, since we are ignorant of its Bounds or Figure; nor do we know the Order of its remoter Parts. But I would be understood to speak of our World; to wit, the *Earth* and the *Visible Heavens.* So that our Assertion returns thus — *The Primitive Earth was of a different Form from the Present, and had another Situation with respect to the Heavens*; This we assert in the first Place, and in a general manner. For we shall in the following Discourse have an Opportunity of shewing wherein this Difference lay, when we come to enquire particularly what were the Properties of that *Primaeval Earth.*

In the meantime, to confirm this general Difference by Authorities, it is in the first Place to be observed, that according to the Sacred Scriptures there is a threefold State, or Order, of the Natural World, or *Heaven* and *Earth*; namely, the *Past*, the *Present*, and the *Future*. For so they are distinguished by the Apostle St. *Peter The Heavens and Earth which then were. The Heavens and the Earth which now are*, [2 Peter 3:

5 and 7] and in the 13th *ver.* he says, *We look for new Heavens, and a new Earth*. By the Heavens and Earth which were past, the Apostle means the *Primogenial* ones, . . . *which*, he says, perished in the Deluge. The Present ones, those which we enjoy, are appointed to a contrary Fate, and *must perish by Fire*. Lastly, by the *New Heavens* and the *New Earth*, which we expect after the Conflagration, are the *Future ones*, which are taken notice of several Times by the Prophet *Isaias*, and mentioned by the Apostle St. *John*. St. *Paul* has likewise touched upon this *threefold* State of the *Natural World*, in his Epistle to the *Romans*, chap. viii, and has made it remarkable by several Characters. In the first place, he supposes a World *not* yet subject to *Vanity*; and then he mentions the present one which is subject to *Vanity*; and lastly, the future one, redeemed and set free from *Vanity*; namely, from that Vanity to which it was before subjected. This future Restoration of the World, which the Apostle here sets forth . . . implies that triple State of the World, of which we are speaking. For a *Renovation* or *Restitution* is made to some past Condition. It is a Return either to the same, or the like Form and Order, which that Thing once had. Now to what former State will the future *Restitution* of the World be made? not to the present one; for that, as the Apostle observes, is *subject* to *Vanity*; but that Restitution is a Freedom from Vanity and Corruption, *they shall be freed from the Bondage of Corruption, into the glorious Liberty of the Sons of God.*

By comparing these Things together, we may justly conclude, That there was another State of this Natural World, before that which is now present, and was also more excellent. These Things I have premised, that so I might shew that our Opinion concerning the *Succession* of Worlds, or the *Diversity* and *Transmutation* of the *Natural World*, as well past as future, is grounded on the *Sacred Scriptures*.

But perhaps you will say, that this Discourse of St. *Paul* does not regard the *natural* and *inanimate* World, but that which is *animated*, and particularly Mankind, and that Renovation which Men were about to experience by the Help of the Gospel. Indeed some late Writers do thus interpret this Place of St. *Paul*. But what can such Expositors say to a like Passage of St. *Peter*, which we just now produced? If they take either of them to be spoken concerning the Natural World, it will be to no Purpose to refuse the other. Now that Dissertation of St. *Peter*, concerning the *triple* World, the *antediluvian, present*, and *new future* One, can by no means be wrested to an Allegorical Sense: For the Apostle particularly, and in exact Order, mentions Heaven and Earth; Parts of the Natural World; and gives us such a Character and Description of the World which he is talking of, as leaves no Room to doubt that he means the Heavenly and Earthly, that is, the Natural One.

*

Hitherto we have treated of the Situation of the *Platonick* Earth, we shall now a little consider those Things which concern the Shape of it, although they do not properly fall under this Head. In the first Place, he [Plato] supposes that Earth to be entire, and unhurt: But ours to be rent, corrupted and decayed. Moreover, he writes many Things about the subterranean Waters, and their Receptacles: And particularly mentions one great Deep (or *Barathrum*) which extended almost through the whole Earth; receiving all the Waters like a pensile Vessel. Now this great Deep or *Tartarus*, unless you will have it a mere Fiction, seems to have taken its Rise from the imperfect and vitiated Memory of the great Abyss, or *Tehom Rabbah*, which inwardly every where went about the primaeval Earth; and was the greatest Vessel and Receptacle of Waters that ever was extant. But as for the other observations which follow, concerning the Rivers of Hell, they have a strong Tincture of poetical Fiction.

But he talks in a pleasanter Strain, concerning the external Form of his Earth: For he says that the Superficies of that Earth is distinguished, or parted, into various Wreaths or Zones, adorned with Variety of Colours; which are exceeding beautiful to behold, even at a Distance, one Part seems to be of a Purple Colour, another Golden, and a third appears Whiter than Snow; and lastly, another Part is embellished with a different Colour. So that the whole Body of Earth seems to glitter in a wreathed and painted Vest. He says moreover, that there are every where Jewels and little lucid Bodies; which imitate Onyx Stones, Jaspars, and Emeralds, or exceed them in Beauty.* If you ask what the meaning of these Things are; I answer, they shew that the primogenial Earth was evidently divided into two Zones or Girdles: which surrounded its whole Body like swadling Bands, and each of them, according to its different Quality and Disposition, reflected the Sunbeams one Way, and another; and by this means appeared to those who beheld them at some Distance, to shine with a Variety of Colours. We may observe some of these Sort of Wreaths in the Planet *Jupiter*, (which seems to me to be yet in its primogenial State, and has not hitherto undergone any Dissolution, or Deluge) but by Reason of the vast Distances and the Weakness of our Eyes, we cannot from our Earth discern any Thing beside Black and watry Zones, which appear like so many Blots.

Lastly, some perhaps may imagine, that when *Plato* talks of his Aethereal Earth's being adorned with Jewels, and filled and beautified with splendid Bodies, he is only indulging a sportive Imagination. But I have often observed (with Admiration) that the Prophets and Sacred Authors always made use of these Figures, in their Descriptions of Paradise, as well as of the *New Jerusalem*, and adorned this Subject with Jewels. Thus did *Moses, Ezekiel,* and especially St. *John*; as if all Things in that State were irradiated with a new and excellent Light, or for the most part were transparent. As by the Help of a Microscope we see the Brightness and

---

*These like the Tartarus above, which Burnet identifies with the white of his 'Mundane Egg', occur towards the end of Plato's *Phaedo*. Ed.

Colours of all Jewels in Sand, little Stones, or Animals, so it might come to pass that, the Eye-sight being strengthened, and the Mind having a Power of forming the same into all the Figures of Glasses, Objects might appear no less splendid and gaudy to the naked Eyes, than now they are represented by the help of Art and Glasses.

JOHN LOCKE (1632–1704)

The major awarenesses in *An Essay Concerning Human Understanding* (1690) are germane to the rise of Romantic poetry; the discussions of time and space, of our complex idea of God, of the association of ideas, and that separation, whose novelty is noted by R.G. Collingwood in *The Principles of Art* (1938), of 'real' ideas from 'fantastical'. It is impossible, furthermore, to think of the rise of Romanticism without the influence of Berkeley, Hume and Hartley, the foremost names in the greatest period of English philosophy, and these men largely pursued further the concepts explored by Locke. As Dryden wrote of Ben Jonson in a different context, 'you track him everywhere in their snow'.

And yet it is largely to the degree to which later epistemology departs from the *Essay* that it appears to have influenced writers most strongly. The distinction between Berkeley's and Locke's idea of space is crucial and seems to surface everywhere – in Young, Thomson, Collins, Gray and Blake – after 1709. Few concepts seem to have been more influential, for example in the poetry especially of Smart, than the same philosopher's denial of the relation of cause and effect and of abstractions. It certainly seems highly unlikely that Edward Young did not have Hume's undermining of time and space before him when writing *Night Thoughts*, whilst Blake's central 'Sea of Time and Space' seems equally Humean as Berkeleyan. The ambiguous universe of Hume's rationality in addition suggests Smollet and Sterne as well as the surrealism of Young. David Hartley's theory of association 'to aery thinness beat' the structures of Locke and influenced directly the poetry of Wordsworth and Coleridge.

In sum, however, one may not ignore the *Essay* in tracing the theories of perception central to the rise of Romanticism. Both Burnet and Locke represent at its most influential the liberating materialization characteristic of their age. In *An Essay Concerning Human Understanding* as in *The Theory of the Earth* the notion arises that the unseen is within the creative purlieus of man, and that arcane mythologies are in the process of disappearance. In Locke, as in Burnet, one senses, if distantly, the beginning of the possibility explored in detail by Wordsworth and Keats in their greatest poems, that myth, whether of Paradise, the Golden Age, the Flood, or God, is not a distant icon borrowed from the ancient dead, but a continuing activity close to man's springs of knowledge in the eternal present.

AN ESSAY CONCERNING HUMAN UNDERSTANDING (1690)

from Chapter XV, Book II, 'Of Duration & Expansion, Considered Together'
1. Though we have in the precedent chapters dwelt pretty long on the

considerations of space and duration, yet, they being *ideas* of general concernment that have something very abstruse and peculiar in their nature, the comparing them one with another may perhaps be of use for their illustration; and we may have the more clear and distinct conception of them by taking a view of them together. Distance or space, in its simple abstract conception, to avoid confusion, I call *expansion*, to distinguish it from *extension*, which by some is used to express this distance only as it is in the solid parts of matter, and so includes, or at least intimates, the *idea* of body: whereas the *idea* of pure distance includes no such thing. I prefer also the word *expansion* to *space*, because *space* is often applied to distance of fleeting successive parts, which never exist together, as well as to those which are permanent. In both these (viz. *expansion* and *duration*) the mind has this common *idea* of continued lengths, capable of greater or less quantities; for a man has as clear an *idea* of the difference of the length of an hour and a day, as of an inch and a foot.

2. The *mind*, having got the *idea* of the length of any part of *expansion*, let it be a span or a pace or what length you will, *can*, as has been said, repeat that *idea* and so, adding it to the former, *enlarge its idea of length* and make it equal to two spans or two paces, and so, as often as it will, till it equals the distance of any parts of the earth one from another, and increase thus till it amounts to the distance of the sun or remotest star. By such a progression as this, setting out from the place where it is or any other place, it can proceed and pass beyond all those lengths and find nothing to stop its going on, either in or without body. It is true, we can easily in our thoughts come to the end of solid extension: the extremity and bounds of all body we have no difficulty to arrive at; but when the mind is there, it finds nothing to hinder its progress into this endless expansion: of that it can neither find nor conceive any end. Nor let anyone say that beyond the bounds of body there is nothing at all, unless he will confine *God* within the limits of matter. *Solomon*, whose understanding was filled and enlarged with wisdom, seems to have other thoughts, when he says, *Heaven, and the heaven of heavens, cannot contain thee*; and he, I think, very much magnifies to himself the capacity of his own understanding who persuades himself that he can extend his thoughts further than *God* exists, or image any expansion where He is not.

3. Just so is it in duration. *The mind, having got the idea of any length of duration, can double, multiply, and enlarge it*, not only beyond its own, but beyond the existence of all corporeal beings, and all the measures of time, taken from the great bodies of the world and their motions. But yet everyone easily admits that, though we make duration boundless, as certainly it is, we cannot yet extend it beyond all being. *God*, everyone easily allows, fills eternity; and it is hard to find a reason why anyone should doubt that he likewise fills immensity. His infinite being is certainly as boundless one way as another; and methinks it ascribes a little too much to matter to say, where there is no body, there is nothing. . . .

*

5. *Time* in general is to *duration* as *place* to *expansion*. They are so much of those boundless oceans of eternity and immensity as is set out and distinguished from the rest, as it were by landmarks; and so are made use of to denote the position of finite real beings, in respect one to another, in those uniform infinite oceans of duration and space. These, rightly considered, are nothing but *ideas* of determinate distances from certain known points, fixed in distinguishable sensible things, and supposed to keep the same distance one from another. From such points fixed in sensible beings we reckon, and from them we measure our portions of those infinite quantities; which, so considered, are that which we call *time* and *place*. For duration and space being in themselves uniform and boundless, the order and position of things, without such known settled points, would be lost in them, and all things would lie jumbled in an incurable confusion.

6. *Time* and *place* taken thus, for determinate distinguishable portions of those infinite abysses of space and duration, set out or supposed to be distinguished from the rest by marks and known boundaries, have each of them a two-fold acceptation.

First, Time in general is commonly taken for so much of infinite duration as is measured out by and co-existent with the existence and motions of the great bodies of the universe, as far as we know anything of them; and in this sense time begins and ends with the frame of this sensible world, as in these phrases before-mentioned, *before all time*, or *when time shall be no more*. *Place* likewise is taken sometimes for that portion of infinite space which is possessed by and comprehended within the material world, and is thereby distinguished from the rest of expansion, though this may be more properly called *extension* than place. Within these two are confined and, by the observable parts of them, are measured and determined the particular time or duration and the particular extension and place of all corporeal beings.

7. *Secondly*, Sometimes the word *time* is used *in a larger sense*, and is applied to parts of that infinite duration, not that were really distinguished and measured out by this real existence and periodical motions of bodies that were appointed from the beginning to be for signs and for seasons and for days and years, and are accordingly our measures of time, but such other portions too of that infinite uniform duration, which we upon any occasion do suppose equal to certain lengths of measured time, and so consider them as bounded and determined. For, if we should suppose the creation, or fall of the angels, was at the beginning of the *Julian* period, we should speak properly enough, and should be understood if we said it is a longer time, since the creation of angels than the creation of the world, by 764 years: whereby we would mark out so

much of that undistinguished duration as we suppose equal to, and would have admitted, 764 annual revolutions of the sun, moving at the rate it now does. And thus likewise we sometimes speak of place, distance, or bulk, in the great *inane*, beyond the confines of the world, when we consider so much of that space as is equal to or capable to receive a body of any assigned dimensions, as a cubic foot, or do suppose a point in it at such a certain distance from any part of the universe.

8. *Where* and *when* are questions belonging to all finite existences, and are by us always reckoned from some known parts of this sensible world, and from some certain epochs marked out to us by the motions observable in it. Without some such fixed parts or periods, the order of things would be lost to our finite understandings, in the boundless invariable oceans of duration and expansion, which comprehend in them all finite beings and in their full extent belong only to the deity. And therefore we are not to wonder that we comprehend them not and do so often find our thoughts at a loss when we would consider them, either abstractly in themselves or as any way attributed to the first incomprehensible being. But when applied to any particular finite beings, the extension of any body is so much of that infinite space as the bulk of that body takes up. And place is the position of any body when considered at a certain distance from some other. As the *idea* of the particular *duration* of anything is an *idea* of that portion of infinite *duration* which passes during the existence of that thing: so the time *when* the thing existed is the *idea* of that space of duration which passed between some known and fixed period of duration and the being of that thing. One shows the distance of the extremities of the bulk or existence of the same thing, as that it is a foot square, or lasted two years; the other shows the distance of it in place or existence from other fixed points of space or duration, as that it was in the middle of *Lincoln's-Inn-Fields*, or the first degree of *Taurus*, and in the year of our Lord 1671, or the 1000th year of the *Julian* period: all which distances we measure by preconceived *ideas* of certain lengths of space and duration, as inches, feet, miles, and degrees, and in the other minutes, days, and years, etc.

9. There is one thing more wherein *space* and *duration* have a great conformity, and that is, though they are justly reckoned amongst our *simple ideas*, yet none of the distinct *ideas* we have of either is without all manner of composition: it is the very nature of both of them to consist of parts; but their parts, being all of the same kind and without the mixture of any other *idea*, hinder them not from having a place amongst simple *ideas*. Could the mind, as in number, come to so small a part of extension or duration as excluded divisibility, *that* would be, as it were, the indivisible unit or *idea*, by repetition of which, it would make its more enlarged *ideas* of extension and duration. But, since the mind is not able to frame an *idea* of any space without parts, instead thereof it makes use of the common measures which, by familiar use in each country, have imprinted themselves on the memory (as inches and feet, cubits and parasangs;

and so seconds, minutes, hours, days, and years in duration): the mind makes use, I say, of such *ideas* as these as simple ones, and these are the component   parts of larger ideas, which the mind upon occasion makes by the addition of such known lengths which it is acquainted with. On the other side, the ordinary smallest measure we have of either is looked on as an unit in number, when the mind by division would reduce them into less fractions, though on both sides, both in addition and division, either of space or duration, when the *idea* under consideration becomes very big or very small, its precise bulk becomes very obscure and confused; and it is the number of its repeated additions or divisions that alone remains clear and distinct; as will easily appear to anyone who will let his thoughts loose in the vast expansion of space, or divisibility of matter. Every part of duration is duration too, and every part of extension is extension, both of them capable of addition or division *in infinitum*. But the least portions of either of them, whereof we have clear and and distinct *ideas*, may perhaps be fittest to be considered by us as the *simple ideas* of that kind out of which our complex modes of space, extension, and duration are made up, and into which they can again be distinctly resolved. Such a small part in duration may be called a *moment*, and is the time of one *idea* in our minds in the train of their ordinary succession there. The other, wanting a proper name, I know not whether I may be allowed to call *a sensible point*, meaning thereby the least particle of matter or space we can discern, which is ordinarily about a minute, and to the sharpest eyes seldom less than thirty seconds of a circle, whereof the eye is the centre.

*

12. *Duration*, and time which is a part of it, *is the idea* we have *of perishing distance, of which no two parts exist together*, but follow each other in succession, as *expansion is the* idea *of lasting distance, all whose parts exist together* and are not capable of succession. And therefore, though we cannot conceive any duration without succession, nor can put it together in our thoughts that any being does now exist tomorrow or possess at once more than the present moment of duration, yet we can conceive the eternal duration of the Almighty far different from that of man, or any other finite being. Because man comprehends not in his knowledge or power all past and future things: his thoughts are but of yesterday, and he knows not what tomorrow will bring forth. What is once past he can never recall; and what is yet to come he cannot make present. What I say of man, I say of all finite beings; who, though they may far exceed man in knowledge and power, yet are no more than the meanest creature in comparison with *God* himself. Finite of any magnitude holds not any proportion to infinite. *God's* infinite duration being accompanied with infinite knowledge and infinite power, he sees all things, past and to come; and they are no more distant from his

knowledge, no further removed from his sight, than the present: they all lie under the same view, and there is nothing which he cannot make exist each moment he pleases. For, the existence of all things depending upon his good pleasure, all things exist every moment that he thinks fit to have them exist. To conclude: expansion and duration do mutually embrace and comprehend each other, every part of space being in every part of duration, and every part of duration in every part of expansion. Such a combination of two distinct *ideas* is, I suppose, scarce to be found in all that great variety we do or can conceive, and may afford matter to further speculation.

*

from Chapter XXIII, Book II, 'Of Our Complex Ideas of Substances'
. . . in the communication of motion by impulse, wherein as much motion is lost to one body as is got to the other, which is the ordinariest case, we can have no other conception but of the passing of motion out of one body into another; which, I think, is as obscure and inconceivable as how our minds move or stop our bodies by thought, which we every moment find they do. The increase of motion by impulse, which is observed or believed sometimes to happen, is yet harder to be understood. We have by daily experience clear evidence of motion produced both by impulse and by thought, but the manner how hardly comes without our comprehension: we are equally at a loss in both. So that however we consider motion and its communication either from body or spirit, *the* idea *which belongs to spirit is at least as clear as that that belongs to body*. And if we consider the active power of moving or, as I may call it, *motivity*, it is much clearer in spirit than body, since two bodies, placed by one another at rest, will never afford us the *idea* of a power in the one to move the other, but by a borrowed motion; whereas the mind every day affords us *ideas* of an active power of moving of bodies; and therefore it is worth our consideration whether active power be not the proper attribute of spirits, and passive power of matter. Hence may be conjectured that created spirits are not totally separate from matter, because they are both active and passive. Pure spirit, viz. *God*, is only active; pure matter is only passive; those beings that are both active and passive we may judge to partake of both. But, be that as it will, I think, we have as many and as clear *ideas* belonging to spirit as we have belonging to body, the substance of each being equally unknown to us, and the *idea* of thinking in spirit as clear as of extension in body; and the communication of motion by thought which we attribute to spirit is as evident as that by impulse, which we ascribe to body. Constant experience makes us sensible to both of these, though our narrow understandings can comprehend neither. For when the mind would look beyond those original *ideas* we have from sensation or reflection and penetrate into their causes and manner of production, we find still it discovers nothing but its own

shortsightedness.

29. To conclude. Sensation convinces us that there are solid, extended substances, and reflection, that there are thinking ones; experience assures us of the existence of such beings, and that the one hath a power to move body by impulse, the other by thought: this we cannot doubt of. Experience, I say, every moment furnishes us with the clear *ideas* both of the one and the other. But beyond these *ideas*, as received from their proper sources, our faculties will not reach. If we would inquire further into their nature, causes, and manner, we perceive not the nature of extension clearer than we do of thinking. If we would explain them any further, one is as easy as the other; and there is no more difficulty to conceive how a substance we know not should, by thought, set body into motion, than how a substance we know not should, by impulse, set body into motion. So that we are no more able to discover wherein the *ideas* belonging to body consist than those belonging to spirit. From whence it seems probable to me that the simple *ideas* we receive from sensation and reflection are the boundaries of our thoughts; beyond which the mind, whatever efforts it would make, is not able to advance one jot; nor can it make any discoveries, when it would pry into the nature and hidden causes of those *ideas*.

*

35. For it is infinity which, joined to our *ideas* of existence, power, knowledge, etc., makes that complex *idea* whereby we represent to ourselves, the best we can, the supreme Being. For, though in his own essence (which certainly we do not know, not knowing the real essence of a pebble, or a fly, or of our own selves) *God* be simple and uncompounded, yet I think I may say we have no other *idea* of him but a complex one of existence, knowledge, power, happiness, etc., infinite and eternal; which are all distinct *ideas*, and some of them, being relative, are again compounded of others; all which, being as has been shown originally got from *sensation* and *reflection*, go to make up the *idea* or notion we have of *God*.

36. This further is to be observed, that there is no *idea* we attribute to *God*, bating infinity, which is not also a part of our complex *idea* of other spirits. Because, being capable of no other simple *ideas*, belonging to anything but body, but those which by reflection we receive from the operation of our own minds, we can attribute to spirits no other but what we receive from thence; and all the difference we can put between them in our contemplation of spirits is only in the several extents and degrees of their knowledge, power, duration, happiness, etc. For that in our *ideas*, as well *of spirits* as of other things, we are *restrained to those we receive from sensation and reflection* is evident from hence: that in our *ideas* of spirits, how much soever advanced in perfection beyond those of bodies, even to that of infinite, we cannot yet have any

idea of the manner wherein they discover their thoughts one to another, though we must necessarily conclude that separate spirits, which are beings that have perfecter knowledge and greater happiness than we, must needs have also a perfecter way of communicating their thoughts than we have who are fain to make use of corporeal signs and particular sounds; which are therefore of most general use as being the best and quickest we are capable of. But of immediate communication, having no experiment in ourselves and consequently no notion of it at all, we have no *idea* how spirits which use not words can, with quickness, or much less, how spirits that have no bodies can be masters of their own thoughts and communicate or conceal them at pleasure, though we cannot but necessarily suppose they have such a power.

37. And thus we have seen *what kind of* ideas *we have of substances of all kinds*, wherein they consist, and how we come by them. From whence, I think, it is very evident:

First, That all our *ideas* of the several sorts of substances are nothing but collections of simple *ideas*, with a supposition of something to which they belong, and in which they subsist, though of this supposed something we have no clear distinct *idea* at all.

Secondly, That all the simple *ideas* that, thus united in one common *substratum*, make up our complex *ideas* of several sorts of the substances are no other but such as we have received from *sensation* or *reflection*. So that even in those which we think we are most intimately acquainted with, and come nearest the comprehension of our most enlarged conceptions, we cannot reach beyond those simple *ideas*. And even in those which seem most remote from all we have to do with and do infinitely surpass anything we can perceive in ourselves by *reflection* or discover by *sensation* in other things, we can attain to nothing but those simple *ideas* which we originally received from *sensation* or *reflection*, as is evident in the complex *ideas* we have of angels and particularly of *God* himself.

Thirdly, That most of the simple *ideas* that make up our complex *ideas* of substances, when truly considered, are only powers, however we are apt to take them for positive qualities: v.g. the greatest part of the *ideas* that make our complex *idea* of *gold* are yellowness, great weight, ductility, fusibility, and solubility in *aqua regia*, etc., all united together in an unknown *substratum*; all which *ideas* are nothing else but so many relations to other substances, and are not really in the gold, considered barely in itself, though they depend on those real and primary qualities of its internal constitution, whereby it has a fitness differently to operate and be operated on by several other substances.

*

from Chapter XXXIII, Book II, 'Of The Association of Ideas'

1. There is scarce anyone that does not observe something that seems

odd to him, and is in itself really extravagant, in the opinions, reasonings, and actions of other men. The least flaw of this kind, if at all different from his own, everyone is quicksighted enough to espy in another, and will by the authority of reason forwardly condemn, though he be guilty of much greater unreasonableness in his own tenets and conduct, which he never perceives and will very hardly, if at all, be convinced of. . . .

5. Some of our *ideas* have a natural correspondence and connexion one with another; it is the office and excellency of our reason to trace these, and hold them together in that union and correspondence which is founded in their peculiar beings. Besides this, there is another connexion of *ideas* wholly owing to chance or custom: *ideas* that in themselves are not at all of kin, come to be so united in some men's minds that it is very hard to separate them, they always keep in company, and the one no sooner at any time comes into the understanding but its associate appears with it; and if they are more than two which are thus united, the whole gang, always inseparable, show themselves together.

6. This strong combination of *ideas*, not allied by nature, the mind makes in itself either voluntarily or by chance; and hence it comes in different men to be very different, according to their different inclinations, educations, interests, etc. Custom settles habits of thinking in the under-standing, as well as of determining in the will, and of motions in the body: all which seem to be but trains of motion in the animal spirits, which, once set a-going, continue in the same steps they have been used to; which, by often treading, are worn into a smooth path, and the motion in it becomes easy and, as it were, natural. As far as we can comprehend thinking, thus *ideas* seem to be produced in our minds; or, if they are not, this may serve to explain their following one another in an habitual train, when once they are put into that track, as well as it does to explain such motions of the body. A musician used to any tune will find that, let it but once begin in his head, the *ideas* of the several notes of it will follow one another orderly in his understanding, without any care or attention, as regularly as his fingers move orderly over the keys of the organ to play out the tune he has begun, though his unattentive thoughts be elsewhere a-wandering. Whether the natural cause of these *ideas*, as well as of that regular dancing of his fingers, be the motion of his animal spirits, I will not determine, how probable soever, by this instance, it appears to be so; but this may help us a little to conceive of intellectual habits and of the tying together of *ideas*.

7. That there are such associations of them made by custom in the minds of most men, I think nobody will question who has well considered himself or others; and to this, perhaps, might be justly attributed most of the sympathies and antipathies observable in men, which work as strongly and produce as regular effects as if they were natural; and are therefore called so, though they at first had no other original but the accidental connexion of two *ideas*, which either the strength of the first impression

or future indulgence so united that they always afterwards kept company together in that man's mind, as if they were but one *idea*. I say most of the antipathies, I do not say all: for some of them are truly natural, depend upon our original constitution, and are born with us; but a great part of those which are counted natural would have been known to be from unheeded, though perhaps early, impressions or wanton fancies at first, which would have been acknowledged the original of them, if they had been warily observed. A grown person surfeiting with honey no sooner hears the name of it, but his fancy immediately carries sickness and qualms to his stomach, and he cannot bear the very *idea* of it; other *ideas* of dislike and sickness and vomiting presently accompany it, and he is disturbed, but he knows from whence to date this weakness and can tell how he got this indisposition: had this happened to him by an overdose of honey when a child, all the same effects would have followed, but the cause would have been mistaken, and the antipathy counted natural.

8. I mention this not out of any great necessity there is in this present argument to distinguish nicely between natural and acquired antipathies, but I take notice of it for another purpose, viz. that those who have children or the charge of their education would think it worth their while diligently to watch and carefully to prevent the undue connexion of *ideas* in the minds of young people. This is the time most susceptible of lasting impressions; and though those relating to the health of the body are by discreet people minded and fenced against, yet I am apt to doubt that those which relate more peculiarly to the mind, and terminate in the understanding or passions, have been much less heeded than the thing deserves: nay, those relating purely to the understanding have, as I suspect, been by most men wholly overlooked.

9. This wrong connexion in our minds of ideas, in themselves loose and independent one of another, has such an influence and is of so great force to set us awry in our actions as well moral as natural, passions, reasonings, and notions themselves, that perhaps there is not any one thing that deserves more to be looked after.

10. The *ideas* of *goblins* and *sprites* have really no more to do with darkness than light: yet let but a foolish maid inculcate these often on the mind of a child and raise them there together, possibly he shall never be able to separate them again so long as he lives, but darkness shall ever afterwards bring with it those frightful *ideas*, and they shall be so joined that he can no more bear the one than the other.

11. A man receives a sensible injury from another, thinks on the man and that action over and over, and by ruminating on them strongly, or much, in his mind, so cements those two *ideas* together that he makes them almost one; never thinks on the man, but the pain and displeasure he suffered comes into his mind with it, so that he scarce distinguishes them, but has as much an aversion for the one as the other. Thus hatreds are often begotten from slight and almost innocent occasions, and quarrels

propagated and continued in the world.

12. A man has suffered pain or sickness in any place, he saw his friend die in such a room: though these have in nature nothing to do one with another, yet when the *idea* of the place occurs to his mind, it brings (the impression being once made) that of the pain and displeasure with it, he confounds them in his mind, and can as little bear the one as the other.

13. When this combination is settled and whilst it lasts, it is not in the power of reason to help us and relieve us from the effects of it. *Ideas* in our minds, when they are there, will operate according to their natures and circumstances; and here we see the cause why time cures certain affections, which reason, though in the right and allowed to be so, has not power over nor is able against them to prevail with those who are apt to hearken to it in other cases. The death of a child, that was the daily delight of his mother's eyes and joy of her soul, rends from her heart the whole comfort of her life and gives her all the torment imaginable; use the consolations of reason in this case, and you were as good preach ease to one on the rack . . .

Fifth edition, 1706

JOHN DENNIS (1657–1734)

At first sight, John Dennis appears an indispensable early Romantic. His championing of passion, his feeling for 'enthusiasm' and 'the Sublime', his sense of religious emotion and of the importance of the obscure, even his antipathy for Pope, all bear a strong resemblance to the positions of the early Romantics.

There is, nevertheless, something only a little stronger than an impression which makes one reluctant to divine in Dennis the true fire. His contemporaries, Burnet, Thomas Warton, Edward Young, even Trapp, assumed less elaborate theories and yet they seem to have divined more, reaching the heart of the matter, as it were, by instinct. For example in Chapter V of *The Advancement and Reformation of Poetry*, itself a puritanical title reminding one of Jeremy Collier's parallel purposes on the stage, Dennis speaks attractively of passion as 'the characteristical mark of poetry' yet the subsequent account of tragedy, epic, and the 'greater ode' shows a preoccupation with form that makes his concept of emotion seem curiously stilted. Similarly, he offers a distinction between 'ordinary passion' and 'enthusiasms' mildly suggestive of Burke's 'Sublime' (see pp. 195-206) 'not clearly comprehended by him who feels them', while labouring towards a kind of Dionysian levelling suggesting the straitjacket at almost every point. There are noble emotions and less noble passions, just as there are religious enthusiasms and lesser enthusiasms. We are reminded that, from Burnet onward, a recognition of the Bible as an anthology of early prophetic poetry seen exclusively as secular, literary creation, fed men's concepts of primitivism and originality. Dennis seems to remain doggedly outside of this movement, intent on retaining traditional structures and hieratic religion.

The Romantic movement may be discerned in its earliest stages in the orientalism, feeling and subjectivism stemming from the ferment of the Royal Society. Perhaps the essential nature of the enormous shift of sensibility which took place at this time is the transference of the *locus* of reality to the individual, variable sensibility through whose lens, as Swift pointed out with trepidation in his greatest works, form and its iconography shifted and altered. Feeling and enthusiasm swept away judgment, rules and *genres*. As we may observe in Burnet, the significant development in contemporary aesthetic thought was the shift of religious feeling away from religion to the great objects of Nature. One of the first casualties in this shift, as Pope's *Peri Bathos*, or *The Art of Sinking* reveals in its satire, was the concept of idealization or ennobling. In Dennis, however, the hieratic is not the victim but the product of enthusiasm; the nobler idea will always ignite the nobler *strata* of the mind, as in the traditional 'Sublime' of Longinus, whose theories, as *Guardian* No. 86 points out, were rapidly being superseded (see pp. 140-143).

Furthest from Dennis's mind apparently was the notion that in the eye of the creator, as in the lens of the new science, space and time, even 'outness' as Berkeley termed externality, became distorted, even dissolved. Most significantly, during the period when we find in every direction traces of the idea that art might be an extension of man, not a mere mirror, and that the poet might — like God — extend Nature through his native, timeless perception, Dennis seems to continue uncritically the concept that art should be an imitation of Nature, defending, like Shadwell in his conflict with Dryden, the most apparently advanced notions while understanding none of their implications.

THE ADVANCEMENT AND REFORMATION OF POETRY (1701)

Chapter V, 'That Passion is the chief Thing in Poetry, and that all Passion is either ordinary Passion, or Enthusiasm'
But before we proceed, let us define Poetry; which is the first Time that a Definition has been given of that noble Art: For neither Ancient nor Modern Criticks have defin'd Poetry in general.

Poetry then is an Imitation of Nature, by a pathetick and numerous Speech. Let us explain it.

As Poetry is an Art, it must be an Imitation of Nature. That the Instrument with which it makes its Imitation, is Speech, need not be disputed. That that Speech must be Musical, no one can doubt: For Numbers distinguish the Parts of Poetick Diction, from the Periods of Prose. Now Numbers are nothing but articulate Sounds, and their Pauses measur'd by their proper proportions of Time. And the Periods of Prosaick Diction are articulate Sounds, and their Pauses unmeasur'd by such Proportions. That the Speech, by which Poetry makes its Imitation, must be pathetick, is evident; for Passion is still more necessary to it than Harmony. For Harmony only distinguishes its Instrument from that of Prose, but Passion distinguishes its very Nature and Character. For, therefore, Poetry is Poetry, because it is more Passionate and Sensual than Prose. A Discourse that is writ in very good Numbers, if it wants Passion, can be but measur'd Prose. But a Discourse that is every where extremely pathetick, and, consequently, every where bold and figurative, is certainly Poetry without Numbers.

Passion then, is the Characteristical Mark of Poetry, and, consequently, must be every where: For where-ever a Discourse is not Pathetick, there it is Prosaick. As Passion in a Poem must be every where, so Harmony is usually diffus'd throughout it. But Passion answers the Two Ends of Poetry better than Harmony can do, and upon that Account is preferable to it: For, first, it pleases more, which is evident: For Passion can please without Harmony, but Harmony tires without Passion. And in Tragedy, and in Epick Poetry, a Man may instruct without Harmony, but never without Passion: For the one instructs by Admiration, and the other by

Compassion and Terror. And as for the greater Ode, if it wants Passion, it becomes hateful and intolerable, and its Sentences grow contemptible.

Passion is the Characteristical Mark of Poetry, and therefore it must be every where; for without Passion there can be no Poetry, no more than there can be Painting. And tho' the Poet and the Painter describe Action, they must describe it with Passion. Let any one who beholds a Piece of Painting, where the Figures are shewn in Action, conclude, that if the Figures are without Passion, the Painting is contemptible. There must be Passion every where, in Poetry and Painting, and the more Passion there is, the better the Poetry and the Painting, unless the Passion is too much for the Subject; and the Painter, and the Poet, arrive at the Height of their Art, when they describe a great deal of Action, with a great deal of Passion. It is plain then, from what has been said, that Passion in Poetry must be every where, for where there is no Passion, there can be no Poetry; but that which we commonly call Passion, cannot be every where in any Poem. There must be Passion then, that must be distinct from ordinary Passion, and that must be Enthusiasm. I call that ordinary Passion, whose Cause is clearly comprehended by him who feels it, whether it be Admiration, Terror or Joy; and I call the very same Passions Enthusiasms, when their Cause is not clearly comprehended by him who feels them. And those Enthusiastick Passions, are sometimes simple, and sometimes complicated, of all which we shall shew Examples lower. And thus I have shewn, that the chief thing in Poetry, is Passion: But here the Reader is desir'd to observe, that by Poetry, we mean Poetry in general, and the Body of Poetry; for as for the Form or Soul of particular Poems, that is allow'd by all to be a Fable. But Passion is the chief Thing in the Body of Poetry; as Spirit is in the Human Body. For without Spirit the Body languishes, and the Soul is impotent: Now every Thing that they call Spirit, or Genius in Poetry, in short, every Thing that pleases, and consequently, moves, in the Poetick Diction, is Passion, whether it be Ordinary or Enthusiastick.

And thus we have shewn, what the chief Excellence in the Body of Poetry is, which we have prov'd to be Passion. Let us now proceed, to the Proofs of what we propounded, That Sacred Subjects, are more susceptible of Passion, than Prophane ones; and that the Subjects of the Ancients, were Sacred in their greater Poetry, I mean either Sacred in their own Natures, or by their Manner of handling them.

*

from Chapter VII, 'The Causes of Poetical Enthusiasm, shewn by Examples'

The Enthusiasm that is found in Poetry, is nothing but the fore-mentioned Passions, Admiration, Joy, Terror, Astonishment, flowing from the Thoughts which naturally produce them. For Admiration, together with that Pride, which exalts the Soul at the conceiving a great Hint, gives

Elevation; Joy, if 'tis great, gives Transport, and Astonishment gives Vehemence. But now let us shew by Examples, how this was done, and let us begin with that admirable Ode of *Horace*, which is the Third of the Third Book.

Justum, & tenacem propositi virum,
Non civium ardor prava jubentium,
Non voltus instantis tyranni
Mente quatit solida; neque Auster,
Dux inquieti turbidus Adriae;
Nec fulminantis magna manus Jovis:
Si fractus illabatur orbis,
Impavidum ferient ruinae.

That is, *The Man, the brave Man, who is resolv'd upon a right and a firm Principle, is sure never to have his solid Vertue shaken, neither by the Rage of the giddy Multitude, nor by the Frowns of an insulting Tyrant, nor by the Fury of the roaring South, that turbulent Ruler of the tempestuous* Adria; *no, nor by the Red Right Hand of Thundring* Jove: *Nay, should the World's disjointed Frame come rushing down with a dismal Sound upon him, its Ruins might Crush, but they could never Shake him.* Now 'tis plain, that in the Original there is a great deal of Enthusiasm. But let us observe a little what this Enthusiasm is. Upon Observation we shall find then, that in the fore-mentioned Verses there is Elevation, Severity and Vehemence, and consequently, there is something Admirable in them, and Terrible, and Astonishing. Now why should we feel these Passions, in reading these Thoughts, unless the Passions naturally attend them, when they are express'd as they should be? But Admiration, as we have said above, must come from something that is Great, and Terror from something that is Powerful, and likely to hurt; and Astonishment from something that is very Terrible, and very likely to hurt; that is, from Things that are so, or from their Ideas. The Reader, upon examining the fore-mentioned Verses, will find, that the Thoughts in them all are Great and Terrible, and some of them are Astonishing.

But here I desire the Reader to observe Three Things: First, The admirable Gradation of Thought here. How the Poet rises from something that is Terrible, to something that is more Terrible, till he comes at last to something Astonishing and Amazing. How from the Rage of the mad Multitude, he proceeds to the Frowns of a Tyrant that stands threatning by: How he rises from thence to a Storm at Sea, and from thence to the to the Wrath of *Jove*, express'd in the dreadful Thunder, and from thence to the final dismal Dissolution of all Things. The next Thing that I desire him to observe, is, How the Spirit of the Poet rises with his Thoughts which is a sure Sign, that the one is nothing but the Passions that attend on the other. And the Third Thing that the Reader is to remark, is, That the Poet could not carry his Enthusiasm higher after the second Thought, without having recourse to Religion. For he who knows any Thing of the Pagan System, knows that the Three last Thoughts are taken from their Religion.

*

from Chapter X, 'That in their Sacred Poetry, in which the Ancients excell'd the Moderns, those Places were greatest and most Poetical, that had most of Religion'

First then, Admiration, which is the reigning Passion of Epick Poetry, I mean, that which is admirable in the Action of the Hero, is heighten'd by Revelations, by Machines, and the Ministration of the Gods. For that Ministration, those Machines, and those Revelations are all miraculous. And the Man who was admirable before for his extraordinary Valour, and his Native Greatness, becomes more wonderful, when we behold him the Esteem and immediate Concern of Heaven, when we see him the peculiar Care of Providence, when we find the Order of Nature inverted, the Skies grown factious upon his Account, and Gods descending to sustain or oppose him.

But, Secondly, Terror and Compassion, which are the reigning Passions in Tragedy, are heighten'd by Religion. Tragedy, says *Aristotle* in his *Poetick*, is the Imitation of an Action which excites Compassion and Terror. Now those two Passions proceed from Surprize, when the Incidents spring one from another against our Expectation: For those Incidents, continues the Philosopher, are always more admirable, than those which arrive by Chance; which is evident from this, says he, That even of accidental Things, those are always the most Wonderful and most Surprizing, which at the same Time that they arrive by Chance, seem to fall out by Design, and by a certain particular secret Conduct; of which Nature was what they relate of the Statue of *Mitys* at *Argos*, which fell upon his Murderer, and kill'd him upon the Spot, in the midst of a great Assembly: For that by no means, says the Philosopher, seems to be the Work of Chance. From whence it follows, says he, of necessity, that those Fables where there is this Conduct, will always seem preferable to those that have it not. Thus *Aristotle* declares, That the Wonderful in Tragedy as well as Epick Poetry, is heightned by Religion, that those Tragical Incidents that appear to have most of Providence in them, are always most Moving and Terrible. The Reason is plain, For all our Passions are grounded upon the Love of Ourselves; and Terror and Compassion spring from the Calamities of our Equals; that is, of those who being in Circumstances resembling ours, and committing Faults which we either commit, or to which we are liable, are upon that, unfortunate. For the more there appears to be of Providence in the Punishment, the more we pity the Persons. For if their Calamities appear to be the Work of Chance, they might as well have happened to those who have not committed such Faults, as to those who have. And therefore a Train of Incidents, which, contrary to our Expectation, surprizingly produce one another, is necessary, because the more plainly the Punishment appears the Result of the Faults, and the more clearly we are convinc'd of this, when we least expect it, Providence appears the more in the Case, and our Security is shaken the more, and the more we are mov'd and terrified. But Religion does not only heighten those Passions which are great in themselves, as Admiration and Terror are; for Admiration raises the Soul, and every Thing that is terrible, is certainly great to him to whom it is terrible, but it ennobles those which are commonly base and dejected; as for Example, Grief; witness that Passage in the Passion of *Dido*:

Testatur moritura Deos, & conscia fati
Sidera.   [*Aeneid*, iv. 519-520]

And that Noble Apostrophe afterwards:

Sol, qui terrarum flammis, &c.   [iv. 607]

And that Sublime Apostrophe of *Sinon*, in the Second Book:

. . . Ille dolis instructus, & arte Pelasga,
Sustulit exutas vinclis, ad sidera palmas:
Vos, aeterni ignes, & non violabile vestrum
Testor numen, ait; vos arae ensesque nefandi,
Quos fugi; vittaeque Deum, quas hostia gessi, &c.   [ii. 152-156]

But to come to the other Sort of Passion, which gives Poetry its Force and its Greatness; Religious Enthusiasm must necessarily be greater than Human Enthusiasm can be, because the Passions that attend on Religious Ideas, when a Man is capable of reflecting on them as he should do, are stronger than those which attend on Prophane Ideas, as has been said above, and has been partly shewn by Examples. And as ordinary Passion is heightned by Religion, so Human Enthusiastick Passions are heightned by Religious Enthusiasm. We shall give an Example of this in Terror, by which I mean, not that common Passion, which *Aristotle* treats of in his Rhetorick, and in his Poetick, and of which we spoke in the former Part of this Chapter; but that Enthusiastick Terror, which springs from the Ideas unknown to him who feels it. *Virgil* in his First Book of the *Aeneis* describes a Tempest, which carries double Terror along with it; the Ordinary one, which springs from the Concern which we have for the Hero; and the Enthusiastick one, which the Ideas would carry along with them, tho' they were separated from that Concern which we feel for the Hero. The Description is Grave and Severe, and Exalted, because the Poet was mov'd by the terrible Ideas. For that which is terrible, is always great to him to whom it is terrible, as we said before; and that which is great is admirable, and then he who is terrified is always serious, and very much in earnest. The same Description where the Terror is at the Height, is vehement.

. . . Insequitur cumulo praeruptus aquae mons,
Hi summo in fluctu pendent: his unda dehiscens
Terram inter fluctus aperit, furit aestus harenis.   [i. 105-107]

Because that which is very terrible, is wonderful and astonishing, and he who is astonish'd, being transported beyond himself, must of necessity express himself with that sort of Fury which we call Vehemence. *Virgil*, by setting so many terrible Images in Motion, had set this Tempest before his Eyes, or rather had transported himself, as it were, into it. Now, any one who has been upon the Brink of a Wreck, and, consequently, has been very much terrify'd himself, and seen others astonish'd, cannot but have felt the same Motions that he feels, in reading this Passage, and cannot but have observ'd, that others who felt them, express'd themselves with the same Fury and Vehemence that the Poet does, tho' not with the same Elegance. But tho' this Storm is terrible in it self, and wonderful, yet the Machines, which prepare, and raise, and allay it, very much add to its Greatness and genuine Terror, and it is quite another Thing when it is consider'd with the Cause of it, which is the Anger of *Juno*, and the Compliance of *Aeolus*, and with that which follow'd upon it, which is the Indignation of *Neptune*, and the Exertion of his absolute Power.

The Passages of the ancient Poets that were most Religious, were their Invocations, Apostrophes, or the like; or those which contain'd the miraculous Part of their Religion, their Signs, Apparitions, Oracles, and other Revelations.

For their Invocations, Apostrophes, and the like, which were all of them either a sort of Prayers, or Divine Attestations, they are most of them very Sublime, and attended with a strong Enthusiasm. And how could it be otherwise, but that the ancient Poets, who were Men of great Learning, of great Passions, great Eloquence, and great Parts, when with Study and Pains, and with all their Endeavours to be Enthusiastick, they address'd themselves to their Gods, should be extremely agitated; when we see very plainly, that a sort of Modern Enthusiasts, who have neither Learning nor Parts, nor the least Tincture of good Letters, are, even in their Extemporary Prayers, disturb'd with very fierce Enthusiasms?

JOSEPH TRAPP (1679–1747)

In the early eighteenth century mythology began to derive from the supposed first years of the globe and from the poetry of the Hebrews and other primitive writers who could be located close to the awe-inspiring beginnings of time. This massive change in the European shape of the past away from the comparatively recent Greeks and Romans occurred, Mark Pattison has suggested in his essay on Joseph Scaliger, under the influence of post-Copernican polymaths who constructed a universal ancient history centred fortuitously on the Hebrews as the tribe most in contact with its neighbours. New skills — for example in ancient languages — led to the dismantling of Renaissance literary commonplaces. The many-talented Vossius (1577–1649), for example, in his influential *De artis poeticae* (1647) dismembered the genealogy, still attractive to Pope in the preface to his Homer, of divine and semi-divine figures named Orpheus, Linus and Musaeus transmitting to men in a direct line from Apollo the art of poetry. Rather, it came to be believed, poetry had originated with Jubal, Biblical inventor of instrumental music, and offspring of Adam. Vossius suggested that 'Orpheus', 'Linus' and 'Musaeus', were not mythological figures but derivatives of oriental roots meaning 'knowledge', 'to murmur', and 'art' or 'discipline'.

The Professorship of Poetry at Oxford was founded in 1708, and, perhaps influenced by the climate of exhaustive enquiry of the scientific age, dwelt from the start on the true, 'original' nature of the poetic art. Trapp, Thomas Warton, Joseph Spence and Robert Lowth, among the first professors, were notably in the forefront of the change from classicism to primitivism. Trapp, for example, echoes Vossius at his most provocative, frequently, as in his statement in the second of his *Praelectiones poeticae*, 'poetry flourished among the Israelites not only before the Trojan war, but before the coming of Cadmus into Boeotia, who first taught the Greeks the use of letters', paraphrasing his mentor almost word for word.

Apparently committed, like Edward Young, to 'orientalism' Trapp wrote an oriental play, *Abra Mule* (1704) and paraphrases of biblical poetry, notably *Psalm 104* (cf. Burnet on Psalm 104, p. 25), which seem to anticipate Smart in their mixture of sublimity and materialistic science. A major contribution of the Professorship of Poetry to the techniques of Romanticism was to be the theory of parallelism first enunciated by Robert Lowth (see pp. 149-167). Trapp anticipates later developments in several instances. The poet was a prophet. The pastoral, he notes, was invented by the Hebrews long before Theocritus. The lyric ode, as superior to other forms of poetry as poetry is to prose, apparently sprang, in Trapp's imagination, spontaneously from the first men, who, as in Herder, seem to be defined by their ability to sing. Perhaps most notable is Trapp's appreciation of the formal consequences of the shift from Mnemosyne to Jubal. In a partial anticipation of parallelism —

interestingly in an ode to Dr Edward Pococke, Professor of Arabic, and crucial figure in contemporary Arabic scholarship – he dwelt on the meandering, digressive, progress of the poetry of the lyric ode, which, whilst it might be found in Horace as in Pindar, appeared so much more characteristic of, indeed to originate in, the East.

LECTURES ON POETRY (1708–18)

from 'The First Lecture'
Not to urge that Poetry is coeval with the World itself, and that the Creator may be said in working up and finishing his beautiful Poem of the Universe, to have performed the Part of a Poet, no less than of a Geometrician; it is well known, that those Books have had the greatest Sanction from Time, that have been dictated by God, or writ by Poets. Those, as it is fit, have the Precedence: But these follow at no very great Distance.

Nay, why should we make this Difference between the sacred Writers and Poets, since the sacred Writers were most of them Poets; on both Accounts deservedly called *Vates* (*a Word expressing either Character*) and acted by no feigned Inspiration? That the Devils, then, heretofore, usurping the Title of Gods, gave out their Oracles in Verse, was owing wholly to their imitating, in this, as well as in other Particulars, the true God, that so they might gain Honour and Reverence from their Votaries. If in the Poems of *Job*, and *David*, and the other sacred Authors, we observe the inexpressible Sublimity of their Words and Matter; their elegant, and more than human Descriptions; the happy Boldness of their Metaphors; their spiritual Ardour breathing Heaven, and winging the Souls of their Readers up to it, triumphing, as it were, by a royal Authority, over the narrow Rules of mortal Writers, it is impossible but we must in Transport own, that nothing is wanting in them, that might be expected from the Strength of Poetry heighten'd by the Energy of Inspiration.

*

from Lecture XIV, 'Of Pastorals'
In the first Ages of the World, before Men were united in Cities, and had learnt the studied Arts of Luxury, they lead in the Country plain harmless Lives; and Cottages, rather than Houses, might be said to be their Habitation. Those happy Times abounded with Leisure and Recreation: To feed the Flock, and cultivate the Land, was the only Employ of its peaceable Inhabitants; the former the joint Care of the Women and the Men. Hence arose abundant Matter for Love and Verse. Nay, when the World was grown older, and Mankind so numerous, that they began to secure themselves in Walls, and to introduce what we call a more civil Life, yet still Shepherds and Husbandmen maintain'd their primitive

Honour. Country Affairs, but especially the Care of the Flock, was not only the Labour of the Vulgar, but the Exercise of the Rich and Powerful, nay, of Princes of either Sex. This appears sufficiently, from sacred History, in the Example of *Jacob, Rachel, Moses*, and the other Patriarchs: From the Testimony of Heathen Writers; as in that of *Virgil*,
Nec te poeniteat pecoris, divine Poeta,
Et formosus oves ad flumina pavit Adonis.   [*Ecl*. x. 17-18]

Them, heav'nly Poet, blush not thou to own:
Ev'n fair *Adonis* did not scorn to tend
Along the River's Side his fleecy Care.
And in another Place, to omit other Instances:
Quem fugis, ah! demens? habitarant Di quoque
    silvas,
Dardaniusque Paris.   [*Ecl*. ii. 60-61]

Whom fly'st thou, thoughtless? Gods have liv'd in
    Woods;
And Trojan Paris.   [*Ecl*. iii. 60–1]
From what has been said, it is easy to see the Origin of *Pastorals*. It appears to have been a very ancient Species of Poetry, tho' I can by no means agree with *Scaliger*, in thinking it the oldest, which is an Honour I shall hereafter shew to be due to the Lyric Kind. Shepherds, 'tis true, were the first Poets; but Odes and Hymns, not Pastorals, were their original Compositions. However, Pastorals, as I said, are undoubtedly of very great Antiquity; and the *Song of Solomon* in sacred Writ comes under this Denomination; from whence, 'tis very observable, *Theocritus* has borrow'd literally many Expressions; making use of the Version of the Seventy-two, with whom he was contemporary.

*

from Lecture XVI, 'Of Lyric Poetry'
That this is the most ancient Kind of Poem, is pretty evident. *Jubal*, in sacred Writ, is said to be the first Inventor of musical Instruments; and little Doubt is to be made, but vocal Music was added to them. And we are farther told, by a *Jewish* Author, of venerable Antiquity, tho' his Works are not admitted into the Canon, that the same *which found out musical Tunes, recited Verses in Writing.* [Ecclesiasticus 44:5.] We have before observ'd, that Poetry took its Rise from those Festival Hymns which were sung at the Conclusion of Harvest, in Gratitude to the Deity. Odes, therefore, and Poetry, date their Original from the same Aera: And, in Truth, if we consider the internal Motions of the Soul, it will seem very probable that Poetry, which is so peculiarly adapted to express the several Emotions of Joy, or Praise, or Gratitude, owes its Rise to Nature herself, and was therefore join'd with Music. We have no Instance of Poetry

older than the celebrated Song, or rather Ode, of *Moses*. [Deuteronomy
15.] The Antiquity of the other Hymns mention'd in sacred History,
and, particularly, the Collection of them in the Book of *Psalms*, is so
well known, that I shall dwell no longer upon this Particular.

As to the Nature of the Lyric Poem, it is, of all Kinds of Poetry, the
most poetical; and is as distinct, both in Style, and Thought, from the rest,
as Poetry in general is from Prose. I have before observ'd, the Peculiarity
of its Diction; the Thought, only, now comes under Consideration. Now
this is the boldest of all other Kinds, full of Rapture, and elevated from
common Language the most that is possible; so that what *Horace* says at
the Beginning of one of his Odes [*Odes*, III. i], may not improperly be
applied to all the rest:

Odi profanum vulgus, & arceo.

I hate, I scorn the Vulgar Throng.

Some Odes there are, likewise, in the free and loose Manner, which seem
to avoid all Method, and yet are conducted by a very clear one; which
affect Transitions, seemingly, without Art, but, for that Reason, have the
more of it; which are above Connexion, and delight in Exclamations, and
frequent Invocation of the Muses; which begin and end abruptly, and
are carried on thro' a Variety of Matter with a sort of divine *Pathos*, above
Rules and Laws, and without Regard to the common Forms of
Grammar.

Hence, then, we learn the chief Property of Lyric Poetry, *viz.* that
it abounds with a Sort of Liberty which consists in Digressions and
Excursions. *Pindar* set his Successors this Example, insomuch that this
Style, when applied to Odes, is generally call'd Pindaric; not that he is
to be esteem'd the Inventor of it: For it is plain that he, and the rest of
the *Grecians*, receiv'd their Learning from the Nations of the East, the
Jews and *Phoenicians*: And it is well known, the Eastern Eloquence
abounded not only with Metaphors, and bold Hyperboles, but in long
Digressions; as is sufficiently evident from the sacred Writings. The
Roman Pindar often imitates the *Theban*, and sometimes exceeds him,
even in his characteristic Excellence. Thus in that Ode [*Odes*, I. iii],
where he addresses himself to the Ship that bore so valuable a Freight
as *Virgil*,

Sic te, Diva potens Cypri, &c.

at the Conclusion of the eighth Verse, he inveighs against the Temerity
of Mankind, and pursues this Argument to the End of the Ode, which is not
a very short one.

*

Nothing can describe the unbounded Nature of this Kind of Ode better
than those Lines of *Horace*, which, at the same Time, give us a lively
Instance of it. We may add, to the same Purpose, his Description of the
Theban Poet;

Monte decurrens velut amnis, imbres
Quem super notas aluere ripas,
Fervet, immensusque ruit profundo
Pindarus ore.   [*Odes,* IV, ii]

Pindar's a mighty raging Flood,
    That from some Mountain flows,
Rapid, and warm, and deep, and loud,
    Whose Force no Limits knows.

From what has been said, some will be induc'd to think, that to write a
Lyric Poem, which is indulg'd with so many Liberties, is the easiest Thing
imaginable: But, in Reality, it is the most difficult in every Respect, except
its Shortness, as it is the most elegant. It demands not only a flowing
Imagination, Brightness, Life, Sublimity, and Elegance, but the nicest
Art, and finest Judgment, so as to seem luxuriant, and not to be so; and
under the Shew of transgressing all Laws, to preserve them. For it is not
impossible but a Writer's Fire may be temper'd with the severest Judgment;
and Poets may be said, tho' Lovers cannot, to be *mad with Reason*.

Those Digressions which quite leave the Subject, and never return to it
again, please me less than some others of a very different Kind. The
former, no doubt, are defensible, and sometimes highly commendable;
for a Poet is not always oblig'd to dwell upon the same Argument from
one End to the other; and I would rather call them Transitions, than
Digressions: But the Digressions which I chiefly admire, are such as *take
Occasion* from some *Adjunct* or *Circumstance* of the Subject, to pass on
to *somewhat else* not totally distinct from it, with which the Imagination
having been diverted for some Time, new Matter starts up, and from some
new Adjunct of that, the Poet is brought back, of a sudden, to his first
Design. I cannot produce a better Instance of this, out of *Horace* himself,
than from a late Ode of one of our own Countrymen,* who, since he has
paid the Debt of Nature, may, without Envy, receive the Tribute of our
Praise; that beautiful Ode, I mean, upon the Death of the famous Dr.
Pocock; where the Poet describes his Travels to the East, in these Words:

Quin nunc requiris tecta virentia
Nini ferocis, nunc Babel arduum,
    Immane opus! crescentibusque
        Vertice sideribus propinquum!
Nequicquam; amici disparibus sonis
Eludit aures nescius artifex,
    Linguasque miratur recentes,
        In patriis peregrinus oris.
Vestitur hinc tot sermo coloribus,
Quot Tu, Pococki, dissimilis Tui

---

*Edmund Smith. Cf. Dr Johnson's praise of this poem in his *Life* of
Smith. Ed.

Orator effers, . . .

Now Ninus' Walls you search with curious Eye,
Now Babel's Tow'r, the Rival of the Sky.
In vain! the mad Attempt new Tongues confound,
The Toil eluded by discordant Sound:
To his own Sire the Son Barbarian grown,
Unletter'd, starts a Language not his own.
Hence various Bounds to Nations set by Speech;
But not to You, who, Orator in each,
His proper Tongue th' admiring Native teach.

With what Elegance does the Poet divert from his Purpose, that he may
bring in a beautiful Description of Babel, and the Confusion of Tongues:
Then, with no less Elegance, he returns to the Praise of his venerable
Traveller, surprizingly skill'd in most of them. Afterwards, with a peculiar
Delicacy, his Comment [*Commentary*] upon *Joel* is hinted at, and from
thence Occasion taken to represent that terrible Day of the Lord, which
the Prophet speaks of, and then the holy Ardour of his Interpreter:

Ac sicut albens perpetua nive
Simul favillas, & cineres sinu
   Eructat ardenti, & pruinis
      Contiguas rotat Aetna flammas:
Sic te trementem, te nive candidum,
Mens intus urget, mens agit ignea
   Sequi reluctantem Joelem
      Per tonitru, aereasque nubes.

Annon pavescis, dum Tuba pallidum
Ciet Sionem? dum tremulum polo
   Caligat astrum, atque incubanti
      Terra nigrans tegitur sub umbra?
Quod agmen! heu! quae turba sequacibus
Tremenda flammis! quis strepitantium
   Flictus rotarum est! O Pococki
      Egregie! O animose Vatis
Interpres abstrusi! O simili fere
Correpte flamma! –

As Aetna's lucid with perpetual Snow,
While heaving Flames within its Entrails glow;
O'er the hoar Frost the raging Fury's spread,
And ruddy Flouds of Fire beam round its Head:
So trembling thou, and venerably white,
Thy urging Soul tries sacred Sion's Height,
Attends thy Joel, clad in dark Array,
Where Clouds and Lightnings mark his awful Way.

Hark! dost not shudder while the Trumpet's Sound
The tott'ring Tow'rs of Solyma rebound?
Behold what Troops come rolling from afar
With Gleams of Terror, and the Din of War!
In the bright Front consuming Fires ride,
And Slaughter stalks indignant by their Side.
Oh! whither, whither tends thy eager Course,
Rapt by thy own, thy kindred Prophet's Force?
The Matter and Thoughts are sublime and elegant, the Transitions artful;
and it is, in short, all over wonderful.
Trans. William Bower and William Clarke, 1742

GEORGE BERKELEY (1685–1753)

The picture of reality in the classical writers of the eighteenth century, for example Samuel Johnson, rests on the fundamental idea of space. That stone we see is, indeed, as we see it, in the place in which we see it. Furthermore, its size and the distance of other objects in relation to it, gives, as it were, a groundplan of the moral perspectives of reality at large. Even the image of past time in Johnson as in Pope, is in essence, a spatial image, distancing and objectifying thoughts. Romanticism was largely concerned with undermining these certainties.

A major early shift in the eighteenth century is that away from the primacy of vision as the iconography of thought to a diffuse metaphor in which mental forms are apprehended rather as intuitive feeling of mass, to which was joined a distrust of reason, clarity and extension. We may observe in Berkeley's *A New Theory of Vision* (1709) one of the levers by which the edifice of classical form was brought down, and the universe of Young's *Night Thoughts* and Blake's *The Four Zoas* came to replace Pope's *Essay on Man*.

The *New Theory of Vision* took as its theme the illusory mechanism by which men convince themselves of the relation between perceived objects and the distance — or space — apparently separating them from the retina. In reality, Berkeley argued, when we thought we saw the size and distance of an object, we in fact experienced an alteration of the fibres in the eye, and recalled ideas, for example of touch, that had nothing to do with vision. It was a sensation or feeling in the eye, simultaneous, we may assume, with the act of seeing, and the transference of unrelated ideas, for example of rough texture, which misled us into concluding that we saw 'outness'. Among the conclusions a reader of Berkeley might be drawn to is the doubtfulness of the relation between an external world and the images of thinking, and of the existence of space as a structural idea of greater importance than other ideas. Not far behind, as it were, he might conclude that simultaneity played a large part in Berkeleyan cognition; knowledge, for example, of the perceived object was apparently created at the same moment as the sensation and was not arrived at after a lapse of time by sequential steps in rational deduction.

In the *Principles of Human Knowledge* (1710) Berkeley went on to attack Locke's concept of abstractions. It followed from the *New Theory* that each idea or sensation, including apparent abstractions, inhabited a separate moment as it were before the Eternal mind, and, in essence was not dependent on a structure of previous thoughts. It is interesting to observe that Berkeley on abstractions parallels the contemporary change in the use of personified abstractions in poetry, and the role of abstractions in the 'primitive' poetry of, for example, Collins (see pp. 186-188). Notoriously, Berkeley cast doubt on cause and effect. In a world of timeless simultaneity, there was no cause and effect. The fire was a signal of the pain which seemed to result from it, but, since each perceived idea did not depend fundamentally on temporal sequence, the pain did not significantly depend on the burning as causation. In the seminal area of association Berkeley appears to have been especially important. If timeless simultaneity were the real nature of thought, ideas must associate — that is, the poet's imagination must get from one image to the next — not by causal, temporal, links but by some other, probably creative, method. Finally, for poetry, words might become equal objects, as they did in Smart (see p. 249), of perception, portions of the minds contemporaneous creativity, not referential signals to masses of abstractions.

With the exception of Smart it is difficult to put one's finger on direct repetitions of Berkeleyan philosophy. However, there are few moments in Thomson, Young, Collins, Gray, as in Blake and Coleridge, when Berkeley does not seem near. Above all, mid-century and later Romanticism exhibited a central decline in a belief in the sequences of rational thought. The rise of orientalism and of primitivism in general was, at root, an abandonment of classical form in poetry, and especially what Coleridge calls in the *Biographia Literaria* the 'conjunction disjunctive' of Pope. Northrop Frye· has ably explained the formal realities of the poetry of sensibility in which each line, like each section of a Gothic window, overwhelms the whole, making the reader aware only of the present, isolated moment. Berkeley's philosophy is the most sophisticated, consistent apology for simultaneity in eighteenth-century English writing.

Berkeley's influence may be detected also in several instances in, for example, Young and Lowth. In Young's *Last Day* (1713), essentially an early *Night Thoughts*, '. . . Time, and Place,/Matter, and Form . . . wait humbly at the footstool of their God.' A decade later the *wunderkind*, Robert Lowth, in verses extravagantly praised by William Cowper in his letters, observes his friends from his *Katherine's Hill* 'measure all the comprehensive space;/Through all the regular confusion run,/And seem to end where they the course begun.' The boy who would become the era's authority on primitive Hebrew poetry (see pp. 149-167) and the major influence on Smart exclaimed 'close join'd the barriers and the goal appear . . . (Delusive sight!) how distant, and how near!' His fellow Wykehamist's *Night Thoughts* found its most Berkeleyan moment in a passage which not only influenced Wordsworth's *Tintern Abbey*, but found echoes in Wallace Stevens's *Sunday Morning*. Outlining a principle of 'creative imagination' little different from Coleridge's, Young celebrated the 'senses, which inherit earth and heavens;/ . . . Take-in, at once, the landscape of the world,/At a small inlet which a grain might close, /And half-create the wondrous world they see.' (*Night Thoughts*, vi. 420–27.)

from *AN ESSAY TOWARDS A NEW THEORY OF VISION (1709)*

16 Now, it being already shewn that distance is suggested to the mind by the mediation of some other idea which is it self perceived in the act of seeing, it remains that we inquire what ideas or sensations there be that attend vision, unto which we may suppose the ideas of distance are connected, and by which they are introduced into the mind. And *first,* It is certain by experience that when we look at a near object with both eyes, according as it approaches or recedes from us, we alter the disposition of our eyes, by lessening or widening the interval between the pupils. This disposition or turn of the eyes is attended with a sensation, which seems to me to be that which in this case brings the idea of greater or lesser distance into the mind.

17 Not that there is any natural or necessary connexion between the sensation we perceive by the turn of the eyes and greater or lesser distance, but because the mind has by constant experience found the different sensations corresponding to the different dispositions of the eyes to be attended each with a different degree of distance in the object, there has grown an habitual or customary connexion between those two sorts of ideas, so that the mind no sooner perceives the sensation arising from the different turn it gives the eyes, in order to bring the pupils nearer or farther asunder, but it withal perceives the different idea of distance which was wont to be connected with that sensation; just as upon hearing a certain sound, the idea is immediately suggested to the understanding which custom had united with it.

18 Nor do I see how I can easily be mistaken in this matter. I know evidently that distance is not perceived of it self. That by consequence it must be perceived by means of some other idea which is immediately perceived, and varies with the different degrees of distance. I know also that the sensation arising from the turn of the eyes is of it self immediately perceived, and various degrees thereof are connected with different distances, which never fail to accompany them into my mind, when I view an object distinctly with both eyes, whose distance is so small that in respect of it the interval between the eyes has any considerable magnitude.

*

44 But for a fuller explication of this point, and to shew that the immediate objects of sight are not so much as the ideas or resemblances of things placed at a distance, it is requisite that we look nearer into the matter and carefully observe what is meant in common discourse, when one says that which he sees is at a distance from him. Suppose, for example, that looking at the moon I should say it were fifty or sixty semidiameters of the earth distant from me. Let us see what moon this

is spoken of: It is plain it cannot be the visible moon, or anything like the visible moon, or that which I see, which is only a round, luminous plain of about thirty visible points in diameter. For in case I am carried from the place where I stand directly towards the moon, it is manifest the object varies, still as I go on; and by the time that I am advanced fifty or sixty semidiameters of the earth, I shall be so far from being near a small, round, luminous flat that I shall perceive nothing like it; this object having long since disappeared, and if I would recover it, it must be by going back to the earth from whence I set out. Again, suppose I perceive by sight the faint and obscure idea of something which I doubt whether it be a man, or a tree, or a tower, but judge it to be at the distance of about a mile. It is plain I cannot mean that what I see is a mile off, or that it is the image or likeness of anything which is a mile off, since that every step I take towards it the appearance alters, and from being obscure, small, and faint, grows clear, large, and vigorous. And when I come to the mile's end, that which I saw first is quite lost, neither do I find any thing in the likeness of it.

45 In these and the like instances the truth of the matter stands thus: Having of a long time experienced certain ideas, perceivable by touch, as distance, tangible figure, and solidity, to have been connected with certain ideas of sight, I do upon perceiving these ideas of sight forthwith conclude what tangible ideas are, by the wonted ordinary course of Nature like to follow. Looking at an object I perceive a certain visible figure and colour, with some degree of faintness and other circumstances, which from what I have formerly observed, determine me to think that if I advance forward so many paces or miles, I shall be affected with such and such ideas of touch: So that in truth and strictness of speech I neither see distance it self, nor anything that I take to be at a distance. I say, neither distance nor things placed at a distance are themselves, or their ideas, truly perceived by sight. This I am persuaded of, as to what concerns my self: and I believe whoever will look narrowly into his own thoughts and examine what he means by saying he sees this or that thing at a distance, will agree with me that what he sees only suggests to his understanding that after having passed a certain distance, to be measured by the motion of his body, which is perceivable by touch, he shall come to perceive such and such tangible ideas which have been usually connected with such and such visible ideas. But that one might be deceived by these suggestions of sense, and that there is no necessary connexion between visible and tangible ideas suggested by them, we need go no farther than the next looking-glass or picture to be convinced. Note that when I speak of tangible ideas, I take the word idea for any the immediate object of sense or understanding, in which large signification it is commonly used by the moderns.

46 From what we have shewn it is a manifest consequence that the ideas of space, outness, and things placed at a distance are not, strictly speaking, the object of sight; they are not otherwise perceived by the eye than by

the ear. Sitting in my study I hear a coach drive along the street; I look through the casement and see it; I walk out and enter into it; thus, common speech would incline one to think I heard, saw, and touched the same thing, to wit, the coach. It is nevertheless certain, the ideas intromitted by each sense are widely different and distinct from each other; but having been observed constantly to go together, they are spoken of as one and the same thing. By the variation of the noise I perceive the different distances of the coach, and know that it approaches before I look out. Thus by the ear I perceive distance, just after the same manner as I do by the eye.

47 I do not nevertheless say I hear distance in like manner as I say that I see it, the ideas perceived by hearing not being so apt to be confounded with the ideas of touch as those of sight are. So likewise a man is easily convinced that bodies and external things are not properly the object of hearing; but only sounds, by the mediation whereof the idea of this or that body or distance is suggested to his thoughts. But then one is with more difficulty brought to discern the difference there is betwixt the ideas of sight and touch: Though it be certain a man no more sees and feels the same thing than he hears and feels the same thing.

48 One reason of which seems to be this. It is thought a great absurdity to imagine that one and the same thing should have any more than one extension and one figure. But the extension and figure of a body, being let into the mind two ways, and that indifferently either by sight or touch, it seems to follow that we see the same extension and the same figure which we feel.

49 But if we take a close and accurate view of things, it must be acknowledged that we never see and feel one and the same object. That which is seen is one thing, and that which is felt is another. If the visible figure and extension be not the same with the tangible figure and extension, we are not to infer that one and the same thing has divers extensions. The true consequence is that the objects of sight and touch are two distinct things. It may perhaps require some thought rightly to conceive this distinction. And the difficulty seems not a little increased, because the combination of visible ideas hath constantly the same name as the combination of tangible ideas wherewith it is connected: Which doth of necessity arise from the use and end of language.

*

52 I have now done with distance, and proceed to shew how it is that we perceive by sight the magnitude of objects. It is the opinion of some that we do it by angles, or by angles in conjunction with distance: but neither angles nor distance being perceivable by sight, and the things we see being in truth at no distance from us, it follows that as we have shewn lines and angles not to be the medium the mind makes use of in apprehending the apparent place, so neither are they the medium whereby

it apprehends the apparent magnitude of objects.

53 It is well known that the same extension at a near distance shall subtend a greater angle, and at a farther distance a lesser angle. And by this principle (we are told) the mind estimates the magnitude of an object, comparing the angle under which it is seen with its distance, and thence inferring the magnitude thereof. What inclines men to this mistake (beside the humour of making one see by geometry) is that the same perceptions or ideas which suggest distance do also suggest magnitude. But if we examine it we shall find they suggest the latter as immediately as the former. I say, they do not first suggest distance, and then leave it to the judgment to use that as a medium whereby to collect the magnitude; but they have as close and immediate a connexion with the magnitude as with the distance; and suggest magnitude as independently of distance as they do distance independently of magnitude. All which will be evident to whoever considers what hath been already said, and what follows.

54 It hath been shewn there are two sorts of objects apprehended by sight; each whereof hath its distinct magnitude, or extension. The one, properly tangible, *i.e.* to be perceived and measured by touch, and not immediately falling under the sense of seeing: The other, properly and immediately visible, by mediation of which the former is brought in view. Each of these magnitudes are greater or lesser, according as they contain in them more or fewer points, they being made up of points or minimums. For, whatever may be said of extension in abstract, it is certain sensible extension is not infinitely divisible. There is a *Minimum Tangibile* and a *Minimum Visibile*, beyond which sense cannot perceive. This every one's experience will inform him.

55 The magnitude of the object which exists without the mind, and is at a distance, continues always invariably the same: But the visible object still changing as you approach to, or recede from, the tangible object, it hath no fixed and determinate greatness. Whenever, therefore, we speak of the magnitude of any thing, for instance a tree or a house, we must mean the tangible magnitude, otherwise there can be nothing steady and free from ambiguity spoken of it. But though the tangible and visible magnitude in truth belong to two distinct objects: I shall nevertheless (especially since those objects are called by the same name, and are observed to coexist), to avoid tediousness and singularity of speech, sometimes speak of them as belonging to one and the same thing.

56 Now in order to discover by what means the magnitude of tangible objects is perceived by sight, I need only reflect on what passes in my own mind, and observe what those things be which introduce the ideas of greater or lesser into my thoughts, when I look on any objects. And these I find to be, *first*, the magnitude or extension of the visible object, which being immediately perceived by sight, is connected with that other which is tangible and placed at a distance. *Secondly*, the confusion or distinctness. And *thirdly*, The vigorousness or faintness of the aforesaid visible appearance. *Caeteris paribus*, by how much the greater or lesser the

visible object is, by so much the greater or lesser do I conclude the tangible object to be. But, be the idea immediately perceived by sight never so large, yet if it be withal confused, I judge the magnitude of the thing to be but small. If it be distinct and clear, I judge it greater. And if it be faint, I apprehend it to be yet greater. . . .

*

73 Faintness, as well as all other ideas or perceptions which suggest magnitude or distance, doth it in the same way that words suggest the notions to which they are annexed. Now, it is known a word pronounced with certain circumstances, or in a certain context with other words, hath not always the same import and signification that it hath when pronounced in some other circumstances or different context of words. The very same visible appearance as to faintness and all other respects, if placed on high, shall not suggest the same magnitude that it would if it were seen at an equal distance on a level with the eye. The reason whereof is that we are rarely accustomed to view objects at a great height; our concerns lie among things situated rather before than above us, and accordingly our eyes are not placed on the top of our heads, but in such a position as is most convenient for us to see distant objects standing in our way. And this situation of them being a circumstance which usually attends the vision of distant objects, we may from hence account for (what is commonly observed) an object's appearing of different magnitude, even with respect to its horizontal extension, on the top of a steeple, for example, an hundred feet high to one standing below, from what it would if placed at an hundred feet distance on a level with his eye. . . .

*

74 If we attentively consider the phaenomenon before us, we shall find the not discerning between the mediate and immediate objects of sight to be the chief cause of the difficulty that occurs in the explication of it. The magnitude of the visible moon, or that which is the proper and immediate object of vision, is no greater when the moon is in the horizon than when it is in the meridian. How comes it, therefore, to seem greater in one situation than the other? What is it can put this cheat on the understanding? It has no other perception of the moon than what it gets by sight: And that which is seen is of the same extent, I say, the visible appearance hath the same, or rather a less, magnitude when the moon is viewed in the horizontal than when in the meridional position: And yet it is esteemed greater in the former than in the latter. Herein consists the difficulty, which doth vanish and admit of a most easy solution, if we consider that as the visible moon is not greater in the horizon than in the meridian, so neither is it thought to be so. It hath been already shewn that in any act of vision the visible object absolutely, or in it self, is

little taken notice of, the mind still carrying its view from that to some tangible ideas which have been observed to be connected with it, and by that means come to be suggested by it. So that when a thing is said to appear great or small, or whatever estimate be made of the magnitude of any thing, this is meant not of the visible but of the tangible object. This duly considered, it will be no hard matter to reconcile the seeming contradiction there is, that the moon should appear of a different bigness, the visible magnitude thereof remaining still the same. For by sect. 56 the very same visible extension, with a different faintness, shall suggest a different tangible extension. When therefore the horizontal moon is said to appear greater than the meridional moon, this must be understood not of a greater visible extension, but of a greater tangible or real extension, which by reason of the more than ordinary faintness of the visible appearance, is suggested to the mind along with it.

Fourth edition, 1732

A TREATISE CONCERNING THE PRINCIPLES OF HUMAN KNOWLEDGE (1710)

from 'Introduction'

17 . . . When men consider the great pains, industry and parts that have for so many ages been laid out on the cultivation and advancement of the sciences, and that notwithstanding all this, the far greater part of them remain full of darkness and uncertainty, and disputes that are like never to have an end, and even those that are thought to be supported by the most clear and cogent demonstrations, contain in them paradoxes which are perfectly irreconcilable to the understandings of men, and that taking all together, a small portion of them doth supply any real benefit to mankind, otherwise than by being an innocent diversion and amusement. I say, the consideration of all this is apt to throw them into a despondency, and perfect contempt of all study. But this may perhaps cease, upon a view of the false principles that have obtained in the world, amongst all which there is none, methinks, hath a more wide influence over the thoughts of speculative men, than this of abstract general ideas.

18 I come now to consider the source of this prevailing notion, and that seems to me to be language. And surely nothing of less extent than reason it self could have been the source of an opinion so universally received. The truth of this appears as from other reasons, so also from the plain confession of the ablest patrons of abstract ideas, who acknowledge that they are made in order to naming; from which it is a clear consequence, that if there had been no such thing as speech or universal signs, there never had been any thought of abstraction. See B. 3 C. 6 Sect. 39 and elsewhere of the *Essay on Human Understanding.* [John Locke, *An Essay Concerning Human Understanding.*] Let us therefore examine

the manner wherein words have contributed to the origin of that mistake. First then, 'tis thought that every name hath, or ought to have, only one precise and settled signification, which inclines men to think there are certain *abstract, determinate ideas*, which constitute the true and only immediate signification of each general name. And that it is by the mediation of these abstract ideas, that a general name comes to signify any particular thing. Whereas, in truth, there is no such thing as one precise and definite signification annexed to any general name, they all signifying indifferently a great number of particular ideas. All which doth evidently follow from what has been already said, and will clearly appear to any one by a little reflexion. To this it will be objected, that every name that has a definition, is thereby restrained to one certain signification. For example, a *triangle* is defined to be a *plane surface comprehended by three right lines*; by which that name is limited to denote one certain idea and no other. To which I answer, that in the definition it is not said whether the surface be great or small, black or white, nor whether the sides are long or short, equal or unequal, nor with what angles they are inclined to each other; in all which there may be great variety, and consequently there is no one settled idea which limits the signification of the word *triangle*. 'Tis one thing for to keep a name constantly to the same definition, and another to make it stand every where for the same idea: the one is necessary, the other useless and impracticable.

19 But to give a farther account how words came to produce the doctrine of abstract ideas, it must be observed that it is a received opinion, that language has no other end but the communicating our ideas, and that every significant name stands for an idea. This being so, and it being withal certain, that names, which yet are not thought altogether insignificant, do not always mark out particular conceivable ideas, it is straightway concluded that they stand for abstract notions. That there are many names in use amongst speculative men, which do not always suggest to others determinate particular ideas, is what no body will deny. And a little attention will discover, that it is not necessary (even in the strictest reasonings) significant names which stand for ideas should, every time they are used, excite in the understanding the ideas they are made to stand for: in reading and discoursing, names being for the most part used as letters are in *algebra*, in which though a particular quantity be marked by each letter, yet to proceed right it is not requisite that in every step each letter suggest to your thoughts, that particular quantity it was appointed to stand for.

20 Besides, the communicating of ideas marked by words is not the chief and only end of language, as is commonly supposed. There are other ends, as the raising of some passion, the exciting to, or deterring from an action, the putting the mind in some particular disposition; to which the former is in many cases barely subservient, and sometimes entirely omitted, when these can be obtained without it, as I think doth not

infrequently happen in the familiar use of language. I entreat the reader to reflect with himself, and see if it doth not often happen either in hearing or reading a discourse, that the passions of fear, love, hatred, admiration, disdain, and the like arise, immediately in his mind upon the perception of certain words, without any ideas coming between. At first, indeed, the words might have occasioned ideas that were fit to produce those emotions; but, if I mistake not, it will be found that when language is once grown familiar, the hearing of the sounds or sight of the characters is oft immediately attended with those passions, which at first were wont to be produced by the intervention of ideas, that are now quite omitted. [Cf. Burke on words, pp. 201-206.] May we not, for example, be affected with the promise of a *good thing*, though we have not an idea of what it is? Or is not the being threatened with danger sufficient to excite a dread, though we think not of any particular evil likely to befall us, nor yet frame to our selves an idea of danger in abstract? If any one shall join ever so little reflection of his own to what has been said, I believe it will evidently appear to him, that general names are often used in the propriety of language without the speaker's designing them for marks of ideas in his own, which he would have them raise in the mind of the hearer. Even proper names themselves do not seem always spoken with a design to bring into our view the ideas of those individuals that are supposed to be marked by them. For example, when a Schoolman tells me *Aristotle hath said it*, all I conceive he means by it, is to dispose me to embrace his opinion with the deference and submission which custom has annexed to that name. And this effect may be so instantly produced in the minds of those who are accustomed to resign their judgment to the authority of that philosopher, as it is impossible any idea either of his person, writings, or reputation should go before. Innumerable examples of this kind may be given, but why should I insist on those things, which every one's experience will, I doubt not, plentifully suggest unto him?

21 We have, I think, shewn the impossibility of *abstract ideas*. We have considered what has been said for them by their ablest patrons; and endeavoured to shew they are of no use for those ends to which they are thought necessary. And lastly, we have traced them to the source from whence they flow, which appears to be language. It cannot be denied that words are of excellent use, in that by their means all that stock of knowledge which has been purchased by the joint labours of inquisitive men in all ages and nations, may be drawn into the view and made the possession of one single person. But at the same time it must be owned that most parts of knowledge have been strangely perplexed and darkened by the abuse of words, and general ways of speech wherein they are delivered. Since therefore words are so apt to impose on the understanding, whatever ideas I consider, I shall endeavour to take them bare and naked into my view, keeping out of my thoughts, so far as I am able, those names which long and constant use hath so strictly united

with them; from which I may expect to derive the following advantages.

*

24 But these being known to be mistakes, a man may with greater ease prevent his being imposed on by words. He that knows he has no other than particular ideas, will not puzzle himself in vain to find out and conceive the abstract idea annexed to any name. And he that knows names do not always stand for ideas, will spare himself the labour of looking for ideas where there are none to be had. It were therefore to be wished that every one would use his utmost endeavours, to obtain a clear view of the ideas he would consider, separating from them all that dress and encumbrance of words which so much contribute to blind the judgment and divide the attention. In vain do we extend our view into the heavens, and pry into the entrails of the earth, in vain do we consult the writings of learned men, and trace the dark footsteps of antiquity; we need only draw the curtain of words, to behold the fairest tree of knowledge, whose fruit is excellent,and within the reach of our hand.

25 Unless we take care to clear the first principles of knowledge from the embarras and delusion of words, we may make infinite reasonings upon them to no purpose; we may draw consequences from consequences, and be never the wiser. The farther we go, we shall only lose our selves the more irrecoverably, and be the deeper entangled in difficulties and mistakes. Whoever therefore designs to read the following sheets, I entreat him to make my words the occasion of his own thinking, and endeavour to attain the same train of thoughts in reading that I had in writing them. By this means it will be easy for him to discover the truth or falsity of what I say. He will be out of all danger of being deceived by my words, and I do not see how he can be led into an error by considering his own naked, undisguised ideas.

*

from Part I

1 It is evident to any one who takes a survey of the objects of human knowledge, that they are either ideas actually imprinted on the senses, or else such as are perceived by attending to the passions and operations of the mind, or lastly ideas formed by help of memory and imagination, either compounding, dividing, or barely representing those originally perceived in the aforesaid ways. By sight I have the ideas of light and colours with their several degrees and variations. By touch I perceive, for example, hard and soft, heat and cold, motion and resistance, and of all these more and less either as to quantity or degree. Smelling furnishes me with odours; the palate with tastes, and hearing conveys sounds to the mind in all their variety of tone and composition. And as several of these are observed to accompany each other, they come to be marked

by one name, and so to be reputed as one thing. Thus, for example, a certain colour, taste, smell, figure and consistence having been observed to go together, are accounted one distinct thing, signified by the name *apple*. Other collections of ideas constitute a stone, a tree, a book, and the like sensible things; which, as they are pleasing or disagreeable, excite the passions of love, hatred, joy, grief, and so forth.

2 But besides all that endless variety of ideas or objects of knowledge, there is likewise something which knows or perceives them, and exercises divers operations, as willing, imagining, remembering about them. This perceiving, active being is what I call *mind, spirit, soul* or *my self.* By which words I do not denote any one of my ideas, but a thing entirely distinct from them, wherein they exist, or, which is the same thing, whereby they are perceived; for the existence of an idea consists in being perceived.

3 That neither our thoughts, nor passions, nor ideas formed by the imagination, exist without the mind, is what every body will allow. And it seems no less evident that the various sensations or ideas imprinted on the sense, however blended or combined together (that is, whatever objects they compose) cannot exist otherwise than in a mind perceiving them. I think an intuitive knowledge may be obtained of this, by any one that shall attend to what is meant by the term *exist* when applied to sensible things. The table I write on, I say, exists, that is, I see and feel it; and if I were out of my study I should say it existed, meaning thereby that if I was in my study I might perceive it, or that some other spirit actually does perceive it. There was an odour, that is, it was smelled; there was a sound, that is to say, it was heard; a colour or figure, and it was perceived by sight or touch. This is all that I can understand by these and the like expressions. For as to what is said of the absolute existence of unthinking things without any relation to their being perceived, that seems perfectly unintelligible. Their *esse* is *percipi*, nor is it possible they should have any existence, out of the minds or thinking things which perceive them.

4 It is indeed an opinion strangely prevailing amongst men, that houses, mountains, rivers, and in a word all sensible objects have an existence natural or real, distinct from their being perceived by the understanding. But with how great an assurance and acquiescence soever this principle may be entertained in the world; yet whoever shall find in his heart to call it in question, may, if I mistake not, perceive it to involve a manifest contradiction. For what are the forementioned objects but the things we perceive by sense, and what do we perceive besides our own ideas or sensations; and is it not plainly repugnant that any one of these or any combination of them should exist unperceived?

5 If we throughly examine this tenet, it will, perhaps, be found at bottom to depend on the doctrine of *abstract ideas*. For can there be a nicer strain of abstraction than to distinguish the existence of sensible objects from their being perceived, so as to conceive them existing un-

perceived? Light and colours, heat and cold, extension and figures, in a word the things we see and feel, what are they but so many sensations, notions, ideas or impressions on the sense; and is it possible to separate, even in thought, any of these from perception? For my part I might as easily divide a thing from it self. I may indeed divide in my thoughts or conceive apart from each other those things which, perhaps, I never perceived by sense so divided. Thus I imagine the trunk of a human body without the limbs, or conceive the smell of a rose without thinking on the rose it self. So far I will not deny I can abstract, if that may properly be called *abstraction* which extends only to the conceiving separately such objects as it is possible may really exist or be actually perceived asunder. But my conceiving or imagining power does not extend beyond the possibility of real existence or perception. Hence as it is impossible for me to see or feel anything without an actual sensation of that thing, so is it impossible for me to conceive in my thoughts any sensible thing or object distinct from the sensation or perception of it.

6 Some truths there are so near and obvious to the mind, that a man need only open his eyes to see them. Such I take this important one to be, to wit, that all the choir of heaven and furniture of the earth, in a word all those bodies which compose the mighty frame of the world, have not any subsistence without a mind, that their being is to be perceived or known; that consequently so long as they are not actually perceived by me, or do not exist in my mind or that of any other created spirit, they must either have no existence at all, or else subsist in the mind of some eternal spirit:* it being perfectly unintelligible and involving all the absurdity of abstraction, to attribute to any single part of them an existence independent of a spirit. To be convinced of which, the reader need only reflect and try to separate in his own thoughts the being of a sensible thing from its being perceived.

7 From what has been said, it follows, there is not any other substance than *spirit*, or that which perceives. But for the fuller proof of this point, let it be considered, the sensible qualities are colour, figure, motion, smell, taste, and such like, that is, the ideas perceived by sense. Now for an idea to exist in an unperceiving thing, is a manifest contradiction; for to have an idea is all one as to perceive: that therefore wherein colour, figure, and the like qualities exist, must perceive them; hence it is clear there can be no unthinking substance or *substratum* of those ideas.

*

43 But for the fuller clearing of this point, it may be worth while to

---

*At this point Berkeleyan philosophy joins with the eighteenth-century 'Sublime'. Ed.

consider, how it is that we perceive distance and things placed at a distance by sight. For that we should in truth see external space, and bodies actually existing in it, some nearer, others farther off, seems to carry with it some opposition to what hath been said, of their existing no where without the mind. The consideration of this difficulty it was, that gave birth to my *Essay towards a new Theory of Vision*, which was published not long since. [See pp. 64-69.] Wherein it is shewn that *distance* or outness is neither immediately of it self perceived by sight, nor yet apprehended or judged of by lines and angles, or any thing that hath a necessary connexion with it: but that it is only suggested to our thoughts, by certain visible ideas and sensations attending vision, which in their own nature have no manner of similitude or relation, either with distance, or things placed at a distance. But by a connexion taught us by experience, they come to signify and suggest them to us, after the same manner that words of any language suggest the ideas they are made to stand for. Insomuch that a man born blind, and afterwards made to see, would not, at first sight, think the things he saw to be without his mind or at any distance from him. *See Sect*. 41 of the forementioned treatise.

44 The ideas of sight and touch make two species, entirely distinct and heterogeneous. The former are marks and prognostics of the latter. That the proper objects of sight neither exist without the mind, nor are the images of external things, was shewn even in that treatise. Though throughout the same, the contrary be supposed true of tangible objects: not that to suppose that vulgar error was necessary for establishing the notion therein laid down; but because it was beside my purpose to examine and refute it in a discourse concerning *vision*. So that in strict truth the ideas of sight, when we apprehend by them distance and things placed at a distance, do not suggest or mark out to us things actually existing at a distance, but only admonish us what ideas of touch will be imprinted in our minds at such and such distances of time, and in consequence of such and such actions. It is, I say, evident from what has been said in the foregoing parts of this treatise, and in *Sect*. 147, and elsewhere of the essay concerning vision, that visible ideas are the language whereby the governing spirit, on whom we depend, informs us what tangible ideas he is about to imprint upon us, in case we excite this or that motion in our own bodies. But for a fuller information in this point, I refer to the essay it self.

45 Fourthly, it will be objected that from the foregoing principles it follows, things are every moment annihilated and created anew. The objects of sense exist only when they are perceived: the trees therefore are in the garden, or the chairs in the parlour, no longer than while there is some body by to perceive them. Upon shutting my eyes all the furniture in the room is reduced to nothing, and barely upon opening them it is again created. In answer to all which, I refer the reader to what has been said in *Sect*. 3, 4, &c-. and desire he will consider whether he means any thing by the actual existence of an idea, distinct from its

being perceived. For my part, after the nicest inquiry I could make, I am not able to discover that any thing else is meant by those words. And I once more entreat the reader to sound his own thoughts, and not suffer himself to be imposed on by words. If he can conceive it possible either for his ideas or their archetypes to exist without being perceived, then I give up the cause: but if he cannot, he will acknowledge it is unreasonable for him to stand up in defence of he knows not what, and pretend to charge on me as an absurdity, the not assenting to those propositions which at bottom have no meaning in them.

*

60 In the eleventh place, it will be demanded to what purpose serves that curious organization of plants, and the admirable mechanism in the parts of animals; might not vegetables grow, and shoot forth leaves and blossoms, and animals perform all their motions, as well without as with all that variety of internal parts so elegantly contrived and put together, which being ideas have nothing powerful or operative in them, nor have any necessary connexion with the effects ascribed to them? If it be a spirit that immediately produces every effect by a *fiat*, or act of his will, we must think all that is fine and artificial in the works, whether of man or Nature, to be made in vain. By this doctrine, though an artist hath made the spring and wheels, and every movement of a watch, and adjusted them in such a manner as he knew would produce the motions he designed; yet he must think all this done to no purpose, and that it is an intelligence which directs the index, and points to the hour of the day. If so, why may not the intelligence do it, without his being at the pains of making the movements, and putting them together? Why does not an empty case serve as well as another? And how comes it to pass, that whenever there is any fault in the going of a watch, there is some corresponding disorder to be found in the movements, which being mended by a skilful hand, all is right again? The like may be said of all the clockwork of Nature, great part whereof is so wonderfully fine and subtle as scarce to be discerned by the best microscope. In short, it will be asked, how upon our principles any tolerable account can be given, or any final cause assigned of an innumerable multitude of bodies and machines framed with the most exquisite art, which in the common philosophy have very apposite uses assigned them, and serve to explain abundance of phenomena.

*

64 To set this matter in a yet clearer light, I shall observe that what has been objected in *Sect.* 60 amounts in reality to no more than this: ideas are not any how and at random produced, there being a certain order and connexion between them, like to that of cause and effect:

there are also several combinations of them, made in a very regular and artificial manner, which seem like so many instruments in the hand of Nature, that being hid as it were behind the scenes, have a secret operation in producing those appearances which are seen on the theatre of the world, being themselves discernible only to the curious eye of the philosopher. But since one idea cannot be the cause of another, to what purpose is that connexion? And since those instruments, being barely *inefficacious perceptions* in the mind, are not subservient to the production of natural effects; it is demanded why they are made, or in other words, what reason can be assigned why God should make us, upon a close inspection into his works, behold so great variety of ideas, so artfully laid together, and so much according to rule; it not being credible, that he would be at the expense (if one may so speak) of all that art and regularity to no purpose?

65 To all which my answer is, first, that the connexion of ideas does not imply the relation of *cause* and *effect*, but only of a mark or *sign* with the thing *signified*. The fire which I see is not the cause of the pain I suffer upon my approaching it, but the mark that forewarns me of it. In like manner, the noise that I hear is not the effect of this or that motion or collision of the ambient bodies, but the sign thereof. Secondly, the reason why ideas are formed into machines, that is, artificial and regular combinations, is the same with that for combining letters into words. That a few original ideas may be made to signify a great number of effects and actions, it is necessary they be variously combined together: and to the end their use be permanent and universal, these combinations must be made by *rule*, and with *wise contrivance*. By this means abundance of information is conveyed unto us, concerning what we are to expect from such and such actions, and what methods are proper to be taken, for the exciting such and such ideas: which in effect is all that I conceive to be distinctly meant when it is said that by discerning the figure, texture, and mechanism of the inward parts of bodies, whether natural or artificial, we may attain to know the several uses and properties depending thereon, or the nature of the thing.

*

90 Ideas imprinted on the senses are real things, or do really exist; this we do not deny, but we deny they can subsist without the minds which perceive them, or that they are resemblances of any archetypes existing without the mind: since the very being of a sensation or idea consists in being perceived, and an idea can be like nothing but an idea. Again, the things perceived by sense may be termed *external*, with regard to their origin, in that they are not generated from within, by the mind it self, but imprinted by a spirit distinct from that which perceives them. Sensible objects may likewise be said to be without the mind, in another sense, namely when they exist in some other mind. Thus when I shut

my eyes, the things I saw may still exist, but it must be in another mind.

91 It were a mistake to think, that what is here said derogates in the least from the reality of things. It is acknowledged on the received principles, that extension, motion, and in a word all sensible qualities, have need of a support, as not being able to subsist by themselves. But the objects perceived by sense, are allowed to be nothing but combinations of those qualities, and consequently cannot subsist by themselves. Thus far it is agreed on all hands. So that in denying the things perceived by sense an existence independent of a substance, or support wherein they may exist, we detract nothing from the received opinion of their *reality*, and are guilty of no innovation in that respect. All the difference is, that according to us the unthinking beings perceived by sense, have no existence distinct from being perceived, and cannot therefore exist in any other substance, than those unextended, indivisible substances, or *spirits*, which act, and think, and perceive them; whereas philosophers vulgarly hold, that the sensible qualities exist in an inert, extended, unperceiving substance, which they call matter, to which they attribute a natural subsistence, exterior to all thinking beings, or distinct from being perceived by any mind whatsoever, even the eternal mind of the Creator, wherein they suppose only ideas of the corporeal substances created by him: if indeed they allow them to be at all created.

92 For as we have shewn the doctrine of matter or corporeal substance to have been the main pillar and support of *scepticism*, so likewise upon the same foundation have been raised all the impious schemes of *atheism* and irreligion. Nay so great a difficulty hath it been thought, to conceive matter produced out of nothing, that the most celebrated among the ancient philosophers, even of these who maintained the being of a God, have thought matter to be uncreated and coeternal with him. How great a friend material substance hath been to *atheists* in all ages, were needless to relate. ...

*

97 Beside the external existence of the objects of perception, another great source of errors and difficulties, with regard to ideal knowledge, is the doctrine of *abstract ideas*, such as it hath been set forth in the Introduction. The plainest things in the world, those we are most intimately acquainted with, and perfectly know, when they are considered in an abstract way, appear strangely difficult and incomprehensible. Time, place, and motion, taken in particular or concrete, are what every body knows; but having passed through the hands of a metaphysician, they become too abstract and fine, to be apprehended by men of ordinary sense. Bid your servant meet you at such a *time*, in such a *place*, and he shall never stay to deliberate on the meaning of those words: in conceiving that particular time and place, or the motion by which he is to get

thither, he finds not the least difficulty. But if *time* be taken, exclusive of all those particular actions and ideas that diversify the day, merely for the continuation of existence, or duration in abstract, then it will perhaps gravel even a philosopher to comprehend it.

98 Whenever I attempt to frame a simple idea of *time*, abstracted from the succession of ideas in my mind, which flows uniformly, and is participated by all beings, I am lost and embrangled in inextricable difficulties. I have no notion of it at all, only I hear others say, it is infinitely divisible, and speak of it in such a manner as leads me to entertain odd thoughts of my existence: since that doctrine lays one under an absolute necessity of thinking, either that he passes away innumerable ages without a thought, or else that he is annihilated every moment of his life: both which seem equally absurd. Time therefore being nothing, abstracted from the succession of ideas in our minds, it follows that the duration of any finite spirit must be estimated by the number of ideas or actions succeeding each other in that same spirit or mind. Hence it is a plain consequence that the soul always thinks: and in truth whoever shall go about to divide in his thoughts, or abstract the *existence* of a spirit from its *cogitation*, will, I believe, find it no easy task.

99 So likewise, when we attempt to abstract extension and motion from all other qualities, and consider them by themselves, we presently lose sight of them, and run into great extravagancies. All which depend on a two-fold abstraction: first, it is supposed that extension, for example, may be abstracted from all other sensible qualities; and secondly, that the entity of extension may be abstracted from its being perceived. But whoever shall reflect, and take care to understand what he says, will, if I mistake not, acknowledge that all sensible qualities are alike *sensations*, and alike *real*; that where the extension is, there is the colour too, to wit, in his mind, and that their archetypes can exist only in some other *mind*: and that the objects of sense are nothing but those sensations combined, blended, or (if one may so speak) concreted together: none of all which can be supposed to exist unperceived.

100 What it is for a man to be happy, or an object good, every one may think he knows. But to frame an abstract idea of *happiness*, prescinded from all particular pleasure, or of *goodness*, from every thing that is good, this is what few can pretend to. So likewise, a man may be just and virtuous, without having precise ideas of *justice* and *virtue*. The opinion that those and the like words stand for general notions abstracted from all particular persons and actions, seems to have rendered morality difficult, and the study thereof of less use to mankind. And in effect, the doctrine of *abstraction* has not a little contributed towards spoiling the most useful parts of knowledge.

Second edition, 1734

ANTHONY ASHLEY COOPER, THIRD EARL OF SHAFTESBURY (1671–1713)

'I found in it almost all of my *Theodicy* before it saw the light of day,' Leibnitz wrote to Coste of *The Moralists*, 'the universe all of a piece, its beauty, its universal harmony, the disappearance of real evil.' In England, however, Shaftesbury's influence on the mainstream of philosophy was more slight. His anticipation of themes of Romantic poetry, however, is extensive, and at times, impressively comprehensive.

As an imaginative writer his foremost achievement was a universe of matter released from time and space, in the labyrinths of which the mind, like that of God, might wander at will in parallel creativity. Shaftesbury was an idealist, but interestingly, his concept of perception led directly to competition with God, in a manner prophetic of Shelley's Prometheus, and of the entire Romantic image of the poet as *Deus Creator*.

Important related concepts of this not entirely unique attitude to the temporal-spatial, are clearer at an earlier date in Shaftesbury than in any contemporary. Without extension there is no structure of value which might consign the dark, evil, and unattractive to the depths, and the bright, good, and proportioned to the heights. The extremely important notion, which leads to the recognition of the crude, ugly, and horrific as of primary importance in aesthetics, appears explicitly in *The Moralists* where the timeless, memoryless, mind exploring, with more than a hint of Blake's *Tyger*, the *fauna* of North Africa, finds, in the freshness of creative discovery that the repellent creatures have their own beauty, in their own terms. Poisonous snakes or hideous crocodiles 'all ghastly and hideous as they appear . . . want not their peculiar beauty' and 'were beauteous in themselves'. Blake's *The Marriage of Heaven and Hell* would not take place for a century, but in Shaftesbury may be observed the proclamation of the banns.

Possibly the most interesting aspect of Shaftesbury is his style. Time and place do, indeed, seem to disappear, to the extent that his writing frequently anticipates the major achievement of mid-century Romantic poets, the disappearance of a sense of a reality external to the poem. Shaftesbury's art seems not to be a mirror held up to Nature, but an obscure, often opaque, externalization of the mind's own cognitive processes, as it extends Nature into the unknown. The prose of *The Moralists* gives a sense of a self-enclosed continuum, as if there were no reality other than the mind's celebration of the words on the page.

Shaftesbury's climactic account of the Atlas Mountains of North Africa, a touchstone of the 'Sublime' which reappears in Spence's *Essay on Pope's Odyssey* (see p. 105) and in Joseph Warton's *Essay on Pope* (see p. 181), reminds us that the perception of the universe without time and space seemed frequently to lead writers of this era into extended image of the east, as if, close to the traditional *locale* of accounts of the

Creation, poetic creativity might most richly be suggested. The mental traveller's ability to foresee in a mixture of horror and delight, the approaching end of the world in 'the irreparable breaches of the wasted mountain' reminds us too that the aesthetic of the ruin was related to the 'sublime' proximity of the Infinite apparent in the wasting of material Nature. The distance from Shaftesbury to Piranesi's prints of ancient Rome is not prohibitive.

'There is no such thing as time and space,' wrote John Keats to his brother from Wordsworth's Lake District, on 25 June 1818, describing 'shores and islands green to the marge − mountains all round up to the clouds.' With Shaftesburian insight into the marvels of uncategorized phenomena, Keats playfully considered, in a manner suggestive of the power of *Hyperion: A Fragment*, the notion of mountains existing out of their usual place, in the poet's imagination *above* not below the clouds. 'I have an amazing partiality for mountains in the clouds,' he noted, adding that such images 'make one forget the divisions of life . . . and refine one's sensual vision into a sort of north star.' It is an indication of the long and continuous intellectual background of Romanticism, that such epoch-making awarenesses might be discovered in Shaftesbury's *The Moralists* as early as 1711.

CHARACTERISTICS OF MEN, MANNERS, OPINIONS, TIMES (1711)

from 'The Moralists, A Rhapsody', Section I

'O Glorious *Nature*! supremely Fair, and sovereignly Good! All-loving and All-lovely, All-divine! Whose Looks are so becoming, and of such infinite Grace; whose Study brings such Wisdom, and whose Contemplation such Delight; whose every single Work affords an ampler Scene, and is a nobler Spectacle than all which ever Art presented! − O mighty *Nature*! Wise Substitute of *Providence*! impower'd *Creatress*! Or Thou impowering *Deity*, Supreme Creator! Thee I invoke, and Thee alone adore. To thee this Solitude, this Place, these Rural Meditations are sacred; whilst thus inspir'd with Harmony of Thought, tho unconfin'd by Words, and in loose Numbers, I sing of Nature's Order in created Beings, and celebrate the Beautys which resolve in Thee, the Source and Principle of all Beauty and Perfection.

Thy Being is boundless, unsearchable, impenetrable. In thy Immensity all Thought is lost; Fancy gives o'er its Flight: and weary'd Imagination spends it-self in vain; finding no Coast nor Limit of this Ocean, nor, in the widest Tract thro which it soars, one Point yet nearer the Circumference than the first Center whence it parted. − Thus having oft essay'd, thus sally'd forth into the wide *Expanse*, when I return again within *My-self* struck with the Sense of this so narrow Being, and of the Fulness of that Immense-one; I dare no more behold the amazing Depths, nor Sound the Abyss of *Deity*. –

Yet since by Thee (O *Sovereign Mind!*) I have been form'd such as I am, intelligent and rational; since the peculiar Dignity of my Nature is to know and contemplate Thee; permit that with due Freedom I exert those Facultys with which thou hast adorn'd me. Bear with my ventrous and bold Approach. And since nor vain Curiosity, nor fond Conceit, nor Love of ought save Thee alone, inspires me with such Thoughts as these, be thou my Assistant, and guide me in this Pursuit; whilst I venture thus to tread the Labyrinth of wide Nature, and endeavour to trace thee in thy Works'. –

Here he stop'd short, and starting, as out of a Dream; 'Now *Philocles*,' said he, 'inform me, How have I appear'd to you in my Fit? Seem'd it a sensible kind of Madness, like those Transports which are permitted to our *Poets*? or was it downright Raving?'

'I *Only* wish,' said I, 'that you had been a little stronger in your Transport, to have proceeded as you began, without ever minding me. For I was beginning to see Wonders in that *Nature* you taught me, and was coming to know the Hand of your *Divine Artificer*. But if you stop here, I shall lose the Enjoyment of the pleasing Vision. And already I begin to find a thousand Difficultys in fancying such a *Universal Genius* as you describe.'

'Why,' said he, 'is there any difficulty in fancying the Universe to be *One Intire Thing*?'

*

'The goodly Bulk so prolifick, kind, and yielding for every-one else, has nothing left at last for its own share; having unhappily lavish'd all away! – By what Chance I wou'd fain understand.'

'How? or by what necessity? – Who gives the Law? – Who orders and distributes thus?'

'*Nature*,' say you.

'And what is *Nature*? Is *It* Sense? Is *It* a Person? Has *She* Reason or Understanding? No. Who then understands for her, or is interested or concern'd in her behalf? No-one; not a Soul; But *Every one for himself.*'

'Come on then. Let us hear further. Is not this *Nature* still a *Self*? Or, tell me, I beseech you, How are *You one*? By what *Token*? or by virtue of *What*?

'By a Principle which joins certain Parts, and which thinks and acts consonantly for the Use and Purpose of those Parts.'

'Say, therefore, What is your whole System a Part of? Or is it, indeed, no *Part*, but *a Whole, by it-self*, absolute, independent, and unrelated to any thing besides? If it be indeed *a Part*, and really *related*; to what else, I beseech you, than to *the Whole of Nature*? Is there then such *a uniting Principle* in *Nature*? If so, how are you then a *Self*, and *Nature* not so?

How have you something to understand and act for you, and *Nature*, who gave this Understanding, nothing at all to understand for her, advise her, or help her out (poor Being!) on any occasion, whatever Necessity she may be in? Has the *World* such ill fortune *in the main*? Are there so many *particular* understanding active Principles every-where? And is there Nothing, at last, which thinks, acts, or understands for *All*? Nothing which administers or looks after *All*?

'No (says one of a modern Hypothesis) for the *World* was from Eternity, as you see it; and is no more than barely what you see: *'Matter modify'd; a Lump in motion, with here and there a Thought, or scatter'd Portion of dissoluble Intelligence.'* –

'No (says one of an antienter Hypothesis) For the World was once without any Intelligence or Thought at all; *Mere Matter, Chaos, and a Play of Atoms*; till *Thought*, by Chance, came into play, and made up a Harmony which was never design'd, or thought of. – Admirable Conceit! – Believe it who can. For my own share (thank Providence) I have a *Mind* in my possession, which serves, such as it is, to keep my Body and its Affections, my Passions, Appetites, Imaginations, Fancys, and the rest, in tolerable *Harmony* and *Order*. But *the Order of the Universe*, I am persuaded still, is much the better of the *two*. Let *Epicurus*, if he please, think his *the better*; and believing no *Genius* or *Wisdom* above his own, inform us by what Chance 'twas dealt him, and how *Atoms* came to be so wise.'

'In fine,' continu'd *Theocles* (raising his Voice and Action) 'being thus, even by *Scepticism* it-self, convinc'd the more still of my own Being, and of this *Self* of mine, "That 'tis a *real Self*, drawn out, and copy'd from another principal and *original Self* (the *Great-one* of the World)." I endeavour to be really *one* with It, and conformable to It, as far as I am able. I consider, That as there is *one* general Mass, *one* Body of the Whole; so to this Body there is *an Order*, to this *Order* a *Mind*: That to this *general Mind* each *particular-one* must have relation; as being of like Substance (as much as we can understand of *Substance*) alike active upon Body, original to Motion and Order; alike simple, uncompounded, individual; of like Energy, Effect, and Operation; and more like still, if it co-operates with It to general Good and strives *to will* according to that best of *Wills*. So that it cannot surely but seem natural, That the *particular Mind* shou'd seek its Happiness in conformity with the *general-one*, and endeavour to resemble it in its highest Simplicity and Excellence.'

*

'The vital Principle is widely shar'd [Theocles continues], and in-finitely vary'd: Dispers'd throughout; nowhere extinct. All lives: and by Succession still revives. The Temporary Beings quit their borrow'd Forms, and yield their Elementary Substance to New-Comers. Call'd, in their several turns, to Life, they view the Light, and viewing pass; that others too may be Spectators of the goodly Scene, and great numbers still enjoy the Privilege of *Nature*. Munificent and Great, she imparts her-self to most; and makes the Subjects of her Bounty infinite. Nought stays her hastning Hand. No Time nor Substance is lost or un-improv'd. New Forms arise: and when the old dissolve, the Matter whence they were compos'd is not left useless, but wrought with equal Management and Art, even in *Corruption*, Nature's seeming Waste, and vile Abhorrence. The abject State appears merely as *the Way* or *Passage* to some better. But cou'd we nearly view it, and with Indifference, remote from the Antipathy of Sense; we then perhaps shou'd highest raise our Admiration: convinc'd that even *the Way it-self* was equal to *the End*. Nor can we judge less favourably of that consummate Art exhibited thro all the Works of Nature; since our weak Eyes, help'd by mechanick Art, discover in these Works a hidden Scene of Wonders; Worlds within Worlds, of infinite Minuteness, tho as to Art still equal to the greatest, and pregnant with more Wonders than the most discerning Sense, join'd with the greatest Art, or the acutest Reason, can penetrate or unfold.

But 'tis in vain for us to search the bulky Mass of *Matter*: seeking to know its Nature; how great *the Whole* it-self, or even how small its *Parts*.

If knowing only some of the Rules of *Motion*, we seek to trace it further, 'tis in vain we follow it into the Bodys it has reach'd. Our tardy Apprehensions fail us, and can reach nothing beyond the Body it-self, thro which it is diffus'd. Wonderful *Being*! (if we may call it so) which Bodys never receive, except from others which lose it; nor ever lose, unless by imparting it to others. Even without Change of Place it has its Force: And Bodys big with Motion labour to move, yet stir not; whilst they express an Energy beyond our Comprehension.

In vain too we pursue that *Phantom Time*, too small, and yet too mighty for our Grasp; when shrinking to a narrow point, it scapes our Hold, or mocks our scanty Thought by swelling to Eternity: an Object unproportion'd to our Capacity, as is Thy Being, O thou Antient *Cause*! older than *Time*, yet young with fresh Eternity.

In vain we try to fathom the Abyss of *Space*, 'the Seat of thy extensive Being; of which no place is empty, no Void which is not full.'

*

*'How oblique and faintly looks the Sun on yonder Climates, far remov'd from him! How tedious are the *Winters* there! How deep the Horrours of the Night, and how uncomfortable even the Light of Day! The freezing Winds employ their fiercest Breath, yet are not spent with

---

*Compare Theocles's spaceless and timeless voyage with the flight to the Pole and tropics in Thomson's *The Seasons*. Ed.

blowing. The Sea, which elsewhere is scarce confin'd within its Limits, lies here immur'd in Walls of Chrystal. The Snow covers the Hills, and almost fills the lowest Valleys. How wide and deep it lies, incumbent o'er the Plains, hiding the sluggish Rivers, the Shrubs, and Trees, the Dens of Beasts, and Mansions of distress'd and feeble Men! — See! where they lie confin'd, hardly secure against the raging Cold, or the Attacks of the wild Beasts, now Masters of the wasted Field, and forc'd by Hunger out of the naked Woods. — Yet not disheartn'd (such is the Force of Human Breasts) but thus provided for, by Art and Prudence, the kind compensating Gifts of Heaven, Men and their Herds may wait for a Release. For at length the Sun approaching, melts the Snow, sets longing Men at liberty, and affords them Means and Time to make provision against the next Return of Cold. It breaks the Icy Fetters of the Main; where vast Sea-Monsters pierce thro floating Islands, with Arms which can withstand the Chrystal Rock: whilst others, who of themselves seem great as Islands, are by their Bulk alone arm'd against all but Man; whose Superiority over Creatures of such stupendous Size and Force, shou'd make him mindful of his Privilege of Reason, and force him humbly to adore the great Composer of these wondrous Frames, and Author of his own superiour Wisdom.

But leaving these dull Climates, so little favour'd by the Sun, for those happier Regions, on which he looks more kindly, making perpetual *Summer*; How great an Alteration do we find? His purer *Light* confounds weak-sighted Mortals, pierc'd by his scorching *Beams*. Scarce can they tread the glowing Ground. The Air they breathe cannot enough abate the *Fire* which burns within their panting Breasts. Their Bodys melt. O'ercome and fainting, they seek the Shade, and wait the cool Refreshments of the Night. Yet oft the *bounteous Creator* bestows other Refreshments. He casts a Veil of *Clouds* before 'em, and raises gentle *Gales*: favour'd by which, the Men and Beasts pursue their Labours; and Plants refresh'd by Dews and Showers, can gladly bear the warmest Sun-beams.

And here the varying Scene opens to new Wonders. We see a Country rich with *Gems*, but richer with the fragrant *Spices* it affords. How gravely move the largest of *Land-Creatures* on the Banks of this fair River! How ponderous are their Arms, and vast their Strength, with Courage, and a Sense superiour to the other Beasts! Yet are they tam'd (we see) by Mankind, and brought even to fight their Battels, rather as Allys and Confederates, than as Slaves. But let us turn our Eyes towards these smaller, and more curious Objects; the numerous and devouring *Insects* on the Trees in these wide Plains. How shining, strong, and lasting are the subtile Threds spun from their artful Mouths! Who beside *The All-wise* has taught 'em to compose the beautiful soft Shells, in which recluse and bury'd, yet still alive, they undergo such a surprizing Change; when not destroy'd by Men, who clothe and adorn themselves with the Labours and Lives of these weak Creatures, and are proud of wearing such inglorious Spoils? How sumptuously apparel'd, gay, and splendid, are all the various *Insects* which feed on the other Plants of this warm Region! How beautiful *the Plants* themselves in all their various Growths, from the triumphant *Palm* down to the humble *Moss*!

Now may we see that *happy* Country where precious *Gums* and *Balsams* flow from Trees; and Nature yields her most delicious Fruits. How tame and tractable, how patient of Labour and of Thirst, are those large Creatures; who lifting up their lofty Heads, go led and loaden thro these dry and barren Places! Their Shape and Temper show them fram'd by Nature to submit to Man, and fitted for his Service: who from hence ought to be more sensible of his Wants, and of the Divine Bounty, thus supplying them.

But see! not far from us, that *Fertilest* of Lands, water'd and fed by a friendly generous Stream, which, e'er it enters the Sea, divides it-self into many Branches, to dispense more equally the rich and nitrous Manure, it bestows so kindly and in due time, on the adjacent Plains. — Fair Image of that fruitful and exuberant Nature, who with a Flood of Bounty blesses all things, and, Parent-like, out of her many Breasts sends the nutritious Draught in various Streams to her rejoicing Offspring! — Innumerable are the dubious Forms and unknown Species which drink the slimy Current: whether they are such as leaving the scorch'd Desarts, satiate here their ardent Thirst, and promiscuously engendring, beget a monstrous Race; or whether (as 'tis said) by the Sun's genial Heat, active on the fermenting Ooze, new Forms are generated, and issue from the River's fertile Bed. — See there the noted Tyrant of the Flood, and Terrour of its Borders! when suddenly displaying his horrid Form, the *amphibious* Ravager invades the Land, quitting his watry Den, and from the Deep emerging, with hideous rush, sweeps o'er the trembling *Plain*. The Natives from afar behold with wonder the enormous Bulk, sprung from so small an Egg. With Horrour they relate the Monster's Nature, cruel and deceitful: how he with dire Hypocrisy, and false Tears, beguiles the Simple-hearted; and inspiring Tenderness and kind Compassion, kills with pious Fraud. — Sad Emblem of that spiritual Plague, dire *Superstition*! Native of this Soil; where first Religion grew unsociable, and among different Worshippers bred mutual Hatred, and Abhorrence of each others Temples. The Infection spreads: and Nations now profane one to another, war fiercer, and in Religion's cause forget Humanity: whilst savage *Zeal*, with meek and pious Semblance, works dreadful Massacre; and for Heaven's sake (horrid Pretence!) makes desolate the Earth. —

Here let us leave these Monsters (glad if we cou'd here confine 'em!) and detesting the dire prolifick Soil, fly to the vast *Desarts* of these Parts. All ghastly and hideous as they appear, they want not their peculiar Beautys. The Wildness pleases. We seem to live alone with Nature. We view her in her inmost Recesses, and contemplate her

with more Delight in these original Wilds, than in the artificial Labyrinths and feign'd Wildernesses of the Palace. The Objects of the place,
the scaly Serpents, the savage Beasts, and poisonous Insects, how
terrible soever, or how contrary to human Nature, are beauteous in
themselves, and fit to raise our Thoughts in Admiration of that
Divine Wisdom, so far superiour to our short Views. Unable to
declare the Use or Service of all things in this Universe, we are
yet assur'd of the Perfection of *all*, and of the Justice of that
Oeconomy, to which all things are subservient, and in respect of
which, Things seemingly deform'd are amiable; Disorder becomes
regular; Corruption wholesome; and Poisons (such as these we have
seen) prove healing and beneficial.

But behold! thro a vast Tract of Sky before us, the mighty ATLAS
rears his lofty Head, cover'd with Snow, above the Clouds. Beneath
the *Mountain's* foot, the rocky Country rises into Hills, a proper
Basis of the ponderous Mass above: where huge embody'd Rocks lie
pil'd on one another, and seem to prop the high Arch of Heaven. –
See! with what trembling Steps poor Mankind tread the narrow
Brink of the deep Precipices! From whence with giddy Horrour
they look down, mistrusting even the Ground which bears 'em;
whilst they hear the hollow Sound of Torrents underneath, and see
the Ruin of the impending Rock; with falling Trees which hang with
their Roots upwards, and seem to draw more Ruin after 'em. Here
thoughtless Men, seiz'd with the Newness of such Objects, become
thoughtful, and willingly contemplate the incessant Changes of this
Earth's Surface. They see, as in one instant, the Revolutions of past
Ages, and Fleeting Forms of Things, and the Decay even of this our
Globe; whose Youth and first Formation they consider, whilst
the apparent Spoil and irreparable Breaches of the wasted Mountain
shew them the World it-self only as a noble Ruin, and make
them think of its approaching Period. – But here mid-way the
Mountain, a spacious Border of thick Wood harbours our weary'd
Travellers: who now are come among the ever-green and lofty Pines, the
Firs, and noble Cedars, whose tow'ring heads seem endless in the Sky;
the rest of Trees appearing only as Shrubs beside them. And here a
different Horrour seizes our shelter'd Travellers, when they see the
Day diminish'd by the deep Shades of the vast Wood; which closing
thick above, spreads Darkness and eternal Night below. The faint and
gloomy Light looks horrid as the Shade it-self: and the profound
Stillness of these Places imposes Silence upon Men struck with the
hoarse Echoings of every Sound within the spacious Caverns of the
Wood. Here *Space* astonishes. *Silence* it-self seems pregnant; whilst
an unknown Force works on the Mind, and dubious Objects move the
wakeful Sense. Mysterious *Voices* are either heard or fancy'd: and
various Forms of *Deity* seem to present themselves, and appear more
manifest in these sacred Silvan Scenes; such as of old gave rise to

Temples, and favour'd the Religion of the antient World. Even we our-selves, who in plain Characters may read *Divinity* from so many bright Parts of Earth, chuse rather these obscurer Places, to spell out that mysterious Being, which to our weak Eyes appears at best under a Veil of Cloud. – –'

Third edition, 1714

JOSEPH ADDISON (1672–1719)

It is only with Locke (Essay, II, xxx) that an attempt is made to distinguish 'real ideas' from 'fantastical', R.G. Collingwood observed in *The Principles of Art* (Oxford, 1938, p. 176). 'By *real ideas*, I mean such as have a foundation in nature, . . . *fantastical or chimerical* I call such as have no foundation in nature', Locke had written (cf. p. 46). Locke's examples of fantastical ideas are fairies and centaurs.

One of the most significant aspects of Addison's 'The Pleasures of the Imagination', as *Spectators* Nos. *411–421* are known, is the attitude to fantasies of the supernatural which Addison, influenced by the New Philosophy displays. The epigraph to his crucial *Spectator* No. *419*, *'mentis gratissimus error'* – 'the most pleasing error of the mind' – is from Horace, *Epistles* II. ii. The man of Argos sat continually in an empty theatre applauding. When cured, he complained of his loss of 'the most pleasing error of my mind'. In writing of 'fairies, witches, magicians, demons and departed spirits', popular especially before the days of the present enlightenment, the poet 'has no pattern to follow . . . and must work altogether out of his own invention', Addison observed. Modifying the phrase 'fairy kind of writing' used in a complimentary manner by Dryden (*King Arthur*), Addison describes a 'fairy way of writing', pointing to the empty theatre which the New Philosophy had revealed. This was the only unnatural way of writing, for, in it alone, the poet had no pattern to follow in nature. In applying Locke's distinction to literary theory, Addison suggests that a significant aspect of Romanticism would be the creation of the supernatural as a direct activity of the imagination. One of the most powerful and characteristic of Romantic agonies might be traced to this point. Formerly, the supernatural had been a common entity shared by nations. Now, it is the uncertain creation of the individual poet sublimely alone in the cosmos. Upon the cultural horizon we may see approaching, clearly, although at a distance, the Wandering Jew, the Ancient Mariner, Mary Shelley's Frankenstein, and all the crew of palely loitering poets in thrall to unspeakable, personal terrors.

The psychology of perception modifies also the related concept of personified abstractions in Addison's pioneering aesthetic. Personifications had been a distinct part of literature for centuries. Milton's *Paradise Lost* which Addison's *Spectators* helped to popularize on the tables of the new rich, had an abundance of these, perhaps notably, Sin and Death. Addison's dislike of Sin and Death in Milton rested on their activity within the epic as three-dimensional actors, with a life apparently distinct from the purely literary images amongst which they appeared. In Addison, moral ideas were not external and 'real' but aesthetic responses related to pleasure. In personifications one caught thrilling glimpses of the mind of the poet fleetingly in action, making images in his own shape under the duress of overwhelming emotion. His praise of Habakkuk's 'Pestilence' (repeated by Lowth in *Lecture 13*) in *Spectator* No. 357 is especially interesting for it ties the new kind of abstraction, closer rather to the philosophy of Berkeley than to that of Locke, to the theory of 'the Sublime' and suggests that in the sublime personification 'greatness' (the Burnetian *sine qua non* of sublimity) was founded on the materiality of the abstraction as an object of thought.

The overall emphasis of 'The Pleasures of the Imagination' is as pioneering as its rarity up until this time as a treatise on the psychology of aesthetic response. Pleasure, relative perception, and subjectivity are taking the place of the morality, assumption of externality, and the objectivity of current Neo-classical thought, as revealed for example in Pope's *Essay on Criticism*. In popularizing in his widely-circulating magazine current theories in which thoughts were object-sensations instead of shadows of a distant unseen, Addison tied for the fashionable world an irreversible knot between the philosophers and poets.

In other matters it is possible to identify Addison too closely with later developments. He is a derivative rather than visionary writer. 'Imagination' for him at large appears to demand a 'pattern in Nature' and means, apparently, little more than the receptive capacity of the retina. His observation in *Spectator 416* that the poet 'seems to get the better of Nature' creating something never seen before, might well be interpreted to indicate, except of course in the instances outlined above, a mere theory of re-arrangement and idealization which would not depart from Renaissance concepts of 'la belle Nature' or Sir Joshua Reynolds.

from SPECTATOR No. 357, Saturday, April 19, 1712

Since the Subject I am upon gives me an Opportunity of speaking more at large of such Shadowy and imaginary Persons as may be introduced into Heroic Poems, I shall beg leave to explain my self in a Matter which is curious in its kind, and which none of the Criticks have treated of. It is certain *Homer* and *Virgil* are full of imaginary Persons, who are very beautiful in Poetry when they are just shown, without being engaged in any Series of Action. *Homer* indeed represents *Sleep* as a Person, and ascribes a short Part to him in his *Iliad*; but we must consider that tho' we now regard such a Person as entirely Shadowy and unsubstantial, the Heathens made Statues of him, placed him in their Temples, and looked upon him as a real Deity. When *Homer* makes use of other such Allegorical Persons, it is only in short Expressions, which convey an ordinary Thought to the Mind in the most pleasing manner, and may rather be looked upon as Poetical Phrases than allegorical Descriptions. Instead of telling us that Men naturally fly when they are terrified, he introduces the Persons of *Flight* and *Fear*, who he tells us are inseparable Companions. Instead of saying that the Time was come when *Apollo* ought to have received his Recompence, he tells us that the *Hours* brought him his Reward. Instead of describing the Effects which *Minerva's Aegis* produced in Battel, he tells us that the Brims of it were encompassed by *Terrour, Rout, Discord, Fury, Pursuit, Massacre* and *Death*. In the same Figure of speaking he represents *Victory* as following *Diomedes*; *Discord* as the Mother of Funerals and Mourning, *Venus* as dressed by the *Graces*, *Bellona* as wearing Terrour and Consternation like a Garment. I might give several other Instances out of *Homer*, as well as a great many out of *Virgil*. *Milton* has likewise very often made use of the same way of speaking, as where he tells us that *Victory* sat on the right hand of the Messiah, when he march'd forth against the Rebel Angels; that at the rising of the Sun the *Hours* unbarr'd the Gates of Light; that *Discord* was the Daughter of *Sin*. Of the same nature are those Expressions where describing the singing of the Nightingale he adds, *Silence was pleased*; and upon   the Messiah's bidding Peace to the *Chaos, Confusion heard his voice*. I might add innumerable Instances of our Poet's writing in this beautiful Figure. It is plain that these I have mentioned, in which Persons of an imaginary Nature are introduced, are such short Allegories as are not designed to be taken in the litteral Sense, but only to convey particular Circumstances to the Reader after an unusual and entertaining Manner. But when such Persons are introduced as principal Actors, and engaged in a Series of Adventures, they take too much upon them, and are by no means proper for an Heroic Poem, which ought to appear credible in its principal Parts. I cannot forbear therefore thinking that *Sin* and *Death* are as improper Agents in a Work of this Nature, as *Strength* and *Necessity* in one of the Tragedies of *Eschylus*, who represented those two Persons nailing down *Prometheus* to a Rock, for which he has been justly censured by the greatest Criticks. I do not know any imaginary Person made use of in a more Sublime manner of thinking than that in one of the Prophets [Habakkuk 3:5], who describing God as descending from Heaven, and visiting the Sins of Mankind, adds that dreadful Circumstance; *Before him went the Pestilence*. It is certain this imaginary Person might have been described in all her purple Spots. The *Fever* might have march'd before her, *Pain* might have stood at her right Hand, *Phrenzy* on her left, and *Death* in her Rear. She might have been introduced as gliding down from the Tail of a Comet, or darted upon the Earth in a Flash of Lightning: She might have tainted the Atmosphere with her Breath; the very glaring of her Eyes might have scattered Infection. But I believe every Reader will think that in such Sublime Writings the mentioning of her as it is done in Scripture has something in it more just, as well as great, than all that the most fanciful Poet could have bestowed upon her in the Richness of his Imagination.

'THE PLEASURES OF THE IMAGINATION', SPECTATOR NOS. 411–421

from SPECTATOR No. 411, Saturday, June 21, 1712

Avia Pieridum peragro loca, nullius ante
Trita solo; juvat integros accedere fontis;
Atque haurire*. . . .

Our Sight is the most perfect and most delightful of all our Senses. It fills the Mind with the largest Variety of Ideas, converses with its Objects at the greatest Distance, and continues the longest in Action without being tired or satiated with its proper Enjoyments. The Sense of Feeling can indeed give us a Notion of Extention, Shape, and all other Ideas that enter at the Eye, except Colours; but at the same time it is very much streightned and confined in its Operations, to the number, bulk, and distance of its particular Objects. Our Sight seems designed to supply all these Defects, and may be considered as a more delicate and diffusive kind of Touch, that spreads it self over an infinite Multitude of Bodies, comprehends the largest Figures, and brings into our reach some of the most remote Parts of the Universe.

It is this Sense which furnishes the Imagination with its Ideas; so that by the Pleasures of the Imagination or Fancy (which I shall use promiscuously) I here mean such as arise from visible Objects, either when we have them actually in our view, or when we call up their Ideas into our Minds by Paintings, Statues, Descriptions, or any the like Occasion. We cannot indeed have a single Image in the Fancy that did not make its first Entrance through the Sight; but we have the Power of retaining, altering and compounding those Images, which we have once received, into all the varieties of Picture and Vision that are most agreeable to the Imagination; for by this Faculty a Man in a Dungeon is capable of entertaining himself with Scenes and Landskips more beautiful than any that can be found in the whole Compass of Nature.

*

from SPECTATOR No. 412, Monday, June 23

. . . Divisum sic breve fiet Opus.
Mart.**

I shall first consider those Pleasures of the Imagination, which arise from the actual View and Survey of outward Objects: And these, I think, all proceed from the Sight of what is *Great, Uncommon* or *Beautiful.* There

---

*Lucretius, *De rerum natura*, I. 926–8: 'The pathless tracts of Pierides never trodden I wander o'er. I rejoice to approach unbroached springs and drink.' Ed.

**Martial, *Epigrams*, IV. lxxxii. 8: 'The work divided will thus become brief.' Ed.

may, indeed, be something so terrible or offensive, that the Horrour or Loathsomness of an Object may over-bear the Pleasure which results from its *Greatness, Novelty,* or *Beauty*; but still there will be such a Mixture of Delight in the very Disgust it gives us, as any of these three Qualifications are most conspicuous and prevailing.

By *Greatness,* I do not only mean the Bulk of any single Object, but the Largeness of a whole View, considered as one entire Piece. Such are the Prospects of an open Champian Country, a vast uncultivated Desart, of huge Heaps of Mountains, high Rocks and Precipices, or a wide Expanse of Waters, where we are not struck with the Novelty or Beauty of the Sight, but with that rude kind of Magnificence which appears in many of these stupendous Works of Nature. Our Imagination loves to be filled with an Object, or to graspe at any thing that is too big for its Capacity. We are flung into a pleasing Astonishment at such unbounded Views, and feel a delightful Stillness and Amazement in the Soul at the Apprehension of them. The Mind of Man naturally hates every thing that looks like a Restraint upon it, and is apt to fancy it self under a sort of Confinement, when the Sight is pent up in a narrow Compass, and shortned on every side by the Neighbourhood of Walls or Mountains. On the contrary, a spacious Horison is an Image of Liberty, where the Eye has Room to range abroad, to expatiate at large on the Immensity of its Views, and to lose it self amidst the Variety of Objects that offer them-selves to its Observation. Such wide and undetermined Prospects are as pleasing to the Fancy, as the Speculations of Eternity or Infinitude are to the Understanding. But if there be a Beauty or Uncommonness joyned with this Grandeur, as in a troubled Ocean, a Heaven adorned with Stars and Meteors, or a spacious Landskip cut out into Rivers, Woods, Rocks, and Meadows, the Pleasure still grows upon us, as it arises from more than a single Principle.

Every thing that is *new* or *uncommon* raises a Pleasure in the Imagination, because it fills the Soul with an agreeable Surprise, gratifies its Curiosity, and gives it an Idea of which it was not before possest. We are, indeed, so often conversant with one Sett of Objects, and tired out with so many repeated Shows of the same Things, that whatever is *new* or *uncommon* contributes a little to vary Human Life, and to divert our Minds, for a while, with the Strangeness of its Appearance: It serves us for a kind of Refreshment, and takes off from that Satiety we are apt to complain of in our usual and ordinary Entertainments. It is this that bestows Charms on a Monster, and makes even the Imperfections of Nature please us. It is this that recommends Variety, where the Mind is every Instant called off to something new, and the Attention not suffered to dwell too long, and waste it self on any particular Object. It is this, likewise, that improves what is great or beautiful, and makes it afford the Mind a double Entertainment. Groves, Fields, and Meadows, are at any Season of the Year pleasant to look upon, but never so much as in the opening of the Spring, when they are all new and fresh, with their first Gloss upon them, and not yet too much accustomed and familiar to the Eye. For this reason there is nothing that more enlivens a Prospect than Rivers, Jetteaus, or Falls of Water, where the Scene is perpetually shifting, and entertaining the Sight every Moment with something that is new. We are quickly tired with looking upon Hills and Valleys, where everything continues fixt and settled in the same Place and Posture, but find our Thoughts a little agitated and relieved at the sight of such Objects as are ever in Motion, and sliding away from beneath the Eye of the Beholder.

*

from SPECTATOR No. 413, Tuesday, June 24
  . . . *Causa latet, vis est notissima . . . ***
Though in Yesterday's Paper we considered how every thing that is *Great, New*, or *Beautiful*, is apt to affect the Imagination with Pleasure, we must own that it is impossible for us to assign the necessary Cause of this Pleasure, because we know neither the Nature of an Idea, nor the Substance of a Human Soul, which might help us to discover the Conformity or Disagreeableness of the one to the other; and therefore, for want of such a Light, all that we can do in Speculations of this kind, is to reflect on those Operations of the Soul that are most agreeable, and to range, under their proper Heads, what is pleasing or displeasing to the Mind, without being able to trace out the several necessary and efficient Causes from whence the Pleasure or Displeasure arises.

Final Causes lye more bare and open to our Observation, as there are often a great Variety that belong to the same Effect; and these, tho' they are not altogether so satisfactory, are generally more useful than the other, as they give us greater Occasion of admiring the Goodness and Wisdom of the first Contriver.

One of the Final Causes of our Delight, in any thing that is *great*, may be this. The Supreme Author of our Being has so formed the Soul of Man, that nothing but himself can be its last, adequate, and proper Happiness. Because, therefore, a great Part of our Happiness must arise from the Contemplation of his Being, that he might give our Souls a just Relish of such a Contemplation, he has made them naturally delight in the Apprehension of what is Great or Unlimited. Our Admiration, which is a very pleasing Motion of the Mind, immediately rises at the Consideration of any Object that takes up a great deal of room in the Fancy, and, by consequence, will improve into the highest pitch of Astonishment and Devotion when we contemplate his Nature, that is neither circumscribed by Time nor Place, nor to be comprehended by the largest Capacity of a Created Being.

---

*Ovid, *Metamorphoses*, IV. 287: 'The cause is secret, but the effect [of the enfeebling fountain] is known.' Ed.

He has annexed a secret Pleasure to the Idea of any thing that is *new* or *uncommon*, that he might encourage us in the Pursuit after Knowledge, and engage us to search into the Wonders of his Creation; for every new Idea brings such a Pleasure along with it, as rewards any Pains we have taken in its Acquisition, and consequently serves as a Motive to put us upon fresh Discoveries.

*

I have here supposed that my Reader is acquainted with that great Modern Discovery, which is at present universally acknowledged by all the Enquirers into Natural Philosophy: Namely, that Light and Colours, as apprehended by the Imagination, are only Ideas of the Mind, and not Qualities that have any Existence in Matter. As this is a Truth which has been proved incontestably by many Modern Philosophers, and is indeed one of the finest Speculations in that Science, if the *English* Reader would see the Notion explained at large, he may find it in the Eighth Chapter of the Second Book of Mr. *Lock's* Essay on Human Understanding. '

*

from SPECTATOR No. 414, Wednesday, June 25

We have before observed, that there is generally in Nature something more Grand and August, than what we meet with in the Curiosities of Art. When, therefore, we see this imitated in any measure, it gives us a nobler and more exalted kind of Pleasure than what we receive from the nicer and more accurate Productions of Art. On this Account our *English* Gardens are not so entertaining to the Fancy as those in *France* and *Italy*, where we see a large Extent of Ground covered over with an agreeable mixture of Garden and Forest, which represent every where an artificial Rudeness, much more charming than that Neatness and Elegancy which we meet with in those of our own Country. It might, indeed, be of ill Consequence to the Publick, as well as unprofitable to private Persons, to alienate so much Ground from Pasturage, and the Plow, in many Parts of a Country that is so well peopled, and cultivated to a far greater Advantage. But why may not a whole Estate be thrown into a kind of Garden by frequent Plantations, that may turn as much to the Profit, as the Pleasure of the Owner? A Marsh overgrown with Willows, or a Mountain shaded with Oaks, are not only more beautiful, but more beneficial, than when they lie bare and unadorned. Fields of Corn make a pleasant Prospect, and if the Walks were a little taken care of that lie between them, if the natural Embroidery of the Meadows were helpt and improved by some small Additions of Art, and the several Rows of Hedges set off by Trees and Flowers, that the Soil was capable of receiving, a Man might make a pretty Landskip of his own Possessions.

Writers, who have given us an Account of *China*, tell us, the Inhabitants of that Country laugh at the Plantations of our *Europeans*, which are laid out by the Rule and Line; because, they say, any one may place Trees in equal Rows and uniform Figures. They chuse rather to shew a Genius in Works of this Nature, and therefore always conceal the Art by which they direct themselves. They have a Word, it seems, in their Language, by which they express the particular Beauty of a Plantation that thus strikes the Imagination at first Sight, without discovering what it is that has so agreeable an Effect. Our *British* Gardeners, on the contrary, instead of humouring Nature, love to deviate from it as much as possible. Our Trees rise in Cones, Globes, and Pyramids. We see the Marks of the Scissars upon every Plant and Bush. I do not know whether I am singular in my Opinion, but, for my own part, I would rather look upon a Tree in all its Luxuriancy and Diffusion of Boughs and Branches, than when it is thus cut and trimmed into a Mathematical Figure; and cannot but fancy that an Orchard in Flower looks infinitely more delightful, than all the little Labyrinths of the most finished Parterre. But as our great Modellers of Gardens have their Magazines of Plants to dispose of, it is very natural for them to tear up all the Beautiful Plantations of Fruit Trees, and contrive a Plan that may most turn to their own Profit, in taking off their Evergreens, and the like Moveable Plants, with which their Shops are plentifully stocked.

*

from SPECTATOR No. 416, Friday, June 27
   Quatenus hoc simile est illi, quod mente videmus. *
I at first divided the Pleasures of the Imagination, into such as arise from Objects that are actually before our Eyes, or that once entered in at our Eyes, and are afterwards called up into the Mind, either barely by its own Operations, or on occasion of something without us, as Statues or Descriptions. We have already considered the first Division, and shall therefore enter on the other, which, for Distinction sake, I have call'd the Secondary Pleasures of the Imagination. When I say the Ideas we receive from Statues, Descriptions, or such like Occasions, are the same that were once actually in our View, it must not be understood that we had once seen the very Place, Action, or Person which are carved or described. It is sufficient, that we have seen Places, Persons, or Actions, in general, which bear a Resemblance, or at least some remote Analogy with what we find represented. Since it is in the Power of the Imagination, when it is once Stocked with particular Ideas, to enlarge, compound, and vary them at her own Pleasure.

*

---

*Lucretius, *De rerum natura*, IV. 750: 'Since what we fancy we see in our mind represents what we behold.' For *illi* Addison has *oculis*. Ed.

Words, when well chosen, have so great a Force in them, that a Description often gives us more lively Ideas than the Sight of Things themselves. The Reader finds a Scene drawn in stronger Colours, and painted more to the Life in his Imagination, by the help of Words, than by an actual Survey of the Scene which they describe. In this Case the Poet seems to get the better of Nature; he takes, indeed, the Landskip after her, but gives it more vigorous Touches, heightens its Beauty, and so enlivens the whole Piece, that the Images, which flow from the Objects themselves, appear weak and faint, in Comparison of those that come from the Expressions. The Reason, probably, may be, because in the Survey of any Object we have only so much of it painted on the Imagination, as comes in at the Eye; but in its Description, the Poet gives us as free a View of it as he pleases, and discovers to us several Parts, that either we did not attend to, or that lay out of our Sight when we first beheld it. As we look on any Object, our Idea of it is, perhaps, made up of two or three simple Ideas; but when the Poet represents it, he may either give us a more complex Idea of it, or only raise in us such Ideas as are most apt to affect the Imagination.

*

from SPECTATOR No. 419, *Tuesday, July 1*
 . . . *mentis gratissimus Error.*
Hor.*

There is a kind of Writing, wherein the Poet quite loses sight of Nature, and entertains his Reader's Imagination with the Characters and Actions of such Persons as have many of them no Existence, but what he bestows on them. Such are Fairies, Witches, Magicians, Demons, and departed Spirits. This Mr. *Dryden* calls *the Fairie way of Writing,* which is, indeed, more difficult than any other that depends on the Poet's Fancy, because he has no Pattern to follow in it, and must work altogether out of his own Invention.

There is a very odd turn of Thought required for this sort of Writing, and it is impossible for a Poet to succeed in it, who has not a particular Cast of Fancy, and an Imagination naturally fruitful and superstitious. Besides this, he ought to be very well versed in Legends and Fables, antiquated Romances, and the Traditions of Nurses and old Women, that he may fall in with our natural Prejudices, and humour those Notions which we have imbibed in our Infancy. For, otherwise, he will be apt to make his Fairies talk like People of his own Species, and not like other Setts of Beings, who converse with different Objects, and think in a different manner from that of Mankind:

 Sylvis deducti caveant, me Judice, Fauni
 Ne velut innati triviis ac poene forenses

---

*Horace, *Epistles* II. ii. 140: 'the most pleasing error of the mind.'

Aut nimium teneris juvenentur versibus . . . *

I do not say with Mr. *Bays* in the *Rehearsal*, that Spirits must not be confined to speak Sense, but it is certain their Sense ought to be a little discoloured, that it may seem particular, and proper to the Person and the Condition of the Speaker.

These Descriptions raise a pleasing kind of Horrour in the Mind of the Reader, and amuse his Imagination with the Strangeness and Novelty of the Persons who are represented in them. They bring up into our Memory the Stories we have heard in our Child-hood, and favour those secret Terrours and Apprehensions to which the Mind of Man is naturally subject. We are pleased with surveying the different Habits and Behaviours of Foreign Countries, how much more must we be delighted and surprised when we are led, as it were, into a new Creation, and see the Persons and Manners of another Species? Men of cold Fancies, and Philosophical Dispositions, object to this kind of Poetry, that it has not Probability enough to affect the Imagination. But to this it may be answered, that we are sure, in general, there are many Intellectual Beings in the World besides our selves, and several Species of Spirits, who are subject to different Laws and Oeconomies from those of Mankind; when we see, therefore, any of these represented naturally, we cannot look upon the Representation as altogether impossible; nay, many are prepossest with such false Opinions, as dispose them to believe these particular Delusions; at least, we have all heard so many pleasing Relations in favour of them, that we do not care for seeing through the Falsehood, and willingly give our selves up to so agreeable an Imposture.

The Ancients have not much of this Poetry among them, for, indeed, almost the whole Substance of it owes its Original to the Darkness and Superstition of later Ages, when pious Frauds were made use of to amuse Mankind, and frighten them into a Sense of their Duty. Our Forefathers looked upon Nature with more Reverence and Horrour, before the World was enlightened by Learning and Philosophy, and loved to astonish themselves with the Apprehensions of Witchcraft, Prodigies, Charms and Enchantments. There was not a Village in *England* that had not a Ghost in it, the Churchyards were all haunted, every large Common had a Circle of Fairies belonging to it, and there was scarce a Shepherd to be met with who had not seen a Spirit.

Among all the Poets of this Kind our *English* are much the best, by what I have yet seen, whether it be that we abound with more Stories of this Nature, or that the Genius of our Country is fitter for this sort of Poetry. For the *English* are naturally Fanciful, and very often disposed

---

*Horace, *Ars poetica* 244–6:

A Satyr that comes staring from the Woods,
Must not at first speak like an Orator:
But, tho' his Language should not be refin'd,
It must not be Obscene, and Impudent. *Roscommon.*

by that Gloominess and Melancholly of Temper, which is so frequent in our Nation, to many wild Notions and Visions, to which others are not so liable.

Among the *English, Shakespear* has incomparably excelled all others. That noble Extravagance of Fancy, which he had in so great Perfection, throughly qualified him to touch this weak superstitious Part of his Reader's Imagination; and made him capable of succeeding, where he had nothing to support him besides the Strength of his own Genius. There is something so wild and yet so solemn in the Speeches of his Ghosts, Fairies, Witches, and the like Imaginary Persons, that we cannot forbear thinking them natural, tho' we have no Rule by which to judge of them, and must confess, if there are such Beings in the World, it looks highly probable they should talk and act as he has represented them.

There is another sort of Imaginary Beings, that we sometimes meet with among the Poets, when the Author represents any Passion, Appetite, Virtue or Vice, under a visible Shape, and makes it a Person or an Actor in his Poem. Of this Nature are the Descriptions of Hunger and Envy in *Ovid*, of Fame in *Virgil*, and of Sin and Death in *Milton*. We find a whole Creation of the like shadowy Persons in *Spencer*, who had an admirable Talent in Representations of this kind. I have discoursed of these Emblematical Persons in former Papers, and shall therefore only mention them in this Place. Thus we see how many ways Poetry addresses it self to the Imagination, as it has not only the whole Circle of Nature for its Province, but makes new Worlds of its own, shews us Persons who are not to be found in Being, and represents even the Faculties of the Soul, with her several Virtues and Vices, in a sensible Shape and Character.

I shall, in my two following Papers, consider in general, how other kinds of Writing are qualified to please the Imagination, with which I intend to conclude this Essay.

JOSEPH SPENCE (1699–1768)

The third noted Professor of Poetry at Oxford has been better known as the author of the *Observations, Anecdotes and Characters of Books and Men* (1820), a storehouse of gossip and contemporary anecdote, and for his *Polymetis* (1747), a presentation of parallel pictorial and verbal images nurtured by the Grand Tour, than for his criticism of Pope's *Odyssey*.

His protection of Stephen Duck, 'thresher-poet' in a rustic tradition culminating in Burns and Clare, suggests interests in 'primitivism' and originality at least as great as those in classical learning or journalism. Duck's *The Shunamite* explicitly rejects epic for the now fashionable poetry of sensibility based on oriental models. 'Nor should my Muse the *Grecian* Monarchs trace,/Nor would I celebrate the *Trojan* race', sings the thresher, accurately echoing the rejection by Thomas Warton, Professor of Poetry prior to Spence, of 'the songs that nobly tell,/How *Troy* was sacked, and *Rome* began'. Spence's thrilled exclamation in his letter to Pope, 'one sees the struggles of a great soul in him', completes our sense of the excitement of recognition of an early native original, not far removed in kind from William Blake.

The participants in *An Essay on Pope's Odyssey*, Antiphaus 'prejudiced for the Ancients, from the purity and justness, which we find in most of their works', and Philypsus whose 'inlarged genius' draws him to 'the flourish and colouring of the moderns', confirm the feeling of a critique of epic consciously undercut by a sensibility some of whose loyalties are elsewhere. Readers who evade the 'Sublime' of the Hebrews are referred to Blackwall's illuminating *Sacred Classics Defended* of the previous year, while it is found acceptable for Ulysses to declare himself and Nestor the wisest of all the Greeks since Moses had said that he was the meekest man upon the earth.

Most interestingly, Spence picks out the incident on Ithaca when Theoclymenus foretells the downfall of the suitors, from the twentieth book ('Nor gives the Sun his golden Orb to roll,/But universal Night Usurps the Pole!'). Affording explicit evidence of the Romantic assumption that all poetry was prophecy and all prophecy poetry (like contemporary philosophy imaging Nature without the dimensions of time and space) Spence goes on to isolate a technique of prophetic poetry, and to coin a new literary-critical term which illuminates a vital range of poems from his friend and successor Robert Lowth's poem on the window of Winchester Chapel, to *Night Thoughts*, Blake's prophecies, and Keats' *Fall of Hyperion*. Excluding by implication the finite qualities of Newtonian optical theories and recalling for the historian of ideas the observations of Burnet (see p. 35) Spence points to 'that *Eastern way of expressing Revolutions in Government, by a confusion or extinction of light in the Heavens*', finding as evidence for the assumptions of the classical epic of Homer, the prophecies of Ezekiel (see pp. 183-185) and others. 'You will pardon me a new word, where we have no old one', Spence pleads, offering a novel term in Homeric criticism, 'an *orientalism*'.

Spence's persistent modern voice is the most telling card in the critical pack. It reinforces the sense that he prefers the colouring of a single broken column to the perspective of the Parthenon. With an interesting echo of 'John Lizard's' emphasis on the emotional value of movement in poetry of feeling (see p. 141) Philypsus observes of the solitary Odysseus awash in mountainous seas that sublime vastness is 'more vigorous and affecting . . . when some more moving Considerations are annext' (Evening V). That Spence's touchstone is the contemporary 'Sublime' of the novel cognitive theories of Shaftesbury (see pp. 00–00) is indicated by his quotation, at this point, of the crucial description of the Atlas Mountains, the peak of *The Moralists*.

One moment in the corridors of subjectivity, a Romantic notion inimical to the extensive forms of Augustanism and, apparently, ultimately derived from the historical enquiries of contemporary scholarship, seems already to have become a crucial explicit criterion. William Darnall MacClintock's short study *Joseph Warton's Essay on Pope* (Chapel Hill, 1933, repr. New York, 1971) conveniently ties a most important knot between Spence and Joseph Warton (see p. 180) at this point. 'One particular passage in this essay influenced Warton greatly', wrote MacClintock (p. 10) pointing to the passage from 'Evening V' (see p. 104) which declares in terms which suggest an end to the general mode of classicism and Pope, 'there is a *Poetical Falsity*, if a strong idea of each particular be not imprinted on the mind'.

It is, of course, important to read between the lines in Spence's *Essay*. As a prophet, himself, he was instinctual. His light weight among critics, is, naturally, the price of his representative value. Frequently he will follow well-worn paths in his discussion of Pope as of Homer. Nevertheless, for the observer of aesthetic history with a taste for irony, he affords the spectacle of one kind of great art, the Augustan epic, criticized in the terms of what would succeed it, the literature of feeling, and a view of Homer beginning the descent crucial to an understanding of classicism in the eighteenth century, from Augustan plinth to the congregation of Hebrew and druidic bards.

AN ESSAY ON POPE'S ODYSSEY (1726)

from 'Evening IV'
Poetical Prophecy, is when we acquaint the Reader before-hand of some Events, which will happen in the Progress of the Poem: *Prevention* is when we speak of such things, yet to come, as if they were already present. *Prevention* gives an uncommon Greatness and Energy to the Language: It places distant Actions full before our Eyes; and carries a certain Boldness

and Assurance with it, that is very becoming: The *other* is of great Strength in possessing and captivating the Reader; We love to look on into Futurity: Thus it flatters the Powers and Capacity of our own Minds, at the same time that it gives an Air of Superior Knowledge and Authority to the Poet.

From the Invocation of the Muse in the entrance to his Poem, the Poet has a Right of Prophecying; and it might be *partly* from this, that the Name of *Prophet* and *Poet* has in some Languages been us'd in common. But tho' he may, and does, prophecy in Person, things of this Nature are usually introduc'd from others: as from Superior Beings; from Priests and Augurs; from Persons in the other State, or just at the Point of Departing from this. This latter Method perhaps may carry the greater *Sanction* with it; but the other is the more *Poetical*.

Some of the strongest Speeches in *Homer* and *Virgil* are deliver'd after this manner, by Men of the Prophetick Character; It is to this Figure (if you will give me leave to call it so) that the *Sixth Book* of the *Aeneid*, and the *Fourth* of the *Odyssey* owe the greatest share of their Beauty. Even the frightful Raptures of *Theoclymenus*, and the *Harpye* of *Virgil*, engage the Reader with a sort of pleasing Terrour. There is something horribly delightful in these Lines.

> Floating in gore, portentous to survey!
> In each discolour'd vase the Viands lay:
> Then down each cheek the Tears spontaneous flow
> And suddain Sighs precede approaching woe.
> In vision rapt, the *Hyperesian* Seer
> Up-rose, and thus divin'd the Vengeance near:
> O Race to Death devote! with *Stygian* shade
> Each destin'd Peer impending Fates invade:
> With tears your wan distorted cheeks are drown'd,
> With sanguin drops the walls are ruby'd round:
> Thick swarms the spacious hall with howling Ghosts,
> To people *Orcus*, and the burning Coasts!
> Nor gives the Sun his golden Orb to roll,
> But universal Night usurps the Pole!   [xx, 417–30]

I beg pardon (says *Antiphaus*) but the Speech of *Theoclymenus* is a particular Favourite of mine: and now you repeat it in *English*, I seem to want something of that strong Pleasure it used to afford me, where the *Greek* speaks *Of the Sun being perisht out of Heaven, and of Darkness rushing over the Earth*; I cannot express the Fulness of the Words — But you know the Original; and, I fear, will never see a Translation equal it. This whole Prophetical Vision of the Fall of the Suitors, is the *True Sublime*; and, in particular, gives us an higher *Orientalism* than we meet with in any other part of *Homer*'s Writings. You will pardon me a new Word, where we have no old one to my Purpose: You know what I mean, That *Eastern way of expressing Revolutions in Government, by a Confusion or Extinction of Light in the Heavens*. It is this manner of

Expression which works up that Speech the nearest of any to those noble Passages in holy Scripture;

I will shew Wonders in the Heavens and in the Earth, Blood and Fire, and Pillars of Smoak; the Sun shall be turn'd into Darkness, and the Moon into Blood [Joel 2:30-1] — I will cause the Sun to go down at Noon, and I will darken the Earth in the clear Day. [Amos 8:9] — All the bright Lights of Heaven will I make dark over thee, and set Darkness upon thy Land. [Ezekiel 32:8]

I have often wonder'd, *Philypsus*, at some particular Persons, who are ever ravish'd with any thing of the Sublime in common Authors, and yet seem to have no taste for the finest touches of this kind, those which are so frequent in our Sacred Writings. With what Greatness and Sublimity do they abound? Such as might persuade, that we are not only blest with *Instructions*, but favour'd too with a *Language* from Heaven. Those Sacred Pages want only to be read with a common regard, that all Men might acknowledge them to contain the greatest Master-pieces of Eloquence. Yes, *Philypsus*, it is there that Eloquence sits beside the Throne of Truth, in all her noblest Attire, and with a Look that strikes us at once with Reverence and Delight. I long to expatiate on so glorious a Subject; but perhaps we may find a Time of joining together in some View of this Nature. There has been a very good Example set the World this last Summer [A. Blackwall, *The Sacred Classics*]; and if ever we should follow it, and enter thoroughly into this sort of Criticism, I dare say it will make any other kind look poor and insipid, when compared with it. — But at present we are in another Sphere; and I have already interrupted you too much. —

*

from 'Evening V'

Intimation is so strong and nervous, that the Ancient Criticks confin'd the name of *Emphasis* to this one Point; tho' (as we use the word) the very contrary of this may be of great Service in making a Discourse *emphatical*. The Soul is sometimes possess'd by the *Number* of great Circumstances. Thus in that Passage of *Homer* which Mr. *Pope* translates after the following manner:

Men, Steeds, and Chariots shake the trembling ground;
The Tumult thickens, and the Skies resound: . . .
Victors and Vanquish'd join promiscuous cries,
Triumphant shouts, and dying groans arise.   [*Iliad*, viii. 73-80]

We meet with the same *tumultuary Figure* in the Description of the Field after the Battle:

Thro' Dust, thro' Blood, o'er Arms, and hills of Slain.   [*Iliad*, x. 356]

This Passage (we are told) is imitated by *Xenophon*; and I am sure the Historian has not weaken'd it, by drawing it into a greater length, and expressing the Circumstances more fully: Allow me the Satisfaction of reading it to you.

When the Battle was over, one might behold thro' the whole extent of the Field, the Ground dy'd red with Blood, the Bodies of Friends and Enemies, stretch'd over each other, the Shields pierc'd, the Spears broken, and the drawn Swords, some scatter'd on the Earth, some plung'd in the Bodies of the Slain, and some yet grasp'd in the Hands of the Soldiers.   [*Agesilaus*, ii. 14]

Now we have faln upon an Historian, give me leave to observe one thing; That, both with Poets and in History, *There may be some Fraud, in saying only the bare Truth*. In either, 'tis not sufficient to tell us, that *such a City*, for Instance, *was taken and ravag'd with a great deal of Inhumanity*. There is a *Poetical Falsity*, if a strong Idea of each particular be not imprinted on the Mind; and an *Historical*, if some things are passed over only with a general mark of Infamy or Dislike. It was in *Quintilian* I first met with this Observation; and I wish our Historians, of all Parties, did not give us so many Examples of it, as we find every-where in their Works.

'Tis the same in Poetry: when all the *Circumstances* are laid out in their proper Colours, and make a complete Piece; its Images strike us with greater Energy, than when the *Whole* of the thing is only mention'd in general. Thus the *diffused Style* has its Propriety under this Head; and makes a larger and more continued Impression: as the force of its contrary Excellence, a just and emphatical *Conciseness*, may be more collected, and pierce the deeper. I do not mean when we *mention* a thing, but when we *shew* it in a few words. There are just Miniatures of Great Objects in Poetry, as well as in Statuary or Painting. A *Hercules* in little, may have all the Nerves of a *Colossus*: and even that prodigious Design of *Dinarchus* might not have been more *Gigantick*, than *Timanthes*'s *Polyphemus*. Noble Images, whether in a larger or smaller Compass, strike the Mind very strongly. Either must be according to the Occasion. Things sometimes demand to be drawn at full length; and the Soul requires to expatiate over them: Sometimes they chuse a more contracted Space: But though they lose from their Size, they lose nothing of their Spirit. It fills us with a noble and enlarg'd Pleasure, to consider the Heavenly Bodies, their Courses, and their immense Distances: at the same time, we are struck with a very particular Admiration, when we view their Situation and Motions in the *Orrery*.

*

This puts me in mind of a Point, that always strikes me very much in Poetry; A sort of *Comprehension*, as I should chuse to call it, for want of some better Name. 'Tis when any Great View is completely contracted into a few Lines; but to come up perfectly to my Notion, it should be such a View as is sufficient to fill the whole Mind: We are, in a manner, surrounded with it on all sides; and which ever way we turn our Eyes, we cannot look out of it. This is the Case, where *Ulysses* is represented in his Shipwreck on the Coast of *Phaeacia*;

> *Above*, sharp Rocks forbid access; *around*,
> Roar the wild Waves; *beneath*, is Sea profound!   [v. 528–9]

If you can fancy yourself in the Place of *Ulysses*, at that juncture, you will apprehend what I mean the more fully. You can then see nothing, but what is painted out in this Couplet.

I apprehend you, (says *Antiphaus*) and indeed have observ'd this Beauty often in Reading. There is a Thought, (if I mistake not) repeated twice in the Eleventh *Odyssey*, of this kind:

> Above, below, on Earth, and in the Sky.   [xi. 139]

I know not whether the Image be total, but it cannot want much of it, in that Description of a shipwreckt Person, just before the Lines you repeated:

> Amidst the rocks he hears a hollow roar
> Of murm'ring surges breaking on the shore;
> Nor peaceful port was there, nor winding bay,
> To shield the vessel from the rolling sea;
> But cliffs, and shaggy shores, a dreadful sight,
> All rough with rocks, with foamy billows white.   [v. 516–21]

If this be not Total, at least it will engross Two of your Senses, whilst you keep in the same Posture; but those, as you say, seem the most complete, which take up the Eye what ever way you turn. – As this (resum'd *Philypsus*) to keep to the same Element:

> And all above is sky, and ocean all around.   [xii. 474]

These Total Views are much more vigorous and affecting, when the Objects are not inanimate: or at least, when some more moving Considerations are annext to them. Thus in the Picture of a rough Sea, terminating in craggy Shores, and Rocks, and a tempestuous Sky, every Object has an additional Terror from our seeing *Ulysses* painted in the midst of these Dangers, and struggling to make so difficult a Shore* – I remember a Passage of this kind in a Writer of a very strong Imagination, which is heighten'd by the same Method. We have it in a Description of Mount *Atlas*, tho' I believe the Author took his Ideas from the *Alps*: 'tis deliver'd in this bold Poetical kind of Prose:

> See, with what trembling steps poor Mankind tread the narrow Brink
> of the deep Precipices! from whence with giddy Horror they look
> down, mistrusting even the Ground which bears them; whilst they hear
> the hollow sound of Torrents underneath, and see the Ruin of the
> impending Rock, with falling Trees, which hang with their Roots
> upwards, and seem to draw more Ruin after them. –
>   [Cf. p. 87 and p. 181]

---

*Cf. Dennis on Aeneas in the storm, p. 54. Dennis's 'Sublime' is hieratic; Spence's 'Sublime', like Shaftesbury's, is post-Berkeleyan, and suggests the dissolving of time and space. Ed.

In these Cases, our Passions, as well as our Senses, are engag'd: and I take such Views to be then entirely complete, when all our Passions, as well as all our Senses, may be engross'd by them.
Second edition, 1737

THOMAS BLACKWELL (1701–1757)

Gibbon observed that *An Enquiry into the Life and Writings of Homer* (1735), was 'by Blackwell of Aberdeen, or rather by Bishop Berkeley, a fine, though sometimes fanciful, effort of genius'. A son of the gown and himself a Professor of Greek in his twenty-second year, Blackwell was greatly admired by the author of *A New Theory of Vision* (see p. 62) who planned his joining the faculty of his Bermuda college. Gibbon's comment, however, is more than circumstantial, for in Blackwell's *Enquiry into Homer* we observe the application of Berkeleyan theories of perception in the writing of a kind of subjective, even Romantic literary history.

The descent of Homer from a radiant semi-divine inventor – after Orpheus, Linus and Musaeus – not only of essentially Augustan poetry but of all the arts in the preface to Pope's *Iliad*, to Romantic genius, one with Job and Ossian, is a lesson in the fluctuating shape of the past during the rise of Romanticism. In Trapp, Thomas Warton and early Young, the first place in time and quality is given to the oriental literature of the Bible at the expense of classical writers. By the second quarter of the eighteenth century, for example in Anthony Blackwall's *The Sacred Classics* (1725, 1727) (see p. 103), classical criteria illuminate Job, Moses and Ezekiel, while biblical forms, for example prophecy, are applied to the classics (see p. 102). By the time of Young's *Conjectures on Original Composition* (1759) and Robert Wood's *On the Original Genius of Homer* (1769) Homer is no longer the pattern of Augustan generality, and, as in Pope, exponent of eighteenth-century concepts of order, but, against an older, Asian backdrop, a unique phenomenon, sublime model for each man's originality.

In Pope's verse the past appears as an external reality. Whilst mirrored in contemporary experience, it is convincingly distanced, perhaps in part as a function of form. For Blackwell, forerunner of generations of gentleman explorers, distance and abstract theories disappear, and we are invited to identify with the uncategorized particulars of Homer's time and place, which, paradoxically, and sublimely, become our own. Once distant and past, Homer, like any other great particular image, becomes aesthetically close, awe-inspiring and overwhelming, like Burnet's mountains and seas. The sense that history, perhaps especially but not exclusively in aesthetic forms, is another aspect of timeless Nature, unites Blackwell's *Enquiry*, Piranesi's Rome and the Salisbury Plain of Wordsworth's poetry. Indeed, the notion of Berkeleyan history even suggests that, like the architecture in Coleridge's *Christabel*, the iconography of the past, is 'all made out of the carver's brain' and is essentially a creation of the imagination. Blackwell's pioneering *Enquiry* reminds us that Giambattista Vico's *New Science*, the most comprehensive study of imaginative history in the history of Romanticism, had first appeared in 1725, and that, through Blackwell as through Vico, we may find reasons for the parallel growth of modern history and theories of the creative imagination in the Romantic era, as well as the intimate co-existence of pastness and futurity which is so marked a characteristic of Collins, Gray, Young, and the later Romantics.

That this imaginative growth was the direct result of the scientific espousal of particulars, which we have already noted in Spence (see p. 101) is suggested by the almost obsessive reiteration that 'a concourse of natural causes conspired to produce and cultivate that mighty genius', that Asia Minor gave him 'mildness of temper, and flow of fancy', and that his genius fed on an accurate knowledge of the manners, 'bracelets, buckles and necklaces' of the time.

from AN ENQUIRY INTO THE LIFE AND WRITINGS OF HOMER (1735)

Were we really of the same Opinion, as the Ancients, that *Homer* was inspired from *Heaven*; that he sung, and wrote as the *Prophet* and *Interpreter* of the Gods, we should hardly be apt to wonder: Nor wou'd it surprize us much, to find a Book of an heavenly Origin without an Equal among human Compositions: to find the Subject of it equally useful and great, the Stile just, and yet sublime, the Order both simple and exquisite, to find the Sentiments natural without lowness, and Manners real, and withal so extensive, as to include even the Varieties of the chief Characters of Mankind; We shou'd expect no less, considering whence it came: And *That* I take to have been the Reason, why none of the Ancients have attempted to account for this Prodigy. They acquiesced, it is probable, in the Pretensions, which the Poet constantly makes to celestial Instruction, and seem to have been of *Tacitus*'s Opinion, 'That it is more pious and respectful to believe, than to enquire into the Works of the Gods.' [*Germania*, xxxiv. 12]

But, *My Lord*, the happy Change that has been since wrought upon the face of religious Affairs, gives us liberty to be of the contrary Opinion: Tho' in ancient times it might have gone near to banish us from *Smyrna* or *Colophon*, yet at present it is become perfectly harmless; and we may any where assert,

That *Homer*'s Poems are of *Human Composition*; inspired by no other Power than his own natural Faculties, and the Chances of his Education: In a word, That a *Concourse* of *natural* Causes, conspired to produce and cultivate that mighty Genius, and gave him the noblest Field to exercise it in, that ever fell to the share of a Poet.

Here, *My Lord*, there seems to be occasion for a little Philosophy, to put us, if possible, upon the *Track* of this singular Phaenomenon: It has shone for upwards of two thousand Years in the *Poetick* World; and so dazzled Men's Eyes, that they have hitherto been more employed in

gazing at it, than in inquiring *What formed it, or How it came there?*
And very fortunately the Author of all Antiquity, who seems to have made
the happiest union of the *Courtier* and the *Scholar*, has determined a
Point that might have given us some trouble. He has laid it down as a
Principle,

> That the greatest Genius cannot excel without *Culture*; Nor the finest
> Education produce any thing *Noble* without *Natural Endowments*.
> [Plato, *Republic*, iii, 400; iv, 424]

Taking this for granted, We may assure ourselves that *Homer* hath been
happy in them both; and must now follow the dark Hints afforded us by
Antiquity, to find out *How a blind and stroling Bard could come by
them.*

I do not choose to entertain your Lordship with the Accidents about his
Birth; tho' some Naturalists would reckon them the Beginnings of his
good Fortune. I incline rather to observe, That he is generally reputed to
have been a Native of *Asia the less*; a Tract of Ground that for the
Temperature of the *Climate*, and Qualities of the *Soil*, may vye with
any in *Europe*. It is not so fat and fruitful as the Plains of *Babylon* or
Banks of the *Nile*, to effeminate the Inhabitants, and beget Laziness and
Inactivity: But the Purity and Benignity of the Air, the Varieties of the
Fruits and Fields, the Beauty and Number of the Rivers, and the
constant Gales from the happy Isles of the Western Sea, *all conspire* to
bring its Productions of every kind to the highest Perfection: They in-
inspire that Mildness of Temper, and Flow of Fancy, which favour the
most extensive Views, and give the finest Conceptions of *Nature* and
Truth.

In the Division commonly made of Climates, the Rough and Cold are
observed to produce the strongest Bodies, and most martial Spirits; the
hotter, lazy Bodies with cunning and obstinate Passions; but the temperate
Regions, lying under the benign Influences of a genial Sky, have the best
Chance for a fine Perception, and a proportioned Eloquence. Good Sense
is indeed said to be the Product of every Country, and I believe it is;
but the richest Growths, and fairest Shoots of it, spring, like other
Plants, from the happiest Exposition and most friendly Soil.

The pursuing a Thought thro' its remotest Consequences, is so familiar
to your Lordship, that I need hardly mention the later History of this
Tract. It has never failed to shew its Virtue, when *Accidents from
abroad* did not stand in the way. In the early Times of Liberty, the first,
and greatest Number of *Philosophers, Historians*, and *Poets*, were
Natives of the *Asiatick* Coast, and adjacent Islands. And after an Interval
of Slavery, when the Influences of the *Roman* Freedom, and of their
mild Government, had reached that happy Country, it repaid them, not
only with the Delicacies of their Fields and Gardens, but with the more
valuable Productions of Men of Virtue and Learning; and in such
Numbers, as to fill their Schools, and the Houses of the Great; to be
Companions for their Princes, and to leave some noble Monuments for

Posterity.

It will probably be thought too great a Refinement to observe, that *Homer* must have been the first or second Generation, after the Transplantation or rather the final Settlement of this Colony, from the rocky *Morea* to these happy Lands: A Situation, in which Nature is observed to make the most vigorous Efforts, and to be most profuse of her genial Treasure. The Curious in Horses, are concerned to have a mixed Breed, a Remove or two from the foreign Parent; and what Influence it might have here, will belong to the Curious in *Mankind* to determine.

If *Homer* then, came into the World, in *such* a Country, and under so propitious an Aspect of Nature, we must next enquire, what Reception he met with upon his Arrival; in what Condition he found things, and what Dispositions they must produce in an exalted Genius, and comprehensive Mind. This is a difficult Speculation, and I should be under no small Apprehensions how to get thro' it, if I did not know that Men moving, like your Lordship, in the higher Spheres of Life, are well acquainted with the Effects of *Culture* and *Education*. They know the Changes they are able to produce; and are not surprized to find them, as it were, new moulding human Creatures, and transforming them more than *Urganda* or *Circe*. The Influence of Example and Discipline is, in effect, so extensive, that some very acute Writers have mistaken it for the only Source of our Morals: tho' their Root lies ˜deeper, and is more interwoven with our *Original* Frame. However, as we have at present only to do with *Homer* in his Poetical Capacity we need give ourselves no further Trouble in considering the Tenour of his Life, than as it served to raise him to be the *Prince* of his Profession.

In this Search, we must remember that *young Minds* are apt to receive such strong Impressions from the Circumstances of the Country where they are born and bred, that they contract a mutual kind of Likeness to those Circumstances, and bear the Marks of the Course of Life thro' which they have passed. A Man who has had great Misfortunes, is easily distinguished from one who has lived all his Days in high Prosperity; and a Person bred to Business, has a very different Appearance from another brought up in Sloth and Pleasure: Both our Understanding and Behaviour receive a Stamp from our Station and Adventures; and as a liberal Education forms a Gentleman, and the contrary a Clown, in the same manner, if we take things a little deeper, are our Thoughts and Manners influenced by the Strain of our Lives. In this view, the Circumstances that may be reasonably thought to have the greatest Effect upon us, may perhaps be reduced to these following: First, The *State of the Country* where a Person is born and bred; in which I include the common *Manners* of the Inhabitants, their *Constitution* civil and religious, with its *Causes* and *Consequences*: Their *Manners* are seen in the *Ordinary* way of living as it happens to be polite or barbarous, luxurious or simple. Next, the *Manners* of the *Times*, or the prevalent Humours and Professions in vogue: These two are publick, and have a common effect on the whole

Generation. Of a more confined Nature is, first, *Private Education*; and after that, *the particular way* of Life we choose and pursue, with our *Fortunes* in it.

From these Accidents, *My Lord*, Men in every Country may be justly said to draw their Character, and derive their Manners. They make us *what we are*, in so far as they reach our Sentiments, and give us a peculiar Turn and Appearance: A Change in any one of them makes an Alteration upon *Us*; and taken together, we must consider them as the Moulds that form us into those Habits and Dispositions, which sway our Conduct and distinguish our Actions.

*

Here then was *Homer's* first Happiness; He took his plain natural Images from *Life*: He saw *Warriors*, and *Shepherds*, and *Peasants*, such as he drew; and was daily conversant among such People as he intended to represent: The Manners used in the *Trojan* Times were not disused in his own: The same way of living in private, and the same Pursuits in publick were still prevalent, and gave him a Model for his Design, which wou'd not allow him to exceed the Truth in his Draught. By frequently and freely looking it over, he cou'd discern what Parts of it were fit to be represented, and what to be passed over.

For so unaffected and simple were the Manners of those Times, that the Folds and Windings of the human Breast lay open to the Eye; nor were People ashamed to avow Passions and Inclinations, which were entirely void of Art and Design. This was *Homer's* Happiness, with respect to Mankind, and the living Part of his Poetry; as for the other Parts, and what a Painter wou'd call *Still-life*, he cou'd have little Advantage: For we are not to imagine, that he cou'd discover the entertaining Prospects, or rare Productions of a Country better than we can. *That* is a Subject still remaining to us, if we will quit our Towns, and look upon it: We find it accordingly, nobly executed by many of the Moderns, and the most illustrious Instance of it [Thomson's *The Seasons*], within these few Years, doing Honour to the *British* Poetry.

In Short, it may be said of *Homer*, and of every *Poet* who has wrote well, That *what* he felt and saw, *that* he described; and that *Homer* had the good Fortune to see and learn the *Grecian* Manners, at their true Pitch and happiest Temper for Verse: Had he been born much sooner, he would have seen nothing but Nakedness and Barbarity: Had he come much later, he had fallen in the Times either of wide Policy and Peace, or of General Wars, when private Passions are buried in the common Order, and established Discipline.

*

It were easy, *My Lord*, to prove these Assertions by abundance of

Grammatical Examples, but they can only be understood by Men who, like your Lordship, have it in their Power to recollect them at pleasure. I will only observe, that the *Turks, Arabs, Indians*, and, in general most of the Inhabitants of the *East*, are a solitary kind of People: They speak but seldom, and never long without Emotion: But when, in their own Phrase, they *open* their *Mouth*, and give a loose to a fiery Imagination, they are poetical, and full of Metaphor. *Speaking*, among such People, is a matter of some Moment, as we may gather from their usual Introductions; for before they begin to deliver their Thoughts, they give notice, *that they will open their Mouth; that they will unloose their Tongue; that they will utter their Voice and pronounce with their Lips.* These Preambles bear a great Resemblance to the old Forms of Introduction in *Homer, Hesiod*, and *Orpheus*, in which they are sometimes followed by *Virgil*.

If there is then an inviolable and necessary Connexion between the Dispositions of a Nation and their Speech, we must believe that there will be an *Alloy* of Simplicity and Wonder in the Beginnings of every Language; and likewise that the Dialect will improve with the Affairs and Genius of the People. Upon a nearer View of that which *Homer* spoke, we find it not *original*, but derived from others more ancient: Yet it seems to have begun upon a very small Stock which the *Pelasgi* spoke, and the old Inhabitants of the Northern Parts of *Greece*. The greater Part of its Acquisitions it drew from *Asia, Phenicia* and *Egypt*, by the Way of *Cyprus* and *Crete*: These, with the other Islands, were first peopled and instructed in the Arts of Life: They lie most conveniently for Merchants sailing from the above-named Countries; and it was either trading People, or Persons who were forced to travel abroad for some bold Actions at Home, that were the first Instructors of the ancient *Greeks*.

These Adventurers came to a Climate which inclines not Men to Solitude, and forbids Idleness: The Necessity of Labour and Contrivance; a growing Commerce, and more than any thing besides, the Number of free Cities and independent Governments, soon raised a nobler Language than either of the Originals. It was at first *simple, unconfined*, and *free*, as was their Life: The *Politick* Stile grew with their *Constitution*; and was at its *height* when they had most Affairs of that kind, and of the *greatest Consequence* to manage: And when a rough warlike People had stripp'd them of their Liberty, they had recourse to *Philosophy* and *Learning*. The Councils of a free State are managed by *Speaking*, which quickly introduces Eloquence, and the Arts of Persuasion: When *these* turn useless, or dangerous in Publick, Men betake themselves to less obnoxious Subjects.

These were the Stages thro' which the *Greek* Language passed. It went thro' them slowly, and had time to receive the Impression of each: It lasted long, and far out-lived the *Latin*, as it had begun before.

*

The next Advantage of *Homer*'s Profession, was the Access it gave him into the Houses and Company of the *Greatest Men*. The Effects of it appear in every Line of his Works; not only in his Characters of them, and Accounts of their Actions; but the more *familiar* Part of Life; their manner of Conversing and method of Entertaining, are accurately and minutely painted. He knows their Rarities and *Plate*, and can hold forth the Neatness and Elegancy of their *Bijouterie*. He has nicely inspected the Trinkets their Ladies wore; their *Bracelets, Buckles* and *Necklaces*, whose Prettinesses he sometimes talks of with great Taste and Exactness. He has a delicious Pair of *three-stoned Ear-rings*. . . . And a curious *Gold Necklace* set in Amber in the form of a *Sun*.

DAVID HUME (1711–1776)

In the essay on Drummond's *Academical Questions* in the *Edinburgh Review* (October, 1805) Francis Jeffrey, hostile critic of Byron, Keats and the 'Methodistical ravings' of Wordsworth's *Excursion* (see pp. 351-363) challenged a basic assumption of Hume's epistemology. Alluding to Hume's *Treatise* Jeffrey wrote:

> 'The table which I see,' says Dr. Hume, 'diminishes as I remove from it; but the real table suffers no alteration; – it could be nothing but its image, therefore, which was present to my mind.' Now this statement, we think, admits pretty explicitly, that there is a real table, the image of which is presented to the mind: but at all events we conceive that the phenomenon may be easily reconciled with the supposition of its real existence.

Jeffrey's distaste for Romantic poetry of the creative imagination was intimately related to his sympathy with a minor school of Scots philosophy. The 'Scottish Commonsense School' of Thomas Reid's *Enquiry* (1764), and the aesthetics of Alison and Stewart, maintained, in conscious opposition to Hume, the assumptions of ordinary folk that the ideas in our minds are dependable substitutes for external things. In this world of perception, as Jeffrey observes in his review of Alison's *Principles of Taste* (May, 1811), association means only the emotions stirred in the mind by any object in art, for example a rural cottage, not the fundamental law by which the mind binds together single impulses into a complete account of reality.

In his remarks on Hume, Jeffrey did not see, as an extended examination of Hume on time, space, and infinity, might have persuaded him, that once the unreliability of the perception of the object – in this case the table – was admitted, the game was lost. The spatial and, perhaps at a short remove, the temporal context governing the image of the table having been admitted unverifiable, the entire reservoir of memory, necessarily a network of spatial and temporal species, collapses. 'Knowing' ceases to be the classical reference to general, similar, necessarily finite, categories, Mnemosyne, the mother of the Muses ends her reign, and the mind, to whatever extent, becomes like that of the prophet, creative in its own infinite moment.

To some extent the *Enquiry Concerning Human Understanding* (1748) superseded the *Treatise*. But for poetry the imaginative dichotomy remains undiminished in its suggestiveness. Hume deals with topics similar to, or related to Berkeley's. He is concerned with our ideas of space, time, abstractions, of cause and effect, and of association at large. But there is a significant distinction in emphasis. Berkeley appears to persuade us that, were we more acute and able to perceive correctly our perceptions, we would dwell in a Berkeleyan world. Hume's macabre and surreal emphasis is of a world comparable, we might say, to that of Locke. The image of time given us by the succession of ideas is convincing; there are only a few models for the association of ideas, for example cause and effect. But, as he argues brilliantly in the example of the billiard balls (see p. 131) there is no way in which we may be sure that any of the picture of the universe's coherence that we absorb is representative. The volcanic suggestion for the susceptible poetic mind can only be that the world is dichotomous; on the one hand, we find a world of space and time, cause and effect, dimension and mass, on the other, the possibility that, as Wallace Stevens says in *Sunday Morning* 'we live in an old chaos of the sun', colourless, meaningless, separated from our perceptions by who knows what mysterious barrier. Imagination, then, remains the only bulwark.

In spite of the relative importance of the *Treatise*, its appearance in 1739 and the general and particular similarity between the world of Hume and that of, for example, Young's *Night Thoughts* (1742–45) are extremely suggestive. Like Hume's world of perception, that of Lorenzo, the young friend to whom *Night Thoughts* is addressed, is rational, causal and finite. The world of the poet, which is opposed to it, undermines every one of these assumptions at every point, giving the poem a rich ambiguity between on the one hand surreal images of a macabre everyday life, and, on the other, a nebulous infinity reducing the cosmos to the dimensions of the mind. The relation of Hume's world to that of several mid-century writers concerned with the strict opposition of the rational and irrational, for example Smollett and Sterne, is equally interesting. 'The Sea of Time and Space' is the major negative image in the dialectic of Blake's letters and poetry, for example in *Milton* (II, xxxiv. 25) and *The Four Zoas* (IV. 265). It may well be that a major link between Young and Blake, and indeed, between the 'poetry of feeling' of the mid-century and the poetry of the imagination, is the bald figure of Time, an amoebic essay in fluctuating space which recedes and shifts on its dubious journey through Blake's illustrations for Young's *Night Thoughts*, casting a Humean shadow over the entire poem and over all our images of perception.

A TREATISE OF HUMAN NATURE (1739)

from Book I, Part ii, Section 5, 'Of Relations'
The word *Relation* is commonly used in two senses considerably different from each other. Either for that quality, by which two ideas are connected together in the imagination, and the one naturally introduces the other, after the manner above-explained; or for that particular circumstance, in which even upon the arbitrary union of two ideas in the fancy, we may think proper to compare them. In common language the former is always the sense, in which we use the word, relation; and 'tis only in philosophy, that we extend it to mean any particular subject of comparison, without

a connecting principle. Thus distance will be allowed by philosophers to be a true relation, because we acquire an idea of it by the comparing of objects: But in a common way we say, *that nothing can be more distant than such or such things from each other, nothing can have less relation*; as if distance and relation were incompatible.

It may perhaps be esteemed an endless task to enumerate all those qualities, which make objects admit of comparison, and by which the ideas of *philosophical* relation are produced. But if we diligently consider them, we shall find that without difficulty they may be compriz'd under seven general heads, which may be considered as the sources of all *philosophical* relation.

1. The first is *resemblance*: And this is a relation, without which no philosophical relation can exist; since no objects will admit of comparison, but what have some degree of resemblance. But tho' resemblance be necessary to all philosophical relation, it does not follow, that it always produces a connexion or association of ideas. When a quality becomes very general, and is common to a great many individuals, it leads not the mind directly to any one of them; but by presenting at once too great a choice, does thereby prevent the imagination from fixing on any single object.

2. *Identity* may be esteem'd a second species of relation. This relation I here consider as apply'd in its strictest sense to constant and unchangeable objects; without examining the nature and foundation of personal identity, which shall find its place afterwards. Of all relations the most universal is that of identity, being common to every being, whose existence has any duration.

3. After identity the most universal and comprehensive relations are those of *Space* and *Time*, which are the sources of an infinite number of comparisons, such as *distant, contiguous, above, below, before, after*, etc.

4. All those objects, which admit of *quantity*, or *number*, may be compar'd in that particular; which is another very fertile source of relation.

5. When any two objects possess the same *quality* in common, the *degrees*, in which they possess it, form a fifth species of relation. Thus of two objects, which are both heavy, the one may be either of greater, or less weight than with the other. Two colours, that are of the same kind, may yet be of different shades, and in that respect admit of comparison.

6. The relation of *contrariety* may at first sight be regarded as an exception to the rule, *that no relation of any kind can subsist without some degree of resemblance*. But let us consider, that no two ideas are in themselves contrary, except those of existence and non-existence, which are plainly resembling, as implying both of them an idea of the object; tho' the latter excludes the object from all times and places, in which it is supposed not to exist.

7. All other objects, such as fire and water, heat and cold, are only

found to be contrary from experience, and from the contrariety of their *causes* or *effects*; which relation of cause and effect is a seventh philosophical relation, as well as a natural one. The resemblance implied in this relation, shall be explain'd afterwards.

It might naturally be expected, that I should join *difference* to the other relations. But that I consider rather as a negation of relation, than as any thing real or positive. Difference is of two kinds as oppos'd either to identity or resemblance. The first is called a difference of *number*; the other of *kind*.

*

from Part ii, Section 3, 'Of the other Qualities of our Ideas of Space and Time'

No discovery cou'd have been made more happily for deciding all controversies concerning ideas, than that above-mention'd, that impressions always take the precedency of them, and that every idea with which the imagination is furnish'd first makes its appearance in a correspondent impression. These latter perceptions are all so clear and evident, that they admit of no controversy; tho' many of our ideas are so obscure, that 'tis almost impossible even for the mind, which forms them, to tell exactly their nature and composition. Let us apply this principle, in order to discover farther the nature of our ideas of space and time.

Upon opening my eyes, and turning them to the surrounding objects, I perceive many visible bodies; and upon shutting them again, and considering the distance betwixt these bodies, I acquire the idea of extension. As every idea is deriv'd from some impression, which is exactly similar to it, the impressions similar to this idea of extension, must either be some sensations deriv'd from the sight, or some internal impressions arising from these sensations.

Our internal impressions are our passions, emotions, desires and aversions; none of which, I believe, will ever be asserted to be the model, from which the idea of space is deriv'd. There remains therefore nothing but the senses, which can convey to us this original impression. Now what impression do our senses here convey to us? This is the principal question, and decides without appeal concerning the nature of the idea.

The table before me is alone sufficient by its view to give me the idea of extension. This idea, then, is borrow'd from, and represents some impression, which this moment appears to the senses. But my senses convey to me only the impressions of colour'd points, dispos'd in a certain manner. If the eye is sensible of any thing farther, I desire it may be pointed out to me. But if it be impossible to shew any thing farther, we may conclude with certainty, that the idea of extension is nothing but a copy of these colour'd points, and of the manner of their appearance.

Suppose that in the extended object, or composition of colour'd points, from which we first receiv'd the idea of extension, the points were of a purple colour; it follows, that in every repetition of that idea we wou'd not only place the points in the same order with respect to each other, but also bestow on them that precise colour, with which alone we are acquainted. But afterwards having experience of the other colours of violet, green, red, white, black, and of all the different compositions of these, and finding a resemblance in the disposition of colour'd points, of which they are compos'd, we omit the peculiarities of colour, as far as possible, and found an abstract idea merely on that disposition of points, or manner of appearance, in which they agree. Nay even when the resemblance is carry'd beyond the objects of one sense, and the impressions of touch are found to be similar to those of sight in the disposition of their parts; this does not hinder the abstract idea from representing both, upon account of their resemblance. All abstract ideas are really nothing but particular ones, consider'd in a certain light; but being annexed to general terms, they are able to represent a vast variety, and to comprehend objects, which, as they are alike in some particulars, are in others vastly wide of each other.

The idea of time, being deriv'd from the succession of our perceptions of every kind, ideas as well as impressions, and impressions of reflection as well as of sensation, will afford us an instance of an abstract idea, which comprehends a still greater variety than that of space, and yet is represented in the fancy by some particular individual idea of a determinate quantity and quality.

As 'tis from the disposition of visible and tangible objects we receive the idea of space, so from the succession of ideas and impressions we form the idea of time, nor is it possible for time alone ever to make its appearance, or be taken notice of by the mind. A man in a sound sleep, or strongly occupy'd with one thought, is insensible of time; and according as his perceptions succeed each other with greater or less rapidity, the same duration appears longer or shorter to his imagination. It has been remark'd by a great philosopher [John Locke] that our perceptions have certain bounds in this particular, which are fix'd by the original nature and constitution of the mind, and beyond which no influence of external objects on the senses is ever able to hasten or retard our thought. If you wheel about a burning coal with rapidity, it will present to the senses an image of a circle of fire; nor will there seem to be any interval of time betwixt its revolutions; merely because 'tis impossible for our perceptions to succeed each other with the same rapidity, that motion may be communicated to external objects. Wherever we have no successive perceptions, we have no notion of time, even tho' there be a real succession in the objects. From these phaenomena, as well as from many others, we may conclude, that time cannot make its appearance to the mind, either alone, or attended with a steady unchangeable object, but is always discover'd by some *perceivable* succession of changeable objects.

To confirm this we may add the following argument, which to me seems perfectly decisive and convincing. 'Tis evident, that time or duration consists of different parts: For otherwise we cou'd not conceive a longer or shorter duration. 'Tis also evident, that these parts are not co-existent: For that quality of the co-existence of parts belongs to extension, and is what distinguishes it from duration. Now as time is compos'd of parts, that are not co-existent; an unchangeable object, since it produces none but co-existent impressions, produces none that can give us the idea of time; and consequently that idea must be deriv'd from a succession of changeable objects, and time in its first appearance can never be sever'd from such a succession.

Having therefore found, that time in its first appearance to the mind is always conjoin'd with a succession of changeable objects, and that otherwise it can never fall under our notice, we must now examine whether it can be *conceiv'd* without our conceiving any succession of objects, and whether it can alone form a distinct idea in the imagination.

In order to know whether any objects, which are join'd in impression, be separable in idea, we need only consider, if they be different from each other; in which case, 'tis plain they may be conceiv'd apart. Every thing, that is different, is distinguishable; and every thing, that is distinguishable, may be separated, according to the maxims above-explain'd. If on the contrary they be not different, they are not distinguishable; and if they be not distinguishable, they cannot be separated. But this is precisely the case with respect to time, compar'd with our successive perceptions. The idea of time is not deriv'd from a particular impression mix'd up with others, and plainly distinguishable from them; but arises altogether from the manner in which impressions appear to the mind, without making one of the number. Five notes play'd on a flute give us the impression and idea of time; tho' time be not a sixth impression, which presents itself to the hearing or any other of the senses. Nor is it a sixth impression, which the mind by reflection finds in itself. These five sounds making their appearance in this particular manner, excite no emotion in the mind, nor produce an affection of any kind, which being observ'd by it can give rise to a new idea. For *that* is necessary to produce a new idea of reflection, nor can the mind, by revolving over a thousand times all its ideas of sensation, ever extract from them any new original idea, unless nature has so fram'd its faculties, that it feels some new original impression arise from such a contemplation. But here it only takes notice of the *manner*, in which the different sounds make their appearance; and that it may afterwards consider without considering these particular sounds, but may conjoin it with any other objects. The ideas of some objects it certainly must have, nor is it possible for it without these ideas ever to arrive at any conception of time; which since it appears not as any primary distinct impression, can plainly be nothing but different ideas, or impressions, or objects dispos'd in a certain manner, that is, succeeding each other.

I know there are some who pretend, that the idea of duration is applicable in a proper sense to objects which are perfectly unchangeable; and this I take to be the common opinion of philosophers as well as of the vulgar. But to be convinc'd of its falsehood we need but reflect on the foregoing conclusion, that the idea of duration is always deriv'd from a succession of changeable objects, and can never be convey'd to the mind by any thing steadfast and unchangeable. For it inevitably follows from thence, that since the idea of duration cannot be deriv'd from such an object, it can never in any propriety or exactness be apply'd to it, nor can any thing unchangeable be ever said to have duration. Ideas always represent the objects or impressions, from which they are deriv'd, and can never without a fiction represent or be apply'd to any other. By what fiction we apply the idea of time, even to what is unchangeable, and suppose, as is common, that duration is a measure of rest as well as of motion, we shall consider afterwards.

There is another very decisive argument, which establishes the present doctrine concerning our ideas of space and time, and is founded only on that simple principle, *that our ideas of them are compounded of parts, which are indivisible.* This argument may be worth the examining.

Every idea that is distinguishable being also separable, let us take one of those simple indivisible ideas, of which the compound one of *extension* is form'd, and separating it from all others, and considering it apart, let us form a judgment of its nature and qualities.

'Tis plain it is not the idea of extension. For the idea of extension consists of parts; and this idea, according to the supposition, is perfectly simple and indivisible. Is it therefore nothing? That is absolutely impossible. For as the compound idea of extension, which is real, is compos'd of such ideas; were there so many non-entities, there wou'd be a real existence compos'd of non-entities; which is absurd. Here therefore I must ask, *What is our idea of a simple and indivisible point?* No wonder if my answer appear somewhat new, since the question itself has scarce ever yet been thought of. We are wont to dispute concerning the nature of mathematical points, but seldom concerning the nature of their ideas.

The idea of space is convey'd to the mind by two senses, the sight and touch; nor does any thing ever appear extended, that is not either visible or tangible. That compound impression, which represents extension, consists of several lesser impressions, that are indivisible to the eye or feeling, and may be call'd impressions of atoms or corpuscles endow'd with colour and solidity. But this is not all. 'Tis not only requisite, that these atoms shou'd be colour'd or tangible, in order to discover themselves to our senses; 'tis also necessary we shou'd preserve the idea of their colour or tangibility in order to comprehend them by our imagination. There is nothing but the idea of their colour or tangibility, which can render them conceivable by the mind. Upon the removal of the ideas of these sensible qualities, they are utterly annihilated to the thought or imagination.

Now such as the parts are, such is the whole. If a point be not consider'd as colour'd or tangible, it can convey to us no idea; and consequently the idea of extension, which is compos'd of the ideas of these points, can never possibly exist. But if the idea of extension really can exist, as we are conscious it does, its parts must also exist; and in order to that, must be consider'd as colour'd or tangible. We have therefore no idea of space or extension, but when we regard it as an object either of our sight or feeling.

The same reasoning will prove, that the indivisible moments of time must be fill'd with some real object or existence, whose succession forms the duration, and makes it be conceivable by the mind.

*

from Part iii, Section 15, 'Rules by which to Judge of Causes and Effects'
According to the precedent doctrine, there are no objects, which by the mere survey, without consulting experience, we can determine to be the causes of any other; and no objects, which we can certainly determine in the same manner not to be the causes. Any thing may produce any thing. Creation, annihilation, motion, reason, volition; all these may arise from one another, or from any other object we can imagine. Nor will this appear strange, if we compare two principles explain'd above, *that the constant conjunction of objects determines their causation*, and *that properly speaking, no objects are contrary to each other, but existence and non-existence*. Where objects are not contrary, nothing hinders them from having that constant conjunction, on which the relation of cause and effect totally depends.

Since therefore 'tis possible for all objects to become causes or effects to each other, it may be proper to fix some general rules, by which we may know when they really are so.

1. The cause and effect must be contiguous in space and time.

2. The cause must be prior to the effect.

3. There must be a constant union betwixt the cause and effect. 'Tis chiefly this quality, that constitutes the relation.

4. The same cause always produces the same effect, and the same effect never arises but from the same cause. This principle we derive from experience, and is the source of most of our philosophical reasonings. For when by any clear experiment we have discover'd the causes or effects of any phaenomenon, we immediately extend our observation to every phaenomenon of the same kind, without waiting for that constant repetition, from which the first idea of this relation is deriv'd.

5. There is another principle, which hangs upon this, *viz.* that where several different objects produce the same effect, it must be by means of some quality, which we discover to be common amongst them. For

as like effects imply like causes, we must always ascribe the causation to the circumstance, wherein we discover the resemblance.

6. The following principle is founded on the same reason. The difference in the effects of two resembling objects must proceed from that particular in which they differ. For as like causes always produce like effects, when in any instance we find our expectation to be disappointed, we must conclude that this irregularity proceeds from some difference in the causes.

7. When any object encreases or diminishes with the encrease or diminution of its cause, 'tis to be regarded as a compounded effect, deriv'd from the union of the several different effects, which arise from the several different parts of the cause. The absence or presence of one part of the cause is here suppos'd to be always attended with the absence or presence of a proportionable part of the effect. This constant conjunction sufficiently proves, that the one part is the cause of the other. We must, however, beware not to draw such a conclusion from a few experiments. A certain degree of heat gives pleasure; if you diminish that heat, the pleasure diminishes; but it does not follow, that if you augment it beyond a certain degree, the pleasure will likewise augment; for we find that it degenerates into pain.

8. The eighth and last rule I shall take notice of is, that an object, which exists for any time in its full perfection without any effect, is not the sole cause of that effect, but requires to be assisted by some other principle, which may forward its influence and operation. For as like effects necessarily follow from like causes, and in a contiguous time and place, their separation for a moment shews, that these causes are not complete ones.

*

from Part iv, Section 5, 'Of the Immateriality of the Soul'
The first notion of space and extension is deriv'd solely from the sense of sight and feeling; nor is there any thing, but what is colour'd and tangible, that has parts dispos'd after such a manner, as to convey that idea. When we diminish or encrease a relish, 'tis not after the same manner that we diminish or increase any visible object; and when several sounds strike our hearing at once, custom and reflection alone make us form an idea of the degrees of the distance and contiguity of those bodies, from which they are deriv'd. Whatever marks the place of its existence either must be extended, or must be a mathematical point, without parts or composition. What is extended must have a particular figure, as square, round, triangular; none of which will agree to a desire, or indeed to any impression or idea, except of these two senses abovemention'd. Neither ought a desire, tho' indivisible, to be consider'd as a mathematical point. For in that case 'twou'd be possible, by the addition of others, to make two, three, four desires, and these dispos'd and

situated in such a manner, as to have a determinate length, breadth and thickness; which is evidently absurd.

'Twill not be surprizing after this, if I deliver a maxim, which is condemn'd by several metaphysicians, and is esteem'd contrary to the most certain principles of human reason. This maxim is *that an object may exist, and yet be no where*: and I assert, that this is not only possible, but that the greatest part of beings do and must exist after this manner. An object may be said to be no where, when its parts are not so situated with respect to each other, as to form any figure or quantity; nor the whole with respect to other bodies so as to answer to our notions of contiguity or distance. Now this is evidently the case with all our perceptions and objects, except those of the sight and feeling. A moral reflection cannot be plac'd on the right or on the left hand of a passion, nor can a smell or sound be either of a circular or a square figure. These objects and perceptions, so far from requiring any particular place, are absolutely incompatible with it, and even the imagination cannot attribute it to them. And as to the absurdity of supposing them to be no where, we may consider, that if the passions and sentiments appear to the perception to have any particular place, the idea of extension might be deriv'd from them, as well as from the sight and touch; contrary to what we have already establish'd. If they *appear* not to have any particular place, they may possibly *exist* in the same manner; since whatever we conceive is possible.

'Twill not now be necessary to prove, that those perceptions, which are simple, and exist no where, are incapable of any conjunction in place with matter or body, which is extended and divisible; since 'tis impossible to found a relation but on some common quality. It may be better worth our while to remark, that this question of the local conjunction of objects does not only occur in metaphysical disputes concerning the nature of the soul, but that even in common life we have every moment occasion to examine it. Thus supposing we consider a fig at one end of the table, and an olive at the other, 'tis evident, that in forming the complex ideas of these substances, one of the most obvious is that of their different relishes; and 'tis as evident, that we incorporate and conjoin these qualities with such as are colour'd and tangible. The bitter taste of the one, and the sweet of the other are suppos'd to lie in the very visible body, and to be separated from each other by the whole length of the table. This is so notable and so natural an illusion that it may be proper to consider the principles, from which it is deriv'd.

Tho' an extended object be incapable of a conjunction in place with another, that exists without any place or extension, yet are they susceptible of many other relations. Thus the taste and smell of any fruit are inseparable from its other qualities of colour and tangibility; and which-ever of them be the cause or effect, 'tis certain they are always co-existent. Nor are they only co-existent in general, but also cotemporary in their appearance in the mind; and 'tis upon the application of the extended body to our senses we perceive its particular taste and smell. These relations, then, of *causation, and contiguity in the time of their appearance,* betwixt the extended object and the quality, which exists without any particular place, must have such an effect on the mind, that upon the appearance of one it will immediately turn its thought to the conception of the other. Nor is this all. We not only turn our thought from one to the other upon account of their relation, but likewise endeavour to give them a new relation, *viz.* that of a *conjunction in place,* that we may render the transition more easy and natural. For 'tis a quality, which I shall often have occasion to remark in human nature, and shall explain more fully in its proper place, that when objects are united by any relation, we have a strong propensity to add some new relation to them, in order to compleat the union. In our arrangement of bodies we never fail to place such as are resembling, in contiguity to each other, or at least in correspondent points of view: Why? but because we feel a satisfaction in joining the relation of contiguity to that of resemblance, or the resemblance of situation to that of qualities. The effects of this propensity have been already observ'd in that resemblance, which we so readily suppose betwixt particular impressions and their external causes. But we shall not find a more evident effect of it, than in the present instance, where from the relations of causation and contiguity in time betwixt two objects, we feign likewise that of a conjunction in place, in order to strengthen the connexion.

But whatever confus'd notions we may form of an union in place betwixt an extended body, as a fig, and its particular taste, 'tis certain that upon reflection we must observe in this union something altogether unintelligible and contradictory. For shou'd we ask ourselves one obvious question, *viz.* if the taste, which we conceive to be contain'd in the circumference of the body, is in every part of it or in one only, we must quickly find ourselves at a loss, and perceive the impossibility of ever giving a satisfactory answer. We cannot reply, that 'tis only in one part: For experience convinces us, that every part has the same relish. We can as little reply, that it exists in every part: For then we must suppose it figur'd and extended; which is absurd and incomprehensible. Here then we are influenc'd by two principles directly contrary to each other, *viz.* that *inclination* of our fancy by which we are determin'd to incorporate the taste with the extended object, and our *reason*, which shows us the impossibility of such an union. Being divided betwixt these opposite principles, we renounce neither one nor the other, but involve the subject in such confusion and obscurity, that we no longer perceive the opposition. We suppose, that the taste exists within the circumference of the body, but in such a manner, that it fills the whole without extension, and exists entire in every part without separation. In short, we use in our most familiar way of thinking, that scholastic principle, which, when crudely propos'd, appears so shocking, of *totum in toto & totum in qualibet parte*: Which is much the same, as if we shou'd say, that a thing is in a certain place, and yet is not there.

All this absurdity proceeds from our endeavouring to bestow a place on what is utterly incapable of it; and that endeavour again arises from our inclination to compleat an union, which is founded on causation, and a contiguity of time, by attributing to the objects a conjunction in place. But if ever reason be of sufficient force to overcome prejudice, 'tis certain that in the present case it must prevail. For we have only this choice left, either to suppose that some beings exist without any place; or that they are figur'd and extended; or that when they are incorporated with extended objects, the whole is in the whole, and the whole in every part. The absurdity of the two last suppositions proves sufficiently the veracity of the first. Nor is there any fourth opinion. For as to the supposition of their existence in the manner of mathematical points, it resolves itself into the second opinion, and supposes, that several passions may be plac'd in a circular figure, and that a certain number of smells, conjoin'd with a certain number of sounds, may make a body of twelve cubic inches; which appears ridiculous upon the bare mentioning of it.

But tho' in this view of things we cannot refuse to condemn the materialists, who conjoin all thought with extension; yet a little reflection will show us equal reason for blaming their antagonists, who conjoin all thought with a simple and indivisible substance. The most vulgar philosophy informs us, that no external object can make itself known to the mind immediately, and without the interposition of an image or perception. That table, which just now appears to me, is only a perception, and all its qualities are qualities of a perception. Now the most obvious of all its qualities is extension. The perception consists of parts. These parts are so situated, as to afford us the notion of distance and contiguity; of length, breadth, and thickness. The termination of these three dimensions is what we call figure. This figure is moveable, separable, and divisible. Mobility, and separability are the distinguishing properties of extended objects. And to cut short all disputes, the very idea of extension is copy'd from nothing but an impression, and consequently must perfectly agree to it. To say the idea of extension agrees to any thing, is to say it is extended.

AN ENQUIRY CONCERNING HUMAN UNDERSTANDING (1748)

from Section ii, 'Of the Origin of Ideas'
11 Every one will readily allow, that there is a considerable difference between the perceptions of the mind, when a man feels the pain of excessive heat, or the pleasure of moderate warmth, and when he afterwards recalls to his memory this sensation, or anticipates it by his

imagination. These faculties may mimic or copy the perceptions of the senses; but they can never entirely reach the force and vivacity of the original sentiment. The utmost we say of them, even when they operate with greatest vigour, is, that they represent their object in so lively a manner, that we could *almost* say we feel or see it: But, except the mind be disordered by disease or madness, they never can arrive at such a pitch of vivacity, as to render these perceptions altogether undistinguishable. All the colours of poetry, however splendid, can never paint natural objects in such a manner as to make the description be taken for a real landskip. The most lively thought is still inferior to the dullest sensation.

We may observe a like distinction to run through all the other perceptions of the mind. A man in a fit of anger, is actuated in a very different manner from one who only thinks of that emotion. If you tell me, that any person is in love, I easily understand your meaning, and form a just conception of his situation; but never can mistake that conception for the real disorders and agitations of the passion. When we reflect on our past sentiments and affections, our thought is a faithful mirror, and copies its objects truly; but the colours which it employs are faint and dull, in comparison of those in which our original perceptions were clothed. It requires no nice discernment or metaphysical head to mark the distinction between them.

12 Here therefore we may divide all the perceptions of the mind into two classes or species, which are distinguished by their different degrees of force and vivacity. The less forcible and lively are commonly denominated *Thoughts* or *Ideas*. The other species want a name in our language, and in most others; I suppose, because it was not requisite for any, but philosophical purposes, to rank them under a general term or appellation. Let us, therefore, use a little freedom, and call them *Impressions*; employing that word in a sense somewhat different from the usual. By the term *impression*, then, I mean all our more lively perceptions, when we hear, or see, or feel, or love, or hate, or desire, or will. And impressions are distinguished from ideas, which are the less lively perceptions, of which we are conscious, when we reflect on any of those sensations or movements above mentioned.

13 Nothing, at first view, may seem more unbounded than the thought of man, which not only escapes all human power and authority, but is not even restrained within the limits of nature and reality. To form monsters, and join incongruous shapes and appearances, costs the imagination no more trouble than to conceive the most natural and familiar objects. And while the body is confined to one planet, along which it creeps with pain and difficulty; the thought can in an instant transport us into the most distant regions of the universe; or even beyond the universe, into the unbounded chaos, where nature is supposed to lie in total confusion. What never was seen, or heard of, may yet be conceived; nor is any thing beyond the power of thought, except what implies an absolute contradiction.

But though our thought seems to possess this unbounded liberty, we shall find, upon a nearer examination, that it is really confined within very narrow limits, and that all this creative power of the mind amounts to no more than the faculty of compounding, transposing, augmenting, or diminishing the materials afforded us by the senses and experience. When we think of a golden mountain, we only join two consistent ideas, *gold*, and *mountain*, with which we were formerly acquainted. A virtuous horse we can conceive; because, from our own feeling, we can conceive virtue; and this we may unite to the figure and shape of a horse, which is an animal familiar to us. In short, all the materials of thinking are derived either from our outward or inward sentiment: the mixture and composition of these belongs alone to the mind and will. Or, to express myself in philosophical language, all our ideas or more feeble perceptions are copies of our impressions or more lively ones.

14 To prove this, the two following arguments will, I hope, be sufficient. First, when we analyze our thoughts or ideas, however compounded or sublime, we always find that they resolve themselves into such simple ideas as were copied from a precedent feeling or sentiment. Even those ideas, which, at first view, seem the most wide of this origin, are found, upon a nearer scrutiny, to be derived from it. The idea of God, as meaning an infinitely intelligent, wise, and good Being, arises from reflecting on the operations of our own mind, and augmenting, without limit, those qualities of goodness and wisdom. We may prosecute this enquiry to what length we please; where we shall always find, that every idea which we examine is copied from a similar impression. Those who would assert that this position is not universally true nor without exception, have only one, and that an easy method of refuting it; by producing that idea, which, in their opinion, is not derived from this source. It will then be incumbent on us, if we would maintain our doctrine, to produce the impression, or lively perception, which corresponds to it.

15 Secondly. If it happen, from a defect of the organ, that a man is not susceptible of any species of sensation, we always find that he is as little susceptible of the correspondent ideas. A blind man can form no notion of colours; a deaf man of sounds. Restore either of them that sense in which he is deficient; by opening this new inlet [cf. Young's use of this term, line 426, p. 143] for his sensations, you also open an inlet for the ideas; and he finds no difficulty in conceiving these objects. The case is the same, if the object, proper for exciting any sensation, has never been applied to the organ. A Laplander or Negro has no notion of the relish of wine. And though there are few or no instances of a like deficiency in the mind, where a person has never felt or is wholly incapable of a sentiment or passion that belongs to his species; yet we find the same observation to take place in a less degree. A man of mild manners can form no idea of inveterate revenge or cruelty; nor can a selfish heart easily conceive the heights of friendship and generosity. It is readily allowed, that other beings may possess many senses of which we can

have no conception; because the ideas of them have never been introduced to us in the only manner by which an idea can have access to the mind, to wit, by the actual feeling and sensation.

16 There is, however, one contradictory phenomenon, which may prove that it is not absolutely impossible for ideas to arise, independent of their correspondent impressions. I believe it will readily be allowed, that the several distinct ideas of colour, which enter by the eye, or those of sound, which are conveyed by the ear, are really different from each other; though, at the same time, resembling. Now if this be true of different colours, it must be no less so of the different shades of the same colour; and each shade produces a distinct idea, independent of the rest. For if this should be denied, it is possible, by the continual gradation of shades, to run a colour insensibly into what is most remote from it; and if you will not allow any of the means to be different, you cannot, without absurdity, deny the extremes to be the same. Suppose, therefore, a person to have enjoyed his sight for thirty years, and to have become perfectly acquainted with colours of all kinds except one particular shade of blue, for instance, which it never has been his fortune to meet with. Let all the different shades of that colour, except that single one, be placed before him, descending gradually from the deepest to the lightest; it is plain that he will perceive a blank, where that shade is wanting, and will be sensible that there is a greater distance in that place between the contiguous colours than in any other. Now I ask, whether it be possible for him, from his own imagination, to supply this deficiency, and raise up to himself the idea of that particular shade, though it had never been conveyed to him by his senses? I believe there are few but will be of opinion that he can: and this may serve as a proof that the simple ideas are not always, in every instance, derived from the correspondent impressions; though this instance is so singular, that it is scarcely worth our observing, and does not merit that for it alone we should alter our general maxim.

17 Here, therefore, is a proposition, which not only seems, in itself, simple and intelligible; but, if a proper use were made of it, might render every dispute equally intelligible, and banish all that jargon, which has so long taken possession of metaphysical reasonings, and drawn disgrace upon them. All ideas, especially abstract ones, are naturally faint and obscure: the mind has but a slender hold of them: they are apt to be confounded with other resembling ideas; and when we have often employed any term, though without a distinct meaning, we are apt to imagine it has a determinate idea annexed to it. On the contrary, all impressions, that is, all sensations, either outward or inward, are strong and vivid: the limits between them are more exactly determined: nor is it easy to fall into any error or mistake with regard to them. When we entertain, therefore, any suspicion that a philosophical term is employed without any meaning or idea (as is but too frequent), we need but enquire, *from what impression is that supposed idea derived?* And if it be impossible

to assign any, this will serve to confirm our suspicion. By bringing ideas into so clear a light we may reasonably hope to remove all dispute, which may arise, concerning their nature and reality.

from Section iii, 'Of the Association of Ideas'

18 It is evident that there is a principle of connexion between the different thoughts or ideas of the mind, and that, in their appearance to the memory or imagination, they introduce each other with a certain degree of method and regularity. In our more serious thinking or discourse this is so observable that any particular thought which breaks in upon the regular tract or chain of ideas, is immediately remarked and rejected. And even in our wildest and most wandering reveries, nay in our very dreams, we shall find, if we reflect, that the imagination ran not altogether at adventures, but that there was still a connexion upheld among the different ideas which succeeded each other. Were the loosest and freest conversation to be transcribed, there would immediately be observed something which connected it in all its transitions. Or where this is wanting, the person who broke the thread of discourse might still inform you, that there had secretly revolved in his mind a succession of thought, which had gradually led him from the subject of conversation. Among different languages, even where we cannot suspect the least connexion or communication, it is found, that the words expressive of ideas the most compounded do yet nearly correspond to each other: a certain proof that the simple ideas, comprehended in the compound ones, were bound together by some universal principle which had an equal influence on all mankind.

19 Though it be too obvious to escape observation that different ideas are connected together; I do not find that any philosopher has attempted to enumerate or class all the principles of association; a subject, however, that seems worthy of curiosity. To me, there appear to be only three principles of connexion among ideas, namely, *Resemblance, Contiguity* in time or place, and *Cause* or *Effect.*

That these principles serve to connect ideas will not, I believe, be much doubted. A picture naturally leads our thoughts to the original: the mention of one apartment in a building naturally introduces an enquiry or discourse concerning the others: and if we think of a wound, we can scarcely forbear reflecting on the pain which follows it. But that this enumeration is complete, and that there are no other principles of association except these, may be difficult to prove to the satisfaction of the reader, or even to a man's own satisfaction. All we can do, in such cases, is to run over several instances, and examine carefully the principle which binds the different thoughts to each other, never stopping till we render the principle as general as possible. The more instances we examine, and the more care we employ, the more assurance shall we acquire, that the enumeration, which we form from the whole, is complete and entire.

*

from Section vii, 'Of Necessary Connexion'

Part 1

48 The great advantage of the mathematical sciences above the moral consists in this, that the ideas of the former, being sensible, are always clear and determinate, the smallest distinction between them is immediately perceptible, and the same terms are still expressive of the same ideas, without ambiguity or variation. An oval is never mistaken for a circle, nor an hyperbola for an ellipsis. The isosceles and scalenum are distinguished by boundaries more exact than vice and virtue, right and wrong. If any term be defined in geometry, the mind readily, of itself, substitutes, on all occasions, the definition for the term defined: Or even when no definition is employed, the object itself may be presented to the senses, and by that means be steadily and clearly apprehended. But the finer sentiments of the mind, the operations of the understanding, the various agitations of the passions, though really in themselves distinct, easily escape us when surveyed by reflection; nor is it in our power to recall the original object, as often as we have occasion to contemplate it. Ambiguity, by this means, is gradually introduced into our reasonings: Similar objects are readily taken to be the same: And the conclusion becomes at last very wide of the premises.

One may safely, however, affirm, that, if we consider these sciences in a proper light, their advantages and disadvantages nearly compensate each other, and reduce both of them to a state of equality. If the mind, with greater facility, retains the ideas of geometry clear and determinate, it must carry on a much longer and more intricate chain of reasoning, and compare ideas much wider of each other, in order to reach the abstruser truths of that science. And if moral ideas are apt, without extreme care, to fall into obscurity and confusion, the inferences are always much shorter in these disquisitions, and the intermediate steps which lead to the conclusion, much fewer than in the sciences which treat of quantity and number. In reality, there is scarcely a proposition in Euclid so simple, as not to consist of more parts, than are to be found in any moral reasoning which runs not into chimera and conceit. Where we trace the principles of the human mind through a few steps, we may be very well satisfied with our progress; considering how soon nature throws a bar to all our enquiries concerning causes, and reduces us to an acknowledgment of our ignorance. The chief obstacle, therefore, to our improvement in the moral or metaphysical sciences is the obscurity of the ideas, and ambiguity of the terms. The principal difficulty in the mathematics is the length of inferences and compass of thought, requisite to the forming of any conclusion. And, perhaps, our progress in natural philosophy is chiefly retarded by the want of proper experiments and phaenomena, which are often discovered by chance, and cannot always be found, when requisite, even by the most diligent and prudent enquiry. As moral philosophy seems hitherto to have received less improvement than either geometry or physics, we may conclude, that, if there be any difference in this respect among these sciences, the difficulties which obstruct the progress of the former, require superior care and capacity to be surmounted.

49 There are no ideas, which occur in metaphysics, more obscure and uncertain, than those of *power, force, energy* or *necessary connexion,* of which it is every moment necessary for us to treat in all our disquisitions. We shall, therefore, endeavour, in this section, to fix, if possible, the precise meaning of these terms, and thereby remove some part of that obscurity, which is so much complained of in this species of philosphy.

It seems a proposition which will not admit of much dispute, that all our ideas are nothing but copies of our impressions, or, in other words, that it is impossible for us to *think* of any thing, which we have not antecedently *felt,* either by our external or internal senses. I have endeavoured to explain and prove this proposition, and have expressed my hopes, that, by a proper application of it, men may reach a greater clearness and precision in philosophical reasonings, than what they have hitherto been able to attain. Complex ideas may, perhaps, be well known by definition, which is nothing but an enumeration of those parts or simple ideas that compose them. But when we have pushed up definitions to the most simple ideas, and find still some ambiguity and obscurity; what resource are we then possessed of? By what invention can we throw light upon these ideas, and render them altogether precise and determinate to our intellectual view? Produce the impressions or original sentiments, from which the ideas are copied. These impressions are all strong and sensible. They admit not of ambiguity. They are not only placed in a full light themselves, but may throw light on their correspondent ideas, which lie in obscurity. And by this means, we may, perhaps, attain a new microscope* or species of optics, by which, in the moral sciences, the most minute, the most simple ideas may be so enlarged as to fall readily under our apprehension, and be equally known with the grossest and most sensible ideas, that can be the object of our enquiry.

50 To be fully acquainted, therefore, with the idea of power or necessary connexion, let us examine its impression; and in order to find the impression with greater certainty, let us search for it in all the sources from which it may possibly be derived.

When we look about us towards external objects, and consider the operation of causes, we are never able, in a single instance, to discover any power or necessary connexion; any quality, which binds the effect to the cause, and renders the one an infallible consequence of the other. We only find, that the one does actually, in fact, follow the other. The impulse of one billiard-ball is attended with motion in the second. This

---

*Note the importance of the lens in Hume's imaging. Cf. Lowth on Comparative Astronomy (p. 153) and see Introduction, p. 8. Ed.

is the whole that appears to the *outward* senses. The mind feels no sentiment or *inward* impression from this succession of objects: Consequently, there is not, in any single, particular instance of cause and effect, any thing which can suggest the idea of power or necessary connexion.

From the first appearance of an object, we never can conjecture what effect will result from it. But were the power or energy of any cause discoverable by the mind, we could foresee the effect, even without experience; and might, at first, pronounce with certainty concerning it, by mere dint of thought and reasoning.

In reality, there is no part of matter, that does ever, by its sensible qualities, discover any power or energy, or give us ground to imagine, that it could produce any thing, or be followed by any other object, which we could denominate its effect. Solidity, extension, motion; these qualities are all complete in themselves, and never point out any other event which may result from them. The scenes of the universe are continually shifting, and one object follows another in an uninterrupted succession; but the power of force, which actuates the whole machine, is entirely concealed from us, and never discovers itself in any of the sensible qualities of body. We know, that, in fact, heat is a constant attendant of flame; but what is the connexion between them, we have no room so much as to conjecture or imagine. It is impossible, therefore, that the idea of power can be derived from the contemplation of bodies, in single instances of their operation; because no bodies ever discover any power, which can be the original of this idea.*

*

53 Shall we then assert, that we are conscious of a power or energy in our own minds, when, by an act or command of our will, we raise up a new idea, fix the mind to the contemplation of it, turn it on all sides, and at last dismiss it for some other idea, when we think that we have surveyed it with sufficient accuracy? I believe the same arguments will prove, that even this command of the will gives us no real idea of force or energy.

First, It must be allowed, that, when we know a power, we know that very circumstance in the cause by which it is enabled to produce the effect: For these are supposed to be synonimous. We must, therefore, know both the cause and effect, and the relation between them. But do

---

*Mr. Locke, in his chapter of power, says that, finding from experience, that there are several new productions in nature, and concluding that there must somewhere be a power capable of producing them, we arrive at last by this reasoning at the idea of power. But no reasoning can ever give us a new, original, simple idea; as this philosopher himself confesses. This, therefore, can never be the origin of that idea.

we pretend to be acquainted with the nature of the human soul and the nature of an idea, or the aptitude of the one to produce the other? This is a real creation; a production of something out of nothing: Which implies a power so great, that it may seem, at first sight, beyond the reach of any being, less than infinite. At least it must be owned, that such a power is not felt, nor known, nor even conceivable by the mind. We only feel the event, namely, the existence of an idea consequent to a command of the will: But the manner, in which this operation is performed, the power by which it is produced, is entirely beyond our comprehension.

Secondly, The command of the mind over itself is limited, as well as its command over the body; and these limits are not known by reason, or any acquaintance with the nature of cause and effect, but only by experience and observation, as in all other natural events and in the operation of external objects.* Our authority over our sentiments and passions is much weaker than that over our ideas; and even the latter authority is circumscribed within very narrow boundaries. Will any one pretend to assign the ultimate reason of these boundaries, or show why the power is deficient in one case, not in another?

Thirdly, This self-command is very different at different times. A man in health possesses more of it than one languishing with sickness. We are more master of our thoughts in the morning than in the evening: Fasting, than after a full meal. Can we give any reason for these variations, except experience? Where then is the power, of which we pretend to be conscious? Is there not here, either in a spiritual or material substance, or both, some secret mechanism or structure of parts, upon which the effect depends, and which, being entirely unknown to us, renders the power or energy of the will equally unknown and incomprehensible?

Volition is surely an act of the mind, with which we are sufficiently acquainted. Reflect upon it. Consider it on all sides. Do you find anything in it like this creative power, by which it raises from nothing a new idea, and with a kind of *Fiat*, imitates the omnipotence of its Maker, if I may be allowed so to speak, who called forth into existence all the various scenes of nature? So far from being conscious of this energy in the will, it requires as certain experience as that of which we are possessed, to convince us that such extraordinary effects do ever result from a simple act of volition.

54 The generality of mankind never find any difficulty in accounting for the more common and familiar operations of nature — such as the descent of heavy bodies, and growth of plants, the generation of animals, or the nourishment of bodies by food: But suppose that, in all these cases, they perceive the very force of energy of the cause, by which it is connected with its effect, and is for ever infallible in its operation. They

---

*Cf. Hartley on 'the command of the mind . . . over the body' (pp. 236-239). Ed.

acquire, by long habit, such a turn of mind, that, upon the appearance of the cause, they immediately expect with assurance its usual attendant, and hardly conceive it possible that any other event could result from it. It is only on the discovery of extraordinary phaenomena, such as earthquakes, pestilence, and prodigies of any kind, that they find themselves at a loss to assign a proper cause, and to explain the manner in which the effect is produced by it. It is usual for men, in such difficulties, to have recourse to some invisible intelligent principle as the immediate cause of that event which surprises them, and which, they think, cannot be accounted for from the common powers of nature. But philosophers, who carry their scrutiny a little farther, immediately perceive that, even in the most familiar events, the energy of the cause is as unintelligible as in the most unusual, and that we only learn by experience the frequent *Conjunction* of objects, without being ever able to comprehend anything like *Connexion* between them.

55 Here, then, many philosophers* think themselves obliged by reason to have recourse, on all occasions, to the same principle, which the vulgar never appeal to but in cases that appear miraculous and supernatural. They acknowledge mind and intelligence to be, not only the ultimate and original cause of all things, but the immediate and sole cause of every event which appears in nature. They pretend that those objects which are commonly denominated *causes*, are in reality nothing but *occasions*; and that the true and direct principle of every effect is not any power or force in nature, but a volition of the Supreme Being, who wills that such particular objects should for ever be conjoined with each other. Instead of saying that one billiard-ball moves another by a force which it has derived from the author of nature, it is the Deity himself, they say, who, by a particular volition, moves the second ball, being determined to this operation by the impulse of the first ball, in consequence of those general laws which he has laid down to himself in the government of the universe. But philosophers advancing still in their inquiries, discover that, as we are totally ignorant of the power on which depends the mutual operation of bodies, we are no less ignorant of that power on which depends the operation of mind on body, or of body on mind; nor are we able, either from our senses or consciousness, to assign the ultimate principle in one case more than in the other. The same ignorance, therefore, reduces them to the same conclusion. They assert that the Deity is the immediate cause of the union between soul and body; and that they are not the organs of sense, which, being agitated by external objects, produce sensations in the mind; but that it is a particular volition of our omnipotent Maker, which excites such a sensation, in consequence of such a motion in the organ. In like manner, it is not any energy in the will that produces local motion in our members: It is God himself, who is pleased to second our will, in itself impotent, and to command that motion which we erroneously attribute

---

*For example, Liebnitz. Ed.

to our own power and efficacy. Nor do philosophers stop at this conclusion. They sometimes extend the same inference to the mind itself, in its internal operations. Our mental vision or conception of ideas is nothing but a revelation made to us by our Maker. When we voluntarily turn our thoughts to any object, and raise up its image in the fancy, it is not the will which creates that idea: It is the universal Creator, who discovers it to the mind, and renders it present to us.

56 Thus, according to these philosophers, every thing is full of God. Not content with the principle, that nothing exists but by his will, that nothing possesses any power but by his concession: They rob nature, and all created beings, of every power, in order to render their dependence on the Deity still more sensible and immediate. They consider not that, by this theory, they diminish, instead of magnifying, the grandeur of those attributes, which they affect so much to celebrate. It argues surely more power in the Deity to delegate a certain degree of power to inferior creatures than to produce every thing by his own immediate volition. It argues more wisdom to contrive at first the fabric of the world with such perfect foresight that, of itself, and by its proper operation, it may serve all the purposes of providence, than if the great Creator were obliged every moment to adjust its parts, and animate by his breath all the wheels of that stupendous machine.

But if we would have a more philosophical confutation of this theory, perhaps the two following reflections may suffice.

57 *First*, it seems to me that this theory of the universal energy and operation of the Supreme Being is too bold ever to carry conviction with it to a man sufficiently apprized of the weakness of human reason and the narrow limits to which it is confined in all its operations. Though the chain of arguments which conduct to it were ever so logical, there must arise a strong suspicion, if not an absolute assurance, that it has carried us quite beyond the reach of our faculties, when it leads to conclusions so extraordinary, and so remote from common life and experience. We are got into fairy land, long ere we have reached the last steps of our theory; and *there* we have no reason to trust our common methods of argument, or to think that our usual analogies and probabilities have any authority. Our line is too short to fathom such immense abysses. And however we may flatter ourselves that we are guided, in every step which we take, by a kind of verisimilitude and experience, we may be assured that this fancied experience has no authority when we thus apply it to subjects that lie entirely out of the sphere of experience. But on this we shall have occasion to touch afterwards.

Secondly, I cannot perceive any force in the arguments on which this theory is founded. We are ignorant, it is true, of the manner in which bodies operate on each other: Their force or energy is entirely incomprehensible: But are we not equally ignorant of the manner or force by which a mind, even the supreme mind, operates either on itself or on body? Whence, I beseech you, do we acquire any idea of it? We have no sentiment or consciousness of this power in ourselves. We have no idea of the Supreme Being but what we learn from reflection on our own faculties. Were our ignorance, therefore, a good reason for rejecting any thing, we should be led into that principle of denying all energy in the Supreme Being as much as in the grossest matter. We surely comprehend as little the operations of one as of the other. Is it more difficult to conceive that motion may arise from impulse than that it may arise from volition? All we know is our profound ignorance in both cases.*

Part 2

58 But to hasten to a conclusion of this argument, which is already drawn out to too great a length: we have sought in vain for an idea of power or necessary connexion in all the sources from which we could suppose it to be derived. It appears that in single instances of the operation of bodies, we never can, by our utmost scrutiny, discover any thing but one event following another, without being able to comprehend any force or power by which the cause operates, or any connexion between it and its supposed effect. The same difficulty occurs in contemplating the operations of mind and body—where we observe the motion of the latter to follow upon the volition of the former, but are not able to observe or conceive the tie which binds together the motion and volition, or the energy by which the mind produces this effect. The authority of the will over its own faculties and ideas is not a whit more comprehensible: So that, upon the whole, there appears not, throughout

---

*I need not examine at length the *vis inertiae* which is so much talked of in the new philosophy, and which is ascribed to matter. We find by experience, that a body at rest or in motion continues for ever in its present state, till put from it by some new cause; and that a body impelled takes as much motion from the impelling body as it acquires itself. These are facts. When we call this a *vis inertiae*, we only mark these facts, without pretending to have any idea of the inert power; in the same manner as, when we talk of gravity, we mean certain effects, without comprehending that active power. It was never the meaning of Sir *Isaac Newton* to rob second causes of all force or energy; though some of his followers have endeavoured to establish that theory upon his authority. On the contrary, that great philosopher had recourse to an etherial active fluid to explain his universal attraction; though he was so cautious and modest as to allow, that it was a mere hypothesis, not to be insisted on, without more experiments. I much confess, that there is something in the fate of opinions a little extraordinary. *Des Cartes* insinuated that doctrine of the universal and sole efficacy of the Deity, without insisting on it. *Malebranche* and other *Cartesians* made it the foundation of all their philosophy. It had, however, no authority in England. *Locke, Clarke,* and *Cudworth*, never so much as take notice of it, but suppose all along, that matter has a real, though subordinate and derived power. By what means has it become so prevalent among our modern metaphysicians?

all nature, any one instance of connexion which is conceivable by us. All events seem entirely loose and separate. One event follows another; but we never can observe any tie between them. They seem *conjoined*, but never *connected*. And as we can have no idea of any thing which never appeared to our outward sense or inward sentiment, the necessary conclusion *seems* to be that we have no idea of connexion or power at all, and that these words are absolutely without any meaning, when employed either in philosophical reasonings or common life.

59 But there still remains one method of avoiding this conclusion, and one source which we have not yet examined. When any natural object or event is presented, it is impossible for us, by any sagacity or penetration, to discover, or even conjecture without experience, what event will result from it, or to carry our foresight beyond that object which is immediately present to the memory and senses. Even after one instance or experiment where we have observed a particular event to follow upon another, we are not entitled to form a general rule, or foretell what will happen in like cases; it being justly esteemed an unpardonable temerity to judge of the whole course of nature from one single experiment, however accurate or certain. But when one particular species of event has always, in all instances, been conjoined with another, we make no longer any scruple of foretelling one upon the appearance of the other, and of employing that reasoning, which can alone assure us of any matter of fact or existence. We then call the one object, *Cause*; the other, *Effect*. We suppose that there is some connexion between them; some power in the one, by which it infallibly produces the other, and operates with the greatest certainty and strongest necessity.

It appears, then, that this idea of a necessary connexion among events arises from a number of similar instances which occur of the constant conjunction of these events; nor can that idea ever be suggested by any one of these instances, surveyed in all possible lights and positions. But there is nothing in a number of instances, different from every single instance, which is supposed to be exactly similar; except only, that after a repetition of similar instances, the mind is carried by habit, upon the appearance of one event, to expect its usual attendant, and to believe that it will exist. This connexion, therefore, which we *feel** in the mind, this customary transition of the imagination from one object to its usual attendant, is the sentiment or impression from which we form the idea of power or necessary connexion. Nothing farther is in the case. Contemplate the subject on all sides; you will never find any other origin of that idea. This is the sole difference between one instance, from which we can never receive the idea of connexion, and a number of similar instances, by which it is suggested. The first time a man saw the communication of motion by impulse, as by the shock of two billiard balls, he could not

---

*Hume's creative *feeling* parallels, of course, the association of ideas in 'the poetry of feeling'. See esp. Lowth, Young, Collins, and Gray. Ed.

pronounce that the one event was *connected*: but only that it was *conjoined* with the other. After he has observed several instances of this nature, he then pronounces them to be *connected*. What alteration has happened to give rise to this new idea of *connexion*? Nothing but that he now *feels* these events to be *connected* in his imagination, and can readily foretell the existence of one from the appearance of the other. When we say, therefore, that one object is connected with another, we mean only that they have acquired a connexion in our thought, and give rise to this inference, by which they become proofs of each other's existence: A conclusion which is somewhat extraordinary, but which seems founded on sufficient evidence. Nor will its evidence be weakened by any general diffidence of the understanding, or sceptical suspicion concerning every conclusion which is new and extraordinary. No conclusions can be more agreeable to scepticism than such as make discoveries concerning the weakness and narrow limits of human reason and capacity.

'A New Edition', 1777

EDWARD YOUNG (1683–1765)

The Spectator and *The Guardian* repeatedly express enthusiasm for primitive poetry, while the latter in particular suggests the influence on theories of poetry of the philosophy especially of Berkeley, one of a group of radical thinkers who wrote for the magazines. The end of the finite world and the emotional impact of such a concept occupies the author of *Guardian* No. *51*, for example, introducing Young's *Last Day* to his readers. Several weeks later, in *Guardian* No. *86*, 'John Lizard' of All Souls, probably Young himself, soon occupied with a 'translation' of *Job*, analysed the reasons for the emotional impact of primitive, original verse in the depiction of the warhorse in *Job* 'the most ancient poem in the world'. Images of motion − a horse in a race − moved us most violently, this writer noted. Secondly, images which appeared as 'in the eye of the Creator', were more effective than those of classical poets. Thirdly, the original poets made 'all the beauties to flow from an inward principle' while classical writers, preoccupied no doubt with perspective and overall form 'chiefly endeavour to paint the outward figure, lineaments, and motions'. Among the fine points of the Job horse − which was to influence Thomson's *Seasons* − was the comparison with a grasshopper and the extraordinary line 'hast thou clothed his neck with thunder?'

In an intriguing blend of current theories of perception and primitive poetry, Young, if it is he, suggests in his appreciation of *Job* 'new laws for the sublime' which clearly will supersede in particular, among 'the great wits of antiquity', Longinus.

The power of poetry for 'John Lizard' apparently, is released when the artist denies space and time. The essentially Romantic figure of the warhorse and grasshopper, like that of the horse's mane and thunder, not only follows the 'primitive' pattern noted by Lowth and Blair, that a comparison should be unlike except in one instance, but depends on a massive denial of spatial expectations. Juxtaposing a horse's neck and thunder (a metaphor redolent of Keats' *Hyperion; A Fragment*, 276f.) and viewing a rampant horse as a grasshopper, was to ignore like the first Creator finite limitation, as if all objects, isolated in infinity, were pregnant with prophetic energy in a continuum of imagination. At a less sophisticated level we might observe that we have entered an era when, unlike their classical predecessors, poets create original metaphors, (following oriental practice rather than classical model), which cut themselves off from precedent and reverberate down the corridors of the individual reader's subjectivity, allowing him to create alongside the poet.

The dubiousness of externality and the likelihood that man 'halfcreates' not only Nature but the concepts of finiteness and externality from his own infinite imagination, is central to Berkeley's philosophy and, of course, to Coleridge's concept of the imagination in Chapter XIII of the *Biographia Literaria*. In a crucial passage in 'Night VI' which has intriguing links with Wallace Stevens's *Sunday Morning*, and from which Wordsworth borrowed the term 'half-create' for *Tintern Abbey*, Young defines perceptive man as the rightful owner of heaven, the bestower of sensual reality upon Nature, and even – like Wordsworth in *The Prelude* – giver of light to the sun itself. With these concepts in mind it is valuable not only to dwell on Blake's illustrations to *Night Thoughts* but also on the composition by Blake of the earliest version of *Vala* or *The Four Zoas* on the working proofs for the illustrations for Young's poem.

It is clear that 'originality' for 'the Bard of Welwyn', as Young became called, meant far more than it does for the twentieth century. In his *Conjectures on Original Composition* (1759) Young called on his readers to put themselves in the place of the first poets of the, as it was believed, five thousand-year-old world, in contagious proximity, we assume, not only to Job, but to the primal Creator. The crucial characteristic of eighteenth-century poetry, a double image of time, which necessarily suggests timelessness and a sense of divine originality, informed not only Young's entire writing career, but enabled Blake to converse with Ezekiel and Isaiah, Smart to write Biblical poems full of West Indian cocoa and quinces, and perhaps prompted Chatterton – and Macpherson – to compose what now seem fraudulent 'primitive' artifacts. Young's *Conjectures* opposes to the structures of time an organic image of creativity, within – not reflective of – Nature, and insists on the development of the individual self in the act of writing in a manner that reminds us that solitary genius, and the artist's life as his major creation, were major characteristics of the Romantic revolution.

GUARDIAN *NO.* 86 *Friday, June 19, 1713*

'To Nestor Ironside, Esq.'

Sir,   *Oxford, June* 16, 1713.
The classical writers, according to your advice, are by no means neglected by me, while I pursue my studies in divinity. I am persuaded that they are fountains of good sense and eloquence; and that it is absolutely necessary for a young mind to form itself upon such models. For by a careful study of their style and manner, we shall at least avoid those faults, into which a youthful imagination is apt to hurry us; such as luxuriance of fancy, licentiousness of style, redundancy of thought, and false ornaments. As I have been flattered by my friends, that I have some genius for poetry, I sometimes turn my thoughts that way: and with pleasure reflect, that I have got over that childish part of life, which delights in points and turns of wit; and that I can take a manly and rational satis-faction in that which is called painting in poetry. Whether it be, that in these copyings of nature, the object is placed in such lights and circum-stances as strike the fancy agreeably; or whether we are surprised to

find objects that are absent, placed before our eyes; or whether it be our admiration of the author's art and dexterity; or whether we amuse ourselves with comparing the picture and the original; or rather (which is most probable) because all these reasons concur to affect us; we are wonderfully charmed with these drawings after the life, this magic that raises apparitions in the fancy.

Landskips or still-life, work much less upon us, than representations of the postures or passions of living creatures. Again, those passions or postures strike us more or less in proportion to the ease or violence of their motions. An horse grazing moves us less than one stretching in a race, and a racer less than one in the fury of a battle. It is very difficult, I believe, to express violent motions which are fleeting and transitory, either in colours, or words. In poetry it requires great spirit in thought, and energy in style; which we find more of in the eastern poetry, than in either the Greek or Roman. The great Creator, who accommodated himself to those he vouchsafed to speak to, hath put into the mouth of his prophets such sublime sentiments and exalted language, as must abash the pride and wit of man. In the book of Job, the most ancient poem in the world, we have such paintings and descriptions as I have spoken of, in great variety. I shall at present make some remarks on the celebrated description of the horse in that holy book, and compare it with those drawn by Homer and Virgil.

Homer hath the following similitude of an horse twice over in the Iliad, which Virgil hath copied from him [see *Iliad* vi. 506ff] ; at least he hath deviated less from Homer, than Mr. Dryden hath from him:

Freed from his keepers, thus with broken reins
The wanton courser prances o'er the plains;
Or in the pride of youth o'erleaps the mounds,
And snuffs the females in forbidden grounds;
Or seeks his watering in the well-known flood,
To quench his thirst, and cool his fiery blood:
He swims luxuriant in the liquid plain,
And o'er his shoulders flows his waving mane;
He neighs, he snorts, he bears his head on high,
Before his ample chest the frothy waters fly.

[Dryden, Aeneis, xi. 743–52]

Virgil's description is much fuller than the foregoing, which, as I said, is only a simile; whereas Virgil professes to treat of the nature of the horse. It is thus admirably translated:

The fiery courser, when he hears from far
The sprightly trumpets, and the shouts of war,
Pricks up his ears, and trembling with delight,
Shifts pace, and paws; and hopes the promis'd fight.
On his right shoulder his thick mane reclin'd,
Ruffles at speed, and dances in the wind.
His horny hoofs are jetty-black and round;

His chine is double; starting, with a bound
He turns the turf, and shakes the solid ground.
Fire from his eyes, clouds from his nostrils flow;
He bears his rider headlong on the foe.   [Dryden, *Georgics*, iii. 130ff]

Now follows that in the book of Job; which under all the disadvantages of having been written in a language little understood; of being expressed in phrases peculiar to a part of the world, whose manner of thinking and speaking seems to us very uncouth; and, above all, of appearing in a prose translation; is nevertheless so transcendently above the heathen descriptions, that hereby we may perceive how faint and languid the images are, which are formed by mortal authors, when compared with that which is figured as it were, just as it appears in the eye of the Creator. God speaking to Job, asks him, 'Hast thou given the horse strength? hast thou clothed his neck with thunder? Canst thou make him afraid as a grasshopper? The glory of his nostrils is terrible. He paweth in the valley, and rejoiceth in his strength. He goeth on to meet the armed men. He mocketh at fear, and is not affrighted; neither turneth he back from the sword. The quiver rattleth against him, the glittering spear, and the shield. He swalloweth the ground with fierceness and rage; neither believeth he that it is the sound of the trumpet. He saith amongst the trumpets, Ha, ha; and he smelleth the battle afar off; the thunder of the captains, and the shouting.'

Here are all the great and sprightly images, that thought can form of this generous beast, expressed in such force and vigour of style, as would have given the great wits of antiquity new laws for the sublime, had they been acquainted with these writings. I cannot but particularly observe, that whereas the classical poets chiefly endeavour to paint the outward figure, lineaments, and motions; the sacred poet makes all the beauties to flow from an inward principle in the creature he describes, and thereby gives great spirit and vivacity to his description. The following phrases and circumstances seem singularly remarkable: 'Hast thou clothed his neck with thunder?' Homer and Virgil mention nothing about the neck of the horse, but his mane. The sacred author, by the bold figure of thunder, not only expresses the shaking of that remarkable beauty in the horse, and the flakes of hair which naturally suggest the idea of lightning; but likewise the violent agitation and force of the neck, which in the oriental tongues had been flatly exprest by a metaphor less than this.

'Canst thou make him afraid as a grasshopper?' There is a twofold beauty in this expression, which not only marks the courage of this beast, by asking if he can be scared? but likewise raises a noble image of his swiftness, by insinuating, that if he could be frighted, he would bound away with the nimbleness of a grasshopper.

'The glory of his nostrils is terrible.' This is more strong and concise than that of Virgil, which yet is the noblest line that was ever written without inspiration:

Collectumque fremens volvit sub naribus ignem.   [*Georg*. iii. 85]

And in his nostrils rolls collected fire.

'He rejoiceth in his strength — He mocketh at fear — neither believeth he that it is the sound of the trumpet — He saith among the trumpets, Ha, ha'; — are signs of courage as I said before, flowing from an inward principle. There is a peculiar beauty in his 'not believing it is the sound of the trumpet:' that is, he cannot believe it for joy; but when he was sure of it, and is 'amongst the trumpets, he saith, Ha, ha . . . '

I am, Sir,

Your ever obliged servant,

John Lizard

NIGHT THOUGHTS (1742–5) 'NIGHT VI', 409–41

With error in ambition justly charged,
Find we *Lorenzo* wiser in his wealth?
What, if thy rental I reform, and draw
An inventory new to set thee right?
Where thy true treasure? Gold says, 'Not in me;'
And, 'Not in me,' the diamond. Gold is poor;
India's insolvent: seek it in thyself;
Seek in thy naked self, and find it there;
In being so descended, form'd, endow'd;
Sky-born, sky-guided, sky-returning race!
Erect, immortal, rational, Divine!
In senses, which inherit earth and heavens;
Enjoy the various riches Nature yields;
Far nobler! give the riches they enjoy;
Give taste to fruits, and harmony to groves,
Their radiant beams to gold, and gold's bright sire;
Take-in, at once, the landscape of the world,
At a small inlet, which a grain might close,
And half-create the wondrous world they see.
Our senses, as our reason, are Divine.
But for the magic organ's powerful charm,
Earth were a rude, uncolour'd chaos still.
Objects are but the' occasion: ours the' exploit;
Ours is the cloth, the pencil, and the paint,
Which Nature's admirable picture draws,
And beautifies Creation's ample dome.
Like Milton's Eve, when gazing on the lake,
Man makes the matchless image man admires.
Say then, shall man, his thoughts all sent abroad,
(Superior wonders in himself forgot,)
His admiration waste on objects round,
When Heaven makes him the soul of all he sees?

Absurd, not rare! so great, so mean, is man!

from *CONJECTURES ON ORIGINAL COMPOSITION (1759)*

The mind of a man of Genius is a fertile and pleasant field, pleasant as *Elysium*, and fertile as *Tempe*; it enjoys a perpetual Spring. Of that Spring, *Originals* are the fairest Flowers: *Imitations* are of quicker growth, but fainter bloom. *Imitations* are of two kinds; one of Nature, one of Authors; The first we call *Originals*, and confine the term *Imitation* to the second. I shall not enter into the curious enquiry of what is, or is not, strictly speaking *Original*, content with what all must allow, that some Compositions are more so than others; and the more they are so, I say, the better. *Originals* are, and ought to be, great Favourites, for they are great Benefactors; they extend the Republic of Letters, and add a new province to its dominion: *Imitators* only give us a sort of Duplicates of what we had, possibly much better, before; increasing the mere Drug of books, while all that makes them valuable, *Knowledge* and *Genius*, are at a stand. The pen of an *Original* Writer, like *Armida*'s wand, out of a barren waste calls a blooming spring: out of that blooming spring an *Imitator* is a transplanter of Laurels, which sometimes die on removal, always languish in a foreign soil.

But suppose an *Imitator* to be most excellent (and such there are), yet still he but nobly builds on another's foundation; his Debt is, at least, equal to his Glory; which therefore, on the ballance, cannot be very great. On the contrary, an *Original*, tho' but indifferent (its *Originality* being set aside,) yet has something to boast; it is something to say with him in *Horace*,

Meo *sum Pauper in aere*;*

and to share ambition with no less than *Caesar*, who declared he had rather be the First in a Village, than the Second at *Rome*.

Still farther: An *Imitator* shares his crown, if he has one, with the chosen Object of his Imitation; an *Original* enjoys an undivided applause. An *Original* may be said to be of a *vegetable* nature; it rises spontaneously from the vital root of Genius; it *grows*, it is not *made*: *Imitations* are often a sort of *Manufacture* wrought up by those *Mechanics*, *Art*, and *Labour*, out of pre-existent materials not their own.

*

An *Original* enters early upon Reputation: *Fame*, fond of new Glories, sounds her Trumpet in Triumph at its birth; and yet how few are awaken'd by it into the noble ambition of like attempts? Ambition is sometimes no Vice in life; it is always a Virtue in Composition. High in the towering

---

*Epl. II. ii. 12. 'I have slender means, but am not in debt.' Ed.

Alps is the Fountain of the *Po*; high in Fame, and in Antiquity, is the Fountain of an *Imitator's* Undertaking; but the River, and the Imitation, humbly creep along the Vale. So few are our *Originals*, that, if all other books were to be burnt, the letter'd World would resemble some Metropolis in flames, where a few incombustible buildings, a Fortress, Temple, or Tower, lift their Heads, in melancholy Grandeur, amid the mighty ruin. Compared with this Conflagration, old *Omar* lighted up but a small Bonfire, when he heated the baths of the Barbarians, for eight months together, with the famed *Alexandrian* Library's inestimable spoils, that no prophane book might obstruct the triumphant progress of his holy *Alcoran* round the Globe.

But why are *Originals* so few? not because the Writer's harvest is over, the great Reapers of Antiquity having left nothing to be gleaned after them; nor because the human mind's teeming time is past, or because it is incapable of putting forth unprecedented births; but because illustrious Examples, *engross, prejudice*, and *intimidate*. They *engross* our attention, and so prevent a due inspection of ourselves; they *prejudice* our Judgment in favour of their abilities, and so lessen the sense of our own; and they *intimidate* us with the splendor of their Renown, and thus under Diffidence bury our strength. Nature's Impossibilities, and those of Diffidence, lie wide asunder.

Let it not be suspected, that I would weakly insinuate any thing in favour of the Moderns, as compared with antient Authors; no, I am lamenting their great Inferiority. But I think it is no *necessary* Inferiority; that it is not from divine Destination, but from some cause far beneath the moon: I think that human Souls, thro' all periods, are equal; that due care, and exertion, would set us nearer our immortal Predecessors than we are at present; and he who questions and confutes this, will show abilities not a little tending toward a proof of that Equality, which he denies.

After all, the first Ancients had no Merit in being *Originals*: They could *not* be *Imitators*. Modern Writers have a *Choice* to make; and therefore have a Merit in their power. They may soar in the Regions of *Liberty* or move in the soft Fetters of easy *Imitation*; and *Imitation* has as many plausible Reasons to urge, as *Pleasure* had to offer to *Hercules*. *Hercules* made the Choice of an Hero, and *so* became immortal.

Yet let not Assertors of Classic Excellence imagine, that I deny the Tribute it so well deserves. He that admires not antient Authors, betrays a secret he would conceal, and tells the world, that he does not understand them. Let us be as far from neglecting, as from copying, their admirable Compositions: Sacred be their Rights, and inviolable their Fame. Let our Understandings feed on theirs; they afford the noblest nourishment: But let them nourish, not annihilate, our own. When we read, let our Imagination kindle at their Charms; when we write, let out Judgment shut them out of our Thoughts; treat even *Homer* himself, as his royal Admirer was treated by the Cynic; bid him stand aside, nor shade our

Composition from the beams of our own Genius; for nothing *Original* can rise, nothing Immortal can ripen, in any other Sun.

Must we then, you say, not imitate antient Authors? Imitate them, by all means; but imitate aright. He that imitates the divine *Iliad*, does not imitate *Homer*; but he who takes the same method, which *Homer* took, for arriving at a capacity of accomplishing a work so great. Tread in his steps to the sole Fountain of Immortality; drink where he drank, at the true *Helicon*, that is, at the breast of Nature: Imitate; but imitate not the *Composition*, but the *Man*. For may not this Paradox pass into a Maxim? *viz*. 'The less we copy the renowned Antients, we shall resemble them the more.'

But possibly you may reply, that you must either imitate *Homer*, or depart from Nature. Not so: For suppose You was to change place, in time, with *Homer*; then, if you write naturally, you might as well charge *Homer* with an imitation of You. Can you be said to imitate *Homer* for writing *so*, as you would have written, if *Homer* had never been? As far as a regard to Nature, and sound Sense, will permit a Departure from your great Predecessors; so far, ambitiously, depart from them; the farther from them in *Similitude*, the nearer are you to them in *Excellence*; you rise by it into an *Original*; become a noble Collateral, not an humble Descendant from them. Let us build our Compositions with the Spirit, and in the Taste, of the Antients; but not with their Materials: Thus will they resemble the structures of *Pericles* at *Athens*, which *Plutarch* commends for having had an air of Antiquity as soon as they were built. All Eminence, and Distinction, lies out of the beaten road; Excursion, and Deviation, are necessary to find it; and the more remote your Path from the Highway, the more reputable; if, like poor *Gulliver* (of whom anon,) you fall not into a Ditch, in your way to Glory.

What glory to come near, what glory to reach, what glory (presumptuous thought!)to surpass, our Predecessors? And is that then in Nature absolutely impossible? Or is it not, rather, contrary to Nature to fail in it? Nature herself sets the Ladder, all wanting is our ambition to climb. For by the bounty of Nature we are as strong as our Predecessors; and by the favour of Time (which is but another Round in Nature's Scale,) we stand on higher ground. As to the *First*, were *they* more than men? Or are *we* less? Are not our minds cast in the same mould with those before the Flood? The flood affected Matter, Mind escaped. As to the *Second*; tho' we are Moderns, the World is an Antient; more antient far, than when they filled it with their Fame, whom we most admire. Have we not their Beauties, as stars, to guide; their Defects, as rocks, to be shunn'd; the Judgment of Ages on both, as a chart to conduct, and a sure helm to steer us in our passage to greater Perfection than Theirs? And shall we be stopt in our rival pretensions to Fame by this just Reproof?

Stat contra, dicitque tibi tua Pagina, Fur es.　　　　　　　MART.*

---

*Martial, *Epigrams* I. 1iii. 12.'Your book stares you in the face and calls you thief'. Ed.

It is by a sort of noble Contagion, from a general familiarity with their Writings, and not by any particular sordid Theft, that we can be the better for those who went before us. Hope we, from Plagiarism, any Dominion in Literature; as that of *Rome* arose from a nest of Thieves?

Rome was a powerful Ally to many States, antient Authors are our powerful Allies; but we must take heed, that they do not succour, till they enslave, after the manner of *Rome*. Too formidable an Idea of their Superiority, like a Spectre, would fright us out of a proper use of our Wits; and dwarf our Understanding, by making a Giant of theirs. Too great Awe for them lays Genius under restraint, and denies it that free scope, that full elbow-room, which is requisite for striking its most masterly strokes. Genius is a Master-workman, Learning is but an Instrument; and an Instrument, tho' most valuable, yet not always indispensable. Heaven will not admit of a Partner in the accomplishment of some favourite Spirits; but rejecting all human means, assumes the whole glory to itself. Have not some, tho' not famed for Erudition, *so* written, as almost to persuade us, that they shone brighter, and soared higher, for escaping the boasted aid of that proud Ally?

Nor is it strange; for what, for the most part, mean we by Genius, but the Power of accomplishing great things without the means generally reputed necessary to that end? A *Genius* differs from a *good Understanding*, as a Magician from a good Architect; *That* raises his structure by means invisible; *This* is by the skilful use of common tools. Hence Genius has ever been supposed to partake of something Divine. *Nemo unquam vir magnus fuit, sine aliquo afflatu Divino.**

Learning, destitute of this superior Aid, is fond, and proud, of what has cost it much pains; is a great Lover of Rules, and Boaster of famed Examples: As Beauties less perfect, who owe half their Charms to cautious Art, she inveighs against natural unstudied Graces, and small harmless Indecorums, and sets rigid Bounds to that Liberty, to which Genius often owes its supreme Glory; but the No-Genius its frequent Ruin. For unprescribed Beauties, and unexampled Excellence, which are characteristics of *Genius*, lie without the Pale of *Learning's* Authorities, and Laws; which Pale, Genius must leap to come at them: But by that Leap, if Genius is wanting, we break our Necks; we lose that little credit, which possibly we might have enjoyed before. For Rules, like Crutches, are a needful Aid to the Lame, tho' an Impediment to the Strong. A *Homer* casts them away; and like his *Achilles*,

> *Jura neget sibi nata, nihil non arroget***

by native force of mind. There is something in Poetry beyond Prose-reason; there are Mysteries in it not to be explained, but admired; which

---

*Cicero, *De Natura Deorum*, II. lxvi, 167. 'No man was ever great without some degree of inspiration.' Ed.

**Horace, *Arts Poetica*, 122. 'He denies that the laws were formed for him. There is nothing that he does not claim by force.' Ed.

renders mere Prose-men Infidels to their Divinity. And here pardon a second Paradox; *viz.*

> *Genius* often then deserves most to be praised, when it is most sure to be condemned; that is, when its Excellence, from mounting high, to weak eyes is quite out of sight.

If I might speak farther of Learning, and Genius, I would compare Genius to Virtue, and Learning to Riches. As Riches are most wanted where there is least Virtue; so Learning where there is least Genius. As Virtue without much Riches can give Happiness, so Genius without much Learning can give Renown. As it is said in *Terence, Pecuniam negligere interdum maximum est Lucrum;** so to neglect of Learning, Genius sometimes owes its greater glory. Genius, therefore, leaves but the second place, among men of letters, to the Learned. It is their Merit, and Ambition, to fling light on the works of Genius, and point out its Charms. We most justly reverence their informing Radius for that favour; but we must much more admire the radiant Stars pointed out by them.

A Star of the first magnitude among the Moderns was *Shakespeare*; among the Antients, *Pindar*; who, (as *Vossius* tells us) boasted of his No-learning, calling himself the Eagle, for his Flight above it. And such Genii as these may, indeed, have much reliance on their own native powers. For Genius may be compared to the Body's natural Strength; Learning to the superinduced Accoutrements of Arms: if the First is equal to the proposed exploit, the Latter rather encumbers, than assists; rather retards, than promotes, the Victory. *Sacer nobis inest Deus,*** says *Seneca*. With regard to the Moral world, *Conscience*, with regard to the Intellectual, *Genius*, is that God within. Genius can set us right in Composition, without the Rules of the Learned; as Conscience sets us right in Life, without the Laws of the Land: *This*, singly, can make us Good, as Men; *That*, singly, as Writers, can, sometimes, make us Great.

---

*Terence, *Adelphoe*, 216. 'To slight money now and then is the way to make it.'

**Seneca, *De Beneficiis*, VII., vi. 3.

ROBERT LOWTH (1710–1787)

At Winchester, Lowth began his affiliation with the most influential literary group until Bloomsbury, Collins, Spence, the Wartons and Young, and wrote brilliant poetry on local archaeology and the Biblical figures of the chapel window which show an acute awareness of the poetic value of temporal ambiguity and earned Cowper's extravagant praise.

At his election from Wykeham's New College to the Professorship of Poetry in his early thirties, Lowth expanded the oriental scholarship of his predecessors, Trapp, Thomas Warton, and Spence, achieving unprecedented heights of elegance and authority, defining with extreme precision of feeling and frequent allusion to eighteenth-century travel, techniques of composition which seem to have strongly influenced Romantic works especially Young's *Night Thoughts* and Smart's *A Song to David* and *Jubilate Agno*.

It is pertinent to a grasp of Romantic primitivism to note that Lowth's *Life of Wykeham* (1758) and the famed *Short Introduction to English Grammar* (1762) show the same imaginative response to the concrete *minutiae* of the English 'first ages' as his *Praelectiones* and parallel translation of *Isaiah* (1778) to that of the primitive orient. Lowth's *Grammar*, still used at Harvard University in the mid-nineteenth century, depended for its sense of the vernacular on the linguistic work of Hickes, Wallis, and others, leading figures of the Royal Society (see p. 1). His account of Gothic in the *Life of Wykeham* (Section VI) indicates a telling parallel, representative of the times, between his taste in architecture and the shape of his own works.

Lowth's *De sacra poesi Hebraeorum praelectiones*, first given between 1741 and 1750, published in 1753 and translated into English in 1787, are perhaps best viewed simply as the most extensive account of the age's alternative to classicism, the counterpart to Blair's *Dissertation on Ossian* (see pp. 264-275). The central concept is that of the newly-created mind of man, sprung to life, more perfect than now, at the beginning of Creation five thousand years before. Aristotelian imitation was not the source of this greatest of all poetry, but the imitation of the mind's processes themselves in memory-less, lyric relation to Nature. Like Bartram in the New World of alligators and Seminoles in Florida without any background of comparison for his novel discoveries, newly-created man combined highly emotional expression with vivid iconography of natural phenomena. Emotion did not lead, like rational discourse, to obscurity, declared Lowth. The melting of the Lebanese snow, female cosmetics, wine-pressing, disappearing streams after rainstorms in the desert, burial practices as described by Chardin, produced the most soaring 'Sublime'. Alluding to poetry descriptive of the first Creator himself, Lowth concludes Lecture XVI, 'from ideas, which in themselves appear coarse, unsuitable, and totally unworthy of so great an object, the mind naturally recedes, and passes suddenly to the contemplation of the object itself, and of its inherent magnitude and importance.' Lowth's 'Sublime' is the indispensable clue to the supposed banality of Young's primitive verse as it is to Smart's cat Jeoffry.

As interesting as his over-all theory is Lowth's crystallization into a scholarly discovery of a movement in poetic syntax which had developed since the epistemology of Berkeley, and which had been suggested distantly by Trapp on the oriental ode (see pp. 59-61). Achieving immediate *éclat* at home and fame in Europe, Lowth analysed the 'parallelismus membrorum' in which most of the Old Testament was composed. The sequential experience of Pope's verse, which Coleridge defined as a 'conjunction-disjunctive' (see p. 337) moved the reader forward in a finite process, imitative of Western concepts of before and after, cause and effect. The primitive poet, (closer to Berkeley, Hume and Hartley, one notes) repeated the pronouncement of the earlier line unit for unit, in a continual experience of stasis and dislocation. Lowth's first example of the first of his kinds – from *Psalm 114* – in a sense tells all:

When Israel went out from Egypt;
The House of Jacob from a strange people:
Judah was as his sacred heritage:
Israel his dominion.
The sea saw, and fled;
Jordan turned back:
The mountains leaped like rams;
The hills like the sons of the flock.

The effect was 'parabolic' giving the thrill of incantatory attack, combining the most imaginative reach with an earthbound awareness of concrete objects, both layers, as it were, vying against and poetically strengthening each other. This theory suggests a poetry of non-elevated objects – sizeless and surreal – seen with prophetic ambiguity and vivid iconography, forming patterns of internal static modification across, or as it were, in opposition to the sequence or process of reading. It was clearly ideal for the perception of the Eternal in the finite, the very form of 'the Sublime'.

Lowth's insights into the nature of so-called 'oriental' primitive poetry, appear to be relevant to the overall concern of the Romantic movement with time, from Chatterton's mediaevalism to Keats's *Hyperion*. Christopher Smart's enthusiastic comparison of Lowth's own verse to the fountains of Versailles (see p. 252) is highly suggestive in this regard, and Smart's instinctual analysis of a verse form of which he was the most skilled modern practitioner suggests concepts important as far at least as the poetry of Walt Whitman and the Imagists. As a critic of international stature, whose work influenced major European theorists, for example Herder (see *The Spirit of Hebrew Poetry*), Lowth stands practically alone in his era. One of the finest productions of the age of sensibility, his work affords one not only a consistently brilliant explication of doctrine, but intimacy with the finest texture of feeling in the mid-eighteenth century.

*

LECTURES ON THE SACRED POETRY OF THE HEBREWS

from Lecture I, 'Of the Uses and Design of Poetry'

Every species of Poetry has in fact its peculiar mode of acting on the human feelings; the general effect is perhaps the same. The Epic accomplishes its design with more leisure, with more consideration and care, and therefore probably with greater certainty. It more gradually insinuates itself, it penetrates, it moves, it delights; now rising to a high degree of sublimity, now subsiding to its accustomed smoothness; and conducting the reader through a varied and delightful scene, it applies a gentle constraint to the mind, making its impression by the forcible nature of this application, but more especially by its continuance. The Ode, on the contrary, strikes with an instantaneous effect, amazes, and as it were storms the affections. The one may be compared to a flame, which fanned by the winds, gradually spreads itself on all sides, and at last involves every object in the conflagration; the other to a flash of lightning, which instantaneously bursts forth, . . .

The amazing power of Lyric Poetry in directing the passions, in forming the manners, in maintaining civil life, and particularly in exciting and cherishing that generous elevation of sentiment, on which the very existence of public virture seems to depend, will be sufficiently apparent by only contemplating those monuments of Genius, which Greece has bequeathed to posterity.

*

These observations are remarkably exemplified in the Hebrew Poetry, than which the human mind can conceive nothing more elevated, more beautiful, or more elegant; in which the almost ineffable sublimity of the subject is fully equalled by the energy of the language, and the dignity of the style. And it is worthy observation, that as some of these writings exceed in antiquity the fabulous ages of Greece, in sublimity they are superior to the most finished productions of that polished people. Thus if the actual origin of Poetry be inquired after, it must of necessity be referred to Religion; and since it appears to be an art derived from nature alone, peculiar to no age or nation, and only at an advanced period of society conformed to rule and method, it must be wholly attributed to the more violent affections of the heart, the nature of which is to express themselves in an animated and lofty tone, with a vehemence of expression far remote from vulgar use. It is also no less observable, that these affections break and interrupt the enunciation by their impetuosity; they burst forth in sentences pointed, earnest, rapid, and tremulous; and in some degree the style as well as the modulation is adapted to the emotions and habits of the mind. This is particularly the case in admiration and delight; and what passions are so likely to be excited by religious contemplations as these? What ideas could so powerfully affect a new-created mind (undepraved by habit or opinion) as the goodness, the wisdom, and the greatness of the Almighty? Is it not probable, that the first effort of rude and unpolished verse would display itself in the praise of the Creator, and flow almost involuntarily from the enraptured mind.

*

from Lecture V, 'Figurative Language'

It is the peculiar design of the figurative style, taken in the sense in which I have explained it, to exhibit objects in a clearer or more striking, in a sublimer or more forcible manner. Since, therefore, whatever is employed with a view to the illustration and elevation of another subject, ought itself to be as familiar and obvious, at the same time as grand and magnificent as possible, it becomes necessary to adduce images from those objects with which both the writers and the persons they address are well acquainted, and which have been constantly esteemed of the highest dignity and importance. On the other hand, if the reader be accustomed to habits of life totally different from those of the author, and be conversant only with different objects; in that case many descriptions and sentiments, which were clearly illustrated and magnificently expressed by the one, will appear to the other mean and obscure, harsh and unnatural: and this will be the case more or less, in proportion as they differ or are more remote from each other in time, situation, customs sacred or profane, in fine, in all the forms of public and private life. On this account difficulties must occur in the perusal of almost every work of literature, and particularly in poetry, where every thing is depicted and illustrated with the greatest variety and abundance of imagery; they must be still more numerous in such of the poets as are foreign and ancient; in the Orientals above all foreigners, they being the farthest removed from our customs and manners; and of all the Orientals more especially in the Hebrews, theirs being confessedly the most ancient compositions extant. To all who apply themselves to the study of their poetry, for the reasons which I have enumerated, difficulties and inconveniencies must necessarily occur. Not only the antiquity of these writings forms a principal obstruction in many respects; but the manner of living, of speaking, of thinking, which prevailed in those times, will be found altogether different from our customs and habits. There is therefore great danger, lest viewing from an improper situation, and rashly estimating all things by our own standard, we form an erroneous judgment.

Of this kind of mistake we are to be always aware, and these inconveniencies are to be counteracted by all possible diligence: nor is it enough to be acquainted with the language of this people, their manners, discipline, rites and ceremonies; we must even investigate their inmost sentiments, the manner and connexion of their thoughts; in one word, we must see all things with their eyes, estimate all things by their opinions: we must endeavour as much as possible to read Hebrew as the Hebrews would have read it. We must act as the Astronomers with regard to that branch of their science which is called comparative, who, in order to form a more perfect idea of the general system, and its different parts, conceive themselves as passing through, and surveying the whole universe, migrating from one planet to another, and becoming for a short time inhabitants of each.* Thus they clearly contemplate, and accurately estimate what each possesses peculiar to itself with respect to situation, celerity, satellites, and its relation to the rest; thus they distinguish what and how different an appearance of the universe is exhibited according to the different situations from which it is contemplated. In like manner, he who would perceive and feel the peculiar and interior elegancies of the Hebrew poetry, must imagine himself exactly situated as the persons for whom it was written, or even as the writers themselves; he must not attend to the ideas which on a cursory reading certain words would obtrude upon his mind; he is to feel them as a Hebrew, hearing or delivering the same words, at the same time, and in the same country. As far as he is able to pursue this plan, so far he will comprehend their force and excellence. This indeed in many cases it will not be easy to do; in some it will be impossible; in all, however, it ought to be regarded, and in those passages particularly in which the figurative style is found to prevail.

In the Metaphor for instance (and what I remark concerning it may be applied to all the rest of the figures, since they are all naturally allied to each other) two circumstances are to be especially regarded, on which its whole force and elegance will depend: first, that resemblance which is the ground-work of the figurative and parabolic style, and which will perhaps be sufficiently apparent, even from a common and indistinct knowledge of the objects; and secondly, the beauty or dignity of the idea which is substituted for another; and this is a circumstance of unusual nicety. An opinion of grace and dignity results frequently, not so much from the objects themselves, in which these qualities are supposed to exist, as from the disposition of the spectator; or from some slight and obscure relation or connexion which they have with some other things. Thus it sometimes happens, that the external form and lineaments may be sufficiently apparent, though the original and intrinsic beauty and elegance be totally erased by time.

For these reasons, it will perhaps not be an useless undertaking, when we treat of the Metaphors of the sacred poets, to enter more fully into the nature of their poetical imagery in general, of which the Metaphor constitutes so principal a part. By this mode of proceeding, we shall be enabled not only to discern the general beauty and elegance of this figure

---

*N.B. The importance of the lens in the new aesthetics. Cf. Hume, p. 131, and see Introduction, p. 8. Ed.

in the Hebrew poetry, but the peculiar elegance, which it frequently possesses, if we only consider how forcible it must have appeared to those for whom it was originally intended; and what a connexion and agreement these figurative expressions must have had with their circumstances, feelings, and opinions. Thus many expressions and allusions, which even now appear beautiful, must, when considered in this manner, shine with redoubled lustre; and many, which now strike the superficial reader as coarse, mean, or deformed, must appear graceful, elegant, and sublime.

The whole course of nature, this immense universe of things, offers itself to human contemplation, and affords an infinite variety, a confused assemblage, a wilderness, as it were, of images, which being collected as the materials of poetry, are selected and produced as occasion dictates. The mind of man is that mirror of Plato, which as he turns about at pleasure, and directs to a different point of view, he creates another sun, other stars, planets, animals, and even another self. In this shadow or image of himself, which man beholds when the mirror is turned inward towards himself, he is enabled in some degree to contemplate the souls of other men: for, from what he feels and perceives in himself, he forms conjectures concerning others; and apprehends and describes the manners, affections, conceptions of others from his own. Of this assemblage of images, which the human mind collects from all nature, and even from itself, that is, from its own emotions and operations, the least clear and evident are those which are explored by reason and argument; the more evident and distinct are those which are formed from the impressions made by external objects on the senses; and of these, the clearest and most vivid are those which are perceived by the eye.* Hence poetry abounds most in those images which are furnished by the senses, and chiefly those of the sight; in order to depict the obscure by the more manifest, the subtile by the more substantial; and as far as simplicity is its object, it pursues those ideas which are most familiar and most evident; of which there is such an abundance, that they serve as well the purpose of ornament and variety, as that of illustration. [Cf. Hume, p. 126.]

*

from Lecture VI, 'The Objects of Nature'
In the first place, the Hebrew poets frequently make use of imagery borrowed from common life, and from objects well known and familiar. On this the perspicuity of figurative language will be found in a great measure to depend: For a principal use of Metaphors is to illustrate the subject by a tacit comparison; but if instead of familiar ideas, we introduce such as are new, and not perfectly understood; if we endeavour to

---

*We note, however, that this eye does not give the classical perspectives of reason. We are to see like Orientals, who, according to Lowth, perceive most clearly by means of emotion. Ed.

demonstrate what is plain by what is occult, instead of making a subject clearer, we render it more perplexed and difficult. To obviate this inconvenience, we must take care, not only to avoid the violent and too frequent use of Metaphors, but also not to introduce such as are obscure and but slightly related. From these causes, and especially from the latter, arises the difficulty of the Latin satyrist Persius; and but for the uncommon accuracy of the sacred poets in this respect, we should now be scarcely able to comprehend a single word of their productions.

In the next place, the Hebrews not only deduce their Metaphors from familiar, or well-known objects, but preserve one constant track and manner in the use and accommodation of them to their subject. The parabolic may indeed be accounted a peculiar style, in which things moral, political, and divine, are marked and represented by comparisons implied or expressed and adopted from sensible objects. As in common and plain language, therefore, certain words serve for signs of certain ideas; so for the most part, in the parabolic style, certain natural images serve to illustrate certain ideas more abstruse and refined. This assertion indeed is not to be understood absolutely without exception; but thus far at least we may affirm, that the sacred poets in illustrating the same subject, make a much more constant use of the same imagery than other poets are accustomed to: and this practice has a surprizing effect in preserving perspicuity.

I must observe in the last place, that the Hebrews employ more freely and more daringly that imagery in particular, which is borrowed from the most obvious and familiar objects, and the figurative effect of which is established and defined by general and constant use. This, as it renders a composition clear and luminous, even where there is the greatest danger of obscurity; so it shelters effectually the sacred poets from the imputation of exuberance, harshness, or bombast.

*

from Lecture XII, 'Simile or Comparison'
There are two operations of the mind, evidently contrary to each other. The one consists in combining ideas, the other in separating and distinguishing them. For in contemplating the innumerable forms of things, one of the first reflexions which occurs is, that there are some which have an immediate agreement, and some which are directly contrary to each other. The mind, therefore, contemplates those objects which have a resemblance in their universal nature in such a manner, as naturally to inquire whether in any respect they so disagree, as to furnish any mark of discrimination; on the contrary, it investigates those which are generally different in such a manner, as to remark whether, in their circumstances or adjuncts, they may not possess something in common, which may serve as a bond of connexion or association to class or unite them. The final cause of the former of these operations seems to be — to caution and guard us against error, in confounding one with another; of the latter, to form a kind

of repository of knowledge, which may be resorted to, as occasion serves, either for utility or pleasure. These constitute the two faculties, which are distinguished by the names of judgment and imagination. As accuracy of judgment is demonstrated by discovering in things, which have in general a very strong resemblance, some partial disagreement; so the genius or fancy is entitled to the highest commendation, when in those objects, which upon the whole have the least agreement, some striking similarity is traced out. In those comparisons, therefore, the chief purpose of which is ornament or pleasure, thus far may pass for an established principle, that they are most likely to accomplish this end, when the image is not only elegant and agreeable, but is also taken from an object, which in the general is materially different from the subject of comparison, and only aptly and pertinently agrees with it in one or two of its attributes.

*

A more complete example is scarcely to be found than that passage, in which Job impeaches the infidelity and ingratitude of his friends, who in his adversity denied him those consolations of tenderness and sympathy, which in his prosperous state, and when he needed them not, they had lavished upon him: he compares them with streams, which, increased by the rains of winter, overflow their borders, and display for a little time a copious and majestic torrent; but with the first impulse of the solar beams are suddenly dried up, and leave those, who unfortunately wander through the deserts of Arabia, destitute of water, and perishing with thirst. [Job 6: 15–20.]

*

from Lecture XIV, 'The Sublime in General'
I proceed to treat of the Sublimity of the sacred poets; a subject which has been already illustrated by many examples quoted upon other occasions; but which, since we have admitted it as a third characteristic of the poetic style, now requires to be distinctly explained. We have already seen, that this is implied in one of the senses of the word *Mashal*, it being expressive of power, or supreme authority, and when applied to style, seems particularly to intimate something eminent or energetic, excellent or important. This is certainly understood in the phrase 'to take (or lift) up his parable'; that is, to express a great or lofty sentiment. The very first instance, in which the phrase occurs, will serve as an example in point. For in this manner Balaam 'took up', as our translation renders it, 'his parable, and said':

From Aram I am brought by Balak,
By the king of Moab from the mountains of the East:
Come, curse me Jacob;
And come, execrate Israel.

How shall I curse whom God hath not cursed?
And how shall I execrate whom God hath not
   execrated?
For from the tops of the rocks I see him,
And from the hills I behold him;
Lo! the people, who shall dwell alone,
Nor shall number themselves among the nations!
Who shall count the dust of Jacob?
Or the number of the fourth of Israel?
Let my soul die the death of the righteous,
And let my end be as his.   [Numbers 23: 7–10]

Let us now consider, on what account this address of the prophet is entitled *Mashal*. The sentences are indeed accurately distributed in parallelisms [see pp. 162-164], as may be discovered even in the translation, which has not entirely obscured the elegance of the arrangement: and compositions in this form, we have already remarked, are commonly classed among the proverbs and adages, which are properly called *Mashalim*, though perhaps they contain nothing of a proverbial or didactic nature. But if we attentively consider this very passage, or others introduced by the same form of expression, we shall find, in all of them, either an extraordinary variety of figure and imagery; or an elevation of style and sentiment; or perhaps an union of all these excellencies; which will induce us to conclude, that something more is meant by the term to which I am alluding than the bare merit of a sententious neatness. If again we examine the same passage in another point of view, we shall discover in it little or nothing of the figurative kind, at least according to our ideas, or according to that acceptation of the word *Mashal* which denotes figurative language; there is evidently nothing in it of the mystical kind, nothing allegorical, no pomp of imagery, no comparison, and in fourteen verses but a single metaphor: as far, therefore, as figurative language is a characteristic of the parabolic style, this is no instance of it. We must then admit the word Parable, when applied to this passage, to be expressive of those exalted sentiments, that spirit of sublimity, that energy and enthusiasm, with which the answer of the prophet is animated. By this example I wished to explain on what reasons I was induced to suppose that the term *Mashal*, as well from its proper power or meaning, as from its usual acceptation, involves an idea of sublimity; and that the Hebrew poetry expresses in its very name and title, the particular quality in which it so greatly excels the poetry of all other nations.

*

The sublime consists either in language or sentiment, or more frequently in an union of both, since they reciprocally assist each other, and since there is a necessary and indissoluble connexion between them: this, however, will not prevent our considering them apart with convenience and advantage. The first object, therefore, which presents itself for our investigation, is, upon what grounds the poetic diction of the Hebrews, whether considered in itself, or in comparison with prose composition, is deserving of an appellation immediately expressive of sublimity.

The poetry of every language has a style and form of expression peculiar to itself; forcible, magnificent, and sonorous; the words pompous and energetic; the composition singular and artificial; the whole form and complexion different from what we meet with in common life, and frequently (as with a noble indignation) breaking down the boundaries by which the popular dialect is confined. The language of Reason is cool, temperate, rather humble than elevated, well arranged and perspicuous, with an evident care and anxiety lest any thing should escape which might appear perplexed or obscure. The language of the Passions is totally different: the conceptions burst out in a turbid stream, expressive in a manner of the internal conflict; the more vehement break out in hasty confusion; they catch (without search or study) whatever is impetuous, vivid, or energetic. In a word, Reason speaks literally, the Passions poetically. The mind, with whatever passion it be agitated, remains fixed upon the object that excited it; and while it is earnest to display it, is not satisfied with a plain and exact description; but adopts one agreeable to its own sensations, splendid or gloomy, jocund or unpleasant. For the passions are naturally inclined to amplification; they wonderfully magnify and exaggerate whatever dwells upon the mind, and labour to express it in animated, bold, and magnificent terms. This they commonly effect by two different methods; partly by illustrating the subject with splendid imagery, and partly by employing new and extraordinary forms of expression, which are indeed possessed of great force and efficacy in this respect especially, that they in some degree imitate or represent the present habit and state of the soul. Hence those theories of Rhetoricians, which they have so pompously detailed, attributing that to art, which above all things is due to nature alone. [Cf. Burke, p. 204.]

*

from Lecture XV, 'Sublimity of Expression'
In this case we ought to consider the proper genius and character of the Hebrew poetry. It is unconstrained, animated, bold, and fervid. The Orientals look upon the language of poetry as wholly distinct from that of common life, as calculated immediately for expressing the passions: if, therefore, it were to be reduced to the plain rule and order of reason, if every word and sentence were to be arranged with care and study, as if calculated for perspicuity alone, it would be no longer what they intended it, and to call it the language of passion would be the grossest of solecisms.

The other observation, to which I alluded as relating both to this poem and to the poetry of the Hebrews in general, is, that you there find a much more frequent change or variation of the tenses than occurs in common language. The chief aim of such a transition, is, to render the subject of a narration or description more striking, and even to embody and give it a visible existence. Thus in all languages, in prose as well as poetry, it is usual to speak of past as well as future events in the present tense, by which means whatever is described or expressed is in a manner brought immediately before our eyes; nor does the mind contemplate a distant object, by looking back to the past or forward to the future.* But in this respect there is a great peculiarity in the Hebrew language. For the Hebrew verbs have no form for expressing the imperfect or indefinite of the present tense, or an action which now is performing: this is usually effected by a participle only, or by a verb substantive understood, neither of which are often made use of in such passages as these, nor indeed can be always conveniently admitted. They, therefore, take another method of attaining this end, and for the sake of clearness and precision, express future events by the past tense, or rather by the perfect present, as if they had actually taken place; and, on the contrary, past events by the future, as if immediately or speedily to happen, and only proceeding towards their completion.

*

from Lecture XVI, 'Sublimity of Sentiment'
In the delineation of the Divine nature, the sacred poets do indeed, in conformity to the weakness of the human understanding, employ terrestrial imagery; but it is in such a manner, that the attributes which are borrowed from human nature and human action, can never in a literal sense be applied to the Divinity. The understanding is continually referred from the shadow to the reality; nor can it rest satisfied with the bare literal application, but is naturally directed to investigate that quality in the Divine nature, which appears to be analogous to the image. This, if I am not mistaken, will supply us with a reason not very obvious, of a very observable effect in the Hebrew writings, namely, why, among those sensible images that are applied to the Deity, those principally, which in a literal sense would seem most remote from the object, and most unworthy of the Divine Majesty, are nevertheless, when used metaphorically, or in the way of comparison, by far the most sublime. That imagery, for instance, which is taken from the parts and members of the human body, is found to be much nobler and more magnificent in its effect, than that which is taken from the passions of the mind; and that, which is taken from the animal creation, frequently exceeds in sublimity that which the nature of man has suggested. For such is our ignorance and blindness in contemplating the Divine nature, that we can

---

*These observations seem peculiarly appropriate to the Romantic displacement of time. Cf. for example, Coleridge's line 'Ancestral voices prophesying war' in *Kubla Khan*. Ed.

by no means attain to a simple and pure idea of it: we necessarily mingle something of the human with the divine: the grosser animal properties, therefore, we easily distinguish and separate, but it is with the utmost difficulty that we can preserve the rational, and even some of the properties of the sensitive, soul perfectly distinct. Hence it is, that in those figurative expressions derived from the nobler and more excellent qualities of human nature, when applied to the Almighty, we frequently acquiesce, as if they were in strict literal propriety to be attributed to him: on the contrary, our understanding immediately rejects the literal sense of those which seem quite inconsistent with the Divine Being, and derived from an ignoble source: and, while it pursues the analogy, it constantly rises to a contemplation, which, though obscure, is yet grand and magnificent. Let us observe whether this observation will apply to the following passages in which the Psalmist ascribes to God the resentment commonly experienced by a human creature for an injury unexpectedly received: there appears in the image nothing to excite our admiration, nothing particularly sublime:

The Lord heard, and he was enraged;
And Israel he utterly rejected.   [Psalm 78:59]

But when, a little after, the same subject is depicted in figurative terms, derived from much grosser objects, and applied in a still more daring manner, nothing can be more sublime:

And the Lord awaked, as out of sleep,
Like a strong man shouting because of wine.   [Ibid.: 65]

On the same principle the sublimity of those passages is founded, in which the image is taken from the roaring of a lion, the clamour of rustic labourers, and the rage of wild beasts:

Jehovah from on high shall roar,
And from his holy habitation shall he utter his voice:
He shall roar aloud against his resting-place,
A shout like that of the vintagers shall he give
Against all the inhabitants of the earth.   [Jeremiah, 25:30]

And I will be unto them as a lion;
As a leopard in the way will I watch them:
I will meet them as a bear bereaved of her whelps:
And I will rent the caul of their heart:
And there will I devour them as a lioness;
A beast of the field shall tear them.   [Hosea, 13:7, 8]

From ideas, which in themselves appear coarse, unsuitable, and totally unworthy of so great an object, the mind naturally recedes, and passes suddenly to the contemplation of the object itself, and of its inherent magnitude and importance.

*

from Lecture XVII, 'The Sublime of Passion'

The language of poetry I have more than once described as the effect of mental emotion. Poetry itself is indebted for its origin, character, complexion, emphasis, and application, to the effects which are produced upon the mind and body, upon the imagination, the senses, the voice, and respiration* by the agitation of passion. Every affection of the human soul, while it rages with violence, is a momentary phrenzy. When therefore a poet is able by the force of genius, or rather of imagination, to conceive any emotion of the mind so perfectly as to transfer to his own feelings the instinctive passion of another, and, agreeably to the nature of the subject, to express it in all its vigour, such a one, according to a common mode of speaking, may be said to possess the true poetic enthusiasm, or, as the ancients would have expressed it, 'to be inspired; full of the God:' not however implying, that their ardour of mind was imparted by the Gods, but that this ecstatic impulse became the God of the moment.

This species of enthusiasm I should distinguish by the term *natural*, were it not that I should seem to connect things which are really different, and repugnant to each other: the true and genuine enthusiasm, that which alone is deserving of the name, that I mean with which the sublimer poetry of the Hebrews, and particularly the prophetic, is animated, is certainly widely different in its nature, and boasts a much higher origin.

As poetry, however, derives its very existence from the more vehement emotions of the mind, so its greatest energy is displayed in the expression of them; and by exciting the passions it more effectually attains its end.

Poetry is said to consist in imitation: whatever the human mind is able to conceive, it is the province of poetry to imitate; things, places, appearances natural and artificial, actions, passions, manners and customs: and since the human intellect is naturally delighted with every species of imitation, that species in particular, which exhibits its own image, which displays and depicts those impulses, inflexions, perturbations, and secret emotions which it perceives and knows in itself, can scarcely fail to astonish and to delight above every other. The delicacy and difficulty of this kind of imitation are among its principal commendations; for to effect that which appears almost impossible naturally excites our admiration. The understanding slowly perceives the accuracy of the description in all other subjects, and their agreement to their archetypes, as being obliged to compare them by the aid and through the uncertain medium, as it were, of the memory:** but when a passion is expressed, the object is clear and distinct at once; the mind is immediately conscious of itself and its

---

*N.B. Lowth's 'modern' notion that art is a bodily phenomenon. Ed.

**Lowth's perception that great poetry is in effect not imitation but the mind's memory-less awareness of itself in process links him with the greatest Romantics, perhaps especially Keats. Ed.

own emotions; it feels and suffers in itself a sensation, either the same or similar to that which is described. Hence that sublimity, which arises from the vehement agitation of the passions, and the imitation of them, possesses a superior influence over the human mind; whatever is exhibited to it from without, may well be supposed to move and agitate it less than what it internally perceives, of the magnitude and force of which it is previously conscious.

*

from Lecture XIX, 'Prophetic Poetry'

The poetical conformation of the sentences, which has been so often alluded to as characteristic of the Hebrew poetry, consists chiefly in a certain equality, resemblance, or parallelism* between the members of each period; so that in two lines (or members of the same period), things for the most part shall answer to things, and words to words, as if fitted to each other by a kind of rule or measure. This parallelism has much variety and many gradations; it is sometimes more accurate and manifest, sometimes more vague and obscure: it may however, on the whole, be said to consist of three species.

The first species is the synonymous parallelism, when the same sentiment is repeated in different, but equivalent terms. This is the most frequent of all, and is often conducted with the utmost accuracy and neatness: examples are very numerous, nor will there be any great difficulty in the choice of them: on this account I shall select such as are most remarkable in other respects.

When Israel went out from Egypt;
The House of Jacob from a strange people:
Judah was as his sacred heritage;
Israel his dominion.
The sea saw, and fled;
Jordan turned back:
The mountains leaped like rams;
The hills like the sons of the flock.   [Psalm 114: 1–4]

*

There is great variety in the form of the synonymous paralellism, some instances of which are deserving of remark. The parallelism is sometimes formed by the iteration of the former member, either in the whole or in part:

Much have they oppressed me from my youth up,
May Israel now say;

---

*In his *Isaiah, A New Translation* (1778) Lowth put these principles into practice and added to his discussion of them. Ed.

Much have they oppressed me from my youth,
Yet have they not prevailed against me.   [Psalm 129: 1, 2]

*

Sometimes also there are triplet parallelisms. In these the second line is
generally synonymous with the first, whilst the third either begins the
period, or concludes it, and frequently refers to both the preceding;
    The floods have lifted up, O *Jehovah*,
    The floods have lifted up their voice;
    The floods have lifted up their waves.
    Than the voice of many waters,
    The glorious waves of the sea,
    Jehovah on high is more glorious.   [Psalm 93: 3, 4]

*

The Antithetic parallelism is the next that I shall specify, when a thing
is illustrated by its contrary being opposed to it. This is not confined to
any particular form: for sentiments are opposed to sentiments, words to
words, singulars to singulars, plurals to plurals, &c. of which the following
are examples:
    The blows of a friend are faithful;
    But the kisses of an enemy are treacherous.
    The cloyed will trample upon an honey-comb;
    But to the hungry every bitter thing is sweet.
    There is who maketh himself rich, and wanteth all things;
    Who maketh himself poor, yet hath much wealth.
    The rich man is wise in his own eyes,
    But the poor man that hath discernment to trace him out will
        despise him.   [Proverbs 27: 6, 7. 13: 7. 28: 11]
There is sometimes a contraposition of parts in the same sentence, such
as occurs once in the above; and as appears in the following:
    I am swarthy but comely, O daughters of Jerusalem;
    As the tents of Kedar, as the pavilions of Solomon.
                                              [Song of Solomon 1: 5]

*

There is a third species of parallelism, in which the sentences answer
to each other, not by the iteration of the same image or sentiment, or the
opposition of their contraries, but merely by the form of construction.
To this, which may be called the Synthetic or Constructive Parallelism,
may be referred all such as do not come within the two former classes:
I shall however produce a few of the most remarkable instances:
    The law of *Jehovah* is perfect, restoring the soul;

The testimony of *Jehovah* is sure, making wise the simple:
The precepts of *Jehovah* are right, rejoicing the heart;
The commandment of *Jehovah* is clear, enlightening the eyes:
The fear of *Jehovah* is pure, enduring for ever.
The judgments of *Jehovah* are truth, they are just altogether;
More desirable than gold, or than much fine gold;
And sweeter than honey, or the dropping of honey-combs.

[Psalm 19: 8, 10]

This kind of parallelism generally consists of verses somewhat longer than usual, of which there are not wanting examples in the prophets:

How hath the oppressor ceased! the exactress of gold ceased!
Jehovah hath broken the staff of the wicked, the sceptre of the rulers.
He that smote the people in wrath with a stroke unremitted;
He that ruled the nations in anger, is persecuted, and none hindereth.

[Isaiah 14: 4–6]

*

from Lecture XXI, 'The Peculiar Character of Each of the Prophets'

Isaiah, the first of the prophets, both in order and dignity, abounds in such transcendent excellencies, that he may be properly said to afford the most perfect model of the prophetic poetry. He is at once elegant and sublime, forcible and ornamented; he unites energy with copiousness, and dignity with variety. In his sentiments there is uncommon elevation and majesty; in his imagery the utmost propriety, elegance, dignity, and diversity; in his language uncommon beauty and energy; and, notwithstanding the obscurity of his subjects, a surprising degree of clearness and simplicity. To these we may add, there is such sweetness in the poetical composition of his sentences, whether it proceed from art or genius, that if the Hebrew poetry at present is possessed of any remains of its native grace and harmony, we shall chiefly find them in the writings of Isaiah: so that the saying of Ezekiel may most justly be applied to this prophet:

Thou art the confirmed exemplar of measures,
Full of wisdom, and perfect in beauty.   [Ezekiel 28: 12]

Isaiah greatly excels too in all the graces of method, order, connexion, and arrangement: though in asserting this we must not forget the nature of the prophetic impulse, which bears away the mind with irresistible violence, and frequently in rapid transitions from near to remote objects, from human to divine: we must also be careful in remarking the limits of particular predictions, since, as they are now extant, they are often improperly connected, without any marks of discrimination; which injudicious arrangement, on some occasions, creates almost insuperable difficulties.

*

Jeremiah, though deficient neither in elegance nor sublimity, must give place in both to Isaiah. Jerome seems to object against him a sort of rusticity of language, no vestige of which, I must however confess, I have been able to discover. His sentiments, it is true, are not always the most elevated, nor are his periods always neat and compact; but these are faults common to those writers, whose principal aim is to excite the gentler affections, and to call forth the tear of sympathy or sorrow. This observation is very strongly exemplified in the Lamentations, where these are the prevailing passions; it is, however, frequently instanced in the prophecies of this author, and most of all in the beginning of the book, which is chiefly poetical. The middle of it is almost entirely historical. The latter part, again, consisting of the six last chapters, is altogether poetical; it contains several different predictions, which are distinctly marked, and in these the prophet approaches very near the sublimity of Isaiah. On the whole, however, I can scarcely pronounce above half the book of Jeremiah to be poetical.

Ezekiel is much inferior to Jeremiah in elegance; in sublimity he is not even excelled by Isaiah: but his sublimity is of a totally different kind. He is deep, vehement, tragical; the only sensation he affects to excite is the terrible:* his sentiments are elevated, fervid, full of fire, indignant; his imagery is crowded, magnificent, terrific, sometimes almost to disgust; his language is pompous, solemn, austere, rough, and at times unpolished: he employs frequent repetitions, not for the sake of grace or elegance, but from the vehemence of passion and indignation. Whatever subject he treats of, that he sedulously pursues, from that he rarely departs, but cleaves as it were to it; whence the connexion is in general evident and well preserved. In many respects he is perhaps excelled by the other prophets; but in that species of composition to which he seems by nature adapted, the forcible, the impetuous, the great and solemn, not one of the sacred writers is superior to him. His diction is sufficiently perspicuous, all his obscurity consists in the nature of the subject. Visions (as for instance, among others, those of Hosea, Amos, and Jeremiah) are necessarily dark and confused. The greater part of Ezekiel, towards the middle of the book especially, is poetical, whether we regard the matter or the diction. His periods, however, are frequently so rude and incompact, that I am often at a loss how to pronounce concerning his performance in this respect.

Isaiah, Jeremiah, and Ezekiel, as far as relates to style, may be said to hold the same rank among the Hebrews, as Homer, Simonides, and Aeschylus among the Greeks.

*

---

*Lowth's father also uses this term. See his introduction to *Ezekiel*: William Lowth, *Commentary on the Prophets* (3rd ed., 1730) p. 254. Ed.

from Lecture XXV, 'Lyric Poetry'

There is scarcely any necessity to mention, that the most ancient of all poems extant (those I mean of which the date is ascertained, and which deserve the name of poems) is the thanksgiving Ode of Moses on passing the Red Sea, the most perfect in its kind, and the true and genuine effusion of the joyful affections. Thus the origin of the ode may be traced into that of poetry itself, and appears to be coeval with the commencement of religion, or more properly the creation of man. [Cf. Trapp, p. 57.]

The Hebrews cultivated this kind of poetry above every other, and therefore may well be supposed to have been peculiarly excellent in it. It was usual in every period of that nation to celebrate in songs of joy their gratitude to God, their Saviour, for every fortunate event, and particularly for success in war. Hence the triumphal odes of Moses, of Deborah, of David. The schools of the prophets were also, in all probability, coeval with the republic; and were certainly antecedent to the monarchy by many years: there, as we have already seen, the youth, educated in the prophetic discipline, applied themselves, among other studies, particularly to sacred poetry, and celebrated the praises of Almighty God in lyric compositions, accompanied with music. Under the government of David, however, the arts of music and poetry were in their most flourishing state. By him no less than four thousand singers or musicians were appointed from among the Levites, under two hundred and eighty-eight principal singers, or leaders of the band, and distributed into twenty-four companies, who officiated weekly by rotation in the temple, and whose whole business was to perform the sacred hymns; the one part chanting or singing, and the other playing upon different instruments. The chief of these were Asaph, Heman, and Iduthun, who also, as we may presume from the titles of the Psalms, were composers of hymns. From so very splendid an establishment, so far surpassing every other appointment of the kind, some reasonable conjectures may be formed concerning the original dignity and grandeur of the Hebrew Ode. We must remember too, that we at present possess only some ruins as it were of that magnificent fabric, deprived of every ornament, except that splendour and elegance, which, notwithstanding the obscurity that antiquity has cast over them, still shine forth in the sentiments and language. Hence, in treating of the Hebrew ode, we must be content to omit entirely what relates to the sacred music, and the nature of the instruments which accompanied the vocal performance; though there is the utmost probability, that these circumstances were not without their influence, as far as respects the form and construction of the different species of ode.

*

Of all the different forms of poetical composition, there is none more agreeable, harmonious, elegant, diversified, and sublime, than the ode; and these qualities are displayed in the order, sentiments, imagery, diction, and versification. The principal beauty of an ode consists in the order and arrangement of the subject; but this excellence, while it is easily felt, is difficult to be described, for there is this peculiarity attending it, that the form of the ode is by no means confined to any certain rule for the exact and accurate distribution of the parts. It is lively and unconstrained: when the subject is sublime, it is impetuous, bold, and sometimes might almost deserve the epithet licentious as to symmetry and method: but even in this case, and uniformly in every order, a certain facility and ease must pervade the whole, which may afford at least the appearance of unaffected elegance, and seem to prefer nature to art. This appearance is best preserved by an exordium plain, simple, and expressive; by a display and detail of incidents and sentiments rising delicately and artfully from each other, yet without any appearance of art; and by a conclusion not pointed or epigrammatic, but finishing by a gentle turn of the sentiment in a part where it is least expected, and sometimes as if by chance. Thus, it is not the metre or versification which constitutes this species of composition: for, unless all these circumstances be adverted to, it is plain, that, whatever be the merit of the production, it cannot with any propriety be termed an ode.

The sentiments and imagery must be suitable to the nature of the subject and the composition, which is varied and unconfined by strict rule or method. . . .

Lectures on the Sacred Poetry of the Hebrews, trans. G. Gregory, 1787

JOSEPH WARTON (1722–1800)

Thomas Warton (c.1688–1745) initiated a tradition and the influence of the most important Romantic family in his *Poems on Several Occasions* composed before he became Professor of Poetry at Oxford in 1718, when he rejected 'the songs that nobly tell,/How *Troy* was sacked and *Rome* began', explicitly praising the Biblical 'Sublime' of Young's *The Last Day* in a dedicatory poem.

His sons consolidated their father's leadership. Joseph composed Romantic poems, but more importantly systematized, especially in the first volume of his *Essay on the Genius and Writings of Pope* (1756), the early impulses of half a century.

Through Warton, for some time headmaster of Winchester, crossed and recrossed the paths of the school's Romantic *alumni*. 'The Sublime and the Pathetic are the two chief nerves of all genuine poesy', he writes in the Dedication of the *Essay* (*Essay*, I. x) to the author of the notably sublime and pathetic *Night Thoughts* (1742–45). Recording Young's superiority to Voltaire in their famous encounter, Warton noted, 'if the friendship with which Dr. Young honoured me does not mislead me, I think I may venture to affirm, that many high strokes of character in Zanga [i.e. *The Revenge*] ; many sentiments and images in his *Night-thoughts*; and many strong and forcible descriptions in his paraphrase on *Job*, mark him for a sublime and original genius' (*Essay*, II. 148–9). Robert Lowth's 'Latin prelections on the inimitable poesy of the Hebrews, abounding in remarks entirely new, delivered in the purest and most expressive language, are the richest augmentation literature has lately received', he writes in the *Essay* (I. 14), while in his edition of Pope, in some ways a continuation of the *Essay on Pope*, he notes that Lowth's lectures 'have been received and read with almost universal approbation at home and abroad', and regrets Pope's lack in writing his *Messiah* of the 'more accurate and animated' translation of *Isaiah* (1778) by Lowth and judges Lowth's translation of *Isaiah 14* 'in the first rank of the sublime' (*Works of Pope*, I. 93n 1 & 106. Cf. also Smart on this *Ode Prophetica*, pp. 250-252). 'I know no critical treatise better calculated to form the taste of young men of genius', he writes of Spence's *Essay on Pope's Odyssey* (see pp. 101-106) which had so strongly influenced his own *Essay on Pope*; 'lest it should be thought that this opinion arises from my partiality to a friend with whom I lived so many years in the happiest intimacy', he added, giving a glimpse of the human relations which so strongly contributed to Romantic theory, 'I will add, that this was also the opinion of three persons, from whose judgement there can be no appeal, Dr. Akenside, Bishop Lowth, and Mr. James Harris' (*Works of Pope*, I. xxxvi).

The *Essay* demotes Pope with comparative praise. Warton offers in the Dedication several categories of excellence, the first the sublime and pathetic, inhabited by Spenser, Shakespeare and Milton; the second, of ethical and moral poets of moderate genius, for example Dryden, Cowley, Gay and Waller; the third, witty, elegant, and fanciful spirits, Swift, Rochester, Donne, *et al*. The essay concludes after two volumes, in suggesting a place for Pope between the first and second groups, '*next* to Milton, and *just* above *Dryden*'. But clouds still obscure even this moon. Warton adds, even in his final paragraph, that this is a judgment about Pope seen whole; he would not dare, we suppose, contrast single passages, 'for there are parts and passages in other modern authors, in *Young* and *Thomson,* for instance, equal to any of Pope; and he has written nothing in a strain so truly sublime, as the *Bard* of *Gray*' (*Essay*, II. 411).

The polarizing of the essay into a progress one by one through Pope's works, and, on the other hand, a fluctuating image drawn from Bassano, Domechino, Rosa and others, of a 'Nature' which is inappropriate to Pope, casts structural doubts even on Warton's moderate warmth. A key contrast is that between Warton on Pope's *Pastorals* and Thomson's *Seasons*. Images appropriate to Theocritus' Sicily in the fourth century B.C. are given short shrift. The images of other times and other places, of central importance to Pope's art, are not found in Thomson. Thomson's scenes are 'frequently as wild and romantic as those of Salvator Rosa' (*Essay*, I, 43). 'Thomson was accustomed to wander away into the country for days and for weeks attentive to "each rural sight, each rural sound"; while many a poet who has dwelt for years in the Strand, has attempted to describe fields and rivers, and generally succeeded accordingly' (*Essay*, I. 42). 'Innumerable are the little circumstances' (p. 178). Warton goes on with a telling phrase which recalls Spence's insistence on particulars in his *Essay on Pope's Odyssey*, 'totally unobserved by all his predecessors'. Fled is the art of 'what oft was thought'. A single leaf in Autumn rustles and then 'slowly circles through the waving air' startling the rapt solitary in the woods (I. 44), downy seeds whiten in the breeze, a shower patters on the leaves, while 'worthy the pencil of Giacamo da Bassano' cattle 'stand/Half in the flood, and often bending sip/The circling surface' (*Essay*, I. 44–46). Most interestingly, each of Warton's examples, the spiralling leaf, the parachuting seeds, the water shaking the leaves, and especially the cattle bending to sip at the ever-circling stream around their knees, are vivid examples of Young's − or 'John Lizard's' − observation on the techniques of primitive poetry in *Guardian* No. *86* (see pp. 140-143) that emotion or feeling is caused by images of motion. In spite of Bassano, perspective, even sight is not paramount.

The crucial distinction is that in Pope all observations had oft been thought. In Thomson no part of a single one had. The poet's perception was a self-contained, we might hazard, solipsistic, event. Through his fibres, in a manner distant from judgment or contrast, movement was apprehended by a parallel disturbance of the senses and emotions, in a totally new event which was at least half-creative. Warton's phrase, 'innumerable are the little circumstances' comes close to Thomson's awareness of 'ten thousand thousand' insect forms extending beyond our sight, and distantly images a notion of Nature as an eternal continuum dependent on man's heuristic partnership. One might argue that we are not yet in the presence of Romanticism, since the medium is emotion, not imagination. However, the absence of any sense of precedent, and hence of memory, suggests a doctrinal and aesthetic relation with, for example, Blake's *The Fly*, or Coleridge's *Frost at Midnight*. In the self-contained moments which are the high points of Thomson, man does not know whether Nature is or is not external to perception or where it begins and the observer commences. Through Warton's *Essay on Pope* runs the high-road to all the poetry of imagination and the heart of Romanticism.

from *AN ESSAY ON THE GENIUS AND WRITINGS OF POPE, Part i, (1756)*

'To the Reverend Dr. Young, Rector of Welwyn in Hertfordshire'
Dear Sir,

Permit me to break into your retirement, the residence of virtue and literature, and to trouble you with a few reflections on the merits and real character of an admired author, and on other collateral subjects, that will naturally arise. No love of singularity, no affectation of paradoxical opinions, gave rise to the following work. I revere the memory of *Pope*, I respect and honour his abilities; but I do not think him at the head of his profession. In other words, in that species of poetry wherein *Pope* excelled, he is superior to all mankind: and I only say, that this species of poetry is not the most excellent one of the art. We do not, it should seem, sufficiently attend to the difference there is, betwixt *a Man of Wit, a Man of Sense*, and *a True Poet*. Donne and Swift, were undoubtedly men of wit, and men of sense: but what traces have they left of *Pure Poetry*? Fontenelle and La Motte are entitled to the former character; but what can they urge to gain the latter? Which of these characters is the most valuable and useful, is entirely out of the question: all I plead for, is, to have their several provinces kept distinct from each other; and to impress on the reader, that a clear head, and acute understanding are not sufficient, alone, to make a *Poet*; that the most solid observations on human life, expressed with the utmost elegance and brevity, are *Morality*, and not *Poetry*; that the *Epistles* of Boileau in *Rhyme*, are no more poetical, than the *Characters* of Bruyere in *Prose*; and that it is a creative and glowing *Imagination*, 'acer spiritus ac vis,* and that alone, that can stamp a writer with this exalted and very uncommon character, which so few possess, and of which so few can properly judge.

For one person, who can adequately relish, and enjoy, a work of

---

*Horace, *Sat.* I. iv. 46. 'The fire and strength of inspiration.' Ed.

imagination, twenty are to be found who can taste and judge of, observations on familiar life, and the manners of the age. The satires of Ariosto,
are more read than the *Orlando Furioso*, or even Dante. Are there so
many cordial admirers of Spenser and Milton, as of *Hudibras*? — If we
strike out of the number of these supposed admirers, those who appear
such out of fashion, and not of feeling. Swift's rhapsody on poetry is far
more popular, than Akenside's noble ode to Lord Huntingdon. The
Epistles on the Characters of men and women, and your sprightly
satires, my good friend, are more frequently perused, and quoted, than
L'Allegro and *Il Penseroso* of Milton. Had you written only these satires,
you would indeed have gained the title of a man of wit, and a man of
sense; but I am confident, would not insist on being denominated a *Poet*,
merely on their account.

Non satis est puris versum perscribere verbis.*

It is amazing this matter should ever have been mistaken, when Horace
has taken particular and repeated pains, to settle and adjust the opinion
in question. He has more than once disclaimed all right and title to the
name of *Poet*, on the score of his ethic and satiric pieces.

—Neque enim concludere versum

Dixeris esse satis—**

are lines, often repeated, but whose meaning is not extended and weighed
as it ought to be. Nothing can be more judicious than the method he
prescribes, of trying whether any composition be essentially poetical or
not; which, is to drop entirely the measures and numbers, and transpose
and invert the order of the words: and in this unadorned manner to
peruse the passage. If there be really in it a true poetical spirit, all your
inversions and transpositions will not disguise and extinguish it; but it
will retain its lustre, like a diamond, unset, and thrown back into the
rubbish of the mine. Let us make a little experiment on the following
well-known lines;

> *Yes, you despise the man that is confined to books, who rails at
> human kind from his study; tho' what he learns, he speaks; and may
> perhaps advance some general maxims, or may be right by chance,
> The coxcomb bird, so grave and so talkative, that cries whore, knave,
> cuckold, from his cage, tho' he rightly call many a passenger, you hold
> him no philosopher. And yet, such is the fate of all extremes, men
> may be read too much, as well as books. We grow more partial, for
> the sake of the observer, to observations which we ourselves make;
> less, so, to written wisdom, because another's. Maxims are drawn
> from notions, and those from guess.*   [Cf. Pope, *Moral Essays*, I. 1ff]

What shall we say of this passage? — Why, that it is most excellent sense,

---

*Horace, *Sat*. I. iv. 54. 'It is not sufficient to write out a line of mere
words.' Ed.

**Horace, *Sat*. I. iv. 40. 'You would not say it was enough to have rounded
off a verse.' Ed.

but just as poetical as the 'Qui fit Maecenas' [first line of Horace's first book of satires. 'Why is it Maecenas?'] of the author who recommends this method of trial. Take any ten lines of the *Iliad*, *Paradise Lost*, or even of the *Georgics* of Virgil, and see whether by any process of critical chymistry, you can lower and reduce them to the tameness of prose. You will find that they will appear like Ulysses in his disguise of rags, still a hero, tho' lodged in the cottage of the herdsman Eumaeus.

The Sublime and the Pathetic are the two chief nerves of all genuine poesy. What is there very Sublime or very Pathetic in *Pope?* In his works there is indeed, 'nihil inane, nihil arcessitum; — puro tamen fonti quam magno flumini propior;'* as the excellent Quintilian remarks of Lysias. And because I am perhaps ashamed or afraid to speak out in plain English, I will adopt the following passage of Voltaire, which, in my opinion, as exactly characterizes *Pope*, as it does his model Boileau, for whom it was originally designed.

'*Incapable peutêtre du sublime qui élève l'âme, et du sentiment qui l'attendrit mais fait pour éclairer ceux à qui la nature accorda l'un et l'autre, laborieux, sévère, précis, pur, harmonieux, il devint, enfin, le poète de la raison.'**

Our English poets may, I think, be disposed in four different classes and degrees. In the first class, I would place, first, our only three sublime and pathetic poets; *Spenser, Shakespeare, Milton*; and then, at proper intervals, *Otway* and *Lee*. In the second class should be placed, such as possessed the true poetical genius, in a more moderate degree, but had noble talents for moral and ethical poesy. At the head of these are *Dryden, Donne, Denham, Cowley, Congreve*. In the third class may be placed, men of wit, of elegant taste, and some fancy in describing familiar life. Here may be numbered, *Prior, Waller, Parnell, Swift, Fenton*. In the fourth class, the mere versifiers, however smooth and mellifluous some of them may be thought, should be ranked. Such as *Pitt, Sandys, Fairfax, Broome, Buckingham, Lansdown*. In which of these classes *Pope* deserves to be placed, the following work is intended to determine.

> I am, Dear Sir,
> Your affectionate
> And faithful servant.

*

That the design of pastoral poesy is, to represent the undisturbed felicity of the golden age, is an empty notion, which, though supported by a Rapin and a Fontenelle, I think, all rational critics have agreed to extirpate and explode. But I do not remember, that even these last-

---

Instit. X. i. 78. 'Nothing formless or laboured, but more a spring than a great river.' Ed.

**Discours à l'Académie, 1746*. Ed.

mentioned critics have remarked the circumstance that gave origin to the opinion that any golden age was intended. Theocritus, the father and the model of this enchanting species of composition, lived and wrote in Sicily. The climate of Sicily was delicious, and the face of the country various, and beautiful: it's vallies and it's precipices, it's grottos and cascades were *Sweetly Interchanged*, and it's fruits and flowers were lavish and luscious. The poet described what he saw and felt: and had no need to have recourse to those artificial assemblages of pleasing objects, which are not to be found in nature. The figs and the honey which he assigns as a reward to a victorious shepherd were in themselves exquisite, and are therefore assigned with great propriety: and the beauties of that luxurious landscape so richly and circumstantially delineated in the close of the seventh idyllium, where all things smelt of summer and smelt of autumn, were present and real. Succeeding writers supposing these beauties too great and abundant to be real, referred them to the fictitious and imaginary scenes of a golden age.

A *Mixture* of British and Grecian ideas may justly be deemed a blemish in the *Pastorals* of *Pope*: and propriety is certainly violated, when he couples Pactolus with Thames, and Windsor with Hybla. Complaints of *immoderate* heat, and wishes to be conveyed to cooling caverns, when uttered by the inhabitants of Greece, have a decorum and consistency, which they totally lose in the character of a British shepherd: and Theocritus, during the ardors of Sirius, must have heard the murmurings of a brook, and the whispers of a pine, with more homefelt pleasure, than Pope could possibly experience upon the same occasion. We can never completely relish, or adequately understand any author especially any Ancient, except we constantly keep in our eye his climate, his country, and his age. [Cf. Lowth, p. 153, and Blackwell, pp. 108-109.] *Pope* himself informs us, in a note, that he judiciously omitted the following verse,

And list'ning wolves grow milder as they hear.   [*Summer*, 79]

on account of the absurdity, which Spenser overlooked, of introducing wolves into England. But on this principle, which is certainly a just one, may it not be asked, why he should speak, the scene lying in Windsor-Forest, of the *Sultry Sirius*, of the *Grateful Clusters of grapes*, of a *pipe of reeds*, the antique fistula, of *thanking Ceres for a plentiful harvest*, of *the sacrifice of lambs* [*Summer*, 21, *Autumn*, 74, *Summer*, 41, 66, *Winter*, 81], with many other instances that might be adduced to this purpose. That *Pope* however was sensible of the importance of adapting images to the scene of action, is obvious from the following example of his judgement; for in translating,

Audiit *Eurotas*, jussitque ediscere *Lauros*

he has dextrously dropt the *laurels* appropriated to Eurotas, as he is speaking of the river Thames, and has rendered it,

Thames heard the numbers, as he flow'd along,
And bade his *willows* learn the moving song.
[Virgil, *Ecl*. vi. 83 and Pope, *Winter*, 13, 14]
In the passages which *Pope* has imitated from Theocritus, and from his
Latin translator Virgil, he has merited but little applause. It may not be
unentertaining to see how coldly and unpoetically *Pope* has copied the
subsequent appeal to the nymphs on the death of Daphnis, in comparison
of Milton on *Lycidas*, one of his juvenile pieces. . . .
Where stray, ye muses, in what lawn or grove,
While your Alexis pines in hopeless love?
In those fair fields where sacred Isis glides,
Or else where Cam his winding vales divides.

Where were ye, nymphs, when the remorseless deep
Clos'd o'er the head of your lov'd Lycidas?
For neither were ye playing on the steep
Where your old bards, the famous Druids, lie;
Nor on the shaggy top of Mona high,
Nor yet where Deva spreads her wizard stream.
[*Summer*, 23–6, *Lycidas*, 50–5]
The mention of places remarkably romantic, the supposed habitation
of Druids, bards, and wizards, is far more pleasing to the imagination, than
the obvious introduction of Cam and Isis, as seats of the Muses.
A *Shepherd* in Theocritus wishes with much tenderness and elegance,
both which must suffer in a literal translation,
Would I could become a murmuring bee, fly into your grotto, and be
permitted to creep among the leaves of ivy and fern that compose
the chaplet which adorns your head.
Pope has thus altered this image,
Oh! were I made by some transforming pow'r,
The captive bird that sings within thy bow'r!
Then might my voice thy list'ning ears employ;
And I, those kisses he receives, enjoy.   [*Idyll* iii, *Summer*, 45–8]
On three accounts the former image is preferable to the latter; for the
pastoral wildness, the delicacy, and the uncommonness of the thought. I
cannot forbear adding, that the riddle of the *Royal Oak*, in the first
Pastoral, invented in imitation of the Virgilian aenigmas in the third
eclogue, favours of pun, and puerile conceit.
Say, Daphnis, say in what glad soil appears
A wondrous tree, that sacred monarchs bears?   [*Spring*, 85–6]
With what propriety could the tree, whose shade protected the king, be
said to be prolific of princes?
That *Pope* has not equalled Theocritus, will indeed appear less sur-
prising, if we *reflect* that no original writer ever remained so unrivalled
by succeeding copyists as this Sicilian master.
If it should be objected, that the barrenness of invention imputed to

Pope from a view of his *Pastorals*, is equally imputable to the *Bucolics* of Virgil, it may be answered, that whatever may be determined of the rest, yet the first and last *Eclogues* of Virgil are indisputable proofs of true genius, and power of fancy. The influence of war on the tranquility of rural life, rendered the subject of the first new, and interesting: its composition is truly dramatic; and the characters of it's two shepherds are well supported, and happily contrasted: and the last has expressively painted the changeful resolutions, the wild wishes, the passionate and abrupt exclamations, of a disappointed and despairing lover.

Upon the whole, the principal merit of the *Pastorals* of *Pope* consists, in their correct and musical versification; musical, to a degree of which rhyme could hardly be thought capable: and in giving the first specimen of that harmony in English verse, which is now become indispensably necessary; and which has so forcibly and universally influenced the publick ear, as to have rendered every moderate rhymer melodious. *Pope* lengthened the abruptness of Waller, and at the same time contracted the exuberance of Dryden.

I *remember* to have been informed, by an intimate friend of *Pope*, that he had once laid a design of writing *American Eclogues*. The subject would have been fruitful of the most poetical imagery; and, if properly executed, would have rescued the author from the accusation here urged, of having written Eclogues without invention.

Our author, who had received an early tincture of religion, a reverence for which he preserved to the last, was with justice convinced, that the scriptures of God contained not only the purest precepts of morality, but the most elevated and sublime strokes of genuine poesy; strokes as much superior to any thing Heathenism can produce, as is Jehovah to Jupiter. This is the case more particularly in the exalted prophesy of *Isaiah*, which *Pope* has so successfully versified in an Eclogue, that incontestably surpasses the Pollio of Virgil: although perhaps the dignity, the energy, and the simplicity of the original are in a few passages weakened and diminished by florid epithets, and useless circumlocutions.

> See nature hastes her earliest wreaths to bring,
> With all the incense of the breathing spring.   [*Messiah*, 23–4]

are lines which have too much prettiness, and too modern an air. The judicious addition of circumstances and adjuncts is what renders poesy a more lively imitation of nature than prose. *Pope* has been happy in introducing the following circumstance: the prophet says, 'The parched ground shall become a pool;' Our author expresses this idea by saying, that the shepherd,

> – *shall start* amid the thirsty wild to hear
> New falls of water murmuring in his ear.   [69–70]

A striking example of a similar beauty may be added from Thompson. Melisander, in the Tragedy of *Agamemnon*, after telling us he was conveyed in a vessel, at mid-night, to the wildest of the Cyclades, adds, when the pitiless mariners had left him in that dreadful solitude,

– I never heard
A sound so dismal as their parting oars.   [III. i.]
On the other hand, the prophet has been sometimes particular, when
Pope has been only general.

Lift up thine eyes round about, and see; all they gather themselves
together, they come to thee: – The multitude of *Camels* shall
cover thee: the *Dromedaries* of Median and Ephah: all they from
Sheba shall come: they shall bring gold and incense, and they
shall shew forth the praise of the Lord. All the *Flocks* of Kedar
shall be gathered together unto thee; the *Rams* of Nebaioth shall
minister unto thee.   [Isaiah, 60: 4–7]

In imitating this passage, *Pope* has omitted the different beasts that in so
picturesque a manner characterize the different countries which were to
be gathered together on this important event, and says only in undis-
tinguishing terms,

See barbarous nations at thy gates attend,
Walk in thy light, and in thy temple bend;
See thy bright altars throng'd with prostrate kings,
And heap'd with products of Sabaean springs.   [Messiah, 91–4]

As prosperity and happiness are described in this Eclogue by a combination of the most pleasing and agreeable objects, so misery and
destruction are as forcibly delineated in the same *Isaiah*, by the circumstances of distress and desolation, that were to attend the fall of
that magnificent city, Babylon: and the latter is perhaps a more proper
and interesting subject for poetry than the former; as such kinds of
objects make the deepest impression on the mind: pity being a stronger
sensation than complacency. Accordingly a noble ode on the destruction
of Babylon, taken from the fourteenth chapter of Isaiah [cf. Smart, pp.
251-252], has been written by Mr Lowth, whose latin prelections on the
inimitable poesy of the Hebrews, abounding in remarks entirely new,
delivered in the purest and most expressive language, are the richest
augmentation literature has lately received; and from which the following
passage gradually unfolding the singular beauties of this prophecy, is here
closely, though faintly, translated, and inserted as a pattern of just
criticism.

'The prophet having predicted the deliverance of the Jews, and their
return into their own country from their rigorous Babylonish captivity,
instantly introduces them singing a certain triumphal song on the fall of
the king of Babylon; a song abounding in the most splendid images, and
carried on by perpetual, and those very beautiful, personifications. The
song begins with a sudden exclamation of the Jews, expressing their joy
and wonder at the unexpected change of their condition, and death of the
tyrant. Earth with her inhabitants triumphs; the firs and cedars of
Libanus, under which images the allegoric style frequently shadows the
kings and princes of the Gentiles, rejoice, and insult with reproaches the
broken power of their most implacable foe.

She is at rest, the whole earth is quiet: they break forth into singing.
Even the firs rejoice at thee, the cedars of Libanus:
Since thou art laid low, no feller is come up against us.*

There follows a most daring prosopopeia of *Orcus*, or the infernal regions: he rouzes his inhabitants, the manes of princes, and the shades of departed kings: immediately all of them arise from their thrones, and walk forward to meet the king of Babylon, they insult and deride him, and gather consolation from his calamity.

Art thou also made weak as we? art thou made like unto us?
Is thy pride dashed down to Orcus, the noise of thy harps?
The worm is strewn under thee, the earth-worm is thy covering!

The Jews are again represented speaking: they most strongly exaggerate his remarkable fall, by an exclamation formed in the manner of funeral lamentations:

How art thou fallen from heaven, O Lucifer, son of the morning!
Thou art dashed down to the earth, thou that didst crush the nations!

They next represent the king himself speaking, and madly boasting of his unbounded power, whence the prodigiousness of his ruin is wonderfully aggravated. Nor is this enough; a new personage is immediately formed: Those are introduced who found the body of the king of Babylon cast out: they survey it closely and attentively, and at last hardly know it.

Is this the man who made earth tremble, who shook the kingdoms?
Who made the world a solitude, and destroyed it's cities?

They reproach him with the loss of the common rite of sepulture, which was deservedly denied to him for his cruelty and oppression, and curse his name, his race, and posterity. The scene is closed by a most awful speech of God himself, menacing a perpetual extirpation to the king of Babylon, to his descendants, and to his city; and confirming the immutability of his councils by the ratification of a solemn oath.

What images, how various, how thicksown, how sublime, exalted with what energy, what expressions, figures, and sentiments, are here accumulated together! we hear the Jews, the cedars of Libanus, the shades of the departed kings, the king of Babylon, those who find his body, and lastly Jehovah himself, all speaking in order; and behold them acting their several parts, as it were in a drama. One continued action is carried on; or rather a various and manifold series of different actions is connected. Every excellence, more peculiarly appropriated to the sublimer ode, is consummately displayed in this poem of *Isaiah*, which is the most perfect and unexampled model, among all the monuments of antiquity. The personages are frequent, but not confused; are bold but not affected; a free, lofty, and truly divine spirit predominates through the whole. Nor is any thing wanting to crown and complete the sublimity of this ode with absolute beauty; nor can the Greek or Roman poesy produce any thing that is similar, or second, to this ode.'

---

*This and the following are from Isaiah 14. Ed.

[Robert Lowth, *On the Sacred Poetry of the Hebrews*, from Lecture XIII.]

*

It would be unpardonable to conclude these remarks on descriptive poesy, without taking notice of the *Seasons* of Thomson, who had peculiar and powerful talents for this species of composition. Let the reader therefore pardon a digression, if such it be, on his merits and character. Thomson was blessed with a strong and copious fancy; he hath enriched poetry with a variety of new and original images, which he painted from nature itself, and from his own actual observations: his descriptions have therefore a distinctness and truth, which are utterly wanting to those, of poets who have only copied from each other, and have never looked abroad on the objects themselves. Thomson was accustomed to wander away into the country for days and for weeks, attentive to, 'each rural sight, each rural sound;' while many a poet who has dwelt for years in the Strand, has attempted to describe fields and rivers, and generally succeeded accordingly. Hence that nauseous repetition of the same circumstances; hence that disgusting impropriety of introducing what may be called a set of hereditary images, without proper regard to the age, or climate, or occasion, in which they were formerly used.* Though the diction of the *Seasons* is sometimes harsh and inharmonious, and sometimes turgid and obscure, and though in many instances, the numbers are not sufficiently diversified by different pauses, yet is this poem on the whole, from the numberless strokes of nature in which it abounds, one of the most captivating and amusing in our language, and which, as its beauties are not of a fugacious kind, as depending on particular customs and manners, will ever be perused with delight. The scenes of Thomson are frequently as wild and romantic as those of Salvator Rosa, pleasingly varied with precipices and torrents, and 'castled cliffs', and deep vallies, with piny mountains, and the gloomiest caverns. Innumerable are the little circumstances in his descriptions, totally unobserved by all his predecessors. What poet hath ever taken notice of the leaf, that towards the end of autumn,

> Incessant rustles from the mournful grove,
> Oft startling such as studious walk below,
> And slowly circles through the waving air.
> > [*The Seasons* (1746), *Autumn*, 990-2]

Or who, in speaking of a summer evening, hath ever mentioned,

> The quail that clamours for his running mate?   [*Summer*, 1657]

Or the following natural image, at the same time of the year?

> Wide o'er the thistly lawn, as swells the breeze,

---

*It would be hard to imagine a more fundamental attack on Neo-classical imitation. See Introduction, pp. 2 and 7. Ed.

A whitening shower of vegetable down
Amusive floats.   [1658–60]
Where do we find the silence and expectation that precedes an April shower
insisted on, as in line 165 of *Spring*, or where,

The stealing shower is scarce to patter heard
By such as wander through the forest walks,
Beneath th' umbrageous multitude of leaves.   [177–9]

How full, particular and picturesque is this assemblage of circumstances
that attend a very keen frost in a night of winter!

Loud rings the frozen earth, and hard reflects
A double noise; while at his evening watch
The village dog deters the nightly thief;
The heifer lows; the distant water-fall
Swells in the breeze; and with the hasty tread
Of traveller, the hollow-sounding plain
Shakes from afar.   [*Winter*, 732–8]

In no one subject are common poets more confused and unmeaning, than
in their descriptions of rivers, which are generally said only to wind and
to murmur, while their qualities and courses are seldom accurately
marked; examine the exactness of the ensuing description, and consider
what a perfect idea it communicates to the mind.

Around th' adjoining brook, that purls along
The vocal grove, now fretting o'er a rock,
Now scarcely moving through a reedy pool,
Now starting to a sudden stream, and now
Gently diffus'd into a limpid plain;
A various group the herds and flocks compose,
Rural confusion!   [*Summer*, 480-6]

A group worthy of the pencil of Giacomo da Bassano, and so minutely
delineated, that he might have worked from this sketch;

. . . On the grassy bank
Some ruminating lie; while others stand
Half in the flood, and often bending sip
The circling surface.   [486–9]

He adds, that the ox in the middle of them,

. . . From his sides
The troublous insects lashes, to his sides
Returning still.   [491–3]

A natural circumstance, that to the best of my remembrance hath
escaped even the natural Theocritus. Nor do I recollect that any poet
hath been struck with the murmurs of the numberless insects, that
swarm abroad at the noon of a summer's day; as attendants of the
evening indeed, they have been mentioned;

Resounds the living surface of the ground:
Nor undelightful is the ceaseless hum
To him who muses through the woods at noon;

Or drowsy shepherd, as he lies reclin'd
With half-shut eyes.   [281–5]

But the novelty and nature we admire in the descriptions of Thomson is
by no means his only excellence; he is equally to be praised, for impressing
on our minds the effects, which the scene delineated would have on the
present spectator or hearer. Thus having spoken of the roaring of the
savages in the wilderness of Africa, he introduces a captive, who though
just escaped from prison and slavery under the tyrant of Morocco, is so
terrified and astonished at the dreadful uproar, that,

The wretch half wishes for his bonds again.   [*Summer*, 936]

Thus also having described a caravan lost and overwhelmed in one of
those whirlwinds that so frequently agitate and lift up the whole sands
of the desert, he finishes his picture by adding that,

— In Cairo's crouded street
Th' impatient merchant, wondering waits in vain,
And Mecca saddens at the long delay.   [977–9]

And thus, lastly, in describing the pestilence that destroyed the British
troops at the seige of Carthagena, he has used a circumstance inimitably
lively, picturesque, and striking to the imagination; for he says that the
admiral not only heard the groans of the sick that echoed from ship to
ship, but that he also pensively stood, and listened, at midnight to the
dashing of the waters, occasioned by the throwing the dead bodies into
the sea;

Heard, nightly, plung'd into the sullen waves,
The frequent corse.   [1048–9]

A minute and particular* enumeration of circumstances judiciously selected,
is what chiefly discriminates poetry from history, and renders the former,
for that reason, a more close and faithful representation of nature than
the latter. And if our poets would accustom themselves to contemplate
fully every object, before they attempted to describe it, they would not
fail of giving their readers more new images than they generally do.

These observations on Thomson, which however would not have been
so large if there had been already any considerable criticism on his
character, might be still augmented by an examination and development
of the beauties in the loves of the birds, in *Spring*, line 580. A view of the
torrid zone in *Summer*, line 626. The rise of fountains and rivers in
Autumn, line 781. A man perishing in the snows, in *Winter*, line 277, and
the wolves descending from the Alps, and a view of winter within the
polar circle, line 809, which are all of them highly finished originals,
excepting a few of those blemishes intimated above.** *Winter* is in my
apprehension the most valuable of these four poems, the scenes of it,
like those of *Il Penseroso* of Milton, being of that awful, and solemn,

---

*See Spence on particulars, pp. 103-104. Ed.
**There is some variation in line numbers between Warton and the edition
   of 1746. Ed.

and pensive kind, on which a great genius best delights to dwell.

*

I am not persuaded that all true genius died with *Pope*: and presume that the *Seasons* of Thomson, the *Pleasures of Imagination*, and *Odes*, of Akenside, the *Night-thoughts* of Young, the *Leonidas* of Glover, the *Elegy* of Gray, together with many pieces in Dodsley's *Miscellanies*, were not published when Dr. Warburton delivered this insinuation of a failure of poetical abilities.

> So pleas'd at first the tow'ring Alps we try,
> Mount o'er the vales, and seem to tread the sky,
> Th' eternal snows appear already past,
> And the first clouds, and mountains seem the last:
> But, those attain'd, we tremble to survey
> The growing labours of the lengthen'd way;
> Th' increasing prospect tires our wand'ring eyes,
> Hills peep o'er hills, and Alps on Alps arise.

[*An Essay on Criticism*, 225–232]

This comparison is frequently mentioned, as an instance of the strength of fancy. The images however appear too general and indistinct, and the last line conveys no new idea to the mind. The following picture in Shaftesbury, on the same sort of subject, appears to be more full and striking, 'Beneath the mountain's foot, the rocky country rises into hills, a proper basis of the ponderous mass above: where huge embodied rocks lie piled on one another, and seem to prop the high arch of heaven. See! with what trembling steps poor mankind tread the narrow brink of the deep precipices! From whence with giddy horror they look down, mistrusting even the ground that bears them; whilst they hear the hollow sound of torrents underneath, and see the ruin of the impending rock; with falling trees, which hang with their roots upwards, and seem to draw more ruin after them.' [See Shaftesbury, *Characteristics*, pp. 86-87.] See Livy's picturesque description of Annibal passing the Alps.

> Soft is the strain when Zephyr gently blows,
> And the smooth stream in smoother numbers flows;
> But when loud surges lash the sounding shore,
> The hoarse, rough verse should like the torrent roar;
> When Ajax strives some rock's vast weight to throw,
> The line too labours, and the words move slow;
> Not so when swift Camilla scours the plain,
> Flies o'er th' unbending corn, and skims along the main.   [366–373]

These lines are usually cited as fine examples of adapting the sound to the sense. But that *Pope* has failed in this endeavour, has been lately demonstrated by the *Rambler*. 'The verse intended to represent the *whisper* of the *vernal breeze* must surely be confessed not much to excell in softness or volubility; and the *smooth stream* runs with a perpetual clash of jarring consonants. The noise and turbulence of the *torrent*, is indeed, distinctly imaged; for it requires very little skill to make our language rough. But in the lines which mention the *effort of Ajax*, there is no particular heaviness or delay. The *swiftness of Camilla* is rather contrasted than exemplified. Why the verse should be lengthened to express speed, will not easily be discovered. In the dactyls, used for that purpose by the ancients, two short syllables were pronounced with such rapidity, as to be equal only to one long; they therefore naturally exhibit the act of passing through a long space in a short time. But the *Alexandrine*, by its pause in the midst, is a tardy and stately measure; and the word *unbending*, one of the most sluggish and slow which our language affords, cannot much accelarate its motion.' [Samuel Johnson, *Rambler* No. *92*.]

Be thou the first true merit to befriend,

His praise is lost, who stays 'till all commend.   [474–5]

When Thomson published his *Winter* it lay a long time neglected, 'till Mr. Spence made honourable mention of it in his *Essay on the Odyssey* [see pp. 100-106]; which becoming a popular book, made the poem universally known. Thomson always acknowledged the use of this early recommendation; and from this circumstance, an intimacy commenced between the critic and the poet, which lasted 'till the lamented death of the latter, who was of a most amiable benevolent temper.

The fourth edition, 1782

EZEKIEL

From an early moment in the emergence of Romanticism poetry was identified with prophecy and the Biblical prophets with poets. Of the three major names, Isaiah, Jeremiah, and Ezekiel, the last, to whom was given a book or the gift of writing, was counted, technically in the terms of Burnet, Addison and Burke the most 'sublime'. His appearances in eighteenth-century literature describe an almost complete account of the path of 'creative imagination'.

From the beginning Ezekiel's jewelled light symbolized the illumination of the infinite, a notion equally as influential in poetic imagery as any derived from Newton's *Optics*. For Burnet (see p. 35) Ezekiel's 'sapphire throne' indicated the 'Mundane Egg', a more sublime and elevated world than our present, finite one. For Joseph Spence (see p. 102) his vision, parallel with Homeric prophecy, was 'an *orientalism*' – the imaging of a revolution in a confusion of light in the heavens. For William Lowth in his *Commentary* (3rd ed., 1730), Ezekiel is the 'terrible' poet of Rapin's 'sublime', forcing the reader into the most disturbing realities. For Young, himself known as 'Bard' or prophet of Welwyn, he was a model for *Night Thoughts*. Robert Lowth's choice of him, influenced no doubt by his father, as 'the most sublime' of the prophets (see p. 165) argues that he had become recognized as the greatest 'oriental' poet, and suggests that the extensive jewelled sections of *A Song to David*, like Smart's versification, had their source in *The Sacred Poetry of the Hebrews*. Blake first saw Ezekiel when he was a young boy. In later life, it was naturally Ezekiel, the greatest primitive poet, who instructed Blake in the pre-eminence of poetry as a form of knowledge, in *The Marriage of Heaven and Hell* (see pp. 292-298). Like *Night Thoughts* on which it was modelled, Blake's greatest poem also derived its governing image from the son of Buzi. 'The likeness of four living creatures' each with four faces, four wings all interconnecting, the feet of calves, the hands of men, and the faces of men, lions, oxen, and eagles, become the overlapping perceptions in *The Four Zoas*.

The two major experiential poems embodying the new poetry of the mid-eighteenth century, Collins's *Ode on the Poetical Character* (see below, pp. 187-188) and Gray's *The Progress of Poesy* (see below, pp. 191-194) both offer the 'sapphire throne' – the sky seen in the dimensionless 'eye of the Creator' (see p. 142) – for their crucial image. Collapsing cosmic distances to the dimensions of a jewelled, royal chair, the single image in itself embodies a Blakean 'marriage of heaven and hell', 'passing' as Gray puts it, 'the flaming bounds of place and time', and marks a meeting point of oriental prophet and eighteenth-century philosopher similarly concerned with the mind's infinite creativity (see pp. 185, 187, 193).

Ezekiel's poetic ability is, clearly, one with his mythologizing. The great shift in personification during this era had been from abstractions which referred to a moral world distinct from literature to anthropomorphic figures suggestive of the poet's mind in mid-creation (see p. 13). In mythology, the localized figures of Greece and Rome gave way to the creation of the poet-prophet's own obscure dimensionless figures from within himself in the eternal here and now of his poem. Ezekiel's 'likenesses' served as a model for the vasty figures of, for example, *Ossian* and Blake, timeless and limitless creations, bearing no resemblance to anything in memory, created from the furnaces of the poet-prophet's own capacities and needs, which included a Collins-like dissolution of the seer's self. Paradoxically, such mythologizing leads directly to a non-hieratic concept of the vatic poet as *Deus Creator*, an imagination creating not only human likenesses but God himself, and to the fearful concept of man's creative control over futurity, and even over the images and materials of Creation.

Wordsworth's *The Excursion* (see pp. 353-363) is especially important both in itself and for its influence on Keats — whose massy Titans of *Hyperion: A Fragment* embody many of these traits — because of its exposition of poetry as unborrowed mythology. It is especially to be noted that a, if not the, climax of *The Excursion* is once more the 'sapphire throne' of the Hebrew prophet.

THE BOOK OF THE PROPHET EZEKIEL

Chapter I

Now it came to pass in the thirtieth year, in the fourth month, in the fifth day of the month, as I was among the captives by the river of Chebar, that the heavens were opened, and I saw visions of God. In the fifth day of the month, which was the fifth year of King Jehoiachin's captivity, the word of the Lord came expressly unto Ezekiel the priest, the son of Buzi, in the land of the Chaldeans by the river Chebar; and the hand of the Lord was there upon him.

And I looked, and, behold, a whirlwind came out of the north, a great cloud, and a fire infolding itself, and a brightness was about it, and out of the midst thereof as the colour of amber, out of the midst of the fire. Also out of the midst thereof came the likeness of four living creatures. And this was their appearance; they had the likeness of a man. And every one had four faces, and every one had four wings. And their feet were straight feet; and the sole of their feet was like the sole of a calf's foot: and they sparkled like the colour of burnished brass. And they had the hands of a man under their wings on their four sides; and they four had their faces and their wings. Their wings were joined one to another; they turned not when they went; they went every one straight forward. As for the likeness of their faces, they four had the face of a man, and the face of a lion, on the right side; and they four had the face of an ox on the left side; they four also had the face of an eagle. Thus were their faces: and their wings were stretched upward; two wings of every one were joined one to another, and two covered their bodies. And they went every one straight forward: whither the spirit was to go, they went; and they turned not when they went. As for the likeness of the living creatures, their appearance was like burning coals of fire, and like the appearance of lamps; it went up and down among the living creatures; and the fire was bright, and out of the fire went forth lightning. And the living creatures ran and returned as the appearance of a flash of lightning.

Now as I beheld the living creatures, behold one wheel upon the earth by the living creatures, with his four faces. The appearance of the wheels and their work was like unto the colour of a beryl: and they four had one likeness: and their appearance and their work was as it were a wheel in the middle of a wheel. When they went, they went upon their four sides: and they turned not when they went. As for their rings, they were so high that they were dreadful; and their rings were full of eyes round about them four. And when the living creatures went, the wheels went by them: and when the living creatures were lifted up from the earth, the wheels were lifted up. Whithersoever the spirit was to go, they went, thither was their spirit to go; and the wheels were lifted up over against them: for the spirit of the living creature was in the wheels. When those went, these went; and when those stood; these stood; and when those were lifted up from the earth, the wheels were lifted up over against them: for the spirit of the living creature was in the wheels. And the likeness of the firmament upon the heads of the living creature was as the colour of the terrible crystal, stretched forth over their heads above. And under the firmament were their wings straight, the one toward the other: every one had two, which covered on this side, and every one had two, which covered on that side, their bodies. And when they went, I heard the noise of their wings, like the noise of great waters, as the voice of the Almighty, the voice of speech, as the noise of a host: when they stood, they let down their wings. And there was a voice from the firmament that was over their heads, when they stood, and had let down their wings.

And above the firmament that was over their heads was the likeness of a throne, as the appearance of a sapphire stone: and upon the likeness of the throne was the likeness as the appearance of a man above upon it. And I saw as the colour of amber, as the appearance of fire round about within it, from the appearance of his loins even upward, and from the appearance of his loins even downward, I saw as it were the appearance of fire, and it had brightness round about. As the appearance of the bow that is in the cloud in the day of rain, so was the appearance of the brightness round about. This was the appearance of the likeness of the glory of the Lord. And when I saw it, I fell upon my face, and I heard a voice of one that spake.

Authorized Version, 1611

WILLIAM COLLINS (1721–1759)

The mid-eighteenth century created a number of works of major importance which demonstrated the chords available to poets following the perceptions of the preceding pages, notably Collins's *Ode on the Poetical Character* (1746) and Gray's *The Progress of Poesy* (see pp. 191-194). The sixteenth-century, 'primitive' poet of Collins's opening, Spenser, gives way to the eternal moment of the day of Creation – parallel to the 'time' of this poem's creation – and to the Hebrew prophet, Ezekiel, and then returns to England and the eighteenth-century or 'Gothic' Milton and a suggestion of the future of poetry. As in Shaftesbury's *Moralists* (see pp. 81-88) freed from time and space each object renders up a novel luminous value in the creativity of the poetic vision in a kind of eternal dance, a form to which the ode was originally related. Among Collins's many types of obscurity, the erasing of expected alignments is primary. The magic girdle or cest out of Spenser, at once fecundity and chastity, girds the loins of prophecy, mixing religion with sexuality in a union between Fancy and a sexually potent God as much Greek Zeus as Jehovah.

Normal associations of ideas, cause and effect and logical progression are fundamentally disoriented, as are all images which, prior to the poem, are dependent on structures. Hence Collins offers a perspectiveless organization of the human mind as if all impulses dance simultaneously in the brain at once finitely still but infinitely moving. Not only do all abstractions, including Truth, become as in Berkeley, merely the momentary aesthetic product of the imagination, interdependent sign rather than product of harmony, in an apparent anticipation of Keats; materiality itself appears to be as much in the power of the poet's present mind as it was in God's on the first day, when he made, as Trapp had noted (see p. 56) this earth as his poem.

Collins is an early and impressive example of the Romantic poet's unearthly exploitation of concepts of the association of ideas current in eighteenth-century philosophy. Demonstrating the poet's necessary association of anomalous categories of ideas, chastity with sexuality, East with West, Jehovah and laughing Jove, past time with prophecy, and, at the fundamental level of the poem's form, the Pindaric ode with what had theoretically preceded it, the original lyric ode of the orient, Collins significantly anticipated Coleridge's poetry, especially *Kubla Khan* and *Frost at Midnight*, and perhaps for the first time, offered the reader the unnerving experience of the 'topic' of a poem dissolving within the poet's treatment of it. The assault on the structures of time and space is actually accomplished on the page with the result that the poet seems to surrender, like Ezekiel, his very self to the furnaces of creativity, threatening, in the process, the parallel integrity of the reader's being.

Collins is the first great poet to reveal successfully the effect of the findings of Berkeley, Hume and Hartley, and of his fellow Wykehamists, Lowth, Young, and Spence, and the possibilities of a poetry in which, freed from finite bonds, the poet's ego in dire jeopardy became a creating god, like the demon lover of *Kubla Khan*, at home with, even procreator of, the forces of the supernatural.

ODE ON THE POETICAL CHARACTER (1746)

As once, if not with light regard
I read aright that gifted bard,
(Him whose school above the rest
His loveliest Elfin Queen has blessed)
One, only one, unrivalled fair
Might hope the magic girdle wear,
At solemn tourney hung on high,
The wish of each love-darting eye;
Lo! to each other nymph in turn applied,
    As if, in air unseen, some hovering hand,   10
Some chaste and angel-friend to virgin-fame,
    With whispered spell had burst the starting band,
It left unblest her loathed, dishonoured side;
        Happier hopeless fair, if never
        Her baffled hand with vain endeavour
Had touched that fatal zone to her denied!
Young Fancy thus, to me divinest name,
        To whom, prepared and bathed in heaven,
        The cest of amplest power is given,
        To few the godlike gift assigns   20
        To gird their blest prophetic loins,
And gaze her visions wild, and feel unmixed her flame!

2.

The band, as fairy legends say,
Was wove on that creating day
When He, who called with thought to birth
Yon tented sky, this laughing earth,
And dressed with springs and forests tall,
And poured the main engirting all,
Long by the loved Enthusiast wooed,
Himself in some diviner mood,   30
Retiring, sat with her alone,
And placed her on his sapphire throne,
The whiles, the vaulted shrine around,
Seraphic wires were heard to sound,

Now sublimest triumph swelling,
Now on love and mercy dwelling;
And she, from out the veiling cloud,
Breathed her magic notes aloud:
And thou, thou rich-haired youth of morn,
And all thy subject life was born!   40
The dangerous Passions kept aloof,
Far from the sainted growing woof;
But near it sat ecstatic Wonder,
Listening the deep applauding thunder;
And Truth, in sunny vest arrayed,
By whose the tarsel's eyes were made;
All the shadowy tribes of Mind
In braided dance their murmurs joined,
And all the bright uncounted powers,
Who feed on heaven's ambrosial flowers.   50
Where is the bard, whose soul can now
Its high presuming hopes avow?
Where he who thinks, with rapture blind,
This hallowed work for him designed?

3.

High on some cliff, to heaven up-piled,
Of rude access, of prospect wild,
Where, tangled round the jealous steep,
Strange shades o'erbrow the valleys deep,
And holy Genii guard the rock,
Its glooms embrown, its springs unlock,   60
While on its rich ambitious head,
An Eden, like his own, lies spread:

I view that oak, the fancied glades among,
By which as Milton lay, his evening ear,
From many a cloud that dropped ethereal dew,
Nigh sphered in heaven, its native strains could hear,
On which that ancient trump he reached was hung:
    Thither oft, his glory greeting,
    From Waller's myrtle shades retreating,
With many a vow from Hope's aspiring tongue,   70

My trembling feet his guiding steps pursue;
    In vain — Such bliss to one alone
    Of all the sons of soul was known;
    And Heaven and Fancy, kindred powers,
Have now o'erturned the inspiring bowers;
Or curtained close such scene from every future view.

THOMAS GRAY (1716–71)

Gray's ode on the new poetry begins with a strong image of the beginnings of poetry in Ancient Greece and of classical progress through perspectives of time and place and proceeds to a prophecy of primitivism like that of Ezekiel and Job who preceded the Greeks. A parallel to Milton's descent out of his heaven in Blake's *Milton*, this movement undoes as it proceeds the source of its beginning and is one with the thematic undermining of the Pindaric ode by a lyric Hebrew original which, as Trapp explicitly (see p. 58) and Lowth more implicitly (see p. 166) had observed, came before it. As it proceeds and then, altering its terms, offers a concept of art greater than sequential progress, Gray's poem demonstrates the capacity of true poetry to outdistance and absorb into the forgetfulness of sublimity the forms of memory.

When the Ancient Mariner blesses the water snakes in Coleridge's poem, he moves into the realm of the creative imagination. In various Romantics, for example Blake and Collins (see p. 187), love, frequently explicitly sexual, parallels aesthetic creation. Dance, within the dance-like ode, Cytherea or Venus represents Greek mythology but, partial product of the creativity she images, also moves — without perspective — opaquely in the texture of Gray's third stanza (cf. Hogarth's Venus, p. 284). The arms of her attendants 'float' sublimely, their motion and density, in an infinite without gravity, dependent only on the creative perception of the poet and on a forming Nature which in art can give the characteristics of one sense to another and to air the substance of water. Reminiscent of the wave-like turf of the *Elegy* (see line 14) this kind of line, anticipating the Gothic chamber of *Christabel* (see line 180), paints the nakedness of the creator's mind in a structureless cosmos and the singleness of perception.

Abstractions tend to belong to the world of time since they are abstracted *from* something, generalizing in a more important moment perceptions which had gone before. Like William Collins and as in the *Elegy*, Gray etches in personifications in the present motions of the poet's mind, after the model of Addison (see pp. 90-91). In II. 1 the 'tribes of mind' Labour, Penury, Pain, Disease, 'sorrow's weeping train', and Death move, noumenal and magical, instancing the power of true verse to include the darkness of grief as well as the brightness of beauty. The categorizing of misery from joy is related to memory. In poetry, it is the strength of feeling not its kind which is significant.

> Full many a gem of purest ray serene
> The dark unfathom'd caves of ocean bear;
> Full many a flower is born to blush unseen
> And waste its sweetness on the desert air,

wrote Gray in the midst of an elegy set in a country churchyard. Similarly, in the *Ode*, Gray images the opposite side of the world. As

Swift suggests in *Gulliver's Travels* and as Coleridge's *Ancient Mariner* confirms, the awareness of the globe as a whole was a major fact in the new thought. Gray sketches in the noble savages of South America in II. 2, extending his image of place to its utmost in preparation for its dissolution along with time as the poem 'progresses'. 'Chile' is in addition an anticipation of the culminating image of the poem, the primitive poetry of Ezekiel and Job.

An organization of perceptions within the harmony of eternity, the creative structures of true art — as in Shelley's *Defence of Poetry* — are a model for political structures. Enslaved Greece has more recently experienced a tyranny so dire that poetry has left the Aegean, and after a short stay in Renaissance Italy, has made its way to 'primitive' England. The river Avon (III. 1) takes up the water image of the opening stanza. The 'flow' of poetry up to this point has the ambiguity of water, for Shakespeare is for Gray, as for the rest of the eighteenth century, a timeless 'original'. A Romantic child-figure after the manner of Chatterton, Wordsworth's 'marvellous boy' and the infant primitives of Blake's *Songs*, Shakespeare lives *within* Nature (cf. Maurice Morgann, p. 255). The 'golden keys' to the Golden Age, are his now in a present Eden located in England. Gray enumerates the 'Bard's' strengths, comedy, the 'Sublime' of Gothic horror, and 'sacred source of sympathetic tears', the poetry of sensibility.

Moving towards modern English poets, Gray, himself a poet of sensibility and Gothic horror, seems to merge with his theme. Identifying Milton with Ezekiel, and the 'sapphire throne' in III. 2, Gray has brought himself to the point at which he too 'passes the flaming bounds of time and place'. The poem as it were turns inside out and the logic of sequence is undercut by the assumption of the prophet's infinite mantle. It is, of course, significant that Gray does not intend that Milton and Ezekiel, any more than himself, be shown as religious visionaries granted a blinding gift of 'higher truths'. Indeed, the ode ends with a denial of even the principle of the hieratic. As in all the major poetry of the mid-century current epistemology blends with eighteenth-century notions of the prophet or bard's capacity in a state of inspiration by his own godlike powers to create futurity. Milton's blindness is caused directly in Gray's poem by his personal creative imagination, which dissolving upwardness along with time and space, becomes one with Ezekiel's in an echo of Berkeley's *New Theory of Vision*.

As if to underline the ageless quality of the poetry he admires, Gray borrows, in line 106, the image out of the description of Job's warhorse 'with necks in thunder cloth'd . . .' which 'John Lizard' (see p. 142) and Burke (see p. 200) both choose as one of the sublimest moments in 'the most ancient poem in the world'.

Gray's greatness lies in his ability to show directly the power of 'sublime' poetry released from memory and the bonds of time and place. Having himself merged with Milton and Ezekiel, he too imaginatively

creates futurity. As if with a foreknowledge of Blake, Gray looks toward
a heuristic future which forms its images as he writes. Bursting the bonds
of the Pindaric ode, he envisions a youthful, original figure, perceiving
not by the light of the sun, great chronometer in the sky, but by the
orient hues of the prophets' jewelled visions, forms of poetry which
avoid traditional moral categories, and in their greatness dissolve even the
ontological hierarchies of tradition.

THE PROGRESS OF POESY. A PINDARIC ODE (1754)

I.1

Awake, Aeolian lyre, awake,
And give to rapture all thy trembling strings.
From Helicon's harmonious springs
A thousand rills their mazy progress take:
The laughing flowers, that round them blow,
Drink life and fragrance as they flow.
Now the rich stream of music winds along,
Deep, majestic, smooth, and strong,
Through verdant vales and Ceres' golden reign:
Now rolling down the steep amain,   10
Headlong, impetuous, see it pour;
The rocks and nodding groves rebellow to the roar.

I. 2

Oh! Sovereign of the willing soul,
Parent of sweet and solemn-breathing airs,
Enchanting shell! the sullen Cares
And frantic Passions hear thy soft control.
On Thracia's hills the Lord of War
Has curbed the fury of his car,
And dropped his thirsty lance at thy command.
Perching on the sceptered hand   20
Of Jove, thy magic lulls the feathered king
With ruffled plumes and flagging wing:
Quenched in dark clouds of slumber lie
The terror of his beak and lightnings of his eye.

I. 3

Thee the voice, the dance, obey,
Tempered to thy warbled lay.
O'er Idalia's velvet-green
The rosy-crowned Loves are seen
On Cytherea's day
With antic Sports and blue-eyed Pleasures,   30

Frisking light in frolic measures;
Now pursuing, now retreating,
Now in circling troops they meet:
To brisk notes in cadence beating
Glance their many-twinkling feet.
Slow melting strains their queen's approach declare:
Where'er she turns the Graces homage pay.
With arms sublime, that float upon the air,
In gliding state she wins her easy way:
O'er her warm cheek and rising bosom move   40
The bloom of young desire and purple light of love.

II. 1

Man's feeble race what ills await,
Labour, and penury, the racks of pain,
Disease, and sorrow's weeping train,
And death, sad refuge from the storms of fate!
The fond complaint, my song, disprove,
And justify the laws of Jove.
Say, has he given in vain the heavenly Muse?
Night and all her sickly dews,
Her spectres wan and birds of boding cry,   50
He gives to range the dreary sky:
Till down the eastern cliffs afar
Hyperion's* march they spy and glittering shafts of war.

II. 2

In climes beyond the solar road,
Where shaggy forms o'er ice-built mountains roam,
The Muse has broke the twilight-gloom
To cheer the shivering native's dull abode.
And oft, beneath the odorous shade
Of Chile's boundless forests laid,
She deigns to hear the savage youth repeat   60
In loose numbers wildly sweet
Their feather-cinctured chiefs and dusky loves.
Her track, where'er the goddess roves,
Glory pursue and generous Shame,
The unconquerable Mind and Freedom's holy flame.

II. 3

Woods that wave o'er Delphi's steep,
Isles that crown the Aegean deep,

---

*Cf. the fate of Hyperion (the sun) in this poem (see esp. line 120) with
Keats's *Hyperion; A Fragment*. Ed.

Fields that cool Ilissus laves,
Or where Maeander's amber waves
In lingering lab'rinths creep,   70
How do your tuneful echoes languish,
Mute but to the voice of anguish?
Where each old poetic mountain
Inspiration breathed around:
Every shade and hallowed fountain
Murmured deep a solemn sound:
Till the sad Nine in Greece's evil hour
Left their Parnassus for the Latian plains.
Alike they scorn the pomp of tyrant-power,
And coward Vice that revels in her chains.   80
When Latium had her lofty spirit lost,
They sought, oh Albion! next thy sea-encircled coast.

III. 1
   Far from the sun and summer-gale,
In thy green lap was Nature's darling laid,
What time, where lucid Avon strayed,
To him the mighty Mother did unveil
Her awful face: the dauntless child
Stretched forth his little arms and smiled,
'This pencil take,' (she said) 'whose colours clear
Richly paint the vernal year: 90
Thine too these golden keys, immortal boy!
This can unlock the gates of joy;
Of horror that and thrilling fears,
Or ope the sacred source of sympathetic tears.'

III. 2
Nor second he, that rode sublime
Upon the seraph-wings of Ecstasy,
The secrets of the abyss* to spy.
He passed the flaming bounds of place and time:
The living throne, the sapphire-blaze,
Where angels tremble while they gaze,   100
He saw; but blasted with excess of light,
Closed his eyes in endless night.
Behold, where Dryden's less presumptuous car,
Wide o'er the fields of glory, bear
Two courses of ethereal race,
With necks in thunder clothed, and long-resounding pace.

---

*Cf. Burnet on the 'sublime' Abyss, pp. 25, 35. Ed.

III. 3

Hark, his hands the lyre explore!
Bright-eyed Fancy hovering o'er
Scatters from her pictured urn
Thoughts that breathe and words that burn.   110
But ah! 'tis heard no more —
Oh! lyre divine, what daring spirit
Wakes thee now? Though he inherit
Nor the pride nor ample pinion,
That the Theban eagle bear
Sailing with supreme dominion
Through the azure deep of air:
Yet oft before his infant eyes would run
Such forms as glitter in the Muse's ray
With orient hues, unborrowed of the sun: 120
Yet shall he mount and keep his distant way
Beyond the limits of a vulgar fate,
Beneath the Good how far — but far above the Great.

EDMUND BURKE (1729–1797)

The core of Burke's psychology in his *Philosophical Enquiry into the Origins of our Ideas of the Sublime and Beautiful* (1757) is not distant from the modern concept that men 'think' with a totality of body and mind. The fibres of the eye give a 'feeling' of distance in Berkeley's *New Theory of Vision* (see pp. 64-69). In Burke we are creatures intended for activity and stress, and, therefore, we feel most 'delight' when danger tautens our fibres. Irrational and organic, the delight we may suppose is physical and mental at one moment, and is scarcely separable from its 'cause'. Burke systematizes, therefore, not only the disappearance of the image of temporality or sequence in art, but also the distinction between pleasure and pain. In Part IV, Section vi, he observes

> Melancholy, dejection, despair and often self-murder is the consequence of the . . . relaxed state of body. The best remedy for all these evils is exercise or *labour*; and labour is a surmounting of *difficulties*, an exertion of the contracting power of the muscles; and as such resembles pain, which consists in tension or contraction, in every thing but degree.

In many ways Burke is the theoretical climax of the disappearance of the unseen which had been in progress since the late seventeenth century. Pain, he adds, is to the 'finer organs' what labour is to the coarser. It is 'these finer and more delicate organs, on which, and by which, the imagination, and perhaps the other mental powers act'.

Undifferentiated knowing by emotional participation is of similar importance in Burke's scheme, which, it is necessary to point out, is a shrewd crystallization of phenomena almost universally detectable in mid-eighteenth-century writing. In a famous passage (Part I, Section xv) suggestive of the volatile nature of the era of 'feeling' and of Wesley, Burke supposed that when a crowd had a choice between a simulated execution in a theatre and a neighbouring hanging, they would choose the latter as more pleasurable. The reason was not that they themselves were happy in their security, pleased not to be killed, but that strong emotion, regardless of kind, was a pleasurable dissolver of identity into the larger experience of society. In so many words (Part I, Section xv) Burke observed that no concept could be more 'sublime' than that of the total destruction of the capital city, London. The pleasure for many of the memory of the Second World War, or the 'sublime' thrill, more intense as more horrid, of political assassination in Dallas, indicates that Burke and his century were right.

The enjoyment of pain as pleasure is a part of Romantic aesthetics from an early time. If we take only the case of Edward Young, prophetically more popular even in Germany than at home, we find that the prologue of each of his plays invites the audience in the terms of *Busiris* (1719) to 'rise in pleasure as you rise in pain'. His *Works* include an enthusiastic poem about Michelangelo's stabbing a criminal 'in such parts . . . as he apprehended would occasion the most excrutiating torture' while painting the agony of Christ, and John Wesley (*Extract* of *Night Thoughts*, 1770) found in Young 'that secret and wonderful endearment which nature has annext to all our sympathetic feelings, whereby we enter into the deepest scenes of stress and sorrow, with a melting softness of heart, far more delightful than all the joys which dissipating and un-thinking mirth can inspire.'

The observation that each cognitive event, especially the terrifying and obscure, is an intensity to be surrendered to for its experience, recalls Shaftesbury's exhortation (see pp. 86-87) that everything in Nature, however loathsome, has its peculiar beauty, and points by way of the continuum of undifferentiated experience, to de Sade, Wagner, D'Annunzio, and finally the aberrations, aesthetic as well as political, of twentieth-century 'blood-knowledge'. Burke's *Enquiry* may be regarded as a summation of a crucial movement which dismissed centuries of almost subliminal hierarchical imaging, for example in the poetry of Pope, in which the bright, smooth, manageable, understood and sunlit, had been held superior to the rough, low, monstrous, lunar and obscure.

Riding in a carriage over an undulating plain, listening to intermittent sounds, the repetition of pillars, are examined among other instances to find reasons for the sense of the infinite first sketched in by Burnet (see pp. 21-36) and Addison (see pp. 90-99). Like Young and Lowth, Burke finds 'primitive' poetry, especially of the Bible, far more sublime than other writing. He appears to have used *Guardian* No. 86 (see pp. 140-143) when writing about the warhorse in *Job*, for his selected quotations coincide with some of the list appearing in that paper.

Interestingly, contradictions may be discovered in Burke. It would appear strange if some creativity were not supposed present in the emotional responses he describes, yet in the *Essay on Taste* which preceded later editions he noted that there was nothing in the imagination which had not previously been experienced, an odd announcement, especially in light of Burke's interesting comments on the nature of words in his final pages. Like Berkeley, Burke seems to suggest that words may function most efficiently when they are free of ideas. He envisions (see pp. 201-206) a kind of poetry in which words affect the reader's emotions without first activating the memory and its visual images. This capacity of words for obscurity leads him far from the concept of 'the sister arts' since painting, before Turner we might note, always depended upon recall, whereas the grandeur of poetry frequently suggested the nebulous obscurities of vast unknowns. It is important to observe that the runic opacity of words functioning in memory-less contexts, for example in Smart, Blake, and Wordsworth (e.g. *We Are Seven*) is an important characteristic and resource of Romantic poetry.

Burke's 'Sublime' is essentially the 'eighteenth-century Sublime', distinct from Longinus in denying structures and hieratic values, and distinct from the later Romantic 'Sublime' in that it is apparently dependent upon extension or dimension and hence, however 'infinite' in its results, tied to the finiteness of materiality. In a way, the *Enquiry into the Sublime and Beautiful* is best read for itself and as a guide to the period of sensibility. Its organization which, in spite of 'parts' and 'sections', does not strongly proceed, suggests a parallel with Lowth's *Sacred Poetry of the Hebrews*, a work which, ostensibly an analysis of 'sublime' poetry, succeeds in becoming what it sets out to examine.

A PHILOSOPHICAL ENQUIRY INTO THE ORIGIN OF OUR IDEAS OF THE SUBLIME AND BEAUTIFUL (1757)

from Part I, Section v, 'Joy and Grief'
It must be observed, that the cessation of pleasure affects the mind three ways. If it simply ceases, after having continued a proper time, the effect is *indifference*; if it be abruptly broken off, there ensues an uneasy sense called *disappointment*; if the object be so totally lost that there is no chance of enjoying it again, a passion arises in the mind, which is called *grief*. Now there is none of these, not even grief, which is the most violent, that I think has any resemblance to positive pain. The person who grieves, suffers his passion to grow upon him; he indulges it, he loves it: but this never happens in the case of actual pain, which no man ever willingly endured for any considerable time. That grief should be willingly endured, though far from a simply pleasing sensation, is not so difficult to be understood. It is the nature of grief to keep its object perpetually in its eye, to present it in its most pleasurable views, to repeat all the circumstances that attend it, even to the last minuteness; to go back to every particular enjoyment, to dwell upon each, and to find a thousand new perfections in all, that were not sufficiently understood before; in grief, the *pleasure* is still uppermost; and the affliction we suffer has no resemblance to absolute pain, which is always odious, and which we endeavour to shake off as soon as possible. The *Odyssey* of Homer, which abounds with so many natural and affecting images, has none more striking than those which Menelaus raises of the calamitous fate of his friends, and his own manner of feeling it. He owns indeed, that he often gives himself some intermission from such melancholy reflections, but he observes too, that melancholy as they are, they give him pleasure.

*

Section vii, 'Of the SUBLIME'
Whatever is fitted in any sort to excite the ideas of pain, and danger, that is to say, whatever is in any sort terrible, or is conversant about terrible objects, or operates in a manner analogous to terror, is a source of the *sublime*; that is, it is productive of the strongest emotion which the

mind is capable of feeling. I say the strongest emotion, because I am satisfied the ideas of pain are much more powerful than those which enter on the part of pleasure. Without all doubt, the torments which we may be made to suffer, are much greater in their effect on the body and mind, than any pleasures which the most learned voluptuary could suggest, or than the liveliest imagination, and the most sound and exquisitely sensible body could enjoy. Nay I am in great doubt, whether any man could be found who would earn a life of the most perfect satisfaction, at the price of ending it in the torments, which justice inflicted in a few hours on the late unfortunate regicide in France [Damiens, who tried to kill Louis XV, Jan. 1757]. But as pain is stronger in its operation than pleasure, so death is in general a much more affecting idea than pain; because there are very few pains, however exquisite, which are not preferred to death; nay, what generally makes pain itself, if I may say so, more painful, is, that it is considered as an emissary of this king of terrors. When danger or pain press too nearly, they are incapable of giving any delight, and are simply terrible; but at certain distances, and with certain modifications, they may be, and they are delightful, as we every day experience. The cause of this I shall endeavour to investigate hereafter.

*

from Part II, Section iii, 'Obscurity'
To make any thing very terrible, obscurity seems in general to be necessary. When we know the full extent of any danger, when we can accustom our eyes to it, a great deal of the apprehension vanishes. Every one will be sensible of this, who considers how greatly night adds to our dread, in all cases of danger, and how much the notions of ghosts and goblins, of which none can form clear ideas, affect minds which give credit to the popular tales concerning such sorts of beings. Those despotic governments which are founded on the passions of men and principally upon the passion of fear, keep their chief as much as may be from the public eye. The policy has been the same in many cases of religion. Almost all the heathen temples were dark. Even in the barbarous temples of the Americans at this day, they keep their idol in a dark part of the hut, which is consecrated to his worship. For this purpose too the Druids performed all their ceremonies in the bosom of the darkest woods, and in the shade of the oldest and most spreading oaks. No person seems better to have understood the secret of heightening, or of setting terrible things, if I may use the expression, in their strongest light by the force of a judicious obscurity, than Milton. His description of Death in the second book is admirably studied; it is astonishing with what a gloomy pomp, with what a significant and expressive uncertainty of strokes and colouring he has finished the portrait of the king of terrors.

The other shape,
If shape it might be called that shape had none
Distinguishable in member, joint, or limb;
Or substance might be called that shadow seemed,
For each seemed either; black he stood as night;
Fierce as ten furies: terrible as hell;
And shook a dreadful dart. What seemed his head
The likeness of a kingly crown had on.   [*Paradise Lost*, II. 666–73]

In this description all is dark, uncertain, confused, terrible, and sublime to the last degree.

*

from Section v 'Power'

Besides these things, which *directly* suggest the idea of danger, and those which produce a similar effect from a mechanical cause, I know of nothing sublime which is not some modification of power. And this branch rises as naturally as the other two branches, from terror, the common stock of every thing that is sublime. The idea of power at first view, seems of the class of these indifferent ones, which may equally belong to pain or to pleasure. But in reality, the affection arising from the idea of vast power, is extremely remote from that neutral character. For first, we must remember, that the idea of pain, in its highest degree, is much stronger than the highest degree of pleasure; and that it preserves the same superiority through all the subordinate gradations. From hence it is, that where the chances for equal degrees of suffering or enjoyment are in any sort equal, the idea of the suffering must always be prevalent. And indeed the ideas of pain, and above all of death, are so very affecting, that whilst we remain in the presence of whatever is supposed to have the power of inflicting either, it is impossible to be perfectly free from terror. Again, we know by experience, that for the enjoyment of pleasure, no great efforts of power are at all necessary; nay we know, that such efforts would go a great way towards destroying our satisfaction: for pleasure must be stolen, and not forced upon us; pleasure follows the will; and therefore we are generally affected with it by many things of a force greatly inferior to our own. But pain is always inflicted by a power in some way superior, because we never submit to pain willingly. So that strength, violence, pain and terror, are ideas that rush in upon the mind together. Look at a man, or any other animal of prodigious strength, and what is your idea before reflection? Is it that this strength will be sub-servient to you, to your ease, to your pleasure, to your interest in any sense? No; the emotion you feel is, lest this enormous strength should be employed to the purposes of rapine and destruction. That power derives all its sublimity from the terror with which it is generally accompanied, will appear evidently from its effect in the very few cases in which it may be possible to strip a considerable degree of strength of its ability to hurt.

When you do this, you spoil it of every thing sublime, and it immediately becomes contemptible. An ox is a creature of vast strength; but he is an innocent creature, extremely serviceable, and not at all dangerous; for which reason the idea of an ox is by no means grand. A bull is strong too; but his strength is of another kind; often very destructive, seldom (at least amongst us) of any use in our business; the idea of a bull is therefore great, and it has frequently a place in sublime descriptions, and elevating comparisons. Let us look at another strong animal in the two distinct lights in which we may consider him. The horse in the light of an useful beast, fit for the plough, the road, the draft, in every social useful light the horse has nothing of the *sublime*; but is it thus that we are affected with him, *whose neck is clothed with thunder, the glory of whose nostrils is terrible, who swalloweth the ground with fierceness and rage, neither believeth that it is the sound of the trumpet?** In this description the useful character of the horse entirely disappears, and the terrible and sublime blaze out together. We have continually about us animals of a strength that is considerable, but not pernicious. Amongst these we never look for the sublime: it comes upon us in the gloomy forest, and in the howling wilderness, in the form of the lion, the tiger, the panther, or rhinoceros.**

*

from Section vii, 'Vastness'
Greatness of dimension, is a powerful cause of the sublime. This is too evident, and the observation too common, to need any illustration; it is not so common, to consider in what ways greatness of dimension, vastness of extent, or quantity, has the most striking effect. For certainly, there are ways, and modes, wherein the same quantity of extension shall produce greater effects than it is found to do in others. Extension is either in length, height, or depth. Of these the length strikes least; an hundred yards of even ground will never work such an effect as a tower an hundred yards high, or a rock or mountain of that altitude. I am apt to imagine likewise, that height is less grand than depth; and that we are more struck at looking down from a precipice, than at looking up at an object of equal height, but of that I am not very positive. A perpendicular has more force in forming the sublime, than an inclined plane; and the effects of a rugged and broken surface seem stronger than where it is smooth and polished.

*

---

*Burke repeats here some of the lines praised in *Guardian* No. *86*. See pp. 140-143 above. Lowth, also, had made the same point about the same passage towards the end of his *Lectures*. Ed.

**In 1976 film makers exploited 'the Sublime' of sharks and bears in *Jaws* and *Grizzly*. Ed.

Section viii, 'Infinity'

Another source of the sublime, is *infinity*; if it does not rather belong to the last. Infinity has a tendency to fill the mind with that sort of delightful horror, which is the most genuine effect, and truest test of the sublime. There are scarce any things which can become the objects of our senses that are really, and in their own nature infinite. But the eye not being able to perceive the bounds of many things, they seem to be infinite, and they produce the same effects as if they were really so. We are deceived in the like manner, if the parts of some large object are so continued to any indefinite number, that the imagination meets no check which may hinder its extending them at pleasure.

Whenever we repeat any idea frequently, the mind by a sort of mechanism repeats it long after the first cause has ceased to operate. After whirling about; when we sit down, the objects about us all seem to whirl. [Cf. Hartley on the prolonging of impressions, p. 223.] After a long succession of noises, as the fall of waters, or the beating of forge hammers, the hammers beat and the water roars in the imagination long after the first sounds have ceased to affect it; and they die away at last by graduations which are scarcely perceptible. If you hold up a strait pole, with your eye to one end, it will seem extended to a length almost incredible. Place a number of uniform and equidistant marks on this pole, they will cause the same deception, and seem multiplied without end. The senses strongly affected in some one manner, cannot quickly change their tenor, or adapt themselves to other things; but they continue in their old channel until the strength of the first mover decays. This is the reason of an appearance very frequent in madmen; that they remain whole days and nights, sometimes whole years, in the constant repetition of some remark, some complaint, or song; which having struck powerfully on their disordered imagination, in the beginning of their phrensy, every repetition reinforces it with new strength; and the hurry of their spirits, unrestrained by the curb of reason, continues it to the end of their lives.

*

from Part V, Section i, 'Of Words'

Natural objects affect us, by the laws of that connexion, which Providence has established between certain motions and configurations of bodies, and certain consequent feelings in our minds. Painting affects in the same manner, but with the superadded pleasure of imitation. Architecture affects by the laws of nature, and the law of reason; from which latter result the rules of proportion, which make a work to be praised or censured, in the whole or in some part, when the end for which it was designed is or is not properly answered. But as to words; they seem to me to affect us in a manner very different from that in which we are affected by natural objects, or by painting or architecture; yet words have as considerable a share in exciting ideas of beauty and of the sublime as any of those, and sometimes a much greater than any of them; therefore an enquiry into the manner by which they excite such emotions is far from being unnecessary in a discourse of this kind.*

*

Section ii, 'The common effect of Poetry, not by raising ideas of things'
The common notion of the power of poetry and eloquence, as well as that of words in ordinary conversation, is; that they affect the mind by raising in it ideas of those things for which custom has appointed them to stand. To examine the truth of this notion, it may be requisite to observe that words may be divided into three sorts. The first are such as represent many simple ideas *united by nature* to form some one determinate composition, as man, horse, tree, castle, &c. These I call *aggregate words*. The second, are they that stand for one simple idea of such compositions and no more; as red, blue, round, square, and the like. These I call *simple abstract* words. The third, are those, which are formed by an union, an *arbitrary* union of both the others, and of the various relations between them, in greater or lesser degrees of complexity; as virtue, honour, persuasion, magistrate, and the like. These I call *compounded abstract* words. Words, I am sensible, are capable of being classed into more curious distinctions; but these seem to be natural, and enough for our purpose; and they are disposed in that order in which they are commonly taught, and in which the mind gets the ideas they are substituted for. I shall begin with the third sort of words; compound abstracts, such as virtue, honour, persuasion, docility. Of these I am convinced, that whatever power they may have on the passions, they do not derive it from any representation raised in the mind of the things for which they stand. As compositions, they are not real essences, and hardly cause, I think, any real ideas. No body, I believe, immediately on hearing the sounds, virtue, liberty, or honour, conceives any precise notion of the particular modes of action and thinking, together with the mixt and simple ideas, and the several relations of them for which these words are substituted; neither has he any *general* idea, compounded of them; for if he had, then some of those particular ones, though indistinct perhaps, and confused, might come soon to be perceived.** But this, I take it, is hardly ever the case. For put yourself upon analysing one of these words, and you must reduce it from one set of general words to another, and then into the simple abstracts and aggregates, in a much longer series than may be at first imagined, before

---

*It is necessary to emphasize that Burke considered words 'sublime' of and by themselves, and not only by reason of the 'things' to which they referred. Ed.

**There is a strong similarity between Burke in this section and Berkeley on both *abstractions* and *words* in his *Principles*. See pp. 69-74 and 78. Ed.

any real idea emerges to light, before you come to discover any thing like the first principles of such compositions; and when you have made such a discovery of the original ideas, the effect of the composition is utterly lost. A train of thinking of this sort, is much too long to be pursued in the ordinary ways of conversation, nor is it at all necessary that it should. Such words are in reality but mere sounds; but they are sounds, which being used on particular occasions, wherein we receive some good, or suffer some evil, or see others affected with good or evil, or which we hear applied to other interesting things or events; and being applied in such a variety of cases that we know readily by habit to what things they belong, they produce in the mind, whenever they are afterwards mentioned, effects similar to those of their occasions. The sounds being often used without reference to any particular occasion, and carrying still their first impressions, they at last utterly lose their connection with the particular occasions that gave rise to them; yet the sound without any annexed notion continues to operate as before.

*

from Section iv, 'The effect of Words'
If words have all their possible extent of power, three effects arise in the mind of the hearer. The first is, the *sound*; the second, the *picture*, or representation of the thing signified by the sound; the third is, the *affection* of the soul produced by one or by both of the foregoing. *Compounded abstract* words, of which we have been speaking, (honour, justice, liberty, and the like,) produce the first and the last of these effects, but not the second. *Simple abstracts*, are used to signify some one simple idea without much adverting to others which may chance to attend it, as blue, green, hot, cold, and the like; these are capable of affecting all three of the purposes of words; as the *aggregate* words, man, castle, horse, &c. are in a yet higher degree. But I am of opinion, that the most general effect even of these words, does not arise from their forming pictures of the several things they would represent in the imagination; because on a very diligent examination of my own mind, and getting others to consider theirs, I do not find that once in twenty times any such picture is formed, and when it is, there is most commonly a particular effort of the imagination for that purpose. But the aggregate words operate as I said of the compound abstracts, not by presenting any image to the mind, but by having from use the same effect on being mentioned, that their original has when it is seen. Suppose we were to read a passage to this effect. 'The river Danube rises in a moist and mountainous soil in the heart of Germany, where winding to and fro it waters several principalities, until turning into Austria and leaving the walls of Vienna it passes into Hungary; there with a vast flood augmented by the Saave and the Drave it quits Christendom, and rolling through the barbarous countries which border on Tartary, it enters by many mouths into the Black Sea.' In this description many things are mentioned, as

mountains, rivers, cities, the sea, &c. But let anybody examine himself, and see whether he has had impressed on his imagination any pictures of a river, mountain, watery soil, Germany, &c.

*

Section vi, 'Poetry not strictly an imitative art'
Hence we may observe that poetry, taken in its most general sense, cannot with strict propriety be called an art of imitation. It is indeed an imitation so far as it describes the manners and passions of men which their words can express; where *animi motus effert interprete lingua*.* There is strictly imitation; and all merely *dramatic* poetry is of this sort. But *descriptive* poetry operates chiefly by *substitution*; by the means of sounds, which by custom have the effect of realities. Nothing is an imitation further than as it resembles some other thing; and words undoubtedly have no sort of resemblance to the ideas for which they stand.

*

Section vii, 'How Words influence the Passions'
Now, as words affect, not by any original power, but by representation, it might be supposed, that their influence over the passions should be but light; yet it is quite otherwise; for we find by experience that eloquence and poetry are as capable, nay indeed much more capable of making deep and lively impressions than any other arts, and even than nature itself in very many cases. And this arises chiefly from these three causes. First, that we take an extraordinary part in the passions of others, and that we are easily affected and brought into sympathy by any tokens which are shewn of them; and there are no tokens which can express all the circum-stances of most passions so fully as words, so that if a person speaks upon any subject, he can not only convey the subject to you, but likewise the manner in which he is himself affected by it. Certain that it is, that the influence of most things on our passions is not so much from the things themselves, as from our opinions concerning them; and these again depend very much on the opinions of other men, conveyable for the most part by words only. Secondly; there are many things of a very affecting nature, which can seldom occur in the reality, but the words which represent them often do; and thus they have an opportunity of making a deep impression and taking root in the mind, whilst the idea of the reality was transient; and to some perhaps never really occurred in any shape, to whom it is notwithstanding very affecting, as war, death, famine, &c. Besides, many ideas have never been at all present to the senses of any men but by words, as God, angels, devils, heaven and hell, all of which

*Horace, *Ars Poetica*, 111. 'With the tongue for interpreter, she proclaims the movement of the soul.' Ed.

have however a great influence over the passions. Thirdly; by words we have it in our power to make such *combinations* as we cannot possibly do otherwise. By this power of combining we are able, by the addition of well-chosen circumstances, to give a new life and force to the simple object. In painting we may represent any fine figure we please; but we never can give it those enlivening touches which it may receive from words. To represent an angel in a picture, you can only draw a beautiful young man winged; but what painting can furnish out any thing so grand as the addition of one word, 'the angel of the *Lord*?' It is true, I have here no clear idea, but these words affect the mind more than the sensible image did, which is all I contend for. A picture of Priam dragged to the altar's foot, and there murdered, if it were well executed would undoubtedly be very moving; but there are very aggravating circumstances which it could never represent.

Sanguine foedantem quos ipse sacraverat *ignes**

As a further instance, let us consider those lines of Milton, where he describes the travels of the fallen angels through their dismal habitation,

— Through many a dark and dreary vale
They pass'd, and many a region dolorous;
O'er many a frozen, many a fiery Alp;
Rocks, caves, lakes, fens, bogs, dens and shades of death,
A universe of Death.   [*Paradise Lost*, II. 618–22]

Here is displayed the force of union in

Rocks, caves, lakes, fens, bogs, dens and shades;

which yet would lose the greatest part of their effect, if they were not the

Rocks, caves, lakes, fens, bogs, dens and shades —

— of *Death*

This idea or this affection caused by a word, which nothing but a word could annex to the others, raises a very great degree of the sublime; and this sublime is raised yet higher by what follows, a *'universe of Death'*. Here are again two ideas not presentable but by language; and an union of them great and amazing beyond conception; if they may properly be called ideas which present no distinct image to the mind; — but still it will be difficult to conceive how words can move the passions which belong to real objects, without representing these objects clearly. This is difficult to us, because we do not sufficiently distinguish, in our observations upon language, between a clear expression, and a strong expression. These are frequently confounded with each other, though they are in reality extremely different. The former regards the understanding; the latter belongs to the passions. The one describes a thing as it is; the other describes it as it is felt. Now, as there is a moving tone of voice, an impassioned countenance, an agitated gesture, which affect independently of the things about which they are exerted, so there are words, and

---

*Virgil, *Aeneid*, II. 502. 'Tainting with his own blood, the fires he had consecrated.' Ed.

certain dispositions of words, which being peculiarly devoted to passionate subjects, and always used by those who are under the influence of any passion; they touch and move us more than those which far more clearly and distinctly express the subject matter. We yield to sympathy what we refuse to description. The truth is, all verbal description, merely as naked description, though never so exact, conveys so poor and insufficient an idea of the thing described, that it could scarcely have the smallest effect, if the speaker did not call in to his aid those modes of speech that mark a strong and lively feeling in himself. Then, by the contagion of our passions, we catch a fire already kindled in another, which probably might never have been struck out by the object described. Words, by strongly conveying the passions, by those means which we have already mentioned, fully compensate for their weakness in other respects. It may be observed that very polished languages, and such as are praised for their superior clearness and perspicuity, are generally deficient in strength. The French language has that perfection, and that defect. Whereas the oriental tongues, and in general the languages of most unpolished people,* have a great force and energy of expression; and this is but natural. Uncultivated people are but ordinary observers of things, and not critical in distinguishing them; but, for that reason, they admire more, and are more affected with what they see, and therefore express themselves in a warmer and more passionate manner. If the affection be well conveyed, it will work its effect without any clear idea; often without any idea at all of the thing which has originally given rise to it.

It might be expected from the fertility of the subject, that I should consider poetry as it regards the sublime and beautiful more at large; but it must be observed that in this light it has been often and well handled already. It was not my design to enter into the criticism of the sublime and beautiful in any art, but to attempt to lay down such principles as may tend to ascertain, to distinguish, and to form a sort of standard for them; which purposes I thought might be best effected by an enquiry into the properties of such things in nature as raise love and astonishment in us; and by shewing in what manner they operated to produce these passions. Words were only so far to be considered, as to shew upon what principle they were capable of being the representatives of these natural things, and by what powers they were able to affect us often as strongly as the things they represent, and sometimes much more strongly.

Second edition, 1759

---

*N.B. Burke's 'Sublime' gave psychological explanations for the taste for the 'orientalism' of Lowth, Young, Smart and Blake, and anticipated the appeal of Ossian; See pp. 264-267. Ed.

MARK AKENSIDE (1721–1770)

Although perhaps predictably more clinical, Dr Akenside's poem on the imagination, like Thomson's *The Seasons*, Young's *Night Thoughts* and Cowper's *The Task*, is a long poem — its revisions not complete at death — on the poet's perception of Nature, in quasi-Miltonic verse, which points the way to Wordsworth's *The Prelude*. Perhaps only distantly related to Addison's *Spectator* Nos. *411–21*, from which it drew its title, it is close also to the odes of Collins and Gray (see pp. 188, 191).

Crucial to Akenside is the parallel of God's creativity and the poet's ' . . . the Great Spirit, whom his works adore,/Within his own deep essence view'd the forms,/The forms eternal of created things . . . ' (I. 106–08). Strongly anticipatory of the ascent of Snowdon in the final book of *The Prelude* the intellectual frame of Nature is perceived by those of 'nobler hopes' (136) who trace the Great Artist's 'lofty sketches' (142) and, enamour'd, 'see portray'd . . . Those lineaments of beauty which delight/The Mind Supreme . . . partake the eternal joy' (145–49).

'The feet of hoary Time/Through their eternal course have travell'd o'er/ No speechless, lifeless desert . . . ' observes the poet (II. 240–41). As if he has read his Blackwell's *Enquiry into Homer* (see pp. 108-113) and imagined Berkeleyan history, Akenside makes the towering figure of Time and the images of history parts of the grand machine of sublime aesthetics:

> Fancy dreams
> Rapt into high discourse with prophets old,
> And wandering through Elysium, Fancy dreams
> Of sacred fountains, of o'ershadowing groves
> Whose walks with godlike harmony resound:
> Fountains which Homer visits . . .   (I. 162–67)

Shaftesbury's image of the mind travelling outside of time and space, creating heuristic perception as a mirror of the Eternal, seems close to Akenside. Most vigorously Akenside has adopted as his own the suggestion that in a restructuring of Nature as a continuum of imagination, the divisions between pleasure and pain, between heaven and hell, aesthetically speaking, disappear, and in a manner suggestive of Burke, the horrific becomes delightful. Few more explicit depictions of the aesthetic of the ruin can be found in eighteenth-century literature than the following:

> . . . ruthless Havoc from the hand of Time
> Tears the destroying scythe, with surer stroke
> To mow the monuments of Glory down;
> Till Desolation o'er the grass-grown street
> Expands her raven wings, and, from the gate
> Where senates once the weal of nations plann'd,
> Hisseth the gliding snake through hoary weeds
> That clasp the mouldering column.   (II. 677–84)

Meanwhile within the reader's 'throbbing bosom' the 'secret soul' repines 'to taste/The big distress' (686–93).

Similarly Akenside delineates the 'pleasing influence' and 'social powers' of pain in his depiction of a shipwreck worthy of Byron or Delacroix. The crowd 'flies impatient from the village walk/To climb the neighbouring cliffs'. Every mother clutches closer her child and with 'distorted limbs and horrent hair'

> . . . pointing where the waves
> Foam through the shatter'd vessel, shrieks aloud
> As one poor wretch, who spreads his piteous arms
> For succour, swallow'd by the roaring surge,
> As now another, dash'd against the rock,
> Drops lifeless down.   (II. 632–37)

The snake gliding in the weeds and the mother shrieking at the shipwreck remind us that in 'sublime' poetry, necessarily removed from general observation, there was from an early moment in the eighteenth century, a patina of undigested particulars — after the manner perhaps of both Spence and Warton (see pp. 104 and 180) — which anticipates Blake's 'minute particulars' and Wordsworth's 'spots of time'. Akenside's delineation of Addison's third category of 'the Sublime' Beauty, with the memorable pearl which 'shines in the concave of its purple bed' (I. 521f.), like 'the mute shell-fish gasping on the shore' (II. 258), reinforces the impression that the closely-observed particular was Akenside's peculiar talent.

A thematic orientalism reminiscent of Young runs throughout the poem It is clearly not necessary to declare that 'the feet of hoary Time' have crossed 'no speechless, lifeless desert', a cluster of images which anticipate Shelley's *Ozymandias*. 'Indus or Ganges rolling his broad wave/Through mountains, plains, thro' spacious cities old,/And regions dark with woods . . . ' (I. 234–36) is a fine oriental affectation anticipating much later Eastern imaging not only in Keats and Shelley. In Keats's *Hyperion: A Fragment*, perhaps the crucial fall of the Titan of the sun, emblem of finite order — and memory — from the sky to the fate of his fellows is completed in these terms:

> . . . a vast shade
> In the midst of his own brightness, like the bulk
> Of Memnon's image at the set of sun
> To one who travels from the dusking East:
> Sighs, too, as mournful as that Memnon's harp
> He utter'd, while his hands contemplative
> He press'd together . . .   (*Hyperion: A Fragment*, II. 372-8)

Memnon's statue in Egyptian Thebes when touched by the light of the sun in the morning, gave off a mournful sound. In the timeless realm of the imagination a perception of an 'external' object, even of stone, is subject to the poet's divine creativity. Touch, sight, and sound imaged in the stone, the light, and the mournful sound, are intermingled in a world without separating categories in an image closer one might observe to 'oriental' theories of poetry than to the sequential world of Western thought. It is important to observe that mid-century theory — as instanced also in Hartley's Proposition III (see p. 224) — had arrived already at this concept of synaesthesia, or the simultaneity of all the senses, and that Akenside, in I, 150ff., images precisely the mythic occurrence central to Keats:

> For as old Memnon's image long renown'd
> Through fabling Egypt, at the genial touch
> Of morning, from its inmost frame sent forth
> Spontaneous music; so doth Nature's hand,
> To certain attributes which matter claims,
> Adapt the finer organs of the mind   (I. 150–55)

The Pleasures of the Imagination has its *longueurs*. In many instances Akenside is contradictory. God seems to be a Creator who parallels human creation in a spaceless and timeless world, and yet he retains his hieratic seat in the sky. Material objects are, clearly, as in the Memnon passage, excitingly sketched as if in the poet's creative sphere, and yet, the 'moral' sense is found to be finer. Most damningly for Akenside, his *Pleasures of the Imagination* gives no hint that the exciting theories of which he speaks affect the present poet. In Thomson, Young, and Cowper, the most interesting aspect of creative imagination is the thematic variability of the self of the poet, which necessarily dependent on memory, wavers into annihilation either frequently or cumulatively. Of the three major poems 'about' poetry in the mid-century, Akenside's, Collins's, and Gray's, this is the weakest for this very reason.

Nevertheless, in spite of the unfruitful tension between didacticism and poetry, Akenside is important. Almost wholly derivative, restatements of almost all the major theorists of the eighteenth century might be found in his lines. At times, his crystallization of earlier thought rises into its own fineness, and suggests, not far off, the more daring but not always more thoughtful, achievements of the major Romantics.

THE PLEASURES OF THE IMAGINATION

from Book I, (1757)

> From Heaven my strains begin: from Heaven
>   descends
> The flame of genius to the chosen breast,
> And beauty with poetic wonder join'd,   100
> And inspiration. Ere the rising sun
> Shone o'er the deep, or, 'mid the vault of night
> The moon her silver lamp suspended: ere
> The vales with springs were water'd, or with groves
> Of oak or pine the ancient hills were crown'd;

Then the Great Spirit, whom his works adore,
Within his own deep essence view'd the forms,
The forms eternal of created things:
The radiant sun; the moon's nocturnal lamp;
The mountains and the streams; the ample stores   110
Of earth, of heaven, of nature. From the first,
On that full scene his love divine he fix'd,
His admiration: till, in time complete,
What he admir'd and lov'd his vital power
Unfolded into being. Hence the breath
Of life informing each organic frame:
Hence the green earth, and wild-resounding waves:
Hence light and shade, alternate; warmth and cold;
And bright autumnal skies, and vernal showers,
And all the fair variety of things.   120
    But not alike to every mortal eye
Is this great scene unveil'd. For while the claims
Of social life to different labours urge
The active powers of man, with wisest care
Hath Nature on the multitude of minds
Impress'd a various bias; and to each
Decreed its province in the common toil.
To some she taught the fabric of the sphere,
The changeful moon, the circuit of the stars,
The golden zones of heaven: to some she gave   130
To search the story of eternal thought;
Of space, and time*; of fate's unbroken chain,
And will's quick movement: others by the hand
She led o'er vales and mountains, to explore
What healing virtue dwells in every vein
Of herbs or trees. But some to nobler hopes
Were destin'd: some within a finer mould
She wrought, and temper'd with a purer flame.
To these the Sire Omnipotent unfolds,
In fuller aspects and with fairer lights,   140
This picture of the world. Through every part
They trace the lofty sketches of his hand:
In earth, or air, the meadow's flowery store,
The moon's mild radiance, or the virgin's mien
Dress'd in attractive smiles, they see portray'd
(As far as mortal eyes the portrait scan)
Those lineaments of beauty which delight
The Mind Supreme. They also feel their force,

---

*Like his contemporaries, Akenside shared the philosophers' awareness
of the limitations of the spatial-temporal. Ed.

Enamour'd: they partake the eternal joy.
   For as old Memnon's image long renown'd   150
Through fabling Egypt, at the genial touch
Of morning, from its inmost frame sent forth
Spontaneous music; so doth Nature's hand,
To certain attributes which matter claims,
Adapt the finer organs of the mind:
So the glad impulse of those kindred powers
(Of form, of colour's cheerful pomp, of sound
Melodious, or of motion aptly sped)
Detains the enliven'd sense; till soon the soul
Feels the deep concord and assents through all   160
Her functions. Then the charm by fate prepar'd
Diffuseth its enchantment. Fancy dreams,
Rapt into high discourse with prophets old,*
And wandering through Elysium, Fancy dreams
Of sacred fountains, of o'ershadowing groves,
Whose walks with godlike harmony resound:
Fountains, which Homer visits; happy groves,
Where Milton dwells: the intellectual power,
On the mind's throne, suspends his graver cares,
And smiles: the passions, to divine repose,   170
Persuaded yield: and love and joy alone
Are waking: love and joy, such as await
An angel's meditation. O! attend,
Whoe'er thou art whom these delights can touch;
Whom Nature's aspect, Nature's simple garb
Can thus command; O! listen to my song;
And I will guide thee to her blissful walks,
And teach thy solitude her voice to hear,
And point her gracious features to thy view.
   Know then, whate'er of the world's ancient store,   180
Whate'er of mimic Art's reflected scenes,
With love and admiration thus inspire
Attentive Fancy, her delighted sons
In two illustrious orders comprehend,
Self-taught: from him whose rustic toil the lark
Cheers warbling, to the bard whose daring thoughts
Range the full orb of being, still the form,
 Which fancy worships, or sublime or fair
Her votaries proclaim. I see them dawn:
I see the radiant visions where they rise,   190
More lovely than when Lucifer displays
His glittering forehead through the gates of morn,

---

*For example, Ezekiel, Ed.

To lead the train of Phoebus and the Spring.
　　Say, why was man so eminently rais'd
Amid the vast creation; why impower'd
Through life and death to dart his watchful eye,
With thoughts beyond the limit of his frame;
But that the Omnipotent might send him forth,
In sight of angels and immortal minds,
As on an ample theatre to join　　　　　　　　　　　　　　200
In contest with his equals, who shall best
The task achieve, the course of noble toils,
By wisdom and by mercy preordain'd?
Might send him forth the sovereign good to learn;
To chase each meaner purpose from his breast;
And through the mists of passion and of sense,
And thro' the pelting storms of chance and pain,
To hold straight on with constant heart and eye
Still fix'd upon his everlasting palm,
The approving smile of Heaven? Else wherefore burns　　210
In mortal bosoms this unquenched hope,
That seeks from day to day sublimer ends;
Happy, though restless? Why departs the soul
Wide from the track and journey of her times,
To grasp the good she knows not? In the field
Of things which may be, in the spacious field
Of science, potent arts, or dreadful arms,
To raise up scenes in which her own desires
Contented may repose; when things, which are,
Pall on her temper, like a twice-told tale:　　　　　　220
Her temper, still demanding to be free;
Spurning the rude control of wilful might;
Proud of her dangers brav'd, her griefs endur'd,
Her strength severely prov'd? To these high aims,
Which reason and affection prompt in man,
Not adverse nor unapt hath Nature fram'd
His bold imagination. For, amid
The various forms which this full world presents
Like rivals to his choice, what human breast
E'er doubts, before the transient and minute,　　　　　230
To prize the vast, the stable, the sublime?
Who, that from heights aërial sends his eye
Around a wild horizon, and surveys
Indus or Ganges rolling his broad wave
Through mountains, plains, thro' spacious cities old,
And regions dark with woods; will turn away
To mark the path of some penurious rill
Which murmureth at his feet? Where does the soul

Consent her soaring fancy to restrain,
Which bears her up, as on an eagle's wings,   240
Destin'd for highest heaven; or which of fate's
Tremendous barriers shall confine her flight
To any humbler quarry? The rich earth
Cannot detain her; nor the ambient air
With all its changes. For a while with joy
She hovers o'er the sun, and views the small
Attendant orbs, beneath his sacred beam,
Emerging from the deep, like cluster'd isles
Whose rocky shores to the glad sailor's eye
Reflect the gleams of morning: for a while   250
With pride she sees his firm, paternal sway
Bend the reluctant planets to move each
Round its perpetual year. But soon she quits
That prospect: meditating loftier views,
She darts adventurous up the long career
Of comets; through the constellations holds
Her course, and now looks back on all the stars
Whose blended flames as with a milky stream
Part the blue region. Empyrean tracts,
Where happy souls beyond this concave heaven   260
Abide, she then explores, whence purer light
For countless ages travels through the abyss,
Nor hath in sight of mortals yet arriv'd.
Upon the wide creation's utmost shore*
At length she stands, and the dread space beyond
Contemplates, half-recoiling: nathless down
The gloomy void, astonish'd, yet unquell'd,
She plungeth; down the unfathomable gulf
Where God alone hath being. There her hopes
Rest at the fated goal. For, from the birth   270
Of human kind, the Sovereign Maker said
That not in humble, nor in brief delight,
Not in the fleeting echoes of renown,
Power's purple robes, nor Pleasure's flowery lap,
The soul should find contentment; but, from these
Turning disdainful to an equal good,
Through Nature's opening walks enlarge her aim,
Till every bound at length should disappear,
And infinite perfection fill the scene.

*

---

*This journey to 'creation's utmost shore' parallels similar sublime responses in Addison, Young's *Night Thoughts*, and Lowth. Ed.

                                    It now remains,
In just gradation through the various ranks
Of being, to contemplate how her gifts
Rise in due measure, watchful to attend   520
The steps of rising Nature. Last and least,
In colours mingling with a random blaze,
Doth Beauty dwell. Then higher in the forms
Of simplest, easiest measure; in the bounds
Of circle, cube, or sphere. The third ascent
To symmetry adds colour: thus the pearl
Shines in the concave of its purple bed,
And painted shells along some winding shore
Catch with indented folds the glancing sun.
Next, as we rise, appear the blooming tribes   530
Which clothe the fragrant earth; which draw from her
Their own nutrition; which are born and die;
Yet, in their seed, immortal: such the flowers
With which young Maia pays the village-maids
That hail her natal morn; and such the groves
Which blithe Pomona rears on Vaga's bank,
To feed the bowl of Ariconian swains
Who quaff beneath her branches. Nobler still
Is Beauty's name where, to the full consent
Of members and of features, to the pride   540
Of colour, and the vital change of growth,
Life's holy flame with piercing sense is given,
While active motion speaks the temper'd soul:
So moves the bird of Juno: so the steed
With rival swiftness beats the dusty plain,
And faithful dogs with eager airs of joy
Salute their fellows. What sublimer pomp
Adorns the seat where Virtue dwells on earth,
And Truth's eternal day-light shines around;
What palm belongs to man's imperial front,   550
And woman powerful with becoming smiles,
Chief of terrestrial natures; need we now
Strive to inculcate? Thus hath Beauty there
Her most conspicuous praise to matter lent,
Where most conspicuous through that shadowy veil
Breaks forth the bright expression of a mind:
By steps directing our enraptur'd search
To Him, the first of minds; the chief; the sole;
From whom, through this wide, complicated world,
Did all her various lineaments begin;   560
To whom alone, consenting and entire,
At once their mutual influence all display.

He, God most high (bear witness, Earth and Heaven)
The living fountains in himself contains
Of beauteous and sublime: with him enthron'd
Ere days or years trod their ethereal way,
In his supreme intelligence enthron'd,
The queen of love holds her unclouded state,
Urania. Thee, O Father! this extent
Of matter; thee the sluggish earth and tract   570
Of seas, the heavens and heavenly splendours feel
Pervading, quickening, moving. From the depth
Of thy great essence, forth didst thou conduct
Eternal Form; and there, where Chaos reign'd,
Gav'st her dominion to erect her seat,
And sanctify the mansion. All her works
Well-pleas'd thou didst behold: the gloomy fires
Of storm or earthquake, and the purest light
Of summer; soft Campania's new-born rose,
And the slow weed which pines on Russian hills,   580
Comely alike to thy full vision stand:
To thy surrounding vision, which unites
All essences and powers of the great world
In one sole order, fair alike they stand,
As features well consenting, and alike
Requir'd by Nature ere she could attain
Her just resemblance to the perfect shape
Of universal Beauty, which with thee
Dwelt from the first. Thou also, ancient mind,
Whom love and free beneficence await   590
In all thy doings; to inferior minds,
Thy offspring, and to man, thy youngest son,
Refusing no convenient gift nor good;
Their eyes did'st open, in this earth, yon heaven
Those starry worlds, the countenance divine
Of Beauty to behold.

*

from Book II, (1765)
                              The feet of hoary Time   240
Through their eternal course have travell'd o'er
No speechless, lifeless desert; but through scenes
Cheerful with bounty still; among a pomp
Of worlds, for gladness round the Maker's throne
Loud-shouting, or, in many dialects
Of hope and filial trust, imploring thence
The fortunes of their people: where so fix'd

Were all the dates of being, so dispos'd
To every living soul of every kind
The field of motion and the hour of rest,   250
That each the general happiness might serve;
And, by the discipline of laws divine
Convinc'd of folly or chastis'd from guilt,
Each might at length be happy. What remains
Shall be like what is pass'd; but fairer still,
And still increasing in the godlike gifts
Of Life and Truth. The same paternal hand,
From the mute shell-fish gasping on the shore,
To men, to angels, to celestial minds,
Will ever lead the generations on   260
Through higher scenes of being: while, supplied
From day to day by his enlivening breath,
Inferior orders in succession rise
To fill the void below. As flame ascends,
As vapours to the earth in showers return,
As the pois'd ocean toward the attracting moon
Swells, and the ever-listening planets charm'd
By the sun's call their onward pace incline,
So all things which have life aspire to God,
Exhaustless fount of intellectual day!   270
Centre of souls! Nor doth the mastering voice
Of Nature cease within to prompt aright
Their steps; nor is the care of Heaven withheld
From sending to the toil external aid;
That in their stations all may persevere
To climb the ascent of being, and approach
For ever nearer to the Life divine.
     But this eternal fabric was not rais'd
For man's inspection. Though to some be given
To catch a transient visionary glimpse   280
Of that majestic scene which boundless power
Prepares for perfect goodness, yet in vain
Would human life her faculties expand
To embosom such an object. Nor could e'er
Virtue or praise have touch'd the hearts of men,
Had not the Sovereign Guide, through every stage
Of this their various journey, pointed out
New hopes, new toils, which to their humble sphere
Of sight and strength might such importance hold
As doth the wide creation to his own.   290

*

                    Ask the faithful youth
Why the cold urn, of her whom long he lov'd,
So often fills his arms; so often draws
His lonely footsteps, silent and unseen,
To pay the mournful tribute of his tears?
Oh! he will tell thee that the wealth of worlds
Should ne'er seduce his bosom to forego   620
Those sacred hours when, stealing from the noise
Of care and envy, sweet remembrance soothes
With Virtue's kindest looks his aching breast,
And turns his tears to rapture! Ask the crowd,
Which flies impatient from the village walk
To climb the neighbouring cliffs, when far below
The savage winds have hurl'd upon the coast
Some helpless bark; while holy Pity melts
The general eye, or Terror's icy hand
Smites their distorted limbs and horrent hair;   630
While every mother closer to her breast
Catcheth her child, and, pointing where the waves
Foam through the shatter'd vessel, shrieks aloud
As one poor wretch, who spreads his piteous arms
For succour, swallow'd by the roaring surge,
As now another, dash'd against the rock,
Drops lifeless down. O! deemest thou indeed
No pleasing influence here by Nature given
To mutual terror and compassion's tears?
No tender charm mysterious, which attracts   640
O'er all that edge of pain the social powers
To this their proper action and their end?
Ask thy own heart; when, at the midnight hour,
Slow through that pensive gloom thy pausing eye,
Led by the glimmering taper, moves around
The reverend volumes of the dead, the songs
Of Grecian bards, the records writ by fame
For Grecian heroes, where the Sovran Power
Of heaven and earth surveys the immortal page
Even as a father meditating all   650
The praises of his son, and bids the rest
Of mankind there the fairest model learn
Of their own nature, and the noblest deeds
Which yet the world hath seen. If then thy soul
Join in the lot of those diviner men;
Say, when the prospect darkens on thy view;
When, sunk by many a wound, heroic states
Mourn in the dust and tremble at the frown
Of hard Ambition; when the generous band

Of youths who fought for freedom and their sires   660
Lie side by side in death; when brutal Force
Usurps the throne of Justice, turns the pomp
Of guardian power, the majesty of rule,
The sword, the laurel, and the purple robe,
To poor dishonest pageants, to adorn
A robber's walk, and glitter in the eyes
Of such as bow the knee; when beauteous works,
Rewards of virtue, sculptur'd forms which deck'd
With more than human grace the warrior's arch
Or patriot's tomb, now victims to appease   670
Tyrannic envy, strew the common path
With awful ruins; when the Muse's haunt,
The marble porch where Wisdom wont to talk
With Socrates or Tully, hears no more
Save the hoarse jargon of contentious monks,
Or female Superstition's midnight prayer;
When ruthless Havoc from the hand of Time
Tears the destroying scythe, with surer stroke
To mow the monuments of Glory down;
Till Desolation o'er the grass-grown street   680
Expands her raven wings, and, from the gate
Where senates once the weal of nations plann'd,
Hisseth the gliding snake through hoary weeds
That clasp the mouldering column: thus when all
The widely-mournful scene is fix'd within
Thy throbbing bosom; when the patriot's tear
Starts from thine eye, and thy extended arm
In fancy hurls the thunderbolt of Jove
To fire the impious wreath on Philip's brow,
Or dash Octavius from the trophied car;   690
Say, doth thy secret soul repine to taste
The big distress? or wouldst thou then exchange
Those heart-ennobling sorrows for the lot
Of him who sits amid the gaudy herd
Of silent flatterers bending to his nod;
And o'er them, like a giant, casts his eye,
And says within himself, 'I am a King,
And wherefore should the clamorous voice of woe
Intrude upon mine ear?' The dregs corrupt
Of barbarous ages, that Circaean draught   700
Of servitude and folly, have not yet,
Bless'd by the Eternal Ruler of the world!
Yet have not so dishonour'd, so deform'd
The native judgment of the human soul,
Nor so effac'd the image of her Sire.

DAVID HARTLEY (1705–1757)

New associations of ideas are the most valuable poetic consequence of the philosophy of the eighteenth century. If a sensation (or idea) might be said to be apprehended by philosopher, bard, or 'sublime' poet, in an absence of time and space, the method by which it conjoins with that 'next' to it might be allowed to consist of a context of new creation. The appearance of Hartley's work on ideas, first in Latin in 1746, then in 1749 as *Observations on Man*, seems inevitable after Berkeley (see pp. 62-79) and Hume (see pp. 114-138). His reappearance in Joseph Priestley's *Hartley's Theory of the Human Mind, on the Principle of the Association of Ideas* (1775) and his early influence on Wordsworth and Coleridge — who named his son 'Hartley' — suggests an indispensable link between the continuing epistemological concerns of the mid and late eighteenth century and the intellectual climate of mature Romanticism.

Every sensation caused by an external object, observed Hartley (Proposition III) is retained after the object is removed as an 'infinitesimal vibration' of 'the medullary particles' of the brain. 'All the senses may be considered as so many kinds of feeling; the taste is nearly allied to the feeling, the smell to the taste, and the sight and the hearing to each other', Hartley noted, in an *aperçu* invaluable for an understanding of the age of feeling. Hartley's closeness to earlier poetic theories of motion, to be observed, for example, in *Guardian* No. 86, is indicated in his fourth proposition 'these vibrations are motions backwards and forwards of the small particles; of the same kind with the oscillations of pendulums and the tremblings of the particles of sounding bodies. . . . ' Up to this point, Hartley has been concerned with simple ideas and vibrations. Now he concentrates on the vibrations. 'Sensations by being often repeated, beget ideas', he declares (Prop. IX), adding 'those vibrations which accompany sensations . . . beget . . . feebler vibrations'. These miniature vibrations or, as he called them, 'vibratiuncles' are the stuff of Hartley's concept of the mind.

Readers of Wordsworth's *Intimations of Immortality* observe with interest that Hartley claims that vibrations occur within the womb. These 'natural vibrations' (Prop. IX) give place to those occasioned after the birth. Hartley's model for growth is paralleled in his tenth proposition which suggests that in any association — say of A and B — the vibrations of one, always recalling by association the other, will cumulatively trespass on those of the other. The vibrations of A stimulating those of B, habit brings about a weakening of B's, until A's vibrations take over.

Growth in association having been established, if not entirely convincingly as Coleridge was to argue (see pp. 339-349), Hartley proposed (Prop. XII) that 'beauty, honour, moral qualities &c. are, in fact, thus composed of parts which, by degrees, coalesce into one complex idea'. Hartley's influence in Wordsworth's early poetry is obvious here. It was not only that 'one impulse from a vernal wood' became an alternative to reason, it was that intellectual concepts might be seen as the product of natural association, since single, simple ideas, were assumed to grow organically into the most complex of awarenesses.

There could be some doubt in a reader's mind at this point whether Hartley was interested more in the nature of complex ideas or in the movement associated with their genesis. Some ambiguity exists but it seems clear that, excitingly, Hartley is largely concerned not with static ideas, however produced, but with their association by and of itself. However vivid − or complex − the ideas, whether of pleasure or of pain, it is the movement of association which is the reality. '*Complex Vibrations attending upon complex Ideas . . . may be as vivid as any of the sensory Vibrations excited by the direct Action of Objects*', he affirms (Prop. XIV). Hartley's own work seems itself to grow automatically through enlarging patterns of association. Now, he focusses on the changes within a personality occasioned by complex associations. We note (Cor. ii of Prop. XIV) that we are in the midst of a psychology of personality and identity, for the affections and the will, he observes, arise from the the same principles as 'ideas, intellect, memory, and fancy'. We grow, we may hazard, with the hindsight afforded by Wordsworth, from memory to forgetfulness, to new clusters of memory, without true individuality other than the stage of complexity reached. It is interesting to observe that *Expostulation and Reply, The Tables Turned*, and *Tintern Abbey*, the poems usually accepted as Hartleyan, not only exploit the growth of organic memory as beneficent Nature's greatest boon. They suggest also, in the processes of the verse, a vulnerability of personality characteristic of much Romantic poetry, as if the reader himself had a Hartleyan stake in the *persona* of the poem and in the identity of the poet.

Up to this point, Hartley has expounded the effect of physical sensation on the mind. Now (Prop. XX) he reverses his viewpoint and observes that every motor or bodily movement is the result of association, the will being a product of association. It is clear that Hartley's theory of the mind suggests comprehensive educational possibilities. Instead of enjoying the vitiating and sensational pleasures of the great towns of the Industrial era, so much the concern of Wordsworth's preface to *Lyrical Ballads*, men influenced early by 'natural' poems might become harmonious creations of an all-wise Nature. Hartley's thematic interest in the minds of children − characteristic of the age and of Romanticism − is clearly related to these perspectives.

Hartley's own writing on memory (see pp. 239-244) is less suggestive than his theory of association at large, although his comments on the mental processes of the old are pertinent to an understanding of the aged in Wordsworth's poetry. In this regard and in an overview of Romanticism it is valuable to observe that at heart Hartley's theory of association is an image of continuing and expanding movement parallel to and in harmony with what might be conceived of as the movement or processes of Nature, a kind of creative memory rather than, perhaps, a creative 'imagination'.

In spite of Coleridge's disagreement, Hartley is not entirely tied to the finite sequences, or spatial image of time. He greatly added to the mystery of organic creation in men, and, as his comments on dreams suggest (see pp. 244-248), reinforced the awareness, fundamental to Romanticism, that the real processes of cognition are far more intriguing than mere fantastic escape.

OBSERVATIONS ON MAN (1749)

Part I, Of 'the Doctrine of Vibrations & Association in General', Chapter i
My chief design in the following chapter is briefly to explain, establish, and apply the doctrine of *vibrations* and *association*. The first of these doctrines is taken from the hints concerning the performance of sensation and motion, which Sir Isaac Newton has given at the end of his *Principia*, and in the Questions annexed to his *Optics*; the last from what Mr Locke, and other ingenious persons since his time, have delivered concerning the influence of *association* over our opinions and affections, and its use in explaining those things in an accurate and precise way, which are commonly referred to the power of habit and custom, in a general and indeterminate one.

The doctrine of *vibrations* may appear at first sight to have no connexion with that of *association*; however, if these doctrines be found in fact to contain the laws of the bodily and mental powers respectively, they must be related to each other, since the body and mind are. One may expect, that *vibrations* should infer *association* as their effect, and *association* point to *vibrations* as its cause. I will endeavour, in the present chapter, to trace out this mutual relation.

The proper method of philosophizing seems to be, to discover and establish the general laws of action, affecting the subject under consideration, from certain select, well-defined, and well-attested phaenomena, and then to explain and predict the other phaenomena by these laws. This is the method of analysis and synthesis recommended and followed by Sir Isaac Newton.

I shall not be able to execute, with any accuracy, what the reader might expect of this kind, in respect of the doctrines of *vibrations* and *association*, and their general laws, on account of the great intricacy, extensiveness, and novelty of the subject. However, I will attempt a sketch in the best manner I can, for the service of future inquirers.

from Section 1
'*Of The Doctrine of Vibrations, And
Its Use For Explaining The Sensations*'
PROP. I:

The white medullary Substance of the Brain, spinal Marrow, and the Nerves, proceeding from them, is the immediate Instrument of Sensation and Motion.

Under the word *brain*, in these observations, I comprehend all that lies within the cavity of the skull, i.e., the *cerebrum*, or *brain* properly so called, the *cerebellum*, and the *medulla oblongata*.

This proposition seems to be sufficiently proved in the writings of physicians and anatomists; from the structure and functions of the several organs of the human body; from experiments on living animals; from the symptoms of diseases, and from dissections of morbid bodies. Sensibility, and the power of motion, seem to be conveyed to all the parts, in their natural state, from the brain and spinal marrow, along the nerves. These arise from the medullary, not the cortical part, every where, and are themselves of a white medullary substance. When the nerves of any part are cut, tied, or compressed in any considerable degree, the functions of that part are either entirely destroyed, or much impaired. When the spinal marrow is compressed by a dislocation of the *vertebrae* of the back, all the parts, whose nerves arise below the place of dislocation, become paralytic. When any considerable injury is done to the medullary substance of the brain, sensation, voluntary motion, memory, and intellect, are either entirely lost, or much impaired; and if the injury be very great, this extends immediately to the vital motions also, *viz.* to those of the heart, and organs of respiration, so as to occasion death. But this does not hold equally in respect of the cortical substance of the brain; perhaps not at all, unless as far as injuries done to it extend themselves to the medullary substance. In dissections after apoplexies, palsies, epilepsies, and other distempers affecting the sensations and motions, it is usual to find some great disorder in the brain, from preternatural tumours, from blood, matter, or serum, lying upon the brain, or in its ventricles, &c. This may suffice as general evidence for the present. The particular reasons of some of these phaenomena, with more definite evidences, will offer themselves in the course of these observations.

PROP. II:

The white medullary Substance of the Brain is also the immediate Instrument, by which Ideas are presented to the Mind: or, in other words, whatever Changes are made in this Substance, corresponding Changes are made in our Ideas; and vice versa.

The evidence for this proposition is also to be taken from the writings of physicians and anatomists; but especially from those parts of these writings which treat of the faculties of memory, attention, imagination, &c. and of mental disorders. It is sufficiently manifest from hence, that the perfection of our mental faculties depends upon the perfection of this substance; that all injuries done to it affect the trains of ideas proportionably; and that these cannot be restored to their natural course till such injuries be repaired. Poisons, spirituous liquors, opiates, fevers, blows upon the head, &c. all plainly affect the mind, by first disordering the medullary substance. And evacuations, rest, medicines, time, &c. as plainly restore the mind to its former state, by reversing the foregoing steps. But there will be more and more definite evidence offered in the course of these observations.

PROP. III:

> *The Sensations remain in the Mind for a short time after the sensible Objects are removed.*

This is very evident in the sensations impressed on the eye. Thus, to use Sir Isaac Newton's words, 'If a burning coal be nimbly moved round in a circle, with gyrations continually repeated, the whole circle will appear like fire; the reason of which is, that the sensation of the coal, in the several places of that circle, remains impressed on the *sensorium* until the coal return again to the same place. And so in a quick consecution of the colours,' (*viz.* red, yellow, green, blue, and purple, mentioned in the experiment, whence this passage is taken,) 'the impression of every colour remains on the *sensorium* until a revolution of all the colours be completed, and that first colour return again. The impressions therefore of all the successive colours are at once in the *sensorium* – and beget a sensation of white.' *Optics*, Bk I, P. 2. Experiment 10.

Thus also, when a person has had a candle, a window, or any other lucid and well-defined object, before his eyes for a considerable time, he may perceive a very clear and precise image thereof to be left in the *sensorium*, fancy, or mind (for these I consider as equivalent expressions in our entrance upon these disquisitions,) for some time after he has closed his eyes. At least this will happen frequently to persons who are attentive to these things in a gentle way; for, as this appearance escapes the notice of those who are entirely inattentive, so too earnest a desire and attention prevents it, by introducing another state of mind or fancy.

To these may be referred the appearance mentioned by Sir Isaac Newton, *Optics*, Qu. 16. *viz.* 'When a man in the dark presses either corner of his eye with his finger, and turns his eye away from his finger, he will see a circle of colours like those in the feather of a peacock's tail. And this appearance continues about a second of time after the eye and finger have remained quiet.' The sensation continues therefore in the mind about a second of time after its cause ceases to act.

The same continuance of the sensations is also evident in the ear. For the sounds which we hear are reflected by the neighbouring bodies, and therefore consist of a variety of sounds, succeeding each other at different distances of time, according to the distances of the several reflecting bodies; which yet causes no confusion or apparent complexity of sound, unless the distance of the reflecting bodies be very considerable, as in spacious buildings. Much less are we able to distinguish the successive pulses of the air, even in the gravest sounds.

As to the senses of taste and smell, there seems to be no clear direct evidence for the continuance of their sensations after the proper objects are removed. But analogy would incline one to believe, that they must resemble the senses of sight and hearing in this particular, though the continuance cannot be perceived distinctly, on account of the shortness of it, or other circumstances. For the sensations must be supposed to bear such an analogy to each other, and so to depend in common upon the brain, that all evidence for the continuance of sensations in any one sense, will extend themselves to the rest. Thus all the senses may be considered as so many kinds of feeling; the taste is nearly allied to the feeling, the smell to the taste and the sight and hearing to each other. All which analogies will offer themselves to view when we come to examine each of these senses in particular.

In the sense of feeling, the continuance of heat, after the heating body is removed, and that of the smart of a wound, after the instant of infliction, seem to be of the same kind with the appearances taken notice of in the eye and ear.

But the greatest part of the sensations of this sense resemble those of taste and smell, and vanish to appearance as soon as the objects are removed.

PROP. IV:

> *External Objects impressed upon the Senses occasion, first in the Nerves on which they are impressed, and then in the Brain, Vibrations of the small, and as one may say, infinitesimal, medullary Particles.*

These vibrations are motions backwards and forwards of the small particles; of the same kind with the oscillations of pendulums, and the tremblings of the particles of sounding bodies. They must be conceived to be exceedingly short and small, so as not to have the least efficacy to disturb or move the whole bodies of the nerves or brain. For that the nerves themselves should vibrate like musical strings, is highly absurd; nor was it ever asserted by Sir Isaac Newton, or any of those who have embraced his notion of the performance of sensation and motion, by means of *vibrations*.

In like manner we are to suppose the particles which vibrate, to be of the inferior orders, and not those biggest particles, on which the operations in chemistry, and the colours of natural bodies, depend, according to the opinion of Sir Isaac Newton. Hence, in the *proposition*, I term the medullary particles, which vibrate, *infinitesimal*.

Now that external objects impress vibratory motions upon the medullary substance of the nerves and brain (which is the immediate instrument of sensation, according to the first proposition) appears from the continuance of the sensations mentioned in the third; since no motion, besides a vibratory one, can reside in any part for the least moment of time. External objects, being corporeal, can act upon the nerves and brain, which are also corporeal, by nothing but impressing motion on them. A vibrating motion may continue for a short time in the small medullary particles of the nerves and brain, without disturbing them, and after a short time would cease; and so would correspond to the above-mentioned short continuance of the sensations; and there seems to be no other species of motion that can correspond thereto.

COR. As this proposition is deduced from the foregoing, so if it could be established upon independent principles, (of which I shall treat under the next,) the foregoing might be deduced from it. And on this supposition there would be an argument for the continuance of the sensations, after the removal of their objects; which would extend to the senses of feeling, taste, and smell, in the same manner as to those of sight and hearing.

*

Section 2
*'Of Ideas, Their Generation and Associations; and
of the Agreement of the Doctrine of Vibrations
With the Phaenomena of Ideas'*
PROP. VIII:

Sensations, by being often repeated, leave certain Vestiges, Types, or Images, of themselves, which may be called, Simple Ideas of Sensation.

I took notice in the Introduction, that those ideas which resemble sensations were called ideas of sensation; and also that they might be called *simple* ideas, in respect of the intellectual ones which are formed from them, and of whose very essence it is to be *complex*. But the ideas of sensation are not entirely simple, since they must consist of parts both co-existent and successive, as the generating sensations themselves do.

Now, that the simple ideas of sensation are thus generated, agreeably to the proposition, appears, because the most vivid of these ideas are those where the corresponding sensations are most vigorously impressed, or most frequently renewed; whereas, if the sensation be faint, or uncommon, the generated idea is also faint in proportion, and, in extreme cases, evanescent and imperceptible. The exact observance of the order of place in visible ideas, and of the order of time in audible ones, may likewise serve to shew, that these ideas are copies and offsprings of the impressions made on the eye and ear, in which the same orders were observed respectively. [Cf. Hume on our ideas of time and space, p. 118 and p. 117.] And though it happens, that trains of visible and audible ideas are presented in sallies of the fancy, and in dreams, in which the order of time and place is different from that of any former impressions, yet the small component parts of these trains are copies of former impressions; and reasons may be given for the varieties of their compositions.

It is also to be observed, that this proposition bears a great resemblance to the third; and that, by this resemblance, they somewhat confirm and illustrate one another. According to the third proposition, sensations remain for a short time after the impression is removed; and these remaining sensations grow feebler and feebler, till they vanish. They are therefore, in some part of their declension, of about the same strength with ideas, and in their first state, are intermediate between sensations and ideas. And it seems reasonable to expect, that, if a single sensation can leave a perceptible effect, trace, or vestige, for a short time, a sufficient repetition of a sensation may leave a perceptible effect of the same kind, but of a more permanent nature, *i.e.*, an idea, which shall recur occasionally, at long distances of time, from the impression of the corresponding sensation, and *vice versa*. As to the occasions and causes, which make ideas recur, they will be considered in the next proposition but one.

The method of reasoning used in the last paragraph is farther confirmed by the following circumstance; *viz.* that both the diminutive declining sensations, which remain for a short space after the impressions of the objects cease, and the ideas, which are the copies of such impressions, are far more distinct and vivid, in respect of visible and audible impressions, than of any others. To which it may be added, that, after travelling, hearing music, &c. trains of vivid ideas are very apt to recur, which correspond very exactly to the late impressions, and which are of an intermediate nature between the remaining sensations of the third proposition, in their greatest vigour, and the ideas mentioned in this.

The sensations of feeling, taste, and smell, can scarce be said to leave ideas, unless very indistinct and obscure ones. However, as analogy leads one to suppose that these sensations may leave traces of the same kind, though not in the same degree, as those of sight and hearing; so the readiness with which we reconnoitre [i.e. re-experience] sensations of feeling, taste, and smell, that have been often impressed, is an evidence that they do so; and these generated traces or dispositions of mind may be called the ideas of feeling, taste, and smell. In sleep, when all our ideas are magnified, those of feeling, taste, and smell, are often sufficiently vivid and distinct; and the same thing happens in some few cases of vigilance.

from PROP. IX:

> *Sensory Vibrations, by being often repeated beget, in the medullary Substance of the Brain, a Disposition to diminutive Vibrations, which may also be called Vibratiuncles, and Miniatures, corresponding to themselves respectively.*

This correspondence of the diminutive vibrations to the original sensory ones, consists in this, that they agree in kind, place, and line of direction; and differ only in being more feeble, *i.e.*, in degree.

This proposition follows from the foregoing. For since sensations, by being often repeated, beget ideas, it cannot but be that those vibrations, which accompany sensations, should beget something which may accompany ideas in like manner; and this can be nothing but feebler vibrations, agreeing with the sensory generating vibrations in kind, place, and line of direction.

Or thus: By the first proposition it appears, that some motion must be excited in the medullary substance, during each sensation; by the fourth, this motion is determined to be a vibratory one: since therefore some motion must also, by the second, be excited in the medullary substance during the presence of each idea, this motion cannot be any other than a vibratory one: else how should it proceed from the original vibration attending the sensation, in the same manner as the idea does from the sensation itself? It must also agree in kind, place, and line of direction, with the generating vibration. A vibratory motion, which recurs t times in a second, cannot beget a diminutive one that recurs $\frac{1}{2} t$, or $2 t$ times; nor one originally impressed on the region of the brain corresponding to the auditory nerves, beget diminutive vibrations in the region corresponding to the optic nerves; and so of the rest. The line of direction must likewise be the same in the original and derivative vibrations. It remains therefore, that each simple idea of sensation be attended by diminutive vibrations of the same kind, place, and line of direction, with the original vibrations attending the sensation itself: or, in the words of the proposition, that sensory vibrations, by being frequently repeated, beget a disposition to diminutive vibrations corresponding to themselves respectively. We may add, that the vibratory nature of the motion which attends ideas, may be inferred from the continuance of some ideas, visible ones for instance, in the fancy for a few moments.

This proof of the present proposition from the foregoing appears to be incontestable, admitting the fourth: however, it will much establish and illustrate the doctrines of vibrations and association, to deduce it directly, if we can, from the nature of vibratory motions, and of an animal body; and not only from the relation between sensations and ideas. Let us see, therefore, what progress we can make in such an attempt.

First, then, if we admit vibrations of the medullary particles at all, we must conceive, that some take place in the *foetus in utero*, both on account of the warmth in which it lies, and of the pulsation of those considerable arteries, which pass through the medullary substance, and which consequently must compress and agitate it upon every contraction of the heart. And these vibrations are probably either uniform in kind and degree, if we consider short spaces of time; or, if long ones, increase in a slow uniform manner, and that in degree only, as the *foetus in utero* increases in bulk and strength. They are also probably the same in all the different regions of the medullary substance. Let these vibrations be called the *natural vibrations*.

Secondly, As soon as the child is born, external objects act upon it violently, and excite vibrations in the medullary substance, which differ from the natural ones, and from each other, in degree, kind, place, and line of direction. We may also conceive that each region of the medullary substance has such a texture as to receive, with the greatest facility, the several specific vibrations, which the objects corresponding respectively to these regions, *i.e.*, to their nerves, are most disposed to excite. Let these vibrations be, for the present, called *preternatural* ones, in contradistinction to those which we just now called natural ones.

Thirdly, Representing now the natural vibrations by N, and the preternatural ones, from various objects, by A, B, C, &c. let us suppose the first object to impress the vibrations A, and then to be removed. It is evident from the nature of vibratory motions, that the medullary substance will not, immediately upon the removal of this object, return to its natural state N, but will remain, for a short space of time, in the preternatural state A, and pass gradually from A to N. Suppose the same object to be impressed again and again, for a sufficient number of times, and it seems to follow, that the medullary substance will be longer in passing from A to N, after the second impression than after the first, after the third impression than second, &c. till, at last, it will not return to its natural original state of vibration N at all, but remain in the preternatural state A, after the vibrations have fallen to a diminutive pitch, their kind and place, or chief seat, and their line of directions, continuing the same. This state may therefore be fitly denoted by a, and, being now in the place of the natural state N, it will be kept up by the heat of the medullary substance, and the pulsation of its arteries. All this seems to follow from the above-mentioned disposition of animal bodies to accommodate themselves to, and continue in, almost any state that is often impressed; which is evident from innumerable both common and medical observations, whatever be determined concerning the manner of explaining and accounting for these facts. For the alterations which habit, custom, frequent impression, &c. make in the small constituent particles, can scarce be anything besides alterations of the distances, and mutual actions, of these particles; and these last alterations must alter the natural tendency to vibrate. We must, however, here resume the supposition made in the last paragraph, viz. that the several regions of the brain have such a texture as disposes them to those specific vibrations, which are to be impressed by the proper objects in the events of life. And this will much facilitate and accelerate the transition of the state N into a: since we are to suppose a predisposition to the state A, or a.

*

from PROP. X:

> *Any Sensations A, B, C, &c. by being associated with one another a sufficient Number of Times, get such a Power over the corresponding Ideas a, b, c, &c. that any one of the Sensations A, when impressed alone, shall be able to excite in the Mind, b, c, &c. the Ideas of the rest.*

. . . the word *association*, in the particular sense here affixed to it, was first brought into use by Mr. Locke. But all that has been delivered by the ancients and moderns, concerning the power of habit, custom, example, education, authority, party-prejudice, the manner of learning the manual and liberal arts, &c. goes upon this doctrine as its foundation, and may be considered as the detail of it, in various circumstances. I here begin with the simplest case, and shall proceed to more and more complex ones continually, till I have exhausted what has occurred to me upon this subject.

This proposition, or first and simplest case of association, is manifest from innumerable common observations. Thus, the names, smells, tastes, and tangible qualities of natural bodies, suggest their visible appearances to the fancy, *i.e.*, excite their visible ideas; and, *vice versa*, their visible appearances impressed on the eye raise up those powers of reconnoitring [i.e. re-experiencing] their names, smells, tastes, and tangible qualities, which may not improperly be called their ideas, as above noted; and in some cases raise up ideas, which may be compared with visible ones, in respect of vividness. All which is plainly owing to the association of the several sensible qualities of bodies with their names, and with each other. It is remarkable, however, as being agreeable to the superior vividness of visible and audible ideas, before taken notice of, that the suggestion of the visible appearance from the name is the most ready of any other; and, next to this, that of the name from the visible appearance; in which last case, the reality of the audible idea, when not evident to the fancy, may be inferred from the ready pronunciation of the name. For it will be shewn hereafter, that the audible idea is most commonly a previous requisite to pronunciation. Other instances of power of association may be taken from compound visible and audible impressions. Thus the sight of part of a large building suggests the idea of the rest instantaneously; and the sound of the words which begin a familiar sentence, brings the remaining part to our memories in order, the association of the parts being synchronous in the first case, and successive in the last.

It is to be observed, that, in successive associations, the power of raising the ideas is only exerted according to the order in which the association is made. Thus, if the impressions A, B, C, be always made in the order of the alphabet, B impressed alone will not raise a, but c only. Agreeably to which it is easy to repeat familiar sentences in the order in which they always occur, but impossible to do it readily in an inverted one. The reason of this is, that the compound idea, c, b, a, corresponds to the compound sensation C, B, A; and therefore requires the impression of C, B, A, in the same manner as a, b, c, does that of A, B, C. This will, however, be more evident, when we come to consider the associations of vibratory motions, in the next proposition.

It is also to be observed, that the power of association grows feebler, as the number either of synchronous or successive impressions is increased, and does not extend, with due force, to more than a small one, in the first and simplest cases. But, in complex cases, or the associations of associations, of which the memory, in its full extent, consists, the powers of the mind, deducible from this source, will be found much greater than any person, upon his first entrance on these inquiries, could well imagine.

from PROP. XI:

> *Any vibrations,* A, B, C, &c. *by being associated together a sufficient Number of Times, get such a Power over* a, b, c, &c. *the corresponding Miniature Vibrations, that any of the Vibrations* A, *when impressed alone, shall be able to excite* b, c, &c. *the Miniatures of the rest.*

This proposition may be deduced from the foregoing, in the same manner as the ninth has been from the eigth.

But it seems also deducible from the nature of vibrations, and of an animal body. Let A and B be two vibrations, associated synchronically. Now, it is evident, that the vibration A (for I will, in this proposition, speak of A and B in the singular number, for the sake of greater clearness), will, by endeavouring to diffuse itself into those parts of the medullary substance which are affected primarily by the vibration B, in some measure modify and change B, so as to make B a little different from what it would be, if impressed alone. For the same reasons the vibration A will be a little affected, even in its primary seat, by the endeavour of B to diffuse itself all over the medullary substance. Suppose now the vibrations A and B to be impressed at the same instant, for a thousand times; it follows, from the ninth proposition, that they will first overcome the disposition to the natural vibrations N, and then leave a tendency to themselves, which will now occupy the place of the original natural tendency to vibrations. When therefore the vibration A is impressed alone, it cannot be entirely such as the object would excite of itself, but must lean, even in its primary seat, to the modifications and changes induced by B, during their thousand joint impressions; and therefore much more, in receding from this primary seat, will it lean that way; and when it comes to the seat of B, it will excite B's miniature a little modified and changed by itself.

Or thus: When A is impressed alone, some vibration must take place in the primary seat of B, both on account of the heat and pulsation of the arteries, and because A will endeavour to diffuse itself over the whole medullary substance. This cannot be that part of the natural vibrations N, which belongs to this region, because it is supposed to be overruled already. It cannot be that which A impressed alone would have propagated into this region, because that has always hitherto been overruled and converted into B; and therefore cannot have begotten a tendency to itself. It cannot be any full vivid vibration, such as B, C, D, &c. belonging to this region, because all full vibrations require the actual impression of an object upon the corresponding external organ. And of miniature vibrations belonging to this region, such as b, c, d, &c. it is evident, that b has the preference, since A leans to it a little, even in its own primary seat, more and more, in receding from this, and almost entirely, when it comes to the primary seat of B. For the same reasons B impressed alone will excite a; and, in general, if A, B, C, &c. be vibrations synchronically impressed on different regions of the medullary substance, A impressed alone will at last excite b, c, &c. according to the proposition.

If A and B be vibrations impressed successively, then will the latter part of A, *viz.* that part which, according to the third and fourth propositions, remains, after the impression of the object ceases, be modified and altered by B, at the same time that it will a little modify and alter it, till at last it be quite overpowered by it, and end in it. It follows therefore, by a like method of reasoning, that the successive impression of

A and B, sufficiently repeated, will so alter the medullary substance, as that when A is impressed alone, its latter part shall not be such as the sole impression of A requires, but lean towards B, and end in b at last. But B will not excite a in retrograde order, since, by supposition, the latter part of B was not modified and altered by A, but by some other vibration, such as C or D. And as B, by being followed by C, may at last raise c; so b, when raised by A, in the method here proposed, may be also suffucient to raise c; inasmuch as the miniature c being a feeble motion, not stronger, perhaps, than the natural vibrations N, requires only to have its kind, place, and line of direction, determined by association, the heat and arterial pulsation conveying to it the requisite degree of strength. And thus A impressed alone will raise b, c, &c. in successive associations, as well as in synchronous ones, according to the proposition.

It seems also, that the influence of A may, in some degree, reach through B to C; so that A of itself may have some effect to raise c, as well as by means of b. However, it is evident, that this chain must break off, at last, in long successions; and that sooner or later, according to the number and vigour of the repeated impressions. The power of miniature vibrations to raise other miniatures may, perhaps, be made clearer to mathematicians, by hinting, that the efficacy of any vibration to raise any other, is not in the simple ratio of its vividness, but as some power thereof less than unity; for thus b may raise c, a weaker vibration than b, c may raise d, &c. with more facility than if the efficacy was in the simple ratio of the vividness, and yet so that the series shall break off at last.

If the ninth proposition be allowed, we may prove this in somewhat a shorter and easier manner, as follows. Since the vibrations A and B are impressed together, they must, from the diffusion necessary to vibratory motions, run into one vibration; and consequently, after a number of impressions sufficiently repeated, will leave a trace, or miniature, of themselves, as one vibration, which will recur every now and then, from slight causes. Much rather, therefore, may the part b of the compound miniature $a + b$ recur, when the part A of the compound original vibration $A + B$ is impressed.

And as the ninth proposition may be thus made to prove the present, so it ought to be acknowledged and remarked here, that unless the ninth be allowed, the present cannot be proved, or that the power of association is founded upon, and necessarily requires, the previous power of forming ideas, and miniature vibrations. For ideas, and miniature vibrations, must first be generated, according to the eighth and ninth propositions, before they can be associated, according to the tenth and this eleventh. But then (which is very remarkable) this power of forming ideas, and their corresponding miniature vibrations, does equally presuppose the power of association. For since all sensations and vibrations are infinitely divisible, in respect of time and place, they could not leave any traces or images of themselves, *i.e.*, any ideas, or miniature vibrations, unless their infinitesimal parts did cohere together through joint impression, *i.e.*, association. Thus, to mention a gross instance, we could have no proper idea of a horse, unless the particular ideas of the head, neck, body, legs, and tail, peculiar to this animal, stuck to each other in the fancy, from frequent joint impression. And, therefore, in dreams, where complex associations are much weakened, and various parcels of visible ideas, not joined in nature, start up together in the fancy, contiguous to each other, we often see monsters, chimeras, and combinations, which have never been actually presented. [N.B. The importance of Hartley for the Romantic interest in dreams, and see pp. 244-48.]

Association seems also necessary to dispose the medullary substance to this or that miniature vibration, in succession, after the miniatures of a large number of original vibrations have been generated.

Nor does there seem to be any precise limit which can be set to this mutual dependence of the powers of generating miniatures, and of association upon each other: however they may both take place together, as the heart and brain are supposed to do, or both depend upon one simple principle; for it seems impossible, that they should imply one another *ad infinitum*. There is no greater difficulty here than in many other cases of mutual indefinite implication, known and allowed by all. Nay, one may almost deduce some presumption in favour of the hypothesis here produced, from this mutual indefinite implication of its parts so agreeable to the tenor of nature in other things. And it is certainly a presumption in its favour, that a less power of generating miniatures will be a foundation for a larger of association and *vice versa*, till, at last, the whole superstructure of ideas and associations observable in human life may, by proceeding upwards according to analysis, and downwards according to synthesis, be built upon as small a foundation as we please. Thus we may observe, that neither does this eleventh proposition necessarily require the ninth, in its full extent, nor *vice versa*, for their demonstration. The least miniatures, with the feeblest cohesions of their parts, will, by degrees, run into larger, with stronger cohesions, from the same principles. . . .

Let me add, that the generation of sensible ideas from sensations, and the power of raising them from association, when considered as faculties of the mind, are evident and unquestionable. Since therefore sensations are conveyed to the mind, by the efficiency of corporeal causes of the medullary substance, as is acknowledged by all physiologists and physicians, it seems to me, that the powers of generating ideas, and raising them by association, must also arise from corporeal causes, and consequently admit of an explication from the subtle influences of the small parts of matter upon each other, as soon as these are sufficiently understood; which is farther evinced from the manifest influences of material causes upon our ideas and associations, taken notice of under the second proposition. And as a vibratory motion is more suitable to the nature of sensation than any other species of motion, so does it seem also more suitable to the powers of generating ideas, and raising them by association. However, these powers are evident independently, as just now observed; so that the doctrine of association may be laid down as a certain foundation, and a clue to direct our future inquiries, whatever becomes of that of vibrations.

from PROP. XII:

Simple Ideas will run into complex ones, by Means of Association.

In order to explain and prove this proposition, it will be requisite to give some previous account of the manner in which simple ideas of sensation may be associated together.

Case 1. Let the sensation A be often associated with each of the sensations B, C, D, &c. *i.e.*, at certain times with B, at certain other times with C, &c. it is evident, from the tenth proposition, that A, impressed alone, will, at last, raise b, c, d, &c. all together, *i.e.*, associate them with one another, provided they belong to different regions of the medullary substance [a, b, c, d, are of course the miniature vibrations or 'vibratiuncles' created by but not dependent on 'real' sensations A, B, C, D, etc.]; for if any two, or more, belong to the same region, since they cannot exist together in their distinct forms, A will raise something intermediate between them.

Case 2. If the sensations A, B, C, D, &c. be associated together, according to various combinations of twos, or even threes, fours, &c, then will A raise b, c, d, &c. also B raise a, c, d, &c. as in case the first.

It may happen, indeed, in both cases, that A may raise a particular miniature, as b, preferably to any of the rest, from its being more associated with B, from the novelty of the impression of B, from a tendency in the medullary substance to favour b, &c. and in like manner, that b may raise c or d preferably to the rest. However, all this will be over-ruled, at least, by the recurrency of the associations; so that any one of the sensations will excite the ideas of the rest at the same instant, *i.e.*, associate them together.

Case 3. Let A, B, C, D, &c. represent successive impressions, it follows from the tenth and eleventh propositions, that A will raise b, c, d, &c. B raise c, d, &c. And though the ideas do not, in this case, rise precisely at the same instant, yet they come nearer together than the sensations themselves did in their original impression; so that these ideas are associated almost synchronically at least, and successively from the first. The ideas come nearer to one another than the sensations, on account of their diminutive nature, by which all that appertains to them is contracted. And this seems to be as agreeable to observation as to theory.

Case 4. All compound impressions $A + B + C + D$, &c. after sufficient repetition leave compound miniatures $a + b + c + d$, &c. which recur every now and then from slight causes, as well such as depend on association, as some which are different from it. Now, in these recurrences of compound miniatures, the parts are farther associated, and approach perpetually nearer to each other, agreeably to what was just now observed; *i.e.*, the association becomes perpetually more close and intimate.

Case 5. When the ideas, *a, b, c, d,* &c. have been sufficiently associated in any one or more of the foregoing ways, if we suppose any single idea of these, *a* for instance, to be raised by the tendency of the medullary substance that way, by the association of *A* with a foreign sensation or idea *X* or *x,* &c. this idea *a,* thus raised, will frequently bring in all the rest, *b, c, d,* &c. and so associate all of them together still farther.

And upon the whole, it may appear to the reader, that the simple ideas of sensation must run into clusters and combinations, by association; and that each of these will, at last, coalesce into one complex idea, by the approach and commixture of the several compounding parts.

It appears also from observation, that many of our intellectual ideas, such as those that belong to the heads of beauty, honour, moral qualities, &c. [i.e. the personifications or personified abstractions of poetry] are, in fact, thus composed of parts, which, by degrees, coalesce into one complex idea.

And as this coalescence of simple ideas into complex ones is thus evinced, both by the foregoing theory, and by observation, so it may be illustrated, and farther confirmed, by the similar coalescence of letters into syllables and words, in which association is likewise a chief instrument.

*

PROP. XIII:

> *When simple Ideas run into a complex one, according to the foregoing Proposition, we are to suppose, that the simple miniature Vibrations corresponding to those simple Ideas, run in like manner, into a complex miniature Vibration, corresponding to the resulting complex Idea.*

This proposition is analogous to the ninth and eleventh, and may be deduced from the last, as they are from the eighth and tenth respectively. It is also an evidence and illustration of the second; shewing, not only that the state of the medullary substance is changed, according to the several natures of the ideas which are presented to the mind; but also shewing, in general, of what kind this change is, and in what manner it is affected.

from PROP. XIV:

> *It is reasonable to think, that some of the complex Vibrations attending upon complex Ideas, according to the last Proposition, may be as vivid as any of the sensory Vibrations excited by the direct Action of Objects.*

For these complex vibrations may consist of so many parts co-existent and successive, and these parts may so alter and exalt one another, as that the resulting agitations in the medullary substance may no longer be miniature vibrations, but vivid ones equal to those excited by objects impressed on the senses. This process may be farther favoured by a mixture of vivid real impressions among the ideas, by the irritability of the medullary substance, by a previous disposition to the vibrations to be excited, &c.

COR. I. When the complex miniature vibrations are thus exalted in degree, we are to conceive, that the corresponding complex ideas are proportionally exalted, and so pass into intellectual affections and passions. We are therefore to deduce the origin of the intellectual pleasures and pains, which are the objects of these affections and passions, from the source here laid open.

COR. II. Since the present proposition unfolds the nature of affections and will, in the same manner, and from the same principles, as the twelfth does that of ideas, intellect, memory, and fancy; it follows, that all these are of the same original and consideration, and differ only in degree, or some accidental circumstances. They are all deducible from the external impressions made upon the senses, the vestiges or ideas of these, and their mutual connexions by means of association, taken together and operating on one another.

COR. III. It follows also from this proposition, that the intellectual pleasures and pains may be greater, equal, or less, than the sensible ones, according as each person unites more or fewer, more vivid or more languid, miniature vibrations in the formation of his intellectual pleasures and pains &c.

*

from PROP. XX:

All that has been delivered above, concerning the Derivation of ideal Vibratiuncles from sensory Vibrations, and concerning their Associations, may be fitly applied to motory Vibrations and Vibratiuncles.

This proposition is the immediate consequence of admitting the doctrines of vibrations and association, in the manner in which they have been asserted in the foregoing propositions. It contains the theory of the voluntary and semi-voluntary motions; to facilitate the application of which theory in the next proposition, I shall deliver the principal cases of this, in the following corollaries.

COR. I. The motory vibrations of the five classes mentioned Prop. XVIII. will generate a propensity to corresponding motory vibratiuncles.

COR. II. These motory vibratiuncles will affect the brain, as well as the motory nerves along which they descend; and, indeed, their descent along the motory nerves will be principally owing to their being first excited in the brain. This is sufficiently evident in the motory vibratiuncles which are derived from the motory vibrations of the second and third classes. As to the motory vibrations of the other classes, it is evident, that the brain is strongly affected by the sensory vibrations which give birth to them, and consequently, that a proportional affection of the brain must take place in the motory vibratiuncles derived from them.

*

from PROP. XXI:

> *The voluntary and semi-voluntary Motions are deducible from Association, in the Manner laid down in the last Proposition.*

In order to verify this proposition, it is necessary to inquire, what connexions each automatic motion has gained by association with other motions, with ideas, or with foreign sensations, according to the third, fourth, and sixth corollaries of the last proposition, so as to depend upon them, *i.e.*, so as to be excited no longer, in the automatic manner described in the nineteenth proposition, but merely by the previous introduction of the associated motion, idea, or sensation. If it follow that idea, or state of mind (*i.e.*, set of compound vibratiuncles), which we term the will, directly, and without our perceiving the intervention of any other idea, or of any sensation or motion, it may be called voluntary, in the highest sense of this word. If the intervention of other ideas, or of sensations and motions (all which we are to suppose to follow the will directly), be necessary, it is imperfectly voluntary; yet still it will be called voluntary, in the language of mankind, if it follow certainly and readily upon the intervention of a single sensation, idea, or motion, excited by the power of the will: but if more than one of these be required, or if the motion do not follow with certainty and facility, it is to be esteemed less and less voluntary, semi-voluntary, or scarce voluntary at all, agreeably to the circumstances. Now, if it be found, upon a careful and impartial inquiry, that the motions which occur every day in common life, and which follow the idea called the will, immediately or mediately, perfectly or imperfectly, do this, in proportion to the number and degree of strength in the associations, this will be sufficient authority for ascribing all which we call voluntary in actions to association, agreeably to the purport of this proposition. And this, I think, may be verified from facts, as far as it is reasonable to expect, in a subject of inquiry so novel and intricate.

In the same manner as any action may be rendered voluntary, the cessation from any, or a forcible restraint upon any, may be also, *viz.* by proper associations with the feeble vibrations in which inactivity consists, or with the strong action of the antagonist muscles.

After the actions, which are most perfectly voluntary, have been rendered so by one set of associations, they may, by another, be made to depend upon the most diminutive sensations, ideas, and motions, such as the mind scarce regards, or is conscious of; and which therefore it can scarce recollect the moment after the action is over. Hence it follows, that association not only converts automatic actions into voluntary, but voluntary into automatic. For these actions, of which the mind is scarce conscious, and which follow mechanically, as it were, some precedent diminutive sensation, idea or motion, and without any effort of the mind, are rather to be ascribed to the body than the mind, *i.e.*, are to be referred to the head of automatic motions. I shall call them automatic motions of the secondary kind, to distinguish them both from those which are originally automatic, and from the voluntary ones; and shall now give a few instances of this double transmutation of motions, *viz.* of automatic into voluntary, and of voluntary into automatic.

The fingers of young children* bend upon almost every impression which is made upon the palm of the hand, thus performing the action of grasping in the original automatic manner. After a sufficient repetition of the motory vibrations which concur in this action, their vibratiuncles are generated, and associated strongly with other vibrations or vibratiuncles, the most common of which, I suppose, are those excited by the sight of a favourite plaything which the child uses to grasp, and hold in his hand. He ought, therefore, according to the doctrine of association, to perform and repeat the action of grasping, upon having such a plaything presented to his sight. But it is a known fact, that children do this. By pursuing the same method of reasoning, we may see how, after a sufficient repetition of the proper associations, the sound of the words, *grasp, take hold*, &c. the sight of the nurse's hand in a state of contraction, the idea of a hand, and particularly of the child's own hand, in that state, and innumerable other associated circumstances, *i.e.*, sensations, ideas, and motions, will put the child upon grasping, till, at last, that idea, or state of mind which we may call the will to grasp, is generated and sufficiently associated with the action to produce it instantaneously. It is therefore perfectly voluntary in this case; and by the innumerable repetitions of it in this perfectly voluntary state, it comes, at last, to obtain a sufficient connexion with so many diminutive sensations, ideas, and motions, as to follow them in the same manner, as originally automatic actions do the corresponding sensations, and consequently to be automatic secondarily. And in the same manner, may all the actions performed with the hands be explained, all those that are very familiar in life passing from the original automatic state through the several degrees of voluntariness till they become perfectly voluntary, and then repassing through the same degrees in an inverted order, till they become secondarily automatic on many occasions, though still perfectly voluntary on some, *viz.* whensoever an express act of the will is exerted.

I will, in the next place, give a short account of the manner in which we learn to speak, as it may be deduced from the foregoing proposition. The new-born child is not able to produce a sound at all, unless the muscles of the trunk and larynx be stimulated thereto by the impression of pain on some part of the body. As the child advances in age, the frequent returns of this action facilitate it; so that it recurs from less and less pains, from pleasures, from mere sensations, and lastly from slight associated circumstances, in the manner already explained. About the same time that this process is thus far advanced, the muscles of speech act

---

*One might find evidence, here and below (see pp. 242-243), to suggest that the Romantic interest in children emerged indirectly from a concern with the nature of perception. Ed.

occasionally, in various combinations, according to the associations of the motory vibratiuncles with each other. Suppose now the muscles of speech to act in these combinations at the same time that sound is produced from some agreeable impression, a mere sensation, or a slight associated cause, which must be supposed to be often the case, since it is so observable, that young children, when in a state of health and pleasure, exert a variety of actions at the same time. It is evident, that an articulate sound, or one approaching thereto, will sometimes be produced by this conjoint action of the muscles of the trunk, larynx, tongue, and lips; and that both these articulate sounds, and inarticulate ones, will often recur, from the recurrence of the same accidental causes. After they have recurred a sufficient number of times, the impression, which these sounds, articulate and inarticulate, make upon the ear, will become an associated circumstance (for the child always hears himself speak, at the same time that he exerts the action) sufficient to produce a repetition of them. And thus it is, that children repeat the same sounds over and over again, for many successions, the impression of the last sound upon the ear exciting a fresh one, and so on, till the organs be tired . . .

*

from PROP. XXII:

It follows, from the Hypothesis here proposed, concerning the voluntary Motions, that a Power of obtaining Pleasure and Removing Pain will be generated early in Children, and increase afterwards every Day.

For the motions which are previous and subservient to the obtaining of pleasure, and the removal of pain, will be much more frequent, from the very instant of birth, than those which occasion pain. The number also of the first will be perpetually increasing, of the last decreasing. Both which positions may be evinced by the following arguments:

First, The pleasures are much more numerous than the pains. Hence the motions which are subservient to them are much more numerous also.

Secondly, The associated circumstances of the pleasures are many more in number than the pleasures themselves. But these circumstances, after a sufficient association, will be able to excite the motions subservient to the pleasures, as well as these themselves. And this will greatly augment the methods of obtaining pleasure.

Thirdly, It favours the position here advanced, that the motions subservient to pleasure are of a moderate nature; and therefore, that they can be excited with the more ease, both in an automatic and voluntary manner.

Fourthly, The pains, and consequently the motions subservient to them, are few, and of a violent nature. These motions are also various, and therefore cannot be united to objects and ideas with constancy and steadiness; and, which is most to be regarded, they end, at last, from the very make of the body, in that species of motion which contributes most to remove or assuage the pain. This species therefore, since it recurs the most frequently, and continues longest, must be confirmed by association, to the exclusion of the rest.

COR. I. Many changes in the actions of young children, very difficult to be explained, according to the usual methods of considering human actions, appear to admit of a solution from this proposition. These changes are such as tend to the ease, convenience, pleasure, of the young child; and they are sufficiently observable in the transition of the originally automatic actions into voluntary ones, as matters of fact, whatever be determined concerning their cause. I shall therefore refer to them occasionally, in the course of these papers, as allowed matters of fact.

COR. II. It seems also, that many very complex propensities and pursuits in adults, by which they seek their own pleasure and happiness, both explicitly and implicitly, may be accounted for, upon the same, or such-like principles.

COR. III. To similar causes we must also refer that propensity to excite and cherish grateful ideas and affections, and trains of these, which is so observable in all mankind. However, this does not hold in so strict a manner, but that ungrateful trains will present themselves, and recur on many occasions, and particularly whenever there is a morbid, and somewhat painful, state of the medullary substance.

COR. IV. Since God is the source of all good, and consequently must at last appear to be so, *i.e.*, be associated with all our pleasures, it seems to follow, even from this proposition, that the idea of God, and of the ways by which his goodness and happiness are made manifest, must, at last, take place of, and absorb all other ideas, and he himself become, according to the language of the Scriptures, *All in all*.

COR. V. This proposition, and its corollaries, afford some very general, and perhaps new, instances of the coincidence of efficient and final causes.

COR. VI. The agreement of the doctrines of vibrations and association, both with each other, and with so great a variety of the phaenomena of the body and mind, may be reckoned a strong argument for their truth.

*

from Chapter iii, Section 4, 'Of Memory'
PROP. XC:
> To examine how far the Phaenomena of Memory are agreeable to the
> foregoing theory.

Memory was defined in the introduction to be the faculty by which traces of sensations and ideas recur, or are recalled, in the same order and proportion, accurately or nearly, as they were once presented.

Now here we may observe,

First, That memory depends entirely or chiefly on the state of the brain.

For diseases, concussions of the brain, spirituous liquors, and some poisons, impair or destroy it; and it generally returns again with the return of health, from the use of proper medicines and methods. And all this is peculiarly suitable to the notion of vibrations. If sensations and ideas arise from peculiar vibrations, and dispositions to vibrate, in the medullary substance of the brain, it is easy to conceive, that the causes above alleged may so confound the sensations and ideas, as that the usual order and proportion of the idea shall be destroyed.

Secondly, The rudiments of memory are laid in the perpetual recurrency of the same impressions, and clusters of impressions. How these leave traces, in which the order is preserved, may be understood from the eighth, ninth, tenth, and eleventh propositions.

The traces which letters, and words, *i.e.*, clusters of letters, leave, afford an instance and example of this. And, as in languages the letters are fewer than the syllables, the syllables than the words, and the words than the sentences, so the single sensible impressions, and the small clusters of them, are comparatively few in respect of the large clusters; and, being so, they must recur more frequently, so as the sooner to beget those traces which I call the rudiments or elements of memory. When these traces or ideas begin to recur frequently, this also contributes to fix them, and their order, in the memory, in the same manner as the frequent impression of the the objects themselves.

Thirdly,* Suppose now a person so far advanced in life, as that he has learnt all these rudiments, *i.e.*, that he has ideas of the common appearances and occurrences of life, under a considerable variety of subordinate circumstances, which recur to his imagination from the slightest causes, and with the most perfect facility; and let us ask, how he can be able to remember or recollect a past fact, consisting of one thousand single particulars, or of one hundred such clusters as are called the rudiments of memory; ten single particulars being supposed to constitute a rudiment? First, then, We may observe, that there are only one hundred links wanting in the chain; for he has already learnt considerable exactness in the subordinate circumstances of the one hundred clusters; and perfect exactness is not to be supposed or required. — Secondly, The one hundred clusters recur again and again to the imagination for some time after the fact, in a quick and transient manner, as those who attend sufficiently to what passes in their own minds may perceive; and this both makes the impression a little deeper, and also serves to preserve the order. If the person attempts to recollect soon after the impression, the effect remaining in the brain is sufficient to enable him to do this with the accuracy required and experienced; if a longer time intervene, before he attempts to recollect, still the number of involuntary recurrences makes up in some measure for the want of this voluntary recollection. However, the power

---

*The following passages are peculiarly appropriate, of course, to Wordworth's *Tintern Abbey*. Ed.

of recollection declines in general, and is entirely lost by degrees. It confirms this reasoning, that a new set of strong impressions destroys this power of recollection. For this must both obliterate the effects of the foregoing impressions, and prevent the recurrency of the ideas. – Thirdly, As the single impressions, which make the small clusters, are not combined together at hazard, but according to a general tenor in nature, so the clusters which make facts succeed each other according to some general tenor likewise. Now this both lessens the number of varieties, and shews that the association between many of the clusters, or rudiments, or one hundred links supposed to be wanting, is cemented already. This may be both illustrated and exemplified by the observation, that it is difficult to remember even well-known words that have no connexion with each other, and more so to remember collections of barbarous terms; whereas adepts in any science remember the things of that science with a surprising exactness and facility. – Fourthly, Some clusters are excluded from succeeding others, by ideas of inconsistency, impossibility, and by the methods of reasoning, of which we become masters as we advance in life. – Fifthly, The visible impressions which concur in the past fact, by being vivid, and preserving the order of place, often contribute greatly to preserve the order of time, and to suggest the clusters which may be wanting. – Sixthly, It is to be observed, that as we think in words,* both the impressions and the recurrences of ideas will be attended with words; and these words, from the great use and familiarity of language, will fix themselves strongly in the fancy, and by so doing bring up the associated trains of ideas in the proper order, accurately or nearly. And thus, when a person relates a past fact, the ideas do in some cases suggest the words, whilst in others the words suggest the ideas. Hence illiterate persons do not remember nearly so well as others, *caeteris paribus* [other things being equal]. And I suppose the same is true of deaf persons in a still greater degree. But it arises hence also, that many mistakes in the subordinate circumstances are committed in the relations of past facts, if the relater descend to minute particulars. For the same reasons these mistakes will be so associated with the true facts after a few relations, that the relater himself shall believe that he remembers them distinctly. – Seventhly, The mistakes which are committed both on the foregoing account and others, make considerable abatements in the difficulty here to be solved.

Fourthly, Let it now be asked, in what the recollection of a past fact, consisting of one hundred clusters, as above, differs from the transit of the same one hundred clusters, over the fancy, in the way of a reverie? I answer, partly in the vividness of the clusters, partly and principally in the readiness and strength of the associations, by which they are cemented together. This follows from what has been already delivered;

---

*Since it was supposed men thought in words, in Hartley's scheme poets might be peculiarly optimistic about the influences of their work for morality. Ed.

but it may be confirmed also by many other observations. – Thus, first, Many persons are known by relating the same false story over and over again, *i.e.*, by magnifying the ideas, and their associations, at last to believe that they remember it. It makes as vivid an impression upon them, and hangs as closely together, as an assemblage of past facts recollected by memory. – Secondly, All men are sometimes at a loss to know whether clusters of ideas that strike the fancy strongly, and succeed each other readily and immediately, be recollections, or mere reveries. And the more they agitate the matter in the mind, the more does the reverie appear like a recollection. It resembles this, that if in endeavouring to recollect a verse, a wrong word, suiting the place, first occurs, and afterwards the right one, it is difficult during the then present agitation to distinguish the right one. But afterwards, when this agitation is subsided, the right word easily regains its place. Persons of irritable nervous systems are more subject to such fallacies than others. And madmen often impose upon themselves in this way, *viz*. from the vividness of their ideas and associations, produced by bodily causes. The same thing often happens in dreams. The vividness of the new scene often makes it appear like one that we remember and are well acquainted with. – Thirdly, If the specific nature of memory consist in the great vigour of the ideas, and their associations, then, as this vigour abates, it ought to suggest to us a length of time elapsed; and *vice versa*, if it be kept up, the distance of time ought to appear contracted. Now this last is the case: for the death of a friend, or any interesting event, often recollected and related, appears to have happened but yesterday, as we term it, *viz*. on account of the vividness of the clusters, and their associations, corresponding to the nature of a recent event. . . .

*

Sixthly, The peculiar imperfection of the memory of children tallies with the foregoing account of this faculty; and indeed this account may be considered as a gross general history of the successive growth of the memory, in passing from childhood to adult age. Children must learn by degrees the ideas of single impressions, the clusters which I call rudiments, and the most usual connexions and combinations of these. They have also the use of words, and of objects and incidents, as signs and symbols, with the proper method of reasoning upon them to learn; and during their novitiate in these things their memories must labour under great imperfections. It appears also, that the imperfections peculiar to children correspond in kind as well as degree to the reasons here assigned for them. Their not being able to digest past facts in order of time is, in great measure, owing to their not having the proper use of the symbols, whereby time is denoted. [See esp. Wordsworth's *We Are Seven*.]

Seventhly, The peculiar imperfection of the memory in aged persons tallies also with the foregoing account. The vibrations, and dispositions to vibrate, in the small medullary particles, and their associations, are all so fixed by the callosity of the medullary substance, and by repeated impressions and recurrences, that new impressions can scarce enter, that they recur seldom, and that the parts which do recur bring in old trains from established associations, instead of continuing those which were lately impressed. Hence one may almost predict what very old persons will say or do upon common occurrences. Which is also the case frequently with persons of strong passions, for reasons that are not very unlike. When old persons relate the incidents of their youth with great precision, it is rather owing to the memory of many preceding memories, recollections, and relations, than to the memory of the thing itself.

Eighthly, In recovering from concussions, and other disorders of the brain, it is usual for the patient to recover the power of remembering the then present common incidents for minutes, hours, and days, by degrees; also the power of recalling the events of his life preceding his illness. At length he recovers this last power perfectly, and at the same time forgets almost all that passed in his illness, even those things which he remembered, at first, for a day or two. Now the reason of this I take to be, that upon a perfect recovery the brain recovers its natural state, *i.e.*, all its former dispositions to vibrate; but that such as took place during the preternatural state of the brain, *i.e.*, during his illness, are all obliterated by the return of the natural state. In like manner dreams, which happen in a peculiar state of the brain, *i.e.*, in sleep, vanish, as soon as vigilance, a different state, takes place, But if they be recollected immediately upon waking, and thus connected with the state of vigilance, they may be remembered. But I shall have occasion to be more explicit on this head in the next Section.

Ninthly, It is very difficult to make any plausible conjectures why some persons of very weak judgments, not much below idiots, are endued with a peculiar extraordinary memory. This memory is generally the power of recollecting a large group of words, suppose, as those of a sermon, in a short time after they are heard, with wonderful exactness and readiness; but then the whole is obliterated, after a longer time, much more completely than in persons of common memories and judgments. [Cf. Wordsworth's *Idiot Boy*.] One may perhaps conjecture, that the brain receives all dispositions to vibrate sooner in these persons, and lets them go sooner, than in others. And the last may contribute to the first: for, new impressions may take place more deeply and precisely, if there be few old ones to oppose them. The most perfect memory is that which can both receive most readily, and retain most durably. But we may suppose, that there are limits, beyond which these two different powers cannot consist with each other.

Tenthly, When a person desires to recollect a thing that has escaped him, suppose the name of a person, or visible object, he recalls the visible idea, or some other associate, again and again, by a voluntary power, the desire generally magnifying all the ideas and associations; and thus bringing in the association and idea wanted, at last. However, if the desire be great, it changes the state of the brain, and has an opposite effect; so that the desired idea does not recur, till all has subsided; perhaps not even then.

Eleventhly, All our voluntary powers are of the nature of memory; as may be easily seen from the foregoing account of it, compared with the account of the voluntary powers given in the first chapter. And it agrees remarkably with this, that, in morbid affections of the memory, the voluntary actions suffer a like change and imperfection.

Twelfthly, For the same reasons the whole powers of the soul may be referred to the memory, when taken in a large sense. Hence, though some persons may have strong memories with weak judgments, yet no man can have a strong judgment with a weak original power of retaining and remembering.

from Section 5
Of Imagination, Reveries, And Dreams
PROP. XCI:

> To examine how far the Phaenomena of Imagination, Reveries, and Dreams, are agreeable to the foregoing Theory.

The recurrence of ideas, especially visible and audible ones, in a vivid manner, but without any regard to the order observed in past facts, is ascribed to the power of imagination or fancy. [Cf. Coleridge, p. 350.] Now here we may observe, that every succeeding thought is the result either of some new impression, or of an association with the preceding. And this is the common opinion. It is impossible indeed to attend so minutely to the succession of our ideas, as to distinguish and remember for a sufficient time the very impression or association which gave birth to each thought; but we can do this as far as it can be expected to be done, and in so great a variety of instances, that our argument for the prevalence of the foregoing principle of association in all instances, except those of new impressions, may be esteemed a complete induction.

A reverie differs from imagination only in that the person being more attentive to his own thoughts, and less disturbed by foreign objects, more of his ideas are deducible from association, and fewer from new impressions.

It is to be observed, however, that in all the cases of imagination and reverie, the thoughts depend, in part, upon the then state of body or mind. A pleasurable or painful state of the stomach or brain, joy or grief, will make all the thoughts warp their own way, little or much. But this exception is as agreeable to the foregoing theory, as the general prevalence of association just laid down.

We come next to dreams. I say then, that dreams are nothing but the imaginations, fancies, or reveries of a sleeping man; and that they are deducible from the three following causes; *viz.* First, The impressions and ideas lately received, and particularly those of the preceding day. Secondly, The state of the body, particularly of the stomach and brain. And, thirdly,

Association.*

That dreams are, in part, deducible from the impression and ideas of the preceding day, appears from the frequent recurrence of these in greater or lesser clusters, and especially of the visible ones, in our dreams. We sometimes take in ideas of longer date, in part, on account of their recency: however, in general, ideas that have not affected the mind for some days, recur in dreams only from the second or third cause here assigned.

That the state of the body affects our dreams, is evident from the dreams of sick persons, and of those who labour under indigestions, spasms, and flatulencies.

Lastly, We may perceive ourselves to be carried on from one thing to another in our dreams partly by association.

It is also highly agreeable to the foregoing theory to expect, that each of the three foregoing causes should have an influence upon the trains of ideas that are presented in dreams.

Let us now see how we can solve the most usual phaenomena of dreams upon these principles.

First, then, The scenes which present themselves are taken to be real. We do not consider them as the work of the fancy; but suppose ourselves present, and actually seeing and hearing what passes. Now this happens, First, Because we have no other reality to oppose to the ideas which offer themselves, whereas in the common fictions of the fancy, while we are awake, there is always a set of real external objects striking some of our senses, and precluding a like mistake there: or, if we become quite in-attentive to external objects, the reverie does so far put on the nature of a dream, as to appear a reality. Secondly, The trains of visible ideas, which occur in dreams, are far more vivid than common visible ideas; and there-fore may the more easily be taken for actual impressions. For what reasons these ideas should be so much more vivid, I cannot presume to say. I guess, that the exclusion of real impressions has some share, and the increased heat of the brain may have some likewise. The fact is more ob-servable in the first approaches of sleep; all the visible ideas beginning then to be more than usually glaring.

Secondly, There is a great wildness and inconsistency in our dreams. For the brain, during sleep, is in a state so different from that in which the usual associations were formed, that they can by no means take place as they do during vigilance. On the contrary, the state of the body suggests such ideas, amongst those that have been lately impressed, as are most suitable to the various kinds and degrees of pleasant and painful

---

*Hartley here provides proof that dreams and prophecies (see p. 247) were viewed in Romantic theory of perception as specific instances of the association of ideas 'without any regard to the order observed in past facts', hence as peculiarly the product of creative imagination. Ed.

vibrations excited in the stomach, brain, or some other part. Thus a person who has taken opium, sees either gay scenes, or ghastly ones, according as the opium excites pleasant or painful vibrations in the stomach. Hence it will follow, that ideas will rise successively in dreams, which have no such connexion as takes place in nature, in actual impressions, nor any such as is deducible from association. And yet, if they rise up quick and vividly one after another as subjects, predicates, and other associates use to do, they will be affirmed of each other, and appear to hang together. Thus the same person appears in two places at the same time; two persons appearing successively in the same place coalesce into one; a brute is supposed to speak (when the idea of voice comes from that quarter), or to handle; any idea, qualification, office, &c. coinciding in the instant of time with the idea of one's self, or of another person adheres immediately, &c. &c.

Thirdly, We do not take notice of, or are offended at, these inconsistencies; but pass on from one to another. For the associations, which should lead us thus to take notice, and be offended, are, as it were, asleep; the bodily causes also hurrying us on to new and new trains successively. But if the bodily state be such as favours ideas of anxiety and perplexity, then the inconsistency and apparent impossibility, occuring in dreams, are apt to give great disturbance and uneasiness. It is to be observed likewise, that we forget the several parts of our dreams very fast in passing from one to another; and that this lessens the apparent inconsistencies, and their influences.

Fourthly, It is common in dreams for persons to appear to themselves to be transferred from one place to another, by a kind of sailing or flying motion. This arises from the change of the apparent magnitude and position of the images excited in the brain, this change being such as a change of distance and position in ourselves would have occasioned. Whatever the reasons be, for which visible images are excited in sleep, like to the objects with which we converse when awake, the same reasons will hold for changes of apparent magnitude and position also; and these changes in fixed objects, being constantly associated with motions in ourselves when awake, will infer these motions when asleep. But then we cannot have the idea of the *vis inertiae* [the power of inertness] of our own bodies, answering to the impressions in walking; because the nerves of the muscles either do not admit of such miniature vibrations in sleep; or do not transmit ideas to the mind in consequence thereof; whence we appear to sail, fly, or ride. Yet sometimes a person seems to walk, and even to strike, just as in other cases he seems to feel the impression of a foreign body on his skin.

Those who walk and talk in their sleep, have evidently the nerves of the muscles concerned so free, as that vibrations can descend from the internal parts of the brain, the peculiar residence of ideas, into them. At the same time the brain itself is so oppressed, that they have scarce any memory. Persons who read inattentively, *i.e.*, see and speak almost without remembering, also those who labour under such a morbid loss of memory, as that though they see, hear, speak, and act, *pro re nata* [for the immediate occasion], from moment to moment, yet they forget all immediately, somewhat resemble the persons who walk and talk in sleep.

Fifthly, Dreams consist chiefly of visible imagery. This agrees remarkably with the perpetual impressions made upon the optic nerves and corresponding parts of the brain during vigilance, and with the distinctness and vividness of the images impressed.

We may observe also, that the visible imagery in dreams is composed, in considerable degree, of fragments of visible appearances lately impressed. For the disposition to these vibrations must be greater than to others, *caeteris paribus*, at the same time that by the imperfection and interruption of the associations, only fragments, not whole images, will generally appear. The fragments are so small, and so intermixed with other fragments and appearances, that it is difficult to trace them up to the preceding day; the shortness of our memory contributing also not a little thereto.

It happens in dreams, that the same fictitious places are presented again and again at the distance of weeks and months, perhaps during the whole course of life. These places are, I suppose, compounded at first, probably early in youth, of fragments of real places, which we have seen. They afterwards recur in dreams, because the same state of brain recurs; and when this has happened for some successions, they may be expected to recur at intervals during life. But they may also admit of variations, especially before frequent recurrency has established and fixed them.

Sixthly, It has been observed already, that many of the things which are presented in dreams, appear to be remembered by us, or, at least, as familiar to us; and that this may be solved by the readiness with which they start up, and succeed one another, in the fancy.

Seventhly, It has also been remarked, that dreams ought to be soon forgotten, as they are in fact; because the state of the brain suffers great changes in passing from sleep to vigilance. The wildness and inconsistency of our dreams render them still more liable to be forgotten. It is said that a man may remember his dreams best by continuing in the same posture in which he dreamt; which, if true, would be a remarkable confirmation of the doctrine of vibrations; since those which take place in the medullary substance of the brain would be least disturbed and obliterated by this means.

Eighthly, the dreams which are presented in the first part of the night are, for the most part, much more confused, irregular, and difficult to be remembered, than those which we dream towards the morning; and these last are often rational to a considerable degree, and regulated according to the usual course of our associations. For the brain begins then to approach to the state of vigilance, or that in which the usual associations were formed and cemented. However, association has some power even in wild and inconsistent dreams.

COR. I. As the prophecies* were, many of them, communicated in the

*Cf. Robert Lowth on the prophets, pp. 162-167. It is interesting to

way of divine visions, trances, or dreams, so they bear many of the foregoing marks of dreams. Thus they deal chiefly in visible imagery; they abound with apparent impossibilities, and deviations from common life, of which yet the prophets take not the least notice: they speak of new things as of familiar ones: they are carried in the spirit from place to place; things requiring a long series of time in real life are transacted in the prophetical visions as soon as seen; they ascribe to themselves and others new names, offices, &c.; every thing has a real existence conferred upon it; there are singular combinations of fragments of visible appearances; and God himself is represented in a visible shape, which of all other things must be most offensive to a pious Jew. And it seems to me that these and such like criterions might establish the genuineness of the prophecies, exclusively of all other evidences.

COR. II. The wildness of our dreams seems to be of singular use to us, by interrupting and breaking the course of our associations. For, if we were always awake, some accidental associations would be so much cemented by continuance, as that nothing could afterwards disjoin them; which would be madness.

COR. III. A person may form a judgment of the state of his bodily health, and of his temperance, by the general pleasantness or unpleasantness of his dreams. There are also many useful hints relating to the strength of our passion deducible from them.

---

observe that Ezekiel, the greatest of the Old Testament prophets (see pp. 183-185), became most prominent after the mid-century when Hartley's associationism became current. Ed.

CHRISTOPHER SMART (1722–1771)

'For my talent is to give an impression upon words by punching, that when
the reader casts his eye upon 'em, he takes up the image from the mould
which I have made', wrote Smart in *Jubilate Agno* (xii. 42). The cutting
edges of the printer's letters, of course, make an indentation downward
into the fabric of the paper – in Smart's image into the perceptions of the
reader – with a local, limited effect and comprehensiveness at variance
with the traditional movement of syntax down the page. The effect of
Smart's major poems, *A Song to David* and *Jubilate Agno* or *Rejoice in the
Lamb*, of a complex and extensive harmony extending as it were into
infinity, and perceived at each point of the poem as if obliquely, is the
high water mark of a long development in the awareness of words which
began at the time of Berkeley half a century earlier. Berkeley's achievement
was to displace externality – or 'outness' – and finite extension, both of
time and space. In Burke's 'Sublime' and in the new oriental prophecy
words tended not to recall anything in memory but, as God's alphabet,
gave a sense impression of the infinite. 'A great number of arbitrary signs,
various and apposite, do constitute a language', Berkeley observed in
The Theory of Vision Vindicated and Explained (40) and went on 'if
such arbitrary connexion be instituted by men, it is an artificial language;
if by the Author of nature, it is a natural language. Infinitely various are
the modifications of light and sound, whence they are each capable of
supplying an endless variety of signs, and, accordingly have been each
employed to form languages; the one by the arbitrary appointment of
mankind, the other by that of God Himself.'

  Berkeley's major benefit for poets was to erect a scientific basis for a
direction in cognition other than the sequential. In Gray, poetry
progresses out of time, to an original sublime perfection before history;
in Blake, Milton moves out of a dissolving heaven through a vortex made
of the opposition of temporal-spatial patterns and their absence; in Smart
the 'gay machine' of the universe is built cumulatively, as it were, at cross-
purposes to the call of the 'conjunction-disjunctive' of Pope (see p. 17).
Smart's poems are joyful, for they are not a celebration of 'spirit' but of
all-comprehending matter. As in Berkeley, knowledge is creative contact
between 'real' things and the mind in infinite contexts. In Smart one is
close to the culmination of the movement, crucial to Romanticism, in
which the imagination is not viewed as an escape from reality, but as the
response of the mind designed, like the printer's fount, for things as
distinct from abstractions. The imagination, therefore, was irreversibly
one with concreteness, which it could only know in the timeless and
spaceless world of poetry. There, freed from the controls of lateral form
and the concept of 'the Whole', the material world – including words
viewed as objects in Nature equal with trees and animals – released its
infinite truth. Of course, it is necessary to observe that the paper, when

the printer's letters strike it, moves away in an opposite direction from the edges of the forming letter. As with any mould or 'negative' what is received is, as it were, the coat or shell, at each point opposite in shape from the cause and direction of the indentation.

The interest in Smart's review of Lowth's *De Sacra Poësi Hebraeorum* which appeared in Smart's *Universal Visiter and Monthly Memorialist* for January and February of 1756, lies in the poet's apparent appreciation of techniques of primitive poetry corresponding to those suggested by his knowledge and implementation of Berkeley. It is, of course, hardly novel to point out the similarity between the organization of Smart's verse and Lowth's theories of parallelism (see pp. 162-164). Other characteristics of Smart suggest a dependence on Lowth's concept of 'oriental primitivism' broader than this. The central concept in Lowth is of the 'new-created mind (undepraved by habit or opinion)' (*Lecture I*). Here, of course, we find a concept of timelessness as in Berkeley and Smart. Lowth's concern, like Smart's, is perception or epistemology. When the mind imitates its own activities as opposed to 'external' nature, 'those impulses, inflexions, perturbations, and secret emotions, which it perceives and knows in itself . . . astonish and delight above every other' (*Lecture XVII*). In this lyric poetry the understanding does not work 'through the uncertain medium . . . of memory'; the 'ecstatic impulse' becomes 'the God of the moment' (*Lecture XVII*). Most importantly, in Lowth, as in Smart, the greatest, most sublime effects derive from the lowliest or commonest concrete objects. 'From ideas which in themselves appear coarse, unsuitable, and totally unworthy. . . ' the astonished intellect 'imperceptibly glides into the void of Infinity: whose vast and formless extent . . . impresses it with the sublimest and most awful sensations, and fills it with a mixture of admiration and terror' (*Lecture XVI*). The mind, we might say, rises in a parabola of admiration and awe at each point of infinite perception, even when the image or word, suggests something coarse, unsuitable, and totally unworthy, for example, Smart's cat, Jeoffry. Of course, the modern equivalent of the 'perpetual splendour' of 'accurate recurrence' (*Lecture V*) of the *mashal* or 'parabolic' style of the Hebrews (see also *Lecture XIV*) is founded on a Berkeleyan view of words from whose 'moulds' – with an absence of time characteristic of oriental prophecy as of Smart – the reader 'takes up the image' and experiences sublimity.

In reading Lowth's *Praelectiones*, Smart was especially impressed with the translation of Chapter XIV of *Isaiah*, the *Ode Prophetica* prophesying the downfall of Babylon, in which the dead kings, as if in the future, dramatically and with heavy sarcasm, welcome the fallen tyrant into their royal sepulchre. Lowth's translation, from Hebrew into Latin, was widely regarded (see pp. 176-178) as one of the 'sublime' achievements of the age. With a poet's interest in technique Smart notes Lowth's omission of the caesura from his lines, an effect which, reinforcing the single thrust of primitive poetry, produces a oneness of syntax and poetry which we have come to recognize as not only Smartian but Whitmanesque. It is, however, the suggestiveness of Smart's central metaphor for the effect of Lowth's orientalism which is of the greatest value in his *critique*. The images of a stream and a fountain, close as they are to Gray's *Progress of Poesy* and Blake's *Introduction* to the *Songs of Innocence*, suggest also the major effect of Smart's own verse, and reinforce the conclusion that in Lowth he had found his model for oriental, primitive poetry at large, and an equivalent for the Berkeleyan ideal: 'The stile is accurate to the most classical exactness, and yet so perspicuous in its purity, that it has all the easiness of a limpid stream, though as elaborate as the water-works of *Versailles*.' Exactness and perspicuousness are the characteristics of Lowth's 'parabolic' style and of Smart's own verse. Even more, however, the conjunction of the limpid profundity of a simple stream with the elaborateness of what was Europe's most extensive system of fountains, images accurately the effect of Smart himself, that of constantly recurring images of profound simplicity suggesting moment by shining moment, the cosmos moulded by a master artist – or printer with his 'fount' of letters.

from *THE UNIVERSAL VISITER AND MONTHLY MEMORIALIST January, 1756*

Literary Observations
Before we give our opinion of a work, which genius, judgement, and learning, have conspired to make truly admirable, we think it proper to declare, that it is not our intention to give an account of books in general; – there are works of that kind to which our readers may refer. But, if any thing extremely striking makes its appearance, we cannot possibly overlook it. We are not in possession of the stamp of fame to signalize the eminent, neither will we hold up the mark to brand persons of a very different denomination. Those, who think themselves neglected, must excuse our want of observation; but we are determined nobody *shall be injured by the proprietors of this work.*
De Sacra Poësi Hebraeorum Praelectiones Academicae. A Roberto Louth.
  This work, which for its elegance, novelty, variety, spirit, and (I had almost said) divinity, is one of the best performances that has been published for a century, cannot need any recommendation; we pretend therefore to do it only justice. There are undoubtedly many gentlemen and scholars, who would be proud to see, but could not conveniently come into the possession of it. For their sakes we have taken the liberty to insert the following ode, which is one of the finest that ever was wrote without inspiration, *if it was wrote without inspiration.* In our next number we intend to be somewhat particular on this head.
                                                                  S.

*Israelitarum Epinikion In Occasum Regis Regnique Babilonici: Ode
Prophetica*
Isaie, Cap. xiv. 4-27.
    Ergo insolentis curruit Imperi
    Infana moles? occidit urbium
        Regina victrix, nec subacto
            Effera jam dominatur orbi?
    Fastus Tyranni contudit impios
    Jehova Vindex, sceptraque ferrea;
        Qui verbere haud unquam remisso
            Fregit atrox populos gementes . . .
[Here Smart prints the rest of Lowth's prophetic ode.]

*

from *THE   UNIVERSAL   VISITER   AND   MONTHLY
MEMORIALIST February, 1756*

Further Remarks on Dr Lowth's celebrated Prelections
Though the *Ode* we inserted in our last, be of so elevated and striking a
nature, that it is impossible it should escape the attention, or fail of the
approbation of any scholar; yet we must beg leave to point out some
beauties, which, as they have a singularity in their excellence, will not in
general be taken notice of, without such pointing out. There is an uncommon degree of merit in what I will venture to call the mechanical
part of the ode, *viz.* the structure of the versification. The doctor has
most judiciously fixed upon the *Alcaie*, as a measure the best adapted to
the sublimity of his subject; and a noble use he has made of it:
    Namque ipse consurgam, Omnipotens ait,
    Et Nomen Extinguam Babylonium
The pause, or breaking-place, usual in the *Alcaie*, being here omitted,
gives a grandeur and rapidity which are due to the magnificence of the
expression. The stile is accurate to the most classical exactness, and yet so
perspicuous in its purity, that it has all the easiness of a limpid stream,
though as elaborate as the water-works of *Versailles.* – The doctor, in his
first lecture, has nobly vindicated the usefulness of his art, and demonstrated, that poetry may be made to answer the best purposes, though
looked upon by the ignorant to be a matter of mere amusement. . . .

MAURICE MORGANN (1726–1802)

Morgann's *Essay on Falstaff*, like Gray's *The Progress of Poesy* (see pp. 191-193) reminds us that the Romantics discovered in Shakespeare, with Milton and Spenser the most admired earlier English poet, the embodiment of the new aesthetics.

Morgann is perhaps especially useful in indicating that the concept of human character had become at this point dominated by 'the Sublime'. Upon the limitless ocean of the infinite, in which time itself was a bubble, distant from the general categories of classical thought, great men were unique particulars who, as the flowering of Romantic biography was to show, could not be plumbed in Morgann's phrase by 'time, reasoning, and authority'. As if fresh from Young's *Conjectures* (see pp. 144-148) 'we cannot indeed do otherwise than admit that there must be distinct principles of character in every distinct individual', observes Morgann, and again, 'he differs essentially from all other writers'. Like perhaps his greatest creation, Shakespeare was cast for the then fashionable part of 'original genius', the *'one man* in the world who could make a more perfect draught of real nature'. It is an interesting comment on the history of ideas that the common term for poet in the later eighteenth century, 'Bard', signifying inspired prophet with special powers over time, has adhered until our day only to Shakespeare.

Morgann's plastic and vegetative sense of the artifact parallels Young's vision of its genesis (see pp. 146-148). Echoing both Hume and Hartley and working with his own preferences, Morgann builds a rhapsodic impression of a drama in which there is a complete gap between rational understanding and the reality of 'feeling', in which the associations of cause and effect are absent, and where an unseen, cumulative process takes place which is never in focus. This 'Bard', in direct contradiction to not only Aristotle but also Johnson's *Preface to Shakespeare*, does not mirror or imitate Nature, but her 'darling' and 'immortal boy' as Gray called him, exists within her timeless, unfolding motion, creating something unique which is a continuum of her. Memory cannot supply terms for this heuristic growth nor, apparently, can the critic deal with it, except by an approximation. Besieged by novelty the reader cannot help but develop in directions for which he has no chart and which the prophet Morgann charmingly images in 'the *Apalachian* mountains' and 'the banks of the *Ohio*' of the New World.

The Romantic discovery of the past, Renaissance or Middle Ages, was not a sympathy for the Elizabethan world picture, just as it did not suggest apostasy to Chaucer's spheres. Shakespeare is an English primitive, 'this uncultivated Barbarian', a poet-prophet to vie with the oriental, and, like Ezekiel, corroborative of eighteenth-century epistemology. Morgann's most intriguing writing which takes us to the very spirit of the third quarter of the eighteenth century, rests in a footnote. The agony of

Romanticism, as we have observed, derives partially from an intimate union between the creative imagination and the supernatural. Morgann nowhere betrays his relation to the eighteenth-century philosophers as clearly as in his account, couched in Lockian terms (see pp. 37-47), of the 'mixed modes' of abstractions and personifications and of 'witches, ghosts, fairies, and the rest' so reminiscent of Addison's 'fairy way of writing' (see pp. 12, 97).

from THE DRAMATIC CHARACTER OF FALSTAFF (1777)

It is a very unpleasant thing to have, in the first setting out, so many and so strong prejudices to contend with. All that one can do in such a case, is, to pray the reader to have a little patience in the commencement; and to reserve his censure, if it must pass, for the conclusion. Under his gracious allowance, therefore, I presume to declare it as my opinion, that Cowardice *is not* the *Impression* which the *whole* character of *Falstaff* is calculated to make on the minds of an unprejudiced audience; tho' there be, I confess, a great deal of something in the *composition* likely enough to puzzle and consequently to mislead the Understanding. — The reader will perceive that I distinguish between *mental Impressions* and the *Understanding.* — I wish to avoid every thing that looks like subtlety and refinement; but this is a distinction which we all comprehend. — There are none of us unconscious of certain feelings or sensations of mind which do not seem to have passed thro' the Understanding; the effects, I suppose, of some secret influences from without, acting upon a certain mental sense, and producing feelings and passions in just correspondence to the force and variety of those influences on the one hand, and to the quickness of our sensibility on the other. [Cf. Hume's distinction between 'sensations' and 'ideas', pp. 125-129.] Be the cause, however, what it may, the fact is undoubtedly so; which is all I am concerned in. And it is equally a fact, which every man's experience may avouch, that the Understanding and those feelings are frequently at variance. The latter often arise from the most minute circumstances, and frequently from such as the Understanding cannot estimate, or even recognize; whereas the Understanding delights in abstraction [cf. Berkeley on abstractions, pp. 69-72], and in general propositions; which, however true considered as such, are very seldom, I had like to have said *never*, perfectly applicable to any particular case. And hence, among other causes, it is, that we often condemn or applaud characters and actions on the credit of some logical process, while our hearts revolt, and would fain lead us to a very different conclusion.

The Understanding seems for the most part to take cognizance of *actions* only, and from these to infer *motives* and *character*; but the sense we have been speaking of proceeds in a contrary course; and determines of *actions* from certain *first principles of character*, which seem wholly out of the reach of the Understanding. We cannot indeed do otherwise than admit that there must be distinct principles of character in every distinct individual: The manifest variety even in the minds of infants will oblige us to this. But what are these first principles of character? Not the objects, I am persuaded, of the Understanding; and yet we take as strong Impressions of them as if we could compare and assort them in a syllogism. We often love or hate at first sight; and indeed, in general, dislike or approve by some secret reference to these *principles*; and we judge even of conduct, not from any idea of abstract good or evil in the nature of actions, but by referring those actions to a supposed original character in the man himself. I do not mean that we *talk* thus; we could not indeed, if we would, explain ourselves in detail on this head; we can neither account for Impressions and passions, nor communicate them to others by *words*: Tones and looks will sometimes convey the *passion* strangely, but the *Impression* is incommunicable. The same causes may produce it indeed at the same time in many, but it is the separate possession of each, and not in its nature transferable: It is an imperfect sort of instinct, and proportionably dumb. – We might indeed, if we chose it, candidly confess to one another that we are greatly swayed by these feelings, and are by no means so *rational* in all points as we could wish; but this would be a betraying of the interests of that high faculty, the Understanding, which we so value ourselves upon, and which we more peculiarly call our own. This, we think, must not be; and so we huddle up the matter, concealing it as much as possible, both from ourselves and others. In Books indeed, wherein character, motive, and action, are all alike subjected to the Understanding, it is generally a very clear case; and we make decisions compounded of them all: And thus we are willing to approve of *Candide*, tho' he kills my Lord the Inquisitor, and runs thro' the body the Baron of *Thunder-ten-tronchk*, the son of his patron, and the brother of his beloved *Cunégonde*: But in real life, I believe, *my Lords the Judges* would be apt to inform the *Gentlemen of the Jury* that my *Lord the Inquisitor* was *ill killed*; as *Candide* did not proceed on the urgency of the moment, but on the speculation only of future evil. And indeed this clear perception, in Novels and Plays, of the union of character and action not seen in nature, is the principal defect of such compositions, and what renders them but ill pictures of human life, and wretched guides of conduct.

But if there was *one man* in the world who could make a more perfect draught of real nature, and steal such Impressions on his audience, without their special notice, as should keep their hold in spite of any error of their Understanding, and should thereupon venture to introduce an apparent incongruity of character and action, for ends which I shall presently endeavour to explain; such an imitation would be worth our nicest curiosity and attention.* But in such a case as this, the reader might

---

*Morgann's observation that Shakespeare does *not* mirror Nature, as

expect that he should find us all talking the language of the Understanding only; that is, censuring the action with very little conscientious investigation even of *that*; and transferring the censure, in every odious colour, to the actor himself; how much soever our hearts and affections might secretly revolt: For as to the *Impression*, we have already observed that it has no tongue; nor is its operation and influence likely to be made the subject of conference and communication.

It is not to the *Courage* only of *Falstaff* that we think these observations will apply: No part whatever of his character seems to be fully settled in our minds; at least there is something strangely incongruous in our discourse and affections concerning him. We all like *Old Jack*; yet, by some strange perverse fate, we all abuse him, and deny him the possession of any one single good or respectable quality. There is something extraordinary in this: It must be a strange art in *Shakespeare* which can draw our liking and good will towards so offensive an object. He has wit, it will be said; cheerfulness and humour of the most characteristic and captivating sort. And is this enough? Is the humour and gaiety of vice so captivating? Is the wit, characteristic of baseness and every ill quality, capable of attaching the heart and winning the affections? Or does not the apparency of such humour, and the flashes of such wit, by more strongly disclosing the deformity of character, but the more effectually excite our hatred and contempt of the man? And yet this is not our *feeling* of *Falstaff*'s character. When he has ceased to amuse us, we find no emotions of disgust; we can scarcely forgive the ingratitude of the Prince in the new-born virtue of the King, and we curse the severity of that poetic justice which consigns our old good-natured delightful companion to the custody of the *warden*, and the dishonours of the *Fleet*.

I am willing, however, to admit that if a Dramatic writer will but preserve to any character the qualities of a strong mind, particularly Courage and ability, that it will be afterwards no very difficult task (as I may have occasion to explain) to discharge that *disgust* which arises from vicious manners; and even to attach us (if such character should contain any quality productive of cheerfulness and laughter) to the cause and subject of our mirth with some degree of affection.

But the question which I am to consider is of a very different nature: It is a question of fact, and concerning a quality which forms the basis of every respectable character; a quality which is the very essence of a Military man; and which is held up to us, in almost every Comic incident of the Play, as the subject of our observation. It is strange then that it should now be a question, whether *Falstaff* is or is not a man of Courage; and whether we do in fact condemn him for the want, or respect him for the possession of that quality: And yet I believe the reader will find that he has by no means decided this question, even for himself. — If then it

---

Johnson had written, separates him from centuries of classical theory and carries us to the heart of Romanticism. Ed.

should turn out that this difficulty has arisen out of the Art of *Shakespeare*, who has contrived to make secret Impressions upon us of Courage, and to preserve those Impressions in favour of a character which was to be held up for sport and laughter on account of actions of apparent Cowardice and dishonour, we shall have less occasion to wonder, as *Shakespeare* is a Name which contains All of Dramatic artifice and genius.

If in this place the reader shall peevishly and prematurely object that the observations and distinctions I have laboured to establish are wholly unapplicable; he being himself unconscious of ever having received any such Impression; what can be done in so nice a case, but to refer him to the following pages; by the number of which he may judge how very much I respect his objection, and by the variety of those proofs which I shall employ to induce him to part with it; and to recognize in its stead certain feelings, concealed and covered over perhaps, but not erased, by time, reasoning, and authority? In the mean while, it may not perhaps be easy for him to resolve how it comes about, that, whilst we look upon *Falstaff* as a character of the like nature with that of *Parolles* or of *Bobadil*, we should preserve for him a great degree of respect and good-will, and yet feel the highest disdain and contempt of the others, tho' they are all involved in similar situations. The reader, I believe, would wonder extremely to find either *Parolles* or *Bobadil* possess himself in danger: What then can be the cause that we are not at all surprized at the gaiety and ease of *Falstaff* under the most trying circumstances; and that we never think of charging *Shakespeare* with departing, on this account, from the truth and coherence of character? Perhaps, after all, the *real* character of *Falstaff* may be different from his *apparent* one; and possibly this difference between reality and appearance, whilst it accounts at once for our liking and our censure, may be the true point of humour in the character, and the source of all our laughter and delight. We may chance to find, if we will but examine a little into the nature of those circum-stances which have accidentally involved him, that he was intended to be drawn as a character of much Natural courage and resolution; and be obliged thereupon to repeal those decisions which may have been made upon the credit of some general tho' unapplicable propositions; the common source of error in other and higher matters. A little reflection may perhaps bring us round again to the point of our departure, and unite our Understandings to our instinct. — Let us then for a moment *suspend* at least our decisions, and candidly and coolly inquire if Sir *John Falstaff* be, indeed, what he has so often been called by critic and commentator, male and female, — a *Constitutional Coward*.

It will scarcely be possible to consider the Courage of *Falstaff* as wholly detached from his other qualities: But I write not professedly of any part of his character, but what is included under the term, *Courage*; however, I may incidentally throw some light on the whole. — The reader will not need to be told that this Inquiry will resolve itself of course into a

Critique on the genius, the arts, and the conduct of *Shakespeare*: For what is *Falstaff*, what *Lear*, what *Hamlet*, or *Othello*, but different modifications of *Shakespeare*'s thought? It is true that this Inquiry is narrowed almost to a single point: But general criticism is as uninstructive as it is easy: *Shakespeare* deserves to be considered in detail; — a task hitherto unattempted.

*

Yet whatever may be the neglect of some, or the censure of others, there are those who firmly believe that this wild, this uncultivated Barbarian has not yet obtained one half of his fame; and who trust that some new Stagyrite* will arise, who instead of pecking at the surface of things will enter into the inward soul of his compositions, and expel, by the force of congenial feelings, those foreign impurities which have stained and disgraced his page. And as to those *spots* which will still remain, they may perhaps become invisible to those who shall seek them thro' the medium of his beauties, instead of looking for those beauties, as is too frequently done, thro' the smoke of some real or imputed obscurity. When the hand of time shall have brushed off his present Editors and Commentators, and when the very name of *Voltaire*, and even the memory of the language in which he has written, shall be no more, the *Apalachian* mountains, the banks of the *Ohio*, and the plains of *Sciota* shall resound with the accents of this Barbarian: In his native tongue he shall roll the genuine passions of nature; nor shall the griefs of *Lear* be alleviated, or the charms and wit of *Rosalind* be abated by time. There is indeed nothing perishable about him, except that very learning which he is said so much to want. He had not, it is true, enough for the demands of the age in which he lived, but he had perhaps too much for the reach of his genius, and the interest of his fame. *Milton* and he will carry the decayed remnants and fripperies of antient mythology into more distant ages than they are by their own force intitled to extend; and the metamorphoses of *Ovid*, upheld by them, lay in a new claim to unmerited immortality.**

Shakespeare is a name so interesting, that it is excusable to stop a moment, nay it would be indecent to pass him without the tribute of some admiration. He differs essentially from all other writers: Him we may profess rather to feel than to understand; and it is safer to say, on many occasions, that we are possessed by him, than that we possess him. And no wonder; — He scatters the seeds of things, the principles of character and action, with so cunning a hand, yet with so careless an air, and,

---

*Aristotle, whose *Poetics* are a *locus classicus* of mimetic criticism, was born at Stagira, Macedonia. Ed.

**It is remarkable that prophecy, made fashionable by Lowth, Young, Gray and others, has become also the vehicle of Shakespeare criticism. Ed.

master of our feelings, submits himself so little to our judgment, that every thing seems superior. We discern not his course, we see no connection of cause and effect, we are rapt in ignorant admiration, and claim no kindred with his abilities. All the incidents, all the parts, look like chance, whilst we feel and are sensible that the whole is design. His Characters not only act and speak in strict conformity to nature, but in strict relation to us; just so much is shewn as is requisite, just so much is impressed; he commands every passage to our heads and to our hearts, and moulds us as he pleases, and that with so much ease, that he never betrays his own exertions. We see these Characters act from the mingled motives of passion, reason, interest, habit, and complection [combinations of humours], in all their proportions, when they are supposed to know it not themselves; and we are made to acknowledge that their actions and sentiments are, from those motives, the necessary result. He at once blends and distinguishes every thing; − everything is complicated, everything is plain. I restrain the further expressions of my admiration lest they should not seem applicable to man; but it is really astonishing that a mere human being, a part of humanity only, should so perfectly comprehend the whole; and that we should possess such exquisite art, that whilst every woman and every child shall feel the whole effect, his learned Editors and Commentators should yet so very frequently mistake or seem ignorant of the cause. A sceptre or a straw are in his hands of equal efficacy; he needs no selection; he converts every thing into excellence; nothing is too great, nothing is too base. Is a character efficient like *Richard*? It is every thing we can wish: Is it otherwise, like *Hamlet*? It is productive of equal admiration: Action produces one mode of excellence, and inaction another: The Chronicle, the Novel, or the Ballad; the king, or the beggar, the hero, the madman, the sot, or the fool; it is all one; − nothing is worse, nothing is better: The same genius pervades and is equally admirable in all. [Cf. the disappearance of hierarchy in, for example, Shaftesbury and Blake; see Introduction, pp. 2-3.] Or is a character to be shewn in progressive change, and the events of years comprized within the hour? With what a Magic hand does he prepare and scatter his spells! The Understanding must, in the first place, be subdued; and lo! how the rooted prejudices of the child spring up to confound the man! The Weird Sisters rise, and order is extinguished. The laws of nature give way, and leave nothing in our minds but wildness and horror. No pause is allowed us for reflection: Horrid sentiment, furious guilt and compunction, air-drawn daggers, murders, ghosts, and enchantment, shake and *possess us wholly*. In the mean time the *process* is completed. *Macbeth* changes under our eye, *the milk of human kindness is converted to gall; he has supped full of horrors,* and his *May of life is fallen into the sear, the yellow leaf*; whilst we, the fools of amazement, are insensible to the shifting of place and the lapse of time [cf. Gray on Milton, *Progress of Poesy*, 98], and, till the curtain drops, never once wake to the truth of things, or recognize the laws of existence. − On such an occasion, a fellow, like *Rymer* [Thomas

Rymer (1641–1713), classical denigrator of 'the Bard'], waking from his trance, shall lift up his Constable's staff, and charge this great Magician, this daring *practicer of arts inhibited* [prohibited], in the name of *Aristotle*, to surrender; whilst *Aristotle* himself, disowning his wretched Officer, would fall prostrate at his feet and acknowledge his supremacy. – O supreme of Dramatic excellence! (*might he say*) not to me be imputed the insolence of fools. The bards of *Greece* were confined within the narrow circle of the Chorus, and hence they found themselves constrained to practice, for the most part the precision, and copy the details of nature. I followed them, and knew not that a larger circle might be drawn, and the Drama extended to the whole reach of human genius. Convinced, I see that a more compendious *nature* may be obtained; a nature of *effects* only, to which neither the relations of place, or continuity of time, are always essential. Nature, condescending to the faculties and apprehensions of man, has drawn through human life a regular chain of visible causes and effects: But Poetry delights in surprise, conceals her steps, seizes at once upon the heart, and obtains the Sublime of things without betraying the rounds of her ascent: True Poesy is *magic*, not *nature*; an effect from causes hidden or unknown. To the Magician I prescribed no laws; his law and his power are one; his power is his law. Him, who neither imitates, nor is within the reach of imitation, no precedent can or ought to bind, no limits to contain. If his end is obtained, who shall question his course? Means, whether apparent or hidden, are justified in Poesy by success; but then most perfect and most admirable when most concealed.* – But

---

*These observations have brought me so near to the regions of Poetic *magic* (using the word here in its strict and proper sense, and not loosely as in the *text*), that, tho' they lie not directly in my course, I yet may be allowed in this place to point the reader that way. A felt propriety, or truth of art, from an unseen, tho' supposed adequate cause, we call *nature*. A like feeling of propriety and truth, supposed without a cause, or as seeming to be derived from causes inadequate, fantastic, and absurd, – such as wands, circles, incantations, and so forth, – we call by the general name *magic*, including all the train of superstition, witches, ghosts, fairies, and the rest. – *Reason* is confined to the line of visible existence; our *passions* and our *fancy* extend far beyond into the *obscure*; but however lawless their operations may seem, the images they so wildly form have yet a relation to truth, and are the shadows at least, however fantastic, of *reality*. I am not investigating but passing this subject, and must therefore leave behind me much curious speculation. Of personifications however we should observe that those which are made out of abstract ideas are the creatures of the Understanding only: Thus, of the mixed modes, virtue, beauty, wisdom and others, – what are they but very obscure ideas of *qualities* considered as abstracted from any *subject* whatever? The mind cannot steadily contemplate such an abstraction: What then does it do? – Invent or imagine a subject in

whither am I going! This copious and delightful topic has drawn me far beyond my design; I hasten back to my subject, and am guarded, for a time at least, against any further temptation to digress.

---

order to support these qualities; and hence we get the Nymphs or Goddesses of virtue, of beauty, or of wisdom; the very obscurity of the ideas being the cause of their conversion into sensible objects, with precision both of feature and of form. But as reason has its person-ifications, so has *passion*. — Every passion has its Object, tho' often distant and obscure; — to be brought nearer then, and rendered more dis-tinct, it is personified; and Fancy fantastically decks, or aggravates the form, and adds 'a local habitation and a name'. But passion is the *dupe* of its own artifice and *realises* the image it had formed. The Grecian theology was mixed of both these kinds of personification. Of the images produced by passion it must be observed that they are the images, for the most part, not of the passions themselves, but of their remote effects. *Guilt* looks through the medium, and beholds a devil; *fear*, spectres of every sort; *hope*, a smiling cherub; *malice* and *envy* see hags, and witches, and enchanters dire; whilst the innocent and the young behold with fearful delight the tripping fairy, whose shadowy form the moon gilds with its softest beams. — Extravagant as all this appears, it has its laws so precise that we are sensible both of a local and temporary and of an universal magic; the first derived from the general nature of the human mind, in-fluenced by particular habits, institutions, and climate; and the latter from the same general nature abstracted from those considerations: Of the first sort the *machinery* in *Macbeth* is a very striking instance; a machinery, which, however exquisite at the time, has already lost more than half its force; and the Gallery now laughs in some places where it ought to shudder: — But the magic of the *Tempest* is lasting and universal.

There is besides a species of writing for which we have no term of art, and which holds a middle place between nature and magic; I mean where fancy either alone, or mingled with reason, or reason assuming the appearance of fancy, governs some real existence; but the whole of this art is portrayed in a single Play; in the real madness of *Lear*, in the assumed wildness of *Edgar*, and in the Professional *Fantasque* of the *Fool*, all operating to contrast and heighten each other. There is yet another feat in this kind, which *Shakespeare* has performed; — he has personified *malice* in his *Caliban*; a character kneaded up of three distinct natures, the dia-bolical, the human, and the brute. The rest of his preternatural beings are images of *effects* only, and cannot subsist but in a surrounding atmos-phere of those passions from which they are derived. *Caliban* is the passion itself, or rather a compound of malice, servility, and lust, *substantiated*; and therefore best shewn in contrast with the lightness of *Ariel* and the innocence of *Miranda*. . . .

HUGH BLAIR (1718–1800)

The poems of James Macpherson (1736–96) reveal a panorama of Romanticism more crude perhaps but more densely-textured than the Lake Poets. They suggest, indeed, that mid-eighteenth century Romanticism was a distinct growth, in many ways more perverse, exciting, and vivid, than the self-consciousness of *The Prelude* and *Frost at Midnight*. Through this crucible the preoccupations of the later poets were refined. Fingal and Oscar, who seem to struggle to shape themselves in the words of the *Scalder* from which reason flies like leaves in the wind, illuminate the mythology of Blake, Keats and Shelley, and early define the elemental formal struggle of this era from the symphonies of Beethoven (and, at a distance, Mendelssohn's *Fingal's Cave*) to the career of Napoleon who decorated Malmaison with pictures of Ossian the Bard and carried the poems on campaign. Ossian was fashioned to suit the developed taste of his era and exploit the aesthetics of Young, Lowth and Burke. As instructive is the preparedness of the Regius Professor of Rhetoric and Belles Lettres at Edinburgh to analyse in his *Dissertation on the Poems of Ossian* the surprising simultaneous eruption of the Gothic, the poetry of feeling, primitivism and 'the Sublime' in a single work.

The spuriousness of Macpherson's 'translations' from the Gaelic, like that of Chatterton's Rowley poems (see pp. 319-332), is related to the iconography of time characteristic of Romanticism. The furthest reach of the antique, or Job, the Druids, or to Homer, fascinated men, as did the psychology of perception. To make time an object in a 'sublime' artifact was the greatest achievement of the Romantic artist. The reader experiences even ancient Ossian recalling a vanished age. In a world without temporal distancing, only the shapes of feeling, constantly contemporaneous and musical, seem profoundly significant, while at the same time remaining opaquely obscure. A psychology like that of Blake's *First Book of Urizen* or Keats's *Hyperion: A Fragment* with its fall of the Titans, is at work. From the vantage point of eternity we experience the central Romantic process, the creation of original mythological figures. In the meantime our contemporary psyche seems at risk while we fashion gods, and, even, God.

Blair seems to share the nebulousness of Macpherson's animistic heroes. Yet for all that he is full of crisp information. From Lowth's *De Sacra Poësi Hebraeorum* (see pp. 151-167) Blair took his chapter on Hebrew poetry in his famed *Lectures on Rhetoric and Belles Lettres* (1783). To the *Dissertation* we owe the admission that the poetry of the Old Testament and of the barbaric North are one not only in their sharing of what Blair calls 'measured prose'. 'Oriental' poetry is not really oriental; 'it is characteristical of an age rather than a country; and belongs, in some measure, to all nations at a certain period' (p. 265). His account of the absence of personified abstractions from primitive poetry (see pp. 268-269) reminds us that Berkeleyan perception was never far from the concept of 'the primitive'. As in the Old Testament, in Ossian there is no allegory. 'The ideas, of men, at first, were all particular. They had not words to express general conceptions' (see p. 268). We might add that in an artifact of constant simultaneity, no portion of perception could be conceived as 'drawn from' or 'abstracted' from any other. Hence 'Fame, Time, Terror, Virtue, and the rest of that class, were unknown to our Celtic bard', he concludes. In Lecture VI (see p. 275) he expands on this point. Like Rousseau and Herder on the origins of language, he notes that early man, again as in Berkeleyan perception, constantly alluded to 'sensible objects . . . Iniquity, or guilt, is expressed by "a spotted garment"; misery, by "drinking the cup of astonishment" . . . hence we have been accustomed to call this sort of style, the Oriental Style . . . whereas, from the American Style, and from many other instances, it plainly appears not to have been peculiar to any one region or climate; but to have been common to all nations, in certain periods of Society and Language' (see p. 278).

Macpherson's heroes seem indistinguishable from the hills of Scotland whose first dawn they were imagined to inhabit. Vastness of size, like obscurity, is an Ossianic quality which greatly influenced later mythologizing especially in Blake. Rejecting received forms from the Daughters of Memory, the poet-prophet conceived on the ever-receding edge of a constantly-created future, in which space and time were problematic. As in contemporary philosophy association also was illogical. In Blair's admiring quotation from Olaus Wormius, source also for both Thomas Warton and Gray, 'the whole ocean was one wound'. This 'sublime' comparison reminds us of the 'sapphire throne' of Ezekiel (see pp. 183-185), of the images of *Job* so much admired by contemporary bards, and suggests the techniques of Wordsworth's vision in *The Excursion* (Book II, 827ff) where the Solitary in a prophetic vision views 'implements of ordinary use/But vast in size . . .'. Like Lowth, Blair crosses his 't's' and dots his 'i's' on comparison. 'As the judgment is principally exercised in distinguishing objects, and remarking the differences among those which seem like; so the highest amusement of the imagination is to trace likenesses and agreements among those which seem different' he writes (p. 271), suggesting a pivotal distinction between the simile of classicism and the ubiquitous metaphor of Romanticism.

Blair fleshes out in detail the contemporary attitudes to a set of ideas which include the fashionable view of Homer as an original genius, and, most valuably, the identification of children with the first age of man, which he finds conveniently localized in such works as George Hickes's *Moeso-Gothic Grammar* (see pp. 1-2 and 266). It is fitting that in the final paragraphs of his *Dissertation on Ossian* Blair seems to cast off the robes of the Edinburgh pedant, and hymning that most artificial of images, the 'first ages' of some five thousand years before, merges with the Bard, imbruing the Scottish landscape with the aura of primitivism and Romanticism from which it, like the Lake District, has not, since this era, been separated.

*

from *A CRITICAL DISSERTATION ON THE POEMS OF OSSIAN, (1763)*

Irregular and unpolished we may expect the productions of uncultivated ages to be; but abounding, at the same time, with that enthusiasm, that vehemence and fire, which are the soul of poetry. For many circumstances of those times which we call barbarous, are favourable to the poetical spirit. That state, in which human nature shoots wild and free, though unfit for other improvements, certainly encourages the high exertions of fancy and passion.

In the infancy of societies, men live scattered and dispersed, in the midst of solitary rural scenes, where the beauties of nature are their chief entertainment. They meet with many objects, to them new and strange; their wonder and surprize are frequently excited; and by the sudden changes of fortune occurring in their unsettled state of life, their passions are raised to the utmost. Their passions have nothing to restrain them: their imagination has nothing to check it. They display themselves to one another without disguise: and converse and act in the uncovered simplicity of nature. As their feelings are strong, so their language, of itself, assumes a poetical turn. Prone to exaggerate, they describe every thing in the strongest colours; which of course renders their speech picturesque and figurative. Figurative language owes its rise chiefly to two causes; to the want of proper names for objects, and to the influence of imagination and passion over the form of expression. Both these causes concur in the infancy of society. Figures are commonly considered as artificial modes of speech, devised by orators and poets, after the world had advanced to a refined state. The contrary of this is the truth. Men never have used so many figures of style, as in those rude ages, when, besides the power of a warm imagination to suggest lively images, the want of proper and precise terms for the ideas they would express, obliged them to have recourse to circumlocution, metaphor, comparison, and all those substituted forms of expression, which give a poetical air to language.

An American chief, at this day, harangues at the head of his tribe, in a more bold metaphorical style, than a modern European would adventure to use in an Epic poem.

In the progress of society, the genius and manners of men undergo a change more favourable to accuracy than to sprightliness and sublimity. As the world advances, the understanding gains ground upon the imagination; the understanding is more exercised; the imagination, less. Fewer objects occur that are new or surprizing. Men apply themselves to trace the causes of things; they correct and refine one another; they subdue or disguise their passions; they form their exterior manners upon one uniform standard of politeness and civility. Human nature is pruned according to method and rule. Language advances from sterility to copiousness, and at the same time, from fervour and enthusiasm, to correctness and precision. Style becomes more chaste; but less animated. The progress of the world in this respect resembles the progress of age in man. The powers of imagination are most vigorous and predominant in youth; those of the understanding ripen more slowly, and often attain not their maturity, till the imagination begins to flag. Hence, poetry, which is the child of imagination, is frequently most glowing and animated in the first ages of society. As the ideas of our youth are remembered with a peculiar pleasure on account of their liveliness and vivacity: so the most ancient poems have often proved the greatest favourites of nations.

Poetry has been said to be more ancient than prose: and however paradoxical such an assertion may seem, yet, in a qualified sense, it is true. Men certainly never conversed with one another in regular numbers; but even their ordinary language would, in ancient times, for the reasons before assigned, approach to a poetical style; and the first compositions transmitted to posterity, beyond doubt, were in a literal sense, poems; that is, compositions in which imagination had the chief hand, formed into some kind of numbers, and pronounced with a musical modulation or tone. Musick or songs has been found coaeval with society among the most barbarous nations. The only subjects which could prompt men, in their first rude state to utter their thoughts in compositions of any length, were such as naturally assumed the tone of poetry; praises of their gods, or of their ancestors; commemorations of their own warlike exploits; or lamentations over their misfortunes. And before writing was invented, no other compositions, except songs or poems, could take such hold of the imagination and memory, as to be preserved by oral tradition, and handed down from one race to another.

Hence we may expect to find poems among the antiquities of all nations. It is probable too, that an extensive search would discover a certain degree of resemblance among all the most ancient poetical productions, from whatever country they have proceeded. In a similar state of manners, similar objects and passions operating upon the imaginations of men, will stamp their productions with the same general character. Some diversity will, no doubt, be occasioned by climate and genius. But mankind never bear such resembling features, as they do in the beginnings of society. Its subsequent revolutions give rise to the principal distinctions among nations; and divert, into channels widely separated, that current of human genius and manners, which descends originally from one spring. What we have been long accustomed to call the oriental vein of poetry, because some of the earliest poetical productions have come to us from the East, is probably no more oriental than occidental; it is characteristical of an age rather than a country; and belongs, in some measure, to all nations at a certain period. Of this the works of Ossian seem to furnish a remarkable proof.

Our present subject leads us to investigate the ancient poetical remains, not so much of the east, or of the Greeks and Romans, as of the northern nations; in order to discover whether the Gothic poetry has any resemblance to the Celtic or Galic, which we were about to consider. Though the Goths, under which name we usually comprehend all the Scandinavian tribes, were a people altogether fierce and martial, and noted, to a proverb, for their ignorance of the liberal arts, yet they too, from the earliest times, had their poets and their songs. Their poets were distinguished by the title of *Scalders*, and their songs were termed *Vyses*.* Saxo Grammaticus, a Danish Historian, of considerable note, who flourished in the thirteenth

---

*Olaus Wormius, in the appendix to his treatise De literatura runica, has given a particular account of the Gothic poetry, commonly called Runic, from *Runes*, which signifies the Gothic letters. He informs us that there were no fewer than 136 different kinds of measure or verse used in their *Vyses*; and tho' we are accustomed to call rhyme a Gothic invention, he says expresly, that among all these measures, rhyme, or correspondence of final syllables, was never employed. He analyses the structure of one of these kinds of verse, that in which the poem of Lodbrog, afterwards quoted, is written; which exhibits a very singular species of harmony, if it can be allowed that name, depending neither upon rhyme nor upon metrical feet, or quantity of syllables, but chiefly upon the number of the syllables, and the disposition of the letters. In every stanza was an equal number of lines: in every line six syllables. In each distich, it was requisite that three words should begin with the same letter; two of the corresponding words placed in the first line of the distich, the third in the second line. In each line were also required two syllables, but never the final ones, formed either of the same consonants, or same vowels. As an example of this measure, Olaus gives us these two Latin lines constructed exactly according to the above rules of Runic verse.

Christus caput nostrum
Coronet te bonis.

The initial letters of Christus, Caput and Coronet, make the three corresponding letters of the distich. In the first line, the first syllables of Christus and of nostrum; in the second line, the *on* in coronet and in bonis make the requisite correspondence of syllables. Frequent inversions and transpositions were permitted in this poetry; which would naturally follow from such laborious attention to the collocation of words.

The curious on this subject may consult likewise Dr. Hicks's Thesaurus Linguarum Septentrionalium; particularly the 23rd chapter of his Grammatica Anglo Saxonica et Maeso Gothica; where they will find a full account of the structure of the Anglo Saxon verse, which nearly resembled the Gothic. They will find also some specimens both of Gothic and Saxon poetry. An extract, which Dr. Hicks has given from the work of one of the Danish Scalders, entitled, Hervarer Saga, containing an evocation from the dead, may be found in the 6th volume of Miscellany Poems, published by Mr. Dryden.

century, informs us that very many of these songs, containing the ancient traditionary stories of the country, were found engraven upon rocks in the old Runic character; several of which he has translated into Latin, and inserted into his History. But his versions are plainly so paraphrastical, and forced into such an imitation of the style and the measures of the Roman poets, that one can form no judgment from them of the native spirit of the original. A more curious monument of the true Gothic poetry is preserved by Olaus Wormius in his book *de Literatura Runica*. It is an Epicedium, or funeral song, composed by Regner Lodbrog; and translated by Olaus, word for word, from the original. This Lodbrog was a king of Denmark, who lived in the eighth century, famous for his wars and victories; and at the same time an eminent *Scalder* or poet. It was his misfortune to fall at last into the hands of one of his enemies, by whom he was thrown into prison, and condemned to be destroyed by serpents.* In this situation he solaced himself with rehearsing all the exploits of his life. The poem is divided into twenty-nine stanzas, of ten lines each; and every stanza begins with these words, 'Pugnavimus ensibus', 'We have fought with our swords'. Olaus's version is in many places so obscure as to be hardly intelligible. I have subjoined the whole below, exactly as he has published it; and shall translate as much as may give the English reader an idea of the spirit and strain of this kind of poetry.

We have fought with our swords, – I was young, when, towards the east, in the bay of Oreon, we made torrents of blood flow, to gorge the ravenous beast of prey, and the yellow-footed bird. There resounded the hard steel upon the lofty helmets of men. The whole ocean was one wound. The crow waded in the blood of the slain. When we had numbered twenty years, we lifted our spears on high, and every where spread our renown. Eight barons we overcame in the east before the port of Diminium; and plentifully we feasted the eagle in that slaughter. The warm stream of wounds ran into the ocean. The army fell before us. When we steered our ships into the mouth of the Vistula, we sent the Helsingians to the Hall of Odin. Then did the sword bite. The waters were all one wound. The earth was dyed red with the warm stream. . . .

*

When we turn from the poetry of Lodbrog to that of Ossian, it is like passing from a savage desert, into a fertile and cultivated country. How is this to be accounted for? Or by what means to be reconciled with the remote antiquity attributed to these poems? This is a curious point; and requires to be illustrated.

That the ancient Scots were of Celtic original, is past all doubt. Their

---

*Thomas Warton the Elder's *Runic Odes* hymned the death of Regner and influenced Gray's *Descent of Odin*. Ed.

conformity with the Celtic nations in language, manners and religion, proves it to a full demonstration. The Celtae, a great and mighty people, altogether distinct from the Goths and Teutons, once extended their dominion over all the west of Europe; but seem to have had their most full and complete establishment in Gaul. Wherever the Celtae or Gauls are mentioned by ancient writers, we seldom fail to hear of their Druids and their Bards; the institution of which two orders was the capital distinction of their manners and policy. The Druids were their philosophers and priests; the Bards, their poets and recorders of heroic actions. And both these orders of men, seem to have subsisted among them, as chief members of the state, from time immemorial. We must not therefore imagine the Celtae to have been altogether a gross and rude nation. They possessed from very remote ages a formed system of discipline and manners, which appears to have had a deep and lasting influence. Ammianus Marcellinus gives them this express testimony, that there flourished among them the study of the most laudable arts, introduced by the Bards, whose office it was to sing in heroic verse, the gallant actions of illustrious men. . . .

*

The manner of composition bears all the marks of the greatest antiquity. No artful transitions; nor full and extended connection of parts; such as we find among the poets of later times, when order and regularity of composition were more studied and known; but a style always rapid and vehement; in narrative concise even to abruptness, and leaving several circumstances to be supplied by the reader's imagination. The language has all that figurative cast, which, as I before showed, partly a glowing and undisciplined imagination, partly the sterility of language and the want of proper terms, have always introduced into the early speech of nations; and in several respects, it carries a remarkable resemblance to the style of the Old Testament. [Cf. Lowth on *The Sacred Poetry of the Hebrews*, pp. 151-167.] It deserves particular notice, as one of the most genuine and decisive characters of antiquity, that very few general terms or abstract ideas, are to be met with in the whole collection of Ossian's works. The ideas, of men, at first, were all particular. They had not words to express general conceptions. These were the consequence of more profound reflection and longer acquaintance with the arts of thought and of speech. Ossian, accordingly, almost never expressed himself in the abstract. His ideas extended little farther than to the objects he saw around him. A public, a community, the universe, were conceptions beyond his sphere. Even a mountain, a sea, or a lake, which he has occasion to mention, though only in a simile, are for the most part particularized; it is the hill of Cromla, the storm of the sea of Malmor, or the reeds of the lake of Lego. A mode of expression, which whilst it is characteristical of ancient ages, is at the same time highly favourable to descriptive poetry. For the same reasons, personification is a poetical figure not very common with Ossian.

Inanimate objects, such as winds, trees, flowers, he sometimes personifies with great beauty. But the personifications which are so familiar to later poets of Fame, Time, Terror, Virtue, and the rest of that class, were unknown to our Celtic bard. These were modes of conception, too abstract for his age. [Cf. Blair below, pp. 277-278, and Berkeley on abstractions pp. 69-79.]

All these are marks so undoubted, and some of them too, so nice and delicate, of the earliest times, as put the high antiquity of these poems out of question. Especially when we consider, that if there had been any imposture in this case, it must have been contrived and executed in the Highlands of Scotland, two or three centuries ago; as up to this period, both by manuscripts, and by the testimony of a multitude of living witnesses, concerning the uncontrovertible tradition of these poems, they can clearly be traced. Now this is a period when that country enjoyed no advantages for a composition of this kind, which it may not 'be supposed to have enjoyed in as great, if not in a greater degree, a thousand years before. To suppose that two or three hundred years ago, when we well know the Highlands to have been in a state of gross ignorance and barbarity, there should have arisen in that country a poet, of such exquisite genius, and of such deep knowledge of mankind, and of history, as to divest himself of the ideas and manners of his own age, and to give us a just and natural picture of a state of society ancienter by a thousand years; one who could support this counterfeited antiquity through such a large collection of poems, without the least inconsistency; and who possessed of all this genius and art, had at the same time the self-denial of concealing himself, and of ascribing his own works to an antiquated bard, without the imposture being detected; is a supposition that transcends all bounds of credibility.

There are, besides, two other circumstances to be attended to, still of greater weight, if possible, against this hypothesis. One is the total absence of religious ideas from this work; for which the translator has, in his preface, given a very probable account, on the footing of its being the work of Ossian. The druidical superstition was, in the days of Ossian, on the point of its final extinction; and for particular reasons, odious to the family of Fingal; whilst the christian faith was not yet established. But had it been the work of one, to whom the idea of christianity were familiar from his. infancy; and who had superadded to them also the bigotted superstition of a dark age and country; it is impossible but in some passage or other, the traces of them would have appeared. The other circumstance is, the entire silence which reigns with respect to all the great clans or families, which are now established in the Highlands. The origin of these several clans is known to be very ancient: And it is as well known, that there is no passion by which a native Highlander is more distinguished, than by attachment to his clan, and jealousy for its honour. That a highland bard in forging a work relating to the antiquities of his country, should have inserted no circumstance which pointed out the rise of his own clan which ascertained its antiquity, or increased its glory, is of all suppositions that can be formed, the most improbable; and the silence on this head, amounts to a demonstration that the author lived before any of the present great clans were formed or known.

Assuming it then, as we well may, for certain, that the poems now under consideration, are genuine venerable monuments of very remote antiquity; I proceed to make some remarks upon their general spirit and strain. The two great characteristics of Ossian's poetry, are, tenderness and sublimity. It breathes nothing of the gay and cheerful kind; an air of solemnity and seriousness is diffused over the whole. Ossian is perhaps the only poet who never relaxes, or lets himself down into the light and amusing strain; which I readily admit to be no small disadvantage to him, with the bulk of readers. He moves perpetually in the high region of the grand and the pathetick. One key note is struck at the beginning, and supported to the end; nor is any ornament introduced, but what is perfectly concordant with the general tone or melody. The events recorded are all serious and grave; the scenery throughout, wild and romantic. The extended heath by the sea-shore; the mountain shaded with mist; the torrent rushing through a solitary valley; the scattered oaks, and the tombs of warriors overgrown with moss; all produce a solemn attention in the mind, and prepare it for great and extraordinary events. We find not in Ossian, an imagination that sports itself, and dresses out gay trifles to please the fancy. His poetry, more perhaps than that of any other writer, deserves to be stiled, *the poetry of the heart*. It is a heart penetrated with noble sentiments, and with sublime and tender passions; a heart that glows, and kindles the fancy; a heart that is full, and pours itself forth. . . .

*

Very often two objects are brought together in a simile, though they resemble one another, strictly speaking, in nothing,* only, because they raise in the mind a train of similar, and what may be called, concordant ideas; so that the remembrance of the one, when recalled, serves to quicken and heighten the impression made by the other. Thus, to give an instance from our poet, the pleasure with which an old man looks back on the exploits of his youth, has certainly no direct resemblance to the beauty of a fine evening; farther than that both agree in producing a certain calm, placid joy. Yet Ossian has founded upon this, one of the most beautiful comparisons that is to be met with in any poet.

Wilt thou not listen, son of the rock, to the song of Ossian? My soul is full of other times; the joy of my youth returns. Thus, the sun appears in the west, after the steps of his brightness have moved behind a storm. The green hills lift their dewy heads. The blue streams rejoice in

---

*Blair would seem to describe here a metaphor, not, as he says, 'a simile'. Ed.

the vale. The aged hero comes forth on his staff; and his grey hair glitters in the beam.

Never was there a finer group of objects. It raises a strong conception of the old man's joy and elation of heart, by displaying a scene, which produces in every spectator, a corresponding train of pleasing emotions; the declining sun looking forth in his brightness after a storm; the cheerful face of all nature; and the still life finely animated by the circumstance of the aged hero, with his staff and his grey locks; a circumstance both extremely picturesque in itself, and peculiarly suited to the main object of the comparison. Such analogies and associations of ideas* as these, are highly pleasing to the fancy. They give opportunity for introducing many a fine poetical picture. They diversify the scene; they aggrandize the subject; they keep the imagination awake and sprightly. For as the judgment is principally exercised in distinguishing objects, and remarking the differences among those which seem like; so the highest amusement of the imagination is to trace likenesses and agreements among those which seem different.

The principal rules which respect poetical comparisons are, that they be introduced on proper occasions, when the mind is disposed to relish them; and not in the midst of some severe and agitating passion, which cannot admit this play of fancy; that they be founded on a resemblance neither too near and obvious, so as to give little amusement to the imagination in tracing it, nor too faint and remote, so as to be apprehended with difficulty; that they serve either to illustrate the principal object, and to render the conception of it, more clear and distinct; or at least to heighten and embellish it by a suitable association of images.

Every country has a scenery peculiar to itself; and the imagery of a good poet will exhibit it. For as he copies after nature, his allusions will of course be taken from those objects which he sees around him, and which have often struck his fancy. For this reason, in order to judge of the propriety of poetical imagery, we ought to be in some measure, acquainted with the natural history of the country where the scene of the poems is laid. The introduction of foreign images betrays a poet, copying not from nature, but from other writers. [Cf. Warton on Pope, p. 173.] Hence so many Lions, and Tygers, and Eagles and Serpents, which we meet in the similes of modern poets; as if these animals had acquired some right to a place in poetical comparisons for ever, because employed by ancient authors. They employed them with propriety, as objects generally known in their country; but they are absurdly used for illustration by us, who know them only at second hand, or by description. To most readers of modern poetry, it were more to the purpose to describe Lions or Tygers by similes taken from men, than to compare men to Lions. Ossian is very correct in this particular. His imagery is, without exception, copied from that face of nature, which he saw before his eyes; and by consequence may

---

*Note Blair's up-to-the-minute terms. Cf. Hartley's 'association of ideas' pp. 221-48. Ed.

be expected to be lively. We meet with no Grecian or Italian scenery; but with the mists, and clouds, and storms of a northern mountainous region.

*

A resemblance may be sometimes observed between Ossian's comparisons, and those employed by the sacred writers. They abound much in this figure, and use it with the utmost propriety.* The imagery of Scripture exhibits a soil and climate altogether different from those of Ossian; a warmer country, a more smiling face of nature, the arts of agriculture and of rural life much farther advanced. The wine press, and the threshing floor, are often presented to us, the Cedar and the Palm-tree, the fragrance of perfumes, the voice of the Turtle, and the beds of Lilies. The similes are, like Ossian's, generally short, touching on one point of resemblance, rather than spread out into little episodes. In the following example may be perceived what inexpressible grandeur poetry receives from the intervention of the Deity.

The nations shall rush like the rushings of many waters; but God shall rebuke them, and they shall fly far off, and shall be chafed as the chaff of the mountains before the wind, and like the down of the thistle before the whirlwind.   [Isaiah 17: 13–14]

*

One of the most exaggerated descriptions in the whole work, is what meets us at the beginning of Fingal, where the scout makes his report to Cuchullin of the landing of the foe. But this is so far from deserving censure that it merits praise, as being, on that occasion, natural and proper. The scout arrives, trembling and full of fears; and it is well known, that no passion disposes men to hyperbolize more than terror. It both annihilates themselves in their own apprehension, and magnifies every object which they view through the medium of a troubled imagination. Hence all those indistinct images of formidable greatness, the natural marks of a disturbed and confused mind, which occur in Moran's description of Swaran's appearance, and his relation of the conference which they held together; not unlike the report, which the affrighted Jewish spies made to their leader of the land of Canaan.

The land through which we have gone to search it, is a land that eateth up the inhabitants thereof; and all the people that we saw in it, are men of a great stature: and there saw we giants, the sons of Anak, which come of the giants; and we were in our own sight as grasshoppers, and so were we in their sight.   [Numbers 13: 32–3]

With regard to personifications, I formerly observed that Ossian was sparing, and I accounted for his being so. Allegorical personages he has

---

*See Dr Lowth, *De Sacra Poësi Hebraeorum*. [Esp. p. 155. Ed.]

none; and their absence is not to be regretted. For the intermixture of those shadowy Beings, which have not the support even of mythological or legendary belief, with human actors, seldom produces a good effect. [Cf. Addison, *Spectator* No. 357, p. 90, and Thomas Burnet's claim that the Old Testament has no allegory, pp. 31-32.] The fiction becomes too visible and phantastick; and overthrows that impression of reality, which the probable recital of human actions is calculated to make upon the mind. In the serious and pathetic scenes of Ossian especially, allegorical characters would have been as much out of place, as in Tragedy; serving only un-seasonably to amuse the fancy, whilst they stopped the current, and weakened the force of passion.

With apostrophes, or addresses to persons absent or dead, which have been, in all ages, the language of passion, our poet abounds; and they are among his highest beauties. Witness the apostrophe, in the first book of Fingal, to the maid of Inistore, whose lover had fallen in battle; and that inimitably fine one of Cuchullin to Bragela at the conclusion of the same book. He commands the harp to be struck in her praise; and the mention of Bragela's name, immediately suggesting to him a crowd of tender ideas; 'Dost thou raise thy fair face from the rocks,' he exclaims 'to find the sails of Cuchullin? The sea is rolling far distant, and its white foam shall deceive thee for my sails.' And now his imagination being wrought up to conceive her as, at that moment, really in this situation he becomes afraid of the harm she may receive from the inclemency of the night; and with an enthusiasm, happy and affecting, though beyond the cautious strain of modern poetry, 'Retire,' he proceeds, 'retire, for it is night, my love, and the dark winds sigh in thy hair. Retire to the hall of my feasts, and think of the times that are past; for I will not return till the storm of war has ceased. O Connal, speak of wars and arms, and send her from my mind; for lovely with her raven hair is the white-bosomed daughter of Sorglan.' This breathes all the native spirit of passion and tenderness.

*

Having now treated fully of Ossian's talents, with respect to description and imagery, it only remains to make some observations on his sentiments. No sentiments can be beautiful without being proper; that is, suited to the character, and situation of those who utter them. In this respect, Ossian is as correct as most writers. His characters, as above observed, are in general well supported; which could not have been the case, had the sentiments been unnatural or out of place. A variety of personages of different ages, sexes, and conditions are introduced into his poems; and they speak and act with a propriety of sentiment and behavior, which it is surprising to find in so rude an age. Let the poem of Darhula, throughout, be taken as an example.

But it is not enough that sentiments be natural and proper. In order to acquire any high degree of poetical merit, they must also be sublime and pathetick.

The sublime is not confined to sentiment alone. It belongs to description also; and whether in description or in sentiment, imports such ideas presented to the mind, as raise it to an uncommon degree of elevation, and fill it with admiration and astonishment. This is the highest effect either of eloquence or poetry; and to produce this effect, requires a genius glowing with the strongest and warmest conception of some object awful, great or magnificent.

*

Upon the whole, if to feel strongly, and to describe naturally, be the two chief ingredients in poetical genius, Ossian must, after fair examination, be held to possess that genius in a high degree. The question is not, whether a few improprieties may be pointed out in his works; whether this, or that passage, might not have been worked up with more art and skill, by some writer of happier times. A thousand such cold and frivolous criticisms, are altogether indecisive as to his genuine merit. But, has he the spirit, the fire, the inspiration of a poet? Does he utter the voice of nature? Does he elevate by his sentiments? Does he interest by his descriptions? Does he paint to the heart as well as to the fancy? Does he make his readers glow, and tremble, and weep? These are the great characteristics of true poetry. Where these are found, he must be a minute critic indeed, who can dwell upon slight defects. A few beauties of this high kind, transcend whole volumes of faultless mediocrity. Uncouth and abrupt, Ossian may sometimes appear by reason of his conciseness. But he is sublime, he is pathetick,* in an eminent degree. If he has not the extensive knowledge, the regular dignity of narration, the fulness and accuracy of description, which we find in Homer and Virgil, yet in strength of imagination, in grandeur of sentiment, in native majesty of passion, he is fully their equal. If he flows not always like a clear stream, yet he breaks forth often like a torrent of fire. Of art too, he is far from being destitute; and his imagination is remarkable for delicacy as well as strength. Seldom or never is he either trifling or tedious; and if he be thought too melancholy, yet he is always moral. Though his merit were in other respects much less than it is, this alone ought to entitle him to high regard, that his writings are remarkably favourable to virtue. They awake the tenderest sympathies, and inspire the most generous emotions. No reader can rise from him, without being warmed with the sentiments of humanity, virtue and honour.

Though unacquainted with the original language, there is no one but must judge the translation to deserve the highest praise, on account of its beauty and elegance. Of its faithfulness and accuracy, I have been assured by persons skilled in the Galic tongue, who, from their youth, were

---

*'The sublime and the pathetic are the two chief nerves of all genuine poesy', Joseph Warton. See p. 172. Ed.

acquainted with many of these poems of Ossian. To transfuse such spirited and fervid ideas from one language into another; to translate literally, and yet with such a glow of poetry; to keep alive so much passion, and support so much dignity throughout, is one of the most difficult works of genius, and proves the translator to have been animated with no small portion of Ossian's spirit.

LECTURES ON RHETORIC AND BELLES LETTRES (1783)

from Lecture VI, 'The Rise and Progress Of Language'
Language, in general, signifies the expression of our ideas by certain articulate sounds, which are used as the signs of those ideas. By articulate sounds, are meant those modulations of simple voice, or of sound emitted from the thorax, which are formed by means of the mouth and its several organs, the teeth, the tongue, the lips, and the palate. How far there is any natural connexion between the ideas of the mind and the sounds emitted, will appear from what I am afterwards to offer. But as the natural connexion can, upon any system, affect only a small part of the fabric of Language; the connexion between words and ideas may, in general, be considered as arbitrary and conventional, owing to the agreement of men among themselves; the clear proof of which is, that different nations have different Languages, or a different set of articulate sounds, which they have chosen for communicating their ideas.

This artificial method of communicating thought, we now behold carried to the highest perfection. Language is become a vehicle by which the most delicate and refined emotions of one mind can be transmitted, or, if we may so speak, transfused into another. Not only are names given to all objects around us, by which means an easy and speedy intercourse is carried on for providing the necessaries of life, but all the relations and differences among these objects are minutely marked, the invisible sentiments of the mind are described, the most abstract notions and conceptions are rendered intelligible; and all the ideas which science can discover, or imagination create, are known by their proper names. Nay, Language has been carried so far, as to be made an instrument of the most refined luxury. Not resting in mere perspicuity, we require ornament also; not satisfied with having the conceptions of others made known to us, we make a farther demand, to have them so decked and adorned as to entertain our fancy; and this demand, it is found very possible to gratify. In this state, we now find Language. In this state, it has been found among many nations for some thousand years. The object is become familiar; and, like the expanse of the firmament, and other great objects, which we are accustomed to behold, we behold it without wonder.

But carry your thoughts back to the first dawn of Language among men. Reflect upon the feeble beginnings from which it must have arisen, and upon the many and great obstacles which it must have encountered in its progress; and you will find reason for the highest astonishment, on viewing the height which it has now attained. We admire several of the inventions of art; we plume ourselves on some discoveries which have been made in latter ages, serving to advance knowledge, and to render life comfortable; we speak of them as the boast of human reason. But certainly no invention is entitled to any such degree of admiration as that of Language; which, too, must have been the product of the first and rudest ages, if indeed it can be considered as a human invention at all.

Think of the circumstances of mankind when Languages began to be formed. They were a wandering scattered race; no society among them except families; and the family society too very imperfect, as their method of living by hunting or pasturage must have separated them frequently from one another. In this situation, when so much divided, and their intercourse so rare, how could any one set of sounds, or words, be generally agreed on as the signs of their ideas? Supposing that a few, whom chance or necessity threw together, agreed by some means upon certain signs, yet by what authority could these be propagated among other tribes or families, so as to spread and grow up into a Language? One would think, that in order to any Language fixing and extending itself, men must have been previously gathered together in considerable numbers; society must have been already far advanced; and yet, on the other hand, there seems to have been an absolute necessity for Speech, previous to the formation of Society. For, by what bond could any multitude of men be kept together, or be made to join in the prosecution of any common interest, until once, by the intervention of Speech, they could communicate their wants and intentions to each other? So that, either how Society could form itself, previously to Language; or how words could rise into a Language, previously to Society formed, seem to be points attended with equal difficulty.

*

We are apt, upon a superficial view, to imagine, that those modes of expression which are called Figures of Speech, are among the chief refinements of Speech, not invented till after Language had advanced to its later periods, and mankind were brought into a polished state; and that, then, they were devised by Orators and Rhetoricians. The quite contrary of this is the truth. Mankind never employed so many figures of Speech, as when they had hardly any words for expressing their meaning.

For first, the want of proper names for every object, obliged them to use one name for many; and, of course, to express themselves by comparisons, metaphors, allusions, and all those substituted forms of Speech which render Language figurative. Next, as the objects with which they were most conversant, were the sensible, material objects around them, names would be given to those objects long before words were invented for signifying the dispositions of the mind, or any sort of moral and intellectual ideas.* Hence, the early Language of men being entirely made up of words descriptive of sensible objects, it became, of necessity, extremely metaphorical.** For, to signify any desire or passion, or any act or feeling of the mind, they had no precise expression which was appropriated to that purpose, but were under a necessity of painting the emotion, or passion, which they felt, by allusion to those sensible objects which had most relation to it, and which could render it, in some sort, visible to others.

But it was not necessity alone, that gave rise to this figured style. Other circumstances also, at the commencement of Language, contributed to it. In the infancy of all societies, men are much under the dominion of imagination and passion. They live scattered and dispersed; they are unacquainted with the course of things; they are, every day, meeting with new and strange objects. Fear and surprise, wonder and astonishment, are their most frequent passions. Their Language will necessarily partake of this character of their minds. They will be prone to exaggeration and hyperbole. They will be given to describe every thing with the strongest colours, and most vehement expressions; infinitely more than men living in the advanced and cultivated periods of Society, when their imagination is more chastened, their passions are more tamed, and a wider experience has rendered the objects of life more familiar to them. Even the manner in which I before showed that the first tribes of men uttered their words, would have considerable influence on their style. Wherever strong exclamations, tones, and gestures, enter much into conversation, the imagination is always more exercised; a greater effort of fancy and passion is excited. Consequently, the fancy kept awake, and rendered more sprightly by this mode of utterance, operates upon style, and enlivens it more.

These reasonings are confirmed by undoubted facts. The style of all the most early Languages, among nations who are in the first and rude periods of Society, is found, without exception, to be full of figures; hyperbolical and picturesque in a high degree. We have a striking instance of this in the American Languages, which are known, by the most authentic accounts, to be figurative to excess. The Iroquois and Illinois, carry on their treaties and public transactions with bolder metaphors, and greater pomp of style, than we use in our poetical productions.***

---

*This point was common. See the essays of Herder and Rousseau 'on the origin of language'. Ed.

**For instance, the 'works' of Ossian. Ed.

***Thus, to give an instance of the singular style of these nations, the Five Nations of Canada, when entering on a treaty of peace with us, expressed themselves by their Chiefs, in the following Language: 'We are happy in having buried under ground the red axe, that has so often been dyed with the blood of our brethren. Now, in this fort, we inter the axe, and plant the tree of Peace. We plant a tree, whose top will

Another remarkable instance is, the style of the Old Testament, which is carried on by constant allusions to sensible objects. Iniquity, or guilt, is expressed by 'a spotted garment'; misery, by 'drinking the cup of astonishment'; vain pursuits, by 'feeding on ashes'; a sinful life, by 'a crooked path'; prosperity, by 'the candle of the Lord shining on our head'; and the like, in innumerable instances. Hence, we have been accustomed to call this sort of style, the Oriental Style; as fancying it to be peculiar to the nations of the East: Whereas, from the American Style, and from many other instances, it plainly appears not to have been peculiar to any one region or climate; but to have been common to all nations, in certain periods of Society and Language.

Hence, we may receive some light concerning that seeming paradox, that Poetry is more ancient than Prose. I shall have occasion to discuss this point fully hereafter, when I come to treat of the Nature and Origin of Poetry. At present, it is sufficient to observe, that, from what has been said it plainly appears, that the style of all Language must have been originally poetical; strongly tinctured with that enthusiasm, and that descriptive, metaphorical expression, which distinguishes Poetry.

As Language, in its progress, began to grow more copious, it gradually lost that figurative style, which was its early character. When men were furnished with proper and familiar names for every object, both sensible and moral, they were not obliged to use so many circumlocutions. Style became more precise, and, of course, more simple. Imagination too, in proportion as Society advanced, had less influence over mankind. The vehement manner of speaking by tones and gestures, became not so universal. The understanding was more exercised; the fancy, less. Intercourse among mankind becoming more extensive and frequent, clearness of style, in signifying their meaning to each other, was the chief object of

---

reach the Sun; and its branches spread abroad, so that it shall be seen afar off. May its growth never be stifled and choked; but may it shade both your country and ours with its leaves! Let us make fast its roots, and extend them to the utmost of your colonies. If the French should come to shake this tree, we would know it by the motion of its roots reaching into our country. May the Great Spirit allow us to rest in tranquility upon our mats, and never again dig up the axe to cut down the tree of Peace! Let the earth be trod hard over it, where it lies buried. Let a strong stream run under the pit, to wash the evil away out of our sight and remembrance. — The fire that had long burned in Albany is extinguished. The bloody bed is washed clean, and the tears are wiped from our eyes. We now renew the covenant chain of friendship. Let it be kept bright and clean as silver, and not suffered to contract any rust. Let not any one pull away his arm from it.' These passages are extracted from Cadwallader Colden's History of the Five Indian Nations; where it appears, from the authentic documents he produces, that such is their genuine style.

attention. In place of Poets, Philosophers became the instructors of men; and, in their reasoning on all different subjects, introduced their plainer and simpler style of composition, which we now call Prose. Among the Greeks, Pherecydes of Scyros, the master of Pythagoras, is recorded to have been the first, who, in this sense, composed any writing in prose. The ancient metaphorical and poetical dress of Language, was now laid aside from the intercourse of men, and reserved for those occasions only, on which ornament was professedly studied.

WILLIAM HOGARTH (1697–1764)

Closely related to the breakdown of what Coleridge calls the 'conjunction disjunctive' of Pope and the rise of the principle of parallelism to be observed in Lowth (see pp. 337 and 162) is the emergence, early in the development of Romanticism, of a distinctive single line. In Gray's *Elegy* the second line of the fourth stanza (line 14) is the most perfect example of this phenomenon. Beneath the 'rugged elms' the 'rude forefathers' sleep '*where*' Gray observes, '*heaves the turf in many a mould'ring heap*'.

The reference or 'outness', in Berkeley's term, of the line is less important than its internal movement. If Pope's is the poetry of allusion, this is the poetry of non-allusion. Apparently poets like Gray had benefitted from contemporary philosophy to the extent that they accepted that the mind created a single impression of anything ostensibly 'exterior' to itself. The weakening, as it were, of a space between the line and whatever it might have been allowed to allude to in 'Nature' is closely related to Gray's apparently conscious attempt to write a 'sublime' line, one in which finite limits disappear. Mid-century poets appear to have taken seriously 'John Lizard's' comment (see p. 141) that motion caused emotion. The unmarked graves heave, in the context of infinity, like waves, an oceanic image relating this line to the 'unfathom'd caves of ocean' of line 54. But, whilst Gray exaggerates the motion of the ground in the first half of the line, he supplies a *diminuendo* in the second half. The artificial climax of 'heaves' is undermined by the anti-climactic 'mould'ring' at the end. Of course, Thomson had anticipated Gray in such lines as that of *Summer* (line 278) in which the rapacious spider having killed the pathetic fly 'strikes . . . grimly pleased' *backwards* out of the line as the reader's eye moves *forward* along the line. As in Keats' *Ode on a Grecian Urn*, one observes, the movement of Nature's process is the highest form of perception, and its paradoxically timeless capturing in the sculpturing of art the greatest achievement of the poet. Temporality and finiteness, the occidental habit of accepting the sequential order of logic as the *locale* of truth, are here held up to criticism. Intriguingly this form of line in which motion is first introduced and exaggerated and then cancelled out, is especially conceived of as relating to the oriental and the prophetic. For Gray it was at the heart of 'the Sublime', as we have observed in *The Progress of Poesy* (see p. 191) where Cytherea, or Venus (cf. Hogarth on the statue of Venus, pp. 284 and 287) 'wins her easy way . . . with arms sublime, that float upon the air', a movement which again sets up a finite expectation, but, in the denial of gravity (and mass) contradicts itself and becomes an image of monumental, infinite harmony.

This kind of line, we observe, is an ambiguous event. Progress seems to occur as the eye moves along the line but such is the force of the static image the process of reading does not seem conclusive. Wherever one concentrates peripheries claim the attention. The beginning of the line appears still to remain with us as we read the middle, and at the end the beginning and middle grow and change by the accretion of new associations. At one point, Hogarth in his *Analysis of Beauty* offers as his ideal a dance, in which the central portion of the line captures our attention, but the peripheries still invite observation, as it were, out of the corners of our mind's eye. For Hogarth, the movement of hair and, 'as the following pages indicate, the curves of muscles, and of a pretty face or handsome torso, like the beauties of capitals, St Paul's, and the cornucopia, persuade us that this ambiguous line, to which he gave the apt name 'serpentine', was the perfect principle of beauty. (Cf. the movement of Smart's cat, Jeoffry, pp. 15 and 150.)

In Coleridge's *Christabel*, the threatening visitor, Geraldine, is both woman and serpent (see lines 250–254), her sinister power imaged again in the pseudo-heraldic dove and snake of lines 523–596. The water snakes of *The Ancient Mariner* (see esp. lines 272–291) occur significantly at a point at which the mariner leaves the temporal-spatial world of direction and extension and enters the realm of timeless imagination. In Keats's *Lamia* an entire poem is devoted to the image of the serpent-woman which juxtaposes sexual guilt and the ambiguous image of the Fall. In Blake's poetry the serpent occurs almost a hundred times. In his illustrations to *Night Thoughts*, one notes, the serpent dominates entire pages, for example the title page of 'Night the Third' where, significantly tail to mouth, it dwarfs Narcissa, and again in the gratuitous oriental illustration towards the end of 'Night the Second' where it decorates the goblet which the Samaritan extends to the reluctant recipient.

The serpent or snake is an image of the greatest importance in the rise of Romanticism. Clearly it represents one of the great juxtapositions of mythology, the opposition of the eternal or infinite Garden of Eden, and the immersion of man in the 'Sea of Time and Space' in which he has seldom been comfortable for long. In the Romantic artist's imagination, the snake or serpent precisely images the opposition of the imagination and the claims of the temporal-spatial in an infinite continuum in which, as Coleridge observes of the architecture of Christabel's chamber, reality is 'all made out of the carver's brain'. It is fascinating to observe that the greatest pictorial artist of the middle of the eighteenth century, William Hogarth, instinctively detected this major development in aesthetics in the period of sensibility and corroborated the intuition of the poets of the period, anticipating not only the concerns of the major Romantics, but also the timeless observations on the undying nature of art of, for example, Gotthold Lessing's *Laocoön*.

THE ANALYSIS OF BEAUTY (1753)

from Chapter X, 'Of Compositions with the Serpentine-Line'
The very great difficulty there is in describing this line, either in words, or

by the pencil (as was hinted before, when I first mention'd it) will make it necessary for me to proceed very slowly in what I have to say in this chapter, and to beg the reader's patience whilst I lead him step by step into the knowledge of what I think the sublime in form, so remarkably display'd in the human body; in which, I believe, when he is once acquainted with the idea of them, he will find this species of lines to be principally concern'd.

First, then, let him consider . . . a straight horn,* with its contents, and he will find, as it varies like the cone, it is a form of some beauty, merely on that account.

Next let him observe in what manner, and in what degree the beauty of this horn is increas'd, . . . where it is supposed to be bent two different ways.

And lastly, let him attend to the vast increase of beauty, even to grace and elegance, in the same horn, [cf. Burke, p. 200] . . . where it is supposed to have been twisted round, at the same time, that it was bent two different ways. . . .

In the first of these figures, the dotted line down the middle expresses the straight lines of which it is composed; which, without the assistance of curve lines, or light and shade, would hardly show it to have contents.

The same is true of the second tho' by the bending of the horn, the straight dotted line is changed into the beautiful waving-line.

But in the last, this dotted line, by the twisting as well as the bending of the horn, is changed from the waving into the serpentine-line; which, as it dips out of sight behind the horn in the middle, and returns again at the smaller end, not only gives play to the imagination, and delights the eye, on that account; but informs it likewise of the quantity and variety of the contents.

I have chosen this simple example, as the easiest way of giving a plain and general idea of the peculiar qualities of these serpentine-lines, and the advantages of bringing them into compositions, where the contents you are to express, admit of grace and elegance. . . .

Though I have distinguish'd these lines so particularly as to give them the titles of *the lines of beauty and grace*, I mean that the use and application of them should still be confined by the principles I have laid down for composition in general; and that they should be judiciously mixt and combined with one another, and even with those I may term *plain* lines, (in opposition to these) as the subject in hand requires. Thus the cornu-copia, . . . is twisted and bent after the same manner, as the last figure of the horn; but more ornamented, and with a greater number of other lines of the same twisted kind, winding round it with as quick returns as those of a screw.

This sort of form may be seen with yet more variations, (and therefore more beautiful) in the goat's horn, from which, in all probability, the ancients originally took the extreme elegant forms they have given their

---

*Hogarth refers here and elsewhere to a chart of illustrations of horns, human bones, muscles, heads and bodies. Ed.

cornu-copias.

There is another way of considering this last figure of the horn I would recommend to my reader, in order to give him a clearer idea of the use both of the waving and serpentine-lines in composition.

This is to imagine the horn, thus bent and twisted, to be cut length-ways by a very fine saw into two equal parts; and to observe one of these in the same position the whole horn is represented in; and these two observations will naturally occur to him. First, that the edge of the saw must run from one end to the other of the horn in the line of beauty; so that the edges of this half of the horn will have a beautiful shape; and, secondly, that wherever the dotted serpentine-line on the surface of the whole horn dips behind, and is lost to the eye, it immediately comes into sight on the hollow surface of the divided horn.

The use I shall make of these observations will appear very considerable in the application of them to the human form, which we are next to attempt.

It will be sufficient, therefore, at present only to observe, first, that the whole horn acquires a beauty by its being thus genteely bent two different ways; secondly, that whatever lines are drawn on its external surface become graceful, as they must all of them, from the twist that is given the horn, partake in some degree or other, of the shape of the serpentine-line: and, lastly, when the horn is split, and the inner, as well as the outward surface of its shell-like form is exposed, the eye is peculiarly entertained and relieved in the pursuit of these serpentine-lines, as in their twistings their concavities and convexities are alternately offer'd to its view. Hollow forms, therefore, composed of such lines are extremely beautiful and pleasing to the eye; in many cases more so, than those of solid bodies.

Almost all the muscles, and bones, of which the human form is composed, have more, or less of these kind of twists in them; and given in a less degree, the same kind of appearance to the parts which cover them, and are the immediate object of the eye; and for this reason it is that I have been so particular in describing these forms of the bent, and twisted, and ornamented horn.

There is scarce a straight bone in the whole body. Almost all of them are not only bent different ways, but have a kind of twist, which in some of them is very graceful; and the muscles annex'd to them, tho' they are of various shapes, appropriated to their particular uses, generally have their component fibres running in these serpentine-lines, surrounding and conforming themselves to the varied shape of the bones they belong to: more especially in the limbs. Anatomists are so satisfied of this, that they take a pleasure in distinguishing their several beauties. I shall only instance in the thigh-bone, and those about the hips.

The thigh-bone . . . has the waving and twisted turn of the horn, . . . but the beautiful bones adjoining, call'd the ossa innominata, have, with greater variety, the same turns and twists of that horn when it is cut;

and its inner and outward surfaces are exposed to the eye.

How ornamental these bones appear, when the prejudice we conceive against them, as being part of a skeleton, is taken off, by adding a little foliage to them, . . . – such shell-like winding forms, mixt with foliage, twisting about them, are made use of in all ornaments; a kind of composition calculated merely to please the eye. Divest these of their serpentine twinings and they immediately lose all grace, and return to the poor gothic taste they were in an hundred years ago. . . . Most of the muscles, (those of the limbs in particular) are twisted round the bones, and conform themselves to their length and shape; but with no anatomical exactness. As to the running of their fibres, some anatomists have compared them to skeins of thread, loose in the middle, and tight at each end, which, when they are thus consider'd as twisted contrary ways round the bone, gives the strongest idea possible of a composition of serpentine-lines.

Of these fine winding forms then is the human body composed, and which, by their varied situations with each other, become more intricately pleasing, and form a continued waving of winding forms from one into the other,* as may be best seen by examining a good anatomical figure . . . which shews the serpentine forms and varied situations of the muscles, as they appear when the skin is taken off. . . . as the skin is taken off the parts are too distinctly traced by the eye, for that intricate delicacy which is necessary to the utmost beauty; yet the winding figures of the muscles, with the variety of their situations, must always be allow'd elegant forms: however, they lose in the imagination some of the beauty, which they really have, by the idea of their being flayed; nevertheless, by what has already been shewn both of them and the bones, the human frame hath more of its parts composed of serpentine-lines than any other object in nature; which is a proof both of its superior beauty to all others, and, at the same time, that its beauty proceeds from those lines: for although they may be required sometimes to be bulging in their twists, as in the thick swelling muscles of the Hercules, yet elegance and greatness of taste is still preserved; but when these lines lose so much of their twists as to become almost straight, all elegance of taste vanishes. . . .

*

In the same manner, divest one of the best antique statues** of all its serpentine winding parts, and it becomes from an exquisite piece of art, a figure of such ordinary lines and unvaried contents, that a common stone-mason or carpenter, with the help of his rule, calipers, and com-

---

*Cf. in this regard, the watercolour drawings of Thomas Rowlandson (1756–1827). Ed.

**Cf. Venus in Gray's *Progress of Poesy*, p. 191, lines 25-41. The *Analysis* was published in 1753, Gray's poem completed in 1755. Ed.

passes, might carve out an exact imitation of it: and were it not for these lines a turner, in his lathe, might turn a much finer neck than that of the Grecian Venus, as according to the common notion of a beautiful neck, it would be more truly round. For the same reason, legs much swoln with disease, are as easy to imitate as a post, having lost their *drawing*, as the painters call it; that is, having their serpentine-lines all effaced, by the skin's being equally puffed up, . . .

If in comparing these three figures one with another, the reader, notwithstanding the prejudice his imagination may have conceiv'd against them, as anatomical figures, has been enabled only to perceive that one of them is not so disagreeable as the others; he will easily be led to see further, that this tendency to beauty in one, is not owing to any greater degree of exactness in the *proportions* of its parts, but merely to the more *pleasing turns, and intertwistings of the lines*, which compose its external form; for in all the three figures the same proportions have been observ'd, and, on that account, they have all an equal claim to beauty.

And if he pursues this anatomical enquiry but a very little further, just to form a true idea of the elegant use that is made of the skin and fat beneath it, to conceal from the eye all that is hard and disagreeable, and at the same time to preserve to it whatever is necessary in the shapes of the parts beneath, to give grace and beauty to the whole limb: he will find himself insensibly led into the principles of that grace and beauty which is to be found in well-turn'd limbs, in fine, elegant, healthy life, or in those of the best antique statues; as well as into the reason why his eye has so often unknowingly been pleased and delighted with them.

Thus, in all other parts of the body, as well as these, wherever, for the sake of the necessary motion of the parts, with proper strength and agility, the insertions of the muscles are too hard and sudden, their swellings too bold, or the hollows between them too deep, for their out-lines to be beautiful; nature most judiciously softens these hardnesses, and plumps up these vacancies with a proper supply of fat, and covers the whole with the soft, smooth, springy, and, in delicate life, almost transparent skin, which, conforming itself to the external shape of all the parts beneath, expresses to the eye the idea of its contents with the utmost delicacy of beauty and grace.

The skin, therefore, thus tenderly embracing, and gently conforming itself to the varied shapes of every one of the outward muscles of the body, soften'd underneath by the fat, where, otherwise, the same hard lines and furrows would appear, as we find come on with age in the face, and with labour, in the limbs, is evidently a shell-like surface (to keep up the idea I set out with) form'd with the utmost delicacy in nature; and therefore the most proper subject of the study of every one, who desires to imitate the works of nature, *as a master should do*, or to judge of the performances of others *as a real connoisseur ought*.

I cannot be too long, I think, on this subject, as so much will be found to depend upon it; and therefore shall endeavour to give a clear idea of the different effect such anatomical figures have on the eye, from what the same parts have, when cover'd by the fat and skin; by supposing a small wire (that has lost its spring and so will retain every shape it is twisted into) to be held fast to the out-side of the hip . . . and thence brought down the other side of the thigh obliquely over the calf of the leg, down to the outward ankle (all the while press'd so close as to touch and conform itself to the shape of every muscle it passes over) and then to be taken off. If this wire be now examined it will be found that the general uninterrupted flowing twist, which the winding round the limbs would otherwise have given to it, is broke into little better than so many separate plain curves, by the sharp indentures it every where has receiv'd on being closely press'd in between the muscles.

Suppose, in the next place, such a wire was in the same manner twisted round a living well-shaped leg and thigh, or those of a fine statue; when you take it off you will find no such sharp indentures, nor any of those regular engralings [indentings of the edge with curvilinear notches] (as the heralds express it) which displeased the eye before. On the contrary, you will see how *gradually* the changes in its shape are produced; how imperceptibly the different curvatures run into each other, and how easily the eye glides along the varied wavings of its sweep. To enforce this still further, if a line was to be drawn by a pencil exactly where these wires have been supposed to pass, the point of the pencil, in the muscular leg and thigh, would perpetually meet with stops and rubs, whilst in the others it would flow from muscle to muscle along the elastic skin, as pleasantly as the lightest skiff dances over the gentlest wave.

This idea of the wire, retaining thus the shape of the parts it passes over, seems of so much consequence, that I would by no means have it forgot; as it may properly be consider'd as one of the threads (or outlines) of the shell (or external surface) of the human form: and the frequently recurring to it will assist the imagination in its conceptions of those parts of it, whose shapes are most intricately varied: for the same sort of observations may be made, with equal justice, on the shapes of ever so many such wires twisted in the same manner in ever so many directions over every part of a well made man, woman, or statue.

And if the reader will follow in his imagination the most exquisite turns of the chisel in the hands of a master when he is putting the finishing touches to a statue; he will soon be led to understand what it is the real judges expect from the hand of such a master, which the Italians call, the little more, *Il poco piu*, and which in reality distinguishes the original master-pieces at Rome from even the best copies of them. . . .

There is an elegant degree of plumpness peculiar to the skin of the softer sex, that occasions these delicate dimplings in all their other joints, as well as these of the fingers; which so perfectly distinguishes them from those even of a graceful man; and which, assisted by the more soften'd shapes of the muscles underneath, presents to the eye all the varieties in the whole figure of the body, with gentler and fewer parts more sweetly connected together, and with such a fine simplicity as will always give the turn of the female frame, represented in the Venus . . . the preference to that of the Apollo.

Now whoever can conceive lines thus constantly flowing, and delicately varying over every part of the body even to the fingers ends, and will call to his remembrance what led us to this last description of what the Italians call, *Il poco piu* (the little more that is expected from the hand of a master) will, in my mind, want very little more than what his own observation on the works of art and nature will lead him to, to acquire a true idea of the word *Taste*, when applied to form; however inexplicable this word may hitherto have been imagined.

We have all along had recourse chiefly to the works of the ancients, not because the moderns have not produced some as excellent; but because the works of the former are more generally known: nor would we have it thought, that either of them have ever yet come up to the utmost beauty of nature. Who but a bigot, even to the antiques, will say that he has not seen faces and necks, hands and arms in living women, that even the Grecian Venus doth but coarsely imitate?

And what sufficient reason can be given why the same may not be said of the rest of the body?*

---

*End of chapter. Ed.

WILLIAM BLAKE (1757–1827)

In Pope's *Pastorals* (1709), which Joseph Warton found so inferior to
Thomson's *The Seasons* (see pp. 170-182), Daphnis offers as prize in the
singing contest a drinking bowl on which

> . . . wanton ivy twines,
> And swelling clusters bend the curling vines:
> Four figures rising from the work appear,
> The various seasons of the rolling year;   (*Spring*, 35–38)

'And what is that?' he concludes 'which binds the radiant sky,/Where
twelve fair signs in beauteous order lie?' (39–40).

The contrast between the assumptions of Pope's *Pastorals* in part revealed
in this artifact within an artifact and those of Blake's *To Spring, To
Summer*, etc., (see below) of the early *Poetical Sketches* casts valuable
light on the shift in English poetry in the eighteenth century especially in
the significant area of a major classical genre, the pastoral. Most obviously
of course, whilst Pope assumes that he is imitating Theocritus, Virgil and
Spenser, and creates as his major image a Neo-classical depiction of time
stretching back to the fourth century B.C., Blake assumes the mantle of the
'original' Biblical and Ossianic (see pp. 151 and 264) bards, who, he
imagines, live – like himself – in a primitive present inimical to extensive
time. Hence, whilst Pope offers an art that is objective and holds up a
mirror to Nature, Blake creates perspectives that dissolve continually in the
processes of the poetry which he images in the *Introduction* to *Songs of
Innocence*, as had Gray (see p. 191), as an ambiguous flow of water.
Whilst Pope depicts a hieratic and subordinating 'order' stretching up to
the heavens, to parallel, as it were, the sequence of the seasons and the
signs of the zodiac depicted on his bowl, Blake, as he reveals at greater
length in *The First Book of Urizen*, denies, as had Berkeley (see pp. 64-
75), the reality of spatial images. Pope's crucial bowl, in its magical and
divine coordination of movement within the stasis of art imitates the
similar bowls and cups of the first idyll of Theocritus, of the third eclogue
of Virgil, and the 'mazers' of Spenser's *August* in *The Shepherd's Calendar*,
encapsulating by allusion the spatial and temporal order which each of them
individually signifies. We are not told that Pope's bowl is made of gold. Its
properties and relation to the 'mighty maze' of Achilles' shield in the
eighteenth book of the *Iliad* suggests this possibility, however. Furthermore, as an artifact within an artifact, it hints at the mythic idealization
of the Golden Age of Virgil's fourth eclogue within and in the background
of the movement of the *Pastorals*. Perhaps it is here more than anywhere
that Blake parts company with Pope. Myth like religion, ossified as it were
in the amber of the historic past, as he makes clear in the mocking lines on
'Ariston, the king of beauty' in *America, a Prophecy* (see lines 107-12), is
for Blake a denial of imagination. Poet-prophets do not allude down the
finite corridors of time to distant golden forms or empty tombs. Like

Ezekiel, they create now eternal myths out of their own subjective imagination. Of course, Joseph Warton did not possess the epistemological genius of Blake. But whilst Warton's reasons for unease over Pope's *Pastorals* in 1756 are not as staggeringly profound as those we might discover in Blake, the assault on classical attitudes is continuous. Far from being a radical departure from his own century, Blake echoes and reinforces not only Warton but Young, Lowth, Shaftesbury and Smart, among others, and notably parallels the work of the philosophers, especially Berkeley and Hume, and even we might add, Hartley.

Crucial as Blake's 'anti-pastorals' are in the course of eighteenth-century poetry, *The Marriage of Heaven and Hell* is an even more significant statement of Romanticism's central myth. In Plates 12–13 Ezekiel, the original poet-prophet explains to Blake 'the philosophy of the east taught the first principles of human perception'. Poetry, we note, is an account of the true epistemological processes of man. In Israel it was believed that 'the Poetic Genius' was the first principle 'and all the others merely derivative'. Ezekiel's Jehovah, Blake clearly states, was the product of the prophet's creative imagination: 'all Gods would at last be proved to originate in ours & . . . be the tributaries of the Poetic Genius'. The poetic genius is for Ezekiel the 'perception of the infinite' and this perception is the natural activity of all primitive peoples, for example 'the North American tribes'. [Cf. Blair, p. 277.] *The Marriage* begins as an attack on Blake's once admired Swedenborg, but ends as a statement of the poetic roots of religion. Inherent in the rise of Romanticism since Shaftesbury (see pp. 85-87) had been the disappearance of the polarities of traditional religion, heaven and hell, and the acceptance of the once-loathed objects of the inferior scale as equally beautiful in the creative imagination. Now the restraints of structure and reason, like the image of heaven itself, are seen as anti-poetic, and the source of the greatest opposition, Satan, replete with energy and imagination, a source of poetry and creativity. Ezekiel's sublimity rests in his closer proximity to the beginnings of time, some six thousand years before for Blake. It is from this vantage point that he can explain to Blake that the senses give man an immediate vision of the infinite, the product of the totality of his being, not the visual perspectives of Lockian epistemology, the 'narrow chinks of his cavern'. In Blake at this point we may see not only the concept expressed perhaps most memorably by Herder, that man is an animal that sings, but that he sang before words were burdened with the weight of memory. At almost every point Blake suggests the presence of the pre-intellectual reality of words, units, as Berkeley and Smart had suggested, of infinite perception.

In Pope's depiction of man and nature in the *Pastorals* man is within the processes of the seasons in his own time, the eighteenth century, and yet he is outside, seeing these processes in the context of Cos, Rome and Elizabethan England. Necessarily he is self-divided. Blake's essential genius rests in his creation of a single texture of poetry in which the perceptual claims of 'the Sea of Time and Space' war on those of the heuristic, primitive imagination, both on the verbal level as 'originality' opposes contemporary structures in the texture of the language, and on the mythic level. The Creation, like all myth, Blake suggests especially in *The First Book of Urizen*, most centrally a satire on the finite depiction of infinity of the book of Genesis, is not a self-dividing objective myth thousands of years away in what Berkeley termed 'outness', but is the central possession of each man's creative psyche, deprived of which he is continually 'beside himself' looking in at the lateral and hieratic structure of his own internal spaces, the delusory domain of Urizen, or reason, which he projects into a cosmos of repression. Words and mythic figures are in Blake one, as they were hypothetically in the original poetry at the dawn of time, organizing all impulses in man's continuing creation of his own universe in which, as the later Romantics optimistically would assume, the infinite, harmonious organization of primitive verse might be extended in the forms of human society.

from *POETICAL SKETCHES (1769–1778)*

TO SPRING

O thou with dewy locks, who lookest down
Thro' the clear windows of the morning, turn
Thine angel eyes upon our western isle,
Which in full choir hails thy approach, O Spring!

The hills tell each other, and the list'ning
Vallies hear; all our longing eyes are turned
Up to thy bright pavillions: issue forth,
And let thy holy feet visit our clime.

Come o'er the eastern hills, and let our winds
Kiss thy perfumed garments; let us taste
Thy morn and evening breath; scatter thy pearls
Upon our love-sick land that mourns for thee.

O deck her forth with thy fair fingers; pour
Thy soft kisses on her bosom; and put
Thy golden crown upon her languish'd head,
Whose modest tresses were bound up for thee!

TO SUMMER

O thou, who passest thro' our vallies in
Thy strength, curb thy fierce steeds, allay the heat
That flames from their large nostrils! thou, O Summer,

Oft pitched'st here thy golden tent, and oft
Beneath our oaks hast slept, while we beheld
With joy thy ruddy limbs and flourishing hair.

Beneath our thickest shades we oft have heard
Thy voice, when noon upon his fervid car
Rode o'er the deep of heaven; beside our springs
Sit down, and in our mossy vallies, on
Some bank beside a river clear, throw thy
Silk draperies off, and rush into the stream:
Our vallies love the Summer in his pride.

Our bards are fam'd who strike the silver wire:
Our youths are bolder than the southern swains:
Our maidens fairer in the sprightly dance:
We lack not songs, nor instruments of joy,
Nor echoes sweet, nor waters clear as heaven,
Nor laurel wreaths against the sultry heat.

TO AUTUMN

O autumn, laden with fruit, and stained
With the blood of the grape, pass not, but sit
Beneath my shady roof; there thou may'st rest,
And tune thy jolly voice to my fresh pipe;
And all the daughters of the year shall dance!
Sing now the lusty song of fruits and flowers.

'The narrow bud opens her beauties to
The sun, and love runs in her thrilling veins;
Blossoms hang round the brows of morning, and
Flourish down the bright cheek of modest eve,
Till clust'ring Summer breaks forth into singing,
And feather'd clouds strew flowers round her head.

The spirits of the air live on the smells
Of fruit; and joy, with pinions light, roves round
The gardens, or sits singing in the trees.'
Thus sang the jolly Autumn as he sat;
Then rose, girded himself, and o'er the bleak
Hills fled from our sight; but left his golden load.

TO WINTER

O Winter! bar thine adamantine doors:
The north is thine; there hast thou built thy dark
Deep-founded habitation. Shake not thy roofs,

Nor bend thy pillars with thine iron car.

He hears me not, but o'er the yawning deep
Rides heavy; his storms are unchain'd, sheathed
In ribbed steel; I dare not lift mine eyes,
For he hath rear'd his sceptre o'er the world.

Lo! now the direful monster, whose skin clings
To his strong bones, strides o'er the groaning rocks:
He withers all in silence, and in his hand
Unclothes the earth, and freezes up frail life.

He takes his seat upon the cliffs; the mariner
Cries in vain. Poor little wretch! that deal'st
With storms, till heaven smiles, and the monster
Is driv'n yelling to his caves beneath mount Hecla.

from *THE MARRIAGE OF HEAVEN AND HELL (1790–93)*

Plate 2
The Argument
Rintrah* roars & shakes his fires in the burdend air;
Hungry clouds swag on the deep

Once meek, and in a perilous path,
The just man kept his course along
The vale of death.
Roses are planted where thorns grow.
And on the barren heath
Sing the honey bees.

Then the perilous path was planted:
And a river, and a spring
On every cliff and tomb;
And on the bleached bones
Red clay brought forth.

Till the villain left the paths of ease,
To walk in perilous paths, and drive
The just man into barren climes.

Now the sneaking serpent walks
In mild humility.

---

*In one aspect, prophetic anger. Ed.

And the just man rages in the wilds
Where lions roam.

Rintrah roars & shakes his fires in the burdend air;
Hungry clouds swag on the deep.

Plate 3
As a new heaven is begun, and it is now thirty-three years since its advent: the Eternal Hell revives. And lo! Swedenborg is the angel sitting at the tomb; his writings are the linen clothes folded up. Now is the dominion of Edom, & the return of Adam into Paradise; see Isaiah xxxiv & XXXV Chap:

Without Contraries is no progression. Attraction and Repulsion, Reason and Energy, Love and Hate, are necessary to Human existence.

From these contraries spring what the religious call Good & Evil. Good is the passive that obeys Reason [.] Evil is the active springing from Energy.

Good is Heaven. Evil is Hell.
Plate 4
The voice of the Devil
All Bibles or sacred codes. have been the causes of the following Errors.
1. That Man has two real existing principles Viz: a Body & a Soul.
2. That Energy. calld Evil. is alone from the Body. & that Reason. calld Good. is alone from the Soul.
3. That God will torment Man in Eternity for following his Energies.
But the following Contraries to these are True
1 Man has no Body distinct from his Soul for that calld Body is a portion of Soul discernd by the five Senses, the chief inlets of Soul in this age
2 Energy is the only life and is from the Body and Reason is the bound or outward circumference of Energy.
3 Energy is Eternal Delight
Plate 5
Those who restrain desire, do so because theirs is weak enough to be restrained; and the restrainer or reason usurps its place & governs the unwilling.

And being restrained it by degrees becomes passive till it is only the shadow of desire.

The history of this is written in Paradise Lost. & the Governor or Reason is call'd Messiah.

And the original Archangel or possessor of the command of the heavenly host, is calld the Devil or Satan and his children are call'd Sin & Death*

But in the Book of Job Miltons Messiah is call'd Satan.

---

*Cf. Addison, *Spectator* 357, pp. 90-91. Ed.

For this history has been adopted by both parties

It indeed appear'd to Reason as if Desire was cast out, but the Devils account is, that the Messi[PL 6]ah fell. & formed a heaven of what he stole from the Abyss

This is shewn in the Gospel, where he prays to the Father to send the comforter or Desire that Reason may have Ideas to build on, the Jehovah of the Bible being no other than he, who dwells in flaming fire. Know that after Christs death, he became Jehovah.

But in Milton; the Father is Destiny, the Son, a Ratio of the five senses. & the Holy-ghost, Vacuum!

Note. The reason Milton wrote in fetters when he wrote of Angels & God, and at liberty when of Devils & Hell, is because he was a true Poet and of the Devils party without knowing it

A Memorable Fancy.

As I was walking among the fires of hell, delighted with the enjoyments of Genius; which to Angels look like torment and insanity. I collected some of their Proverbs: thinking that as the sayings used in a nation, mark its character, so the Proverbs of Hell, shew the nature of Infernal wisdom better than any description of buildings or garments.

When I came home; on the abyss of the five senses, where a flat sided steep frowns over the present world. I saw a mighty Devil folded in black clouds, hovering on the sides of the rock, with cor[PL 7]roding fires he wrote the following sentence now percieved* by the minds of men, & read by them on earth.

How do you know but ev'ry Bird that cuts the airy way,
Is an immense world of delight, clos'd by your senses five?

Proverbs of Hell.

In seed time learn, in harvest teach, in winter enjoy.

Drive your cart and your plow over the bones of the dead.

The road of excess leads to the palace of wisdom.

Prudence is a rich ugly old maid courted by Incapacity.

He who desires but acts not, breeds pestilence.

The cut worm forgives the plow.

Dip him in the river who loves water.

A fool sees not the same tree that a wise man sees.

He whose face gives no light, shall never become a star.

Eternity is in love with the productions of time.

The busy bee has no time for sorrow.

The hours of folly are measur'd by the clock, but of wisdom: no clock can measure.

All wholsom food is caught without a net or a trap.

Bring out number weight & measure in a year of dearth.

No bird soars too high. if he soars with his own wings.

---

*This and other odd spellings and punctuation, Blake's. Ed.

A dead body. revenges not injuries.

The most sublime act is to set another before you.

If the fool would persist in his folly he would become wise

Folly is the cloke of knavery

Shame is Prides cloke.

*

Plate 10

The head Sublime, the heart Pathos, the genitals Beauty, the hands & feet Proportion.

As the air to a bird or the sea to a fish, so is contempt to the contemptible.

The crow wish'd every thing was black, the owl, that every thing was white.

Exuberance is Beauty.

If the lion was advise'd by the fox, he would be cunning.

Improve [me] nt makes strait roads, but the crooked roads without Improvement, are roads of Genius.

Sooner murder an infant in its cradle than nurse unacted desires

Where man is not nature is barren.

Truth can never be told so as to be understood, and not be believ'd.

Enough! or Too much

Plate 11

The ancient Poets animated all sensible objects with Gods or Geniuses, calling them by the names and adorning them with the properties of woods, rivers, mountains, lakes, cities, nations, and whatever their enlarged & numerous senses could perceive.*

And particularly they studied the genius of each city & country. placing it under its mental deity.

Till a system was formed, which some took advantage of & enslav'd the vulgar by attempting to realize or abstract the mental deities from their objects; thus began Priesthood.

Choosing forms of worship from poetic tales.

And at length they pronounced that the Gods had ordered such things.

Thus men forgot that All deities reside in the human breast.

Plate 12

A Memorable Fancy.

The Prophets Isaiah and Ezekiel dined with me, and I asked them how they dared so roundly to assert. that God spake to them: and whether they did not think at the time, that they would be misunderstood, & so be the cause of imposition.

Isaiah answer'd. I saw no God, nor heard any, in a finite organical perception; but my senses discover'd the infinite in every thing, and as I was then perswaded, & remain confirm'd; that the voice of honest indignation

---

*Cf. Blair on Ossian, pp. 270-273. Ed.

is the voice of God, I cared not for consequences but wrote.

Then I asked: does a firm perswasion that a thing is so, make it so?

He replied. All poets believe that it does, & in ages of imagination this firm perswasion removed mountains; but many are not capable of a firm perswasion of any thing.

Then Ezekiel said. The philosophy of the east taught the first principles of human perception some nations held one principle for the origin & some another, we of Israel taught that the Poetic Genius (as you now call it) was the first principle and all the others merely derivative, which was the cause of our despising the Priests & Philosophers of other countries, and prophecying that all Gods [PL 13] would at last be proved to originate in ours & to be the tributaries of the Poetic Genius, it was this. that our great poet King David desired so fervently & invokes so patheticly, saying by this he conquers enemies & governs kingdoms; and we so loved our God. that we cursed in his name all the deities of surrounding nations, and asserted that they had rebelled; from these opinions the vulgar came to think that all nations would at last be subject to the jews.

This said he, like all firm perswasions, is come to pass, for all nations believe the jews code and worship the jews god, and what greater subjection can be

I heard this with some wonder, & must confess my own conviction. After dinner I ask'd Isaiah to favour the world with his lost works, he said none of equal value was lost. Ezekiel said the same of his.

I also asked Isaiah what made him go naked and barefoot three years? he answered, the same that made our friend Diogenes the Grecian.

I then asked Ezekiel. why he eat dung, & lay so long on his right & left side? he answered. the desire of raising other men into a perception of the infinite this the North American tribes practise.* & is he honest who resists his genius or conscience, only for the sake of present ease or gratification?

Plate 14

The ancient tradition that the world will be consumed in fire at the end of six thousand years is true. as I have heard from Hell.

For the cherub with his flaming sword is hereby commanded to leave his guard at tree of life, and when he does, the whole creation will be consumed, and appear infinite. and holy whereas it now appears finite & corrupt.

This will come to pass by an improvement of sensual enjoyment.

But first the notion that man has a body distinct from his soul, is to be expunged; this I shall do, by printing in the infernal method, by corrosives, which in Hell are salutary and medicinal, melting apparent surfaces away, and displaying the infinite which was hid.

If the doors of perception were cleansed every thing would appear to man as it is, infinite.

---

*Cf. Blair, p. 277. Ed.

For man has closed himself up, till he sees all things thro' narrow chinks of his cavern.

*

Plate 25
A Song of Liberty
1. The Eternal Female groand! it was heard over all the Earth:
2. Albions coast is sick silent; the American meadows faint!
3. Shadows of Prophecy shiver along by the lakes and the rivers and mutter across the ocean? France rend down thy dungeon;
4. Golden Spain burst the barriers of old Rome;
5. Cast thy keys O Rome into the deep down falling, even to eternity down falling,
6. And weep
7. In her trembling hands she took the new born terror howling:
8. On those infinite mountains of light now barr'd out by the atlantic sea, the new born fire stood before the starry king!
9. Flag'd with grey brow'd snows and thunderous visages the jealous wings wav'd over the deep.
10. The speary hand burned aloft, unbuckled was the shield, forth went the hand of jealousy among the flaming hair, and [PL 26] hurl'd the new born wonder thro' the starry night.
11. The fire, the fire, is falling!
12. Look up! look up! O citizen of London. enlarge thy countenance; O Jew, leave counting gold! return to thy oil and wine; O African! black African! (go. winged thought widen his forehead.)
13. The fiery limbs, the flaming hair, shot like the sinking sun into the western sea.
14. Wak'd from his eternal sleep, the hoary element roaring fled away:
15. Down rushd beating his wings in vain the jealous king: his grey brow'd councellors, thunderous warriors, curl'd veterans, among helms, and shields, and chariots [,] horses, elephants: banners, castles, slings and rocks,
16. Falling, rushing, ruining! buried in the ruins, on Urthona's dens.
17. All night beneath the ruins, then their sullen flames faded emerge round the gloomy king,
18. With thunder and fire: leading his starry hosts thro' the waste wilderness [PL 27] he promulgates his ten commands, glancing his beamy eyelids over the deep in dark dismay,
19. Where the son of fire in his eastern cloud, while the morning plumes her golden breast,
20. Spurning the clouds written with curses, stamps the stony law to dust, loosing the eternal horses from the dens of night, crying
Empire is no more! and now the lion & wolf shall cease.

Chorus

Let the Priests of the Raven of dawn, no longer in deadly black. with hoarse note curse the sons of joy. Nor his accepted brethren whom, tyrant, he calls free: lay the bound or build the roof. Nor pale religious letchery call that virginity, that wishes but acts not!   For every thing that lives is Holy

*

THE FIRST BOOK OF URIZEN (1794)

Plate 2

PRELUDIUM TO THE [FIRST] BOOK OF URIZEN

Of the primeval Priests assum'd power,
When Eternals spurn'd back his religion;
And gave him a place in the north,
Obscure, shadowy, void, solitary.

Eternals I hear your call gladly,
Dictate swift winged words, & fear not
To unfold your dark visions of torment.

Plate 3

Chap: I

1. Lo, a shadow of horror is risen
In Eternity! Unknown, unprolific!
Self-closd, all-repelling: what Demon
Hath form'd this abominable void
This soul-shudd'ring vacuum? — Some said
'It is Urizen', But unknown, abstracted
Brooding secret, the dark power hid.

2. Times on times he divided, & measur'd
Space by space in his ninefold darkness*
Unseen, unknown! changes appeard
In his desolate mountains rifted furious
By the black winds of perturbation

3. For he strove in battles dire
In unseen conflictions with shapes
Bred from his forsaken wilderness,
Of beast, bird, fish, serpent & element
Combustion, blast, vapour and cloud.

4. Dark revolving in silent activity:
Unseen in tormenting passions;

---

*Cf. Locke on time and space, Introduction p. 10 and pp. 38-42. Ed.

An activity unknown and horrible;
A self-contemplating shadow,
In enormous labours occupied

5. But Eternals beheld his vast forests
Age on ages he lay, clos'd, unknown,
Brooding shut in the deep; all avoid
The petrific abominable chaos

6. His cold horrors silent, dark Urizen
Prepar'd: his ten thousands of thunders
Rang'd in gloom'd array stretch out across
The dread world, & the rolling of wheels
As of swelling seas, sound in his clouds
In his hills of stor'd snows, in his mountains
Of hail & ice; voices of terror,
Are heard, like thunders of autumn,
When the cloud blazes over the harvests

Chap: II.
1. Earth was not: nor globes of attraction
The will of the Immortal expanded
Or contracted his all flexible senses.
Death was not, but eternal life sprung

2. The sound of a trumpet the heavens
Awoke & vast clouds of blood roll'd
Round the dim rocks of Urizen, so nam'd
That solitary one in Immensity

3. Shrill the trumpet: & myriads of Eternity,
Plate 4
Muster around the bleak desarts
Now fill'd with clouds, darkness & waters
That roll'd perplex'd labring & utter'd
Words articulate, bursting in thunders
That roll'd on the tops of his mountains

4. From the depths of dark solitude. From
The eternal abode in my holiness,
Hidden set apart in my stern counsels
Reserv'd for the days of futurity,
I have sought for a joy without pain,
For a solid without fluctuation
Why will you die O Eternals?
Why live in unquenchable burnings?

5. First I fought with the fire; consum'd

Inwards, into a deep world within:
A void immense, wild dark & deep,
Where nothing was; Natures wide womb[.]
And self balanc'd stretch'd o'er the void
I alone, even I! the winds merciless
Bound; but condensing, in torrents
They fall & fall; strong I repell'd
The vast waves, & arose on the waters
A wide world of solid obstruction

6. Here alone I in books formd of metals
Have written the secrets of wisdom
The secrets of dark contemplation
By fightings and conflicts dire,
With terrible monsters Sin-bred:
Which the bosoms of all inhabit;
Seven deadly Sins of the soul.

7. Lo! I unfold my darkness: and on
This rock, place with strong hand the Book
Of eternal brass, written in my solitude.

8. Laws of peace, of love, of unity:
Of pity, compassion, forgiveness.
Let each chuse one habitation:
His ancient infinite mansion:
One command, one joy, one desire,
One curse, one weight, one measure
One King, one God, one Law.

*

Chap: V.
1. In terrors Los shrunk from his task:
His great hammer fell from his hand:
His fires beheld, and sickening,
Hid their strong limbs in smoke.
For with noises ruinous loud;
With hurtlings & clashings & groans
The Immortal endur'd his chains,
Tho' bound in a deadly sleep.

2. All the myriads of Eternity:
All the wisdom & joy of life:
Roll like a sea around him,
Except what his little orbs

Of sight by degrees unfold

3. And now his eternal life
Like a dream was obliterated

4. Shudd'ring, the Eternal Prophet smote
With a stroke, from his north to south region
The bellows & hammer are silent now
A nerveless silence, his prophetic voice
Siez'd; a cold solitude & dark void
The Eternal Prophet & Urizen clos'd

5. Ages on ages rolld over them
Cut off from life & light frozen
Into horrible forms of deformity
Los suffer'd his fires to decay
Then he look'd back with anxious desire
But the space undivided by existence
Struck horror into his soul.

6. Los wept obscur'd with mourning:
His bosom earthquak'd with sighs;
He saw Urizen deadly black,
In his chains bound, & Pity began,

7. In anguish dividing & dividing
For pity divides the soul
In pangs eternity on eternity
Life in cataracts pourd down his cliffs
The void shrunk the lymph into Nerves
Wand'ring wide on the bosom of night
And left a round globe of blood
Trembling upon the Void
Plate 15
Thus the Eternal Prophet was divided
Before the death-image of Urizen
For in changeable clouds and darkness
In a winterly night beneath,
The Abyss of Los stretch'd immense:
And now seen now obscur'd, to the eyes
Of Eternals the visions remote
Of the dark seperation appear'd.
As glasses discover Worlds
In the endless Abyss of space,
So the expanding eyes of Immortals
Beheld the dark visions of Los,

And the globe of life blood trembling.
Plate 18
8. The globe of life blood trembled
Branching out into roots;
Fibrous, writhing upon the winds;
Fibres of blood, milk and tears;
In pangs, eternity on eternity.
At length in tears & cries imbodied
A female form trembling and pale
Waves before his deathy face

9. All Eternity shudderd at sight
Of the first female now separate
Pale as a cloud of snow
Waving before the face of Los

10. Wonder, awe, fear, astonishment,
Petrify the eternal myriads;
At the first female form now separate
Plate 19
They call'd her Pity, and fled

11. 'Spread a Tent, with strong curtains around them
Let cords & stakes bind in the Void
That Eternals may no more behold them'

12. They began to weave curtains of darkness
They erected large pillars round the Void
With golden hooks fastend in the pillars
With infinite labour the Eternals
A woof wove, and called it Science

*

Chap. VIII.
1. Urizen explor'd his dens
Mountain, moor, & wilderness,
With a globe of fire lighting his journey
A fearful journey, annoy'd
By cruel enormities: forms
Plate 23
Of life on his forsaken mountains

2. And his world teemd vast enormities
Frightning; faithless; fawning
Portions of life; similitudes

Of a foot, or a hand, or a head
Or a heart, or an eye, they swam mischevous
Dread terrors! delighting in blood

3. Most Urizen sicken'd to see
His eternal creations appear
Sons & daughters of sorrow on mountains
Weeping! wailing! first Thiriel appear'd
Astonish'd at his own existence
Like a man from a cloud born, & Utha
From the waters emerging, laments!
Grodna rent the deep earth howling
Amaz'd! his heavens immense cracks
Like the ground parch'd with heat; then Fuzon
Flam'd out! first begotten, last born.
All his eternal sons in like manner
His daughters from green herbs & cattle
From monsters, & worms of the pit.

4. He in darkness clos'd, view'd all his race
And his soul sicken'd! he curs'd
Both sons & daughters; for he saw
That no flesh nor spirit could keep
His iron laws one moment.

5. For he saw that life liv'd upon death
The Ox in the slaughter house moans
Plate 25
The Dog at the wintry door
And he wept, & he called it Pity
And his tears flowed down on the winds

6. Cold he wander'd on high, over their cities
In weeping & pain & woe!
And where-ever he wanderd in sorrows
Upon the aged heavens
A cold shadow follow'd behind him
Like a spiders web, moist, cold & dim
Drawing out from his sorrowing soul
The dungeon-like heaven dividing
Where ever the footsteps of Urizen
Walk'd over the cities in sorrow.

7. Till a Web dark & cold throughout all
The tormented element stretch'd
From the sorrows of Urizens soul

And the Web is a Female in embrio.
None could break the Web, no wings of fire.

8. So twisted the cords, & so knotted
The meshes: twisted like to the human brain

9. And all calld it, The Net of Religion.

Chap: IX.
1. Then the Inhabitants of those Cities:
Felt their Nerves change into Marrow
And hardening Bones began
In swift diseases and torments,
In throbbings & shootings & grindings
Thro' all the coasts; till weaken'd
The Senses inward rush'd shrinking,
Beneath the dark net of infection.

2. Till the shrunken eyes clouded over
Discernd not the woven hipocrisy
But the streaky slime in their heavens
Brought together by narrowing perceptions
Appeard transparent air; for their eyes
Grew small like the eyes of a man
And in reptile forms shrinking together
Of seven feet stature they remaind

3. Six days they shrunk up from existence
And on the seventh day they rested
And they bless'd the seventh day, in sick hope:
And forgot their eternal life

4. And their thirty cities divided
In form of a human heart
No more could they rise at will
In the infinite void, but bound down
To earth by their narrowing perceptions
Plate 28
They lived a period of years
Then left a noisom body
To the jaws of devouring darkness

5. And their children wept, & built
Tombs in the desolate places,
And form'd laws of prudence, and call'd them
The eternal laws of God

6. And the thirty cities remaind
Surrounded by salt floods, now call'd
Africa: its name was then Egypt.

7. The remaining sons of Urizen
Beheld their brethren shrink together
Beneath the Net of Urizen;
Perswasion was in vain;
For the ears of the inhabitants
Were wither'd, & deafen'd, & cold.
And their eyes could not discern,
Their brethren of other cities.

8. So Fuzon call'd all together
The remaining children of Urizen:
And they left the pendulous earth:
They called it Egypt, & left it.

9. And the salt ocean rolled englob'd

   The End of the [*first*] book of Urizen

RICHARD HURD (1720–1808)

In the response to Lowth's *Praelectiones* (see pp. 149-167) William War-burton's attack led all the rest. His bizarre *Divine Legations of Moses* (1738-41) had made him the major authority on 'the first ages' and he was slighted by Lowth's omission of him in his discussion of *Job*. Warburton was, of course, executor to and editor of Pope, and defender of the *Essay on Man* against charges of deism. Characteristically in his battle with Gibbon he had maintained that Aeneas' descent into the Underworld was an Eleusinian initiation. For this 'knock-knee'd colossus' in Leslie Stephen's phrase, the earliest literature was allegorical. For more acute thinkers like Lowth, who might today be spoken of as a cultural anthropologist with a special interest in linguistics, even the Old Testament was a manifestation of the psychology of perception, revealing not 'higher' truths, but human creativity. It is of special interest, there-fore, that Warburton's symbiotic ally, Richard Hurd, himself Bishop of Worcester, who eerily kept alive the battle in his editions of his friend after the participants were buried, in effect came down on the less traditional side of the debate in his own work on primitive poetry.

The major religious dispute between deism and revelation which exer-cised all thinking men in the eighteenth century informed literary theory at the deepest level. If early man formed language and myth by his own efforts unaided, then, language was autonomous, as Romantic theorists believed it was in children, and he had made myth, and God, in his own image. The supernatural, as in *The Ancient Mariner* and *Christabel* for example became only the most vivid area of man's imaginative creativity, without 'a pattern in nature' in Addison's phrase. A reading of Hurd's *Letters on Chivalry and Romance* makes clear that for him the 'fairies, witches, magicians, demons, and departed spirits' (see pp. 97-99) of Spenser and other 'primitive' English writers was, as in Maurice Morgann, the definitive mark of the barbaric, Gothic imagination, of the very essence of the Romance. Mirroring Nature, the classical author used rules which were ancient and universal. Following a totally different principle, the mind of Spenser in *The Fairy Queen* voyaged entirely alone in the strangest seas of fancy and autonomous undisciplined imagination. Interes-tingly, Hurd's Spenser is very close to Blake's notion of the original and primitive. He made up his own mythology as he went along, like Ezekiel searching inside himself for anthropomorphic shapes in the deepest thickets of his unique creativity, the very model of the 'original' poet. It goes without saying, perhaps, that the Spenser of Hurd and the eighteenth century is not the Renaissance artist of the modern scholar.

Drawing, as for example Thomas Warton did also, from a sharp sense of the customs of the Middle Ages, the product of a century of antiquarianism stretching back to the Royal Society, Hurd further explained the form of Spenser's poem in terms of its inner demands. Spenser's world was not, for Hurd, structured. Neither was his poem, in any classical sense. Because there were always twelve days in a joust, there were to be twelve books in *The Fairy Queen*. To Hurd's dogged explicitness we owe a whole range of considerations related to the modern concept of organic form. If the form were related thus intimately to the content, then, content and form might be one. If the form occurs only in a single work of art for which it is adapted, then, in practical terms, the artist is not imitative but timeless, and creates unique, hence sublime artifacts. In Hurd, a not atypical literary cleric, we may detect again the principle that the artist is always in a new relation to Nature, seeing her, as *Guardian* No. *86* observed of Job, as if 'in the eye of the Creator', and Nature herself might be viewed as a continuum of unlike moments, endlessly extended through the imagination of the 'original' poet.

LETTERS ON CHIVALRY AND ROMANCE (1762)

from Letter VII
But nothing shews the difference of the two systems under consideration more plainly, than the effect they really had on the two greatest of our Poets; at least the Two which an English reader is most fond to compare with Homer, I mean Spenser and Milton.

It is not to be doubted but that each of these bards had kindled his poetic fire from classic fables. So that, of course, their prejudices would lie that way. Yet they both appear, when most inflamed, to have been more particularly rapt with the Gothic fables of chivalry.

Spenser, tho' he had been long nourished with the spirit and substance of Homer and Virgil, chose the times of chivalry for his theme, and fairy land for the scene of his fictions. He could have planned, no doubt, an heroic design on the exact classic model: Or, he might have trimmed between the Gothic and Classic, as his contemporary Tasso did. But the charms of *fairy* prevailed. And if any think, he was seduced by Ariosto into this choice, they should consider that it could be only for the sake of his subject; for the genius and character of these poets was widely different.

Under this idea then of a Gothic, not classical poem, the *Faery Queen* is to be read and criticized. And on these principles, it would not be difficult to unfold it's merit in another way than has been hitherto attempted.

Milton, it is true, preferred the classic model to the Gothic. But it was after long hesitation; and his favourite subject was *Arthur and his Knights of the round table*. On this he had fixed for the greater part of his life. What led him to change his mind was, partly, as I suppose, his growing fanaticism; partly, his ambition to take a different rout from Spenser; but chiefly perhaps, the discredit into which the stories of chivalry had now fallen by the immortal satire of Cervantes. Yet we see thro' all his poetry, where his enthusiasm flames out most, a certain predilection for the legends of chivalry before the fables of Greece.

This circumstance, you know, has given offence to the austerer and more mechanical critics. They are ready to censure his judgment, as juvenile and unformed, when they see him so delighted, on all occasions, with the Gothic romances. But do these censors imagine that Milton did not perceive the defects of these works, as well as they? No: it was not the *composition* of books of chivalry, but the manners described in them, that took his fancy; as appears from his *Allegro* —

Tower'd cities please us then
And the busy hum of men,
Where throngs of knights and barons bold
In weeds of peace high triumphs hold,
With store of ladies, whose bright eyes
Rain influence, and judge the prize
Of wit, or arms, while both contend
To win her grace, whom all commend.   [117–124]

And when in the *Penseroso* he draws, by a fine contrivance, the same kind of image to sooth melancholy which he had before given to excite mirth, he indeed extolls an *author* of one of these romances, as he had before, in general, extolled the *subject* of them; but it is an author worthy of his praise; not the writer of *Amadis*, or *Sir Launcelot of the Lake*, but Chaucer himself, who has left an unfinished story on the Gothic or feudal model.

Or, call up him that left half-told
The story of Cambuscan bold,
Of Camball and of Algarsife,
And who had Canace to wife
That own'd the virtuous ring and glass,
And of the wondrous horse of brass,
On which the Tartar king did ride;
And if ought else great bards beside
In sage and solemn tunes have sung
Of turneys and of trophies hung,
Of forests and inchantments drear,
Where more is meant than meets the ear.   [109–20]

The conduct then of these two poets may incline us to think with more respect, than is commonly done of the *Gothic manners*, I mean as adapted to the uses of the greater poetry.

I say nothing of Shakespear, because the sublimity (the divinity, let it be, if nothing else will serve) of his genius kept no certain rout, but rambled at hazard into all the regions of human life and manners. So that we can hardly say what he preferred, or what he rejected, on full deliberation. Yet one thing is clear, that even he is greater when he uses Gothic manners and machinery, than when he employs classical: which brings us again to the same point, that the former have, by their nature and genius, the advantage of the latter in producing the *sublime*.

*

from Letter VIII

I spoke 'of criticizing Spenser's poem, under the idea, not of a classical but Gothic composition.'

It is certain much light might be thrown on that singular work, were an able critic to consider it in this view. For instance, he might go some way towards explaining, perhaps justifying, the general plan and *conduct* of the *Faery Queen*, which, to classical readers has appeared indefensible.

I have taken the fancy, with your leave, to try my hand on this curious subject.

When an architect examines a Gothic structure by Grecian rules, he finds nothing but deformity. But the Gothic architecture has it's own rules, by which when it comes to be examined, it is seen to have it's merit, as well as the Grecian. The question is not, which of the two is conducted in the simplest or truest taste: but, whether there be not sense and design in both, when scrutinized by the laws on which each is projected.

The same observation holds of the two sorts of poetry. Judge of the *Faery Queen* by the classic models, and you are shocked with it's disorder: consider it with an eye to it's Gothic original, and you find it regular. The unity and simplicity of the former are more complete: but the latter has that sort of unity and simplicity, which results from it's nature.

The *Faery Queen* then, as a Gothic poem, derives it's *Method*, as well as the other characters of it's composition, from the established modes and ideas of chivalry.

It was usual, in the days of knight-errantry, at the holding of any great feast, for Knights to appear before the Prince, who presided at it, and claim the privilege of being sent on any adventure, to which the solemnity might give occasion. For it was supposed that, when such a *throng of knights and barons bold*, as Milton speaks of, were got together, the distressed would flock in from all quarters, as to a place where they knew they might find and claim redress for all their grievances.

This was the real practice, in the days of pure and ancient chivalry. And an image of this practice was afterwards kept up in the castles of the great, on any extraordinary festival or solemnity: of which, if you want an instance, I refer you to the description of a feast made at Lisle in 1453, in the court of Philip the Good, Duke of Burgundy, for a crusade against the Turks: As you may find it given at large in the memoirs of *Matthieu de Conci, Olivier de la Marche*, and *Monstrelet* [Mediaeval French chroniclers].

That feast was held for *twelve* days: and each day was distinguished by the claim and allowance of some adventure.

Now laying down this practice, as a foundation for the poet's design, you will see how properly the *Faery Queen* is conducted.

– 'I devise', says the poet himself in his Letter to Sir W. Raleigh, 'that
the Faery Queen kept her annual feaste xii days: upon which xii several
days, the occasions of the xii several adventures hapened; which being
undertaken by xii several knights, are in these xii books severally
handled.'

Here you have the poet delivering his own method, and the reason of
it. It arose out of the order of his subject. And would you desire a better
reason for his choice?

Yes; you will say, a poet's method is not that of his subject. I grant you,
as to the order of *time*, in which the recital is made; for here, as Spenser
observes (and his own practice agrees to the Rule) lies the main difference
between *the poet historical, and the historiographer*: The reason of which
is drawn from the nature of Epic composition itself, and holds equally, let
the subject be what it will, and whatever the system of manners be, on
which it is conducted. Gothic or Classic makes no difference in this
respect.

But the case is not the same with regard to the general plan of a work,
or what may be called the order of *distribution*, which is and must be
governed by the subject-matter itself. It was as requisite for the *Faery
Queen* to consist of the adventures of twelve knights, as for the *Odyssey*
to be confined to the adventures of one Hero: Justice had otherwise not
been done to his subject.

So that if you will say any thing against the poet's method, you must
say that he should not have chosen this subject. But this objection arises
from your classic ideas of Unity, which have no place here; and are in
every view foreign to the purpose, if the poet has found means to give his
work, tho' consisting of many parts, the advantage of Unity. For in some
reasonable sense or other, it is agreed, every work of art must be *one*, the
very idea of a work requiring it.

If you ask then, what is this *Unity* of Spenser's Poem? I say, It consists
in the relation of it's several adventures to one common *original*, the
appointment of the Faery Queen; and to one common *end*, the completion
of the Faery Queen's injunctions. The knights issued forth on their
adventures on the breaking up of this annual feast, and the next annual
feast, we are to suppose, is to bring them together again from the achievement of their several charges.

This, it is true, is not the classic Unity, which consists in the representation of one entire action: but it is an Unity of another sort, an unity
resulting from the respect which a number of related actions have to one
common purpose. In other words, It is an unity of *design*, and not of
action.

This Gothic method of design in poetry may be, in some sort, illustrated
by what is called the Gothic method of design in Gardening. [Cf.
Addison on Chinese gardens, pp. 95-96.] A wood or grove cut out into
many separate avenues or glades was amongst the most favourite of the
works of art, which our fathers attempted in this species of cultivation.

These walks were distinct from each other, had, each, their several destination, and terminated on their own proper objects. Yet the whole was brought together and considered under one view by the relation which these various openings had, not to each other, but to their common and concurrent center. You and I are, perhaps, agreed that this sort of gardening is not of so true a taste as that which *Kent* and *Nature* [William Kent (1684–1748), artist and landscape gardener] have brought us acquainted with; where the supreme art of the Designer consists of disposing his ground and objects into an *entire landskip*; and grouping them, if I may use the term, in so easy a manner, that the careless observer, tho' he be taken with the symmetry of the whole, discovers no art in the combination:

In lieto aspetto, il bel giardin s'aperse,
Acque stagnanti, mobili cristalli
Fior vari, e varie piante, herbe diverse,
Apriche Collinette, ombrose valli
Selve, e spelunche in *Una Vista* offerse:
E quel che'l bello, e'l caro accresce a l'opre
L'Arte, che tutto fa, nulla si scopre.

Tasso XVI. ix.*

This, I say, may be the truest taste in gardening, because the simplest: Yet there is a manifest regard to unity in the other method; which has had it's admirers, as it may have again, and is certainly not without it's *design* and beauty.

But to return to our poet. Thus far he drew from Gothic ideas, and these ideas, I think, would lead him no farther. But, as Spenser knew what belonged to classic composition, he was tempted to tie his subject still closer together by *one* expedient of his own, and by *another* taken from his classic models.

His *own* was to interrupt the proper story of each book, by dispersing it into several; involving by this means, and as it were intertwisting** the several actions together, in order to give something like the appearance of one action to his twelve adventures. And for this conduct, as absurd as it seems, he had some great examples in the Italian poets, tho' I believe, they were led into it by different motives.

The *other* expedient which he borrowed from the classics, was by adopting one superior character, which should be seen throughout. Prince Arthur, who had a separate adventure of his own, was to have his part in each of the other; and thus several actions were to be embodied by the interest which one principal Hero had in them all. It is even observable,

---

*For Hurd the point of the description of the garden from *Gerusalemme Liberata* is the last line, 'The art which had made all this might be seen nowhere.' Ed.

**Hurd's appreciation of the serpentine or parallel principle, common in Romantic art, relates to contemporary images of time in e.g. Lowth (see pp. 162-164) and Hogarth (pp. 280-287). Ed.

that Spenser gives this adventure of Prince Arthur, in quest of Gloriana, as the proper subject of his poem. And upon this idea the late learned editor of the *Faery Queen* [see the edition of John Upton (1758)] has attempted, but I think without success, to defend the Unity and simplicity of it's fable. The truth was the violence of classic prejudices forced the poet to affect this appearance of unity, tho' in contradiction to his gothic system. And, as far as we can judge of the tenour of the whole work from the finished half of it, the adventure of Prince Arthur, whatever the author pretended, and his critic too easily believed, was but an after thought; and at least with regard to the *historical fable*, which we are now considering, was only one of the expedients by which he would conceal the disorder of his Gothic plan.

And if this was his design, I will venture to say that both his expedients were injudicious. Their purpose was to ally two things, in nature incompatible, the Gothic, and the classic unity; the effect of which misalliance was to discover and expose the nakedness of the Gothic.

I am of opinion then, considering the *Faery Queen* as an epic or *narrative* poem constructed on Gothic ideas, that the Poet had done well to affect no other unity than that of *design*, by which his subject was connected. But his poem is not simply narrative; it is throughout *Allegorical*:* he calls it *a perpetual allegory or dark conceit*: and this character, for reasons I may have occasion to observe hereafter, was ever predominant in the *Faery Queen*. His narration is subservient to his moral, and but serves to colour it. This he tells us himself at setting out.

Fierce wars and faithful loves shall *moralize* my song,   [I. i. 9]
that is, shall serve for a vehicle, or instrument to convey the moral.

Now under this idea, the *Unity* of the *Faery Queen* is more apparent, His twelve knights are to exemplify as many virtues, out of which one illustrious character is to be composed. And in this view the part of Prince Arthur in each book becomes *essential*, and yet not *principal*; exactly, as the poet has contrived it. They who rest in the literal story, that is, who criticize it on the footing of a narrative poem, have constantly objected to this management. They say, it necessarily breaks the unity of design. Prince Arthur, they affirm, should either have had no part in the other adventures, or he should have had the chief part. He should either have done nothing, or more. And the objection is unanswerable; at least I know of nothing that can be said to remove it but what I have supposed above might be the purpose of the poet, and which I myself have rejected as insufficient.

But how faulty soever this conduct be in the literal story, it is perfectly right in the *moral*: and that for an obvious reason, tho' his critics seem not to have been aware of it. His chief hero was not to have the twelve virtues in the *degree* in which the knights had, each of them, their own;

---

*Hurd's somewhat contradictory insistence here is explained perhaps in part by loyalty to Warburton, Ed.

(such a character would be a monster) but he was to have so much of each as was requisite to form his superior character. Each virtue, in it's perfection, is exemplified, in it's own knight: they are all, in a due degree, concenter'd in Prince Arthur.

This was the poet's *moral*: And what way of expressing this moral in the *history*, but by making Prince Arthur appear in each adventure, and in a manner subordinate to it's proper hero? Thus, tho' inferior to each in in his own specific virtue, he is superior to all by uniting the whole circle of their virtues in himself: And thus he arrives, at length, at the possession of that bright form of *Glory*, whose ravishing beauty, as seen in a dream or vision, had led him out into these miraculous adventures in the land of Faery.

The conclusion is, that, as an *allegorical* poem, the method of the *Faery Queen* is governed by the justness of the *moral*: As a *narrative* poem, it is conducted on the ideas and usages of *chivalry*. In either view, if taken by itself, the plan is defensible. But from the union of the two designs there arises a perplexity and confusion, which is the proper, and only considerable, defect of this extraordinary poem.

*

from Letter X

But here, to prevent mistakes, an explanation will be necessary. We must distinguish between the *popular belief*, and *that of the Reader*. The fictions of poetry, do in some degree at least, require the *first*; (They would, otherwise, deservedly pass for *dreams* indeed): But when the poet has the advantage on his side, and his fancies have, or may be supposed to have, a countenance from the current superstitions of the age, in which he writes, he dispenses with the last, and gives his Reader leave to be as skeptical and as incredulous, as he pleases.

An eminent French critic diverts himself with imagining 'what a person, who comes fresh from reading Mr. Addison and Mr. Locke, would be apt to think of Tasso's Enchantment.'*

The English reader will, perhaps, smile at seeing these two writers so coupled together: And, with the critic's leave, we will put Mr. Locke out of the question. But if he be desirous to know what a reader of Mr. Addison would pronounce in the case, I can undertake to give him satisfaction.

Speaking of what Mr. Dryden calls, *the Faery way of writing*, [see pp. 97-99]

> Men of cold fancies and philosophical dispositions, says he, object to this kind of poetry, that it has not probability enough to affect the imagination. But – many are prepossessed with such false opinions, as dispose them to *believe* these particular delusions: At least, we have all

---

*Voltaire, *Essai sur la Poèsie Epique*, Ch. vii. Ed.

heard so many pleasing relations in favour of them, that we do not care for seeing thro' the *falsehood*, and willingly give ourselves up to so agreeable an imposture.

Apply, now, this sage judgment of Mr. Addison to *Tasso's Enchantments*, and you see that a *falsehood convict* is not to be pleaded against a *supposed belief*, or even the *slightest hear-say*.

So little account does this wicked poetry make of philosophical or historical truth: All she allows us to look for, is *poetical truth*; a very slender thing indeed, and which the poet's eye, when rolling in it's finest frenzy, can but just lay hold of. To speak in the philosophic language of Mr. Hobbes, It is something much *beyond the actual bounds, and only within the conceived possibility, of nature.* [*Answer to D'Avenant's Preface to Gondibert.*]

But the source of bad criticism, as universally of bad philosophy, is the abuse of terms. A poet, they say, must follow *Nature*; and by Nature we are to suppose can only be meant the known and experienced course of affairs in this world. Whereas the poet has a world of his own, where experience has less to do, than consistent imagination.

He has, besides, a supernatural world to range in. He has Gods, and Faeries, and Witches at his command And,

　　　– O! who can tell
The hidden *pow'r* of herbes, and might of magic spell?
　　　　　　　　　　　　　　　　[*Fairy Queen*, I. ii. 10]
Thus in the poet's world, all is marvellous and extraordinary; yet not *unnatural* in one sense, as it agrees to the conceptions that are readily entertained of these magical and wonder-working Natures.

　　　　　　　　　　　　　*

Still further, in those species that address themselves to the heart and would obtain their end, not thro' the Imagination, but thro' the *Passions*, there the liberty of transgressing nature, I mean the real powers and properties of human nature, is infinitely restrained; and *poetical* truth is, under these circumstances, almost as severe a thing as *historical*.

The reason is, we must first *believe*, before we can be *affected*.

But the case is different with the more sublime and creative poetry. This species, addressing itself solely or principally to the Imagination; a young and credulous faculty, which loves to admire and to be deceived; has no need to observe those cautious rules of credibility so necessary to be followed by him, who would touch the affections and interest the heart.

This difference, you will say, is obvious enough. How came it then to be overlooked? From another mistake, in extending a particular precept of the drama into a general maxim.

The *incredulus odi** of Horace ran in the heads of these critics, tho' his

---

**Ars Poetica*, 188. 'I discredit and hate'. Ed.

own words confine the observation singly to the stage.

Segnius irritant animos demissa per aurem
Quam quae sunt oculis subjecta fidelibus, et quae
Ipse sibi tradit Spectator –   [*Ars Poetica*, 180–2]*

That, which passes in *representation* and challenges, as it were, the
scrutiny of the eye, must be truth itself, or something very nearly
approaching to it. But what passes in *narration*, even on the stage, is
admitted without much difficulty –

multaque tolles
Ex oculis, quae mox, narret facundia praesens.   [183–4]**

In the epic narration, which may be called *absens facundia*, [narration
in absense] the reason of the thing shews this indulgence to be still
greater. It appeals neither to the *eye* nor the *ear*, but simply to the
imagination, and so allows the poet a liberty of multiplying and enlarging
his impostures at pleasure, in proportion to the easiness and comprehension of that faculty.

These general reflexions hardly require an application to the present
subject. The tales of faery are exploded, as fantastic and incredible. They
would merit this contempt, if presented on the stage; I mean, if they
were given as the proper subject of dramatic imitation, and the interest
of the poet's plot were to be wrought out of the adventures of these
marvellous persons. But the *epic muse* runs no risk in giving way to such
fanciful exhibitions.

You may call them, as one does, 'extraordinary dreams, such as excellent
poets and painters, by being over studious, may have in the beginning of
fevers'. [Sir W. Davenant's *Preface* (to *Gondibert*. Ed.)]

The epic poet would acknowledge the charge, and even value himself
upon it. He would say, 'I leave to the stage dramatist the merit of being
always broad awake, and always in his senses: The *divine dream*. . . and
delirious fancy, are among the noblest of my prerogatives.'

But the injustice done the Italian poets does not stop here. The cry is,
'Magic and enchantments are senseless things. Therefore the Italian poets
are not worth the reading.' As if, because the superstitions of Homer and
Virgil are no longer believed, their poems, which abound in them, are good
for nothing.

Yes, you will say, their fine pictures of life and manners. . .

And may not I say the same, in behalf of Ariosto and Tasso? For it is not
true that all is *unnatural* and monstrous in their poems, because of this
mixture of the wonderful. Admit, for example, Armida's marvellous con-
veyance to the happy Island, and all the rest of the love-story is as natural,

---

*'Less vividly is the mind moved by what enters through the ears than
by what is brought before the faithful eyes, and what the spectator can
himself see.' Ed.

**'You will keep much from our eyes which soon will be narrated in our
presence.' Ed.

that is, as suitable to our common notions of that passion, as any thing in Virgil or (if you will) Voltaire.

Thus you see the apology of the Italian poets is easily made on every supposition. But I stick to my point and maintain that the faery tales of Tasso do him more honour than what are called the more natural, that is, the classical parts of his poem. His imitations of the ancients have indeed their merit; for he was a genius in every thing. But they are faint and cold and almost insipid, when compared with his original fictions. We make a shift to run over the passages he has copied from Virgil. We are all on fire amidst the magical feats of Ismen, and the enchantments of Armida.

THOMAS WARTON THE YOUNGER (1728–1790)

The study of literature might well be described as the investigation of useful fantasy. The decline in classical literature, fantasy shared with a Europe stretching back as far as Greece and Rome, was attended by the rise of individual fantasy celebrating the subjective imagination of modern man, significantly in the newly popular novel frequently referred to as 'romance', and in the romances of the Middle Ages, which gave rise to the term 'Romantic'.

A number of aesthetic ingredients indispensable in late eighteenth-century taste constituted the romance. First of all the romance was primitive. Curious and 'antique', it was the product of the 'original' period of English literature before classicism, and like the poetry of the Old Testament it had been composed comparatively close to the imaginative beginnings of the world, before memory and society had shaped man's identity along the paths of imitation. As Blair remarked (see pp. 265-266) northern and oriental primitivism were a common flowering. It is to be noted not only that Warton's earlier work was in Chinese literature, but that he insisted on the oriental sources of *The Fairy Queen*, and that 'the revival of learning was due to the Arabians'. The minstrel or bard, whom he, like Percy, Ritson, and Scott, hymned was of course blood-brother to the Hebrew prophet, while the prosody of primitive English literature, especially perhaps noticeable in *Piers Plowman*, was close to the Hebrew form which Lowth had described in his theory of parallelism (see pp. 162-164). Secondly, the mediaeval romance was 'sublime'. Technically one experienced 'sublimity' wherever an image of overwhelming immensity, suggestive of infinity, was present. In a work as apparently 'antique' as an Arthurian romance, *The Seven Champions of Christendom*, or even Walter Scott's *Sir Tristrem*, the shape of time stretched back to the comparative proximity of Creation (five thousand years before) and the earliest of men. As in the appreciation of *Job* the romantic reader seemed to view millennia and even to overhear echoes of the voice of the Creator. This projection, supported by feudal, religious, and even architectural images of structure, as the related taste for the Gothic novel reminds us, was combined with powerful elements of chaotic imagination. 'Barbaric', 'wild', 'uncivilized' are terms frequently used with reference to *The Fairy Queen* and other romances. Massive structure, therefore, and its continuing dissolution, complemented each other in the same work. This 'sublime' mixture is organically related to the eighteenth-century concept of uniqueness. Not holding up a mirror to Nature, the Gothic artist – as Hurd had announced – seemed to have produced a form appropriate only to the work which he had in hand. Creative imagination demanded not old terms for its creations, but those never seen on land or sea. As Thomson's *Seasons* noted, Nature held 'ten thousand forms, ten thousand . . . tribes' (*Summer*, 248). In league with the imagination she grew in a never-ending continuum. One might observe in passing that the opposition of the mighty structures of time, mediaeval society, and Gothic architecture on the one hand, and the heuristic, solitary human imagination, dissolving and reforming, on the other, is at the heart of such poems as Coleridge's *Christabel* and Keats's *Eve of St Agnes*, and more obvious beneficiaries of the research which we are discussing. Perhaps most significantly, the mediaeval world was one in which a distinct supernatural reality was shared by the populace at large and the reading and composing aristocracy in particular. Catholicism and the underworld of demons, magicians, witches, and fairies, was property common to all classes. In this regard more than any it is clear that the significance of the Middle Ages for the poet of creative imagination in the Romantic era was notably dissimilar from that for the subjects, say, of Henry II. Lastly, it is important to observe that the movement of which Warton's *History* is a culmination was antiquarian. In his discussion of Chatterton's poems, it is the chest in St Mary Redcliffe in Bristol, the material touchstone, which looms so convincingly. The investigation which had begun into the origin of things under the aegis of the Royal Society (see pp. 1 and 8) had produced a number of manifestations, including the British Museum. The lens of science was peculiarly equipped to investigate the properties of material objects in isolation. For Warton, when it is not Chatterton's chest in Bristol, it is the tapestries on the walls of mediaeval castles or the payment of wandering minstrels which hold his attention and prove the point. As in Lowth (see pp. 159-160) the ground of the most sublime poetry was everyday things. Once again we come across the mixture, paradoxical but of the utmost importance in an understanding of the roots of Romanticism, that as in the greatest poems of the era and the mediaeval ballad, the most compelling flights of imagination were inseparable from the most sharply, and obsessively etched objects of sense.

The work of Thomas Warton the Younger is not, in effect, a departure from that of his family. In Thomas Warton the Elder's *Poems on Several Occasions*, written in 1717 and 1718 before he became Professor of Poetry at Oxford, the orientalism and mediaevalism, the rejection of classicism, and, perhaps most remarkably, the contemporary sense of the fabric of times past, had already woven the texture his son would embroider. The image of time in Joseph Warton's *Essay on Pope* (see pp. 169-182) suggests a view of the perceptions of poetry not far distant from that of his brother. Many were the researchers into mediaeval literature contemporaneous with Warton making available, as was he, the remoter reaches of literary history to the intelligent non-specialist reader. In Thomas Percy's *Reliques of Ancient English Poetry* (1765–75), praised by Wordsworth in the supplement to the 1815 preface of the significantly named *Lyrical Ballads*, in Hurd, in Joseph Ritson's *Select Collection of English Songs* (1783) and *Ancient Songs* (1790), Arthur, Bede, Gildas, Gawaine, *King Horn, Orfeo*, Tristram, William of Malmesbury, and a hundred others were awakened from their long sleep, and started on journeys to the studies of the nineteenth century and the examination halls of the twentieth. But Thomas Warton the Younger has a special place, if not that of innovator.

It has been observed that the creation of the past as a collection of material particulars, the product of the scientific investigation into 'origins', is a pronounced activity of the eighteenth century. At the same time, the belief had arisen in the 'creative imagination' both by reason of the philosophy of the greatest age of English epistemology and because of the analysis of the work of primitive prophet-poets. We have noted Gibbon's comment that in Blackwell might be observed history as it might have been written by Bishop Berkeley (see pp. 107 and 207). In Warton imaginative history based on antiquarian *minutiae*, and the manifestation of imagination, come together in the invention of a significant new artifact, the extended English literary history. In Warton only, in this period, may be observed the image with which in the twentieth century we are long familiar, the cavalcade of literary development, the long procession of succeeding ages making its way towards modernity. It is only if we can avoid a conviction of the absoluteness of his scheme and allow ourselves in turn to imagine the finally subjective and eighteenth-century nature of his achievement that we can give Warton his due.

In a work as sublimely extensive as *The History of English Poetry* it is, of course, difficult to select a representative passage. It is perhaps permissible, therefore, to cultivate irony and concentrate on Warton's regretful account of a contemporary who for a briefer period derived his major inspiration also from the image of past time, Thomas Chatterton, with the possible exception of Macpherson, composer of the largest body of antique verse in the eighteenth century. This boy's short life ending in suicide struck several of the chords we have isolated. Not only did he write 'original' which is to say primitive verse. In the figure of untutored genius the 'marvellous boy' of Wordsworth's phrase fitted precisely the age's belief in the archetypal originality of children, and hence offered as it were double proof of the primitive imagination at work. It is sad that he has been dealt with severely by later moralists, and that Warton himself labours over the authenticity of poems so close to his own sensibility. In essence Chatterton's muse like that of his contemporaries was faithful to the seductions of the twin, and, on the surface, ill-paired enchantresses Time and Imagination. No doubt, before long, he will be seen, like Warton, as a true progenitor of nineteenth-century mediaevalism.

THE HISTORY OF ENGLISH POETRY (1774–81)

from Section XXVI. 'Chatterton'*

But a want of genius will no longer be imputed to this period of our

---

*The numbered footnotes are Warton's. Ed.

poetical history, if the poems lately discovered at Bristol, and said to have been written by Thomas Rowlie, a secular priest of the place, about the year 1470, are genuine.

It must be acknowledged that there are some circumstances which incline us to suspect these pieces to be a modern forgery. On the other hand, as there is some degree of plausibility in the history of their discovery, as they possess considerable merit, and are held to be the real productions of Rowlie by many respectable critics; it is my duty to give them a place in this series of our poetry,[1] if it was for no other reason than that the world might be furnished with an opportunity of examining their authenticity. By exhibiting therefore the most specious evidences, which I have been able to collect, concerning the manner in which they were brought to light, and by producing such specimens, as in another respect cannot be deemed unacceptable; I will endeavour, not only to gratify the curiosity of the public on a subject which has long engaged the general attention, and has never yet been fairly or fully stated, but to supply the more inquisitive reader with every argument, both external and internal, for determining the merits of this interesting controversy. I shall take the liberty to add my own opinion, on a point at least doubtful: but with the greatest deference to decisions of much higher authority.

About the year 1470, William Cannynge,[2] an opulent merchant and an alderman of Bristol, afterwards an ecclesiastic, and dean of Westbury

---

[1] It will be sufficient to throw some of the obscurer rhymers of this period into the Notes. Osbern Bokenham wrote or translated metrical lives of the saints, about 1445. See supr. vol. i, p. 14. *Notes.* Gilbert Banester wrote in English verse the *Miracle of St. Thomas*, in the year 1467. *CCCC. MSS. Q.* viii. See supr. vol. i, p. 75. *Notes.* And. Lel. *Collectan.* tom. i. (p. ii.) pag. 510. edit. 1770. Wydville earl of Rivers, already mentioned, translated into English distichs, *The morale Proverbes of Crystyne of Pyse*, printed by Caxton, 1477. They consist of two sheets in folio. This is a couplet; Little vailleth good example to see/For him that wole not the contrarie flee. [I omit here a portion of Warton's more obscure antiquarian learning. Ed.] This nobleman's only original piece is a *Balet* of four stanzas, preserved by Rouse, a contemporary historian, Ross. Hist. p. 213. edit. Hearn. apud Leland. Itin. tom. x edit. Oxon. 1745. I refer also the *Notbrown Mayde* to this period. Capel's *Prolusions* p. 23. seq. edit. 1760. Of the same date is perhaps the *Delectable Historie of king Edward* IV *and the Tanner of Taniworth* &c. &c. Percy, ubi supr. p. 81. Hearne affirms, that in this piece there are some 'romantic *assertions:* — otherwise 'tis a book of *value*, and more *authority* is to be given to it than is given to *poetical books* of *Late Years*.' Hearne's Leland, ut supr. vol. ii. p. 103.

[2] I acknowledge myself greatly indebted to Dr. Harrington, of Bath, for facilitating my enquiries on this subject.

college, erected the magnificent church of St. Mary of Redcliffe, or Radcliff, near Bristol.[1] In a muniment-room over the northern portico of the church, the founder placed an iron chest, secured by six different locks[2]; which seems to have been principally intended to receive instruments relating to his new structure, and perhaps to his other charities[3], inventories of vestments and ornaments[4]. accompts of church-wardens, and other parochial evidences. He is said to have directed, that this venerable chest should be annually visited and opened by the mayor and other chief magistrates of Bristol, attended by the vicar and church-wardens of the parish: and that a feast should be celebrated every year, on the day of visitation. But this order, that part at least which relates to the inspection of the chest was soon neglected.

In the year 1768, when the present new bridge at Bristol was finished and opened for passengers, an account of the ceremonies observed on occasion of opening the old bridge, appeared in one of the Bristol Journals; taken, as it was declared, from an ancient manuscript[5]. Curiosity was naturally raised to know from whence it came. At length, after much enquiry concerning the person who sent this singular memoir to the newspaper, it was discovered that he was a youth about seventeen years old, whose name was Chatterton; and whose father had been sexton of Redcliffe church for many years, and also master of a writing-school in that parish, of which the church-wardens were trustees. The father however was now dead: and the son was at first unwilling to acknowledge, from whom, or by what means, he had procured so valuable an original. But after many promises, and some threats, he confessed that he received

---

[1] He is said to have rebuilt Westbury college. Dugd. *Warwicksh.* p. 634, edit. 1730. And Atkyns, *Glocestersh.* p. 802. On his monument in Redcliffe church, he is twice represented, both in an alderman's and a priest's habit. He was five times mayor of Bristol. See Godwin's *Bish.* p. 446. (But see edit. fol. p. 467.)

[2] It is said there were four chests; but this is a circumstance of no consequence.

[3] These will be mentioned below.

[4] See an inventory of ornaments given to this church by the founder, Jul. 4, 1470, formerly kept in this chest, and printed by Walpole, *Anecd. Paint.* i. p. 45.

[5] The old bridge was built about the year 1248. *History of Bristol*, MSS. Archiv. Bodl. C. iii. By Abel Wantner.

Archdeacon Furney, in the year 1755, left by will to the Bodleian library, large collections, by various hands, relating to the history and antiquities of the city, church, and county of Gloucester, which are now preserved there, Archiv. C. ut supr. At the end of N. iii. is the MSS. *History* just mentioned, supposed to have been compiled by Abel Wantner, of Minchin-Hampton in Gloucestershire, who published proposals and specimens for a history of that county, in 1683.

a MSS. on parchment containing the narrative above-mentioned, together with many other MSS. on parchment, from his father; who had found them in an iron chest, the same that I have mentioned, placed in a room situated over the northern entrance of the church.

It appears that the father became possessed of these MSS. in the year 1748. For in that year, he was permitted, by the church-wardens of Redcliffe church, to take from this chest several written pieces of parchment, supposed to be illegible and useless, for the purpose of converting them into covers for the writing-books of his scholars. It is impossible to ascertain, what, or how many, writings were destroyed, in consequence of this unwarrantable indulgence. Our school-master, however, whose accomplishments were much above his station, and who was not totally destitute of a taste for poetry, found, as it is said, in this immense heap of obsolete MSS., many poems written by Thomas Rowlie above mentioned, priest of St. John's church in Bristol, and the confessor of alderman Cannynge, which he carefully preserved. These at his death, of course fell into the hands of the son of Cannynge.

Of the extraordinary talents of this young man [i.e. Chatterton] more will be said hereafter. It will be sufficient to observe at present, that he saw the merit and value of these poems, which he diligently transcribed. In the year 1770, he went to London, carrying with him these transcripts, and many originals, in hopes of turning so inestimable a treasure to his great advantage. But from these flattering expectations, falling into a dissipated course of life, which ill-suited with his narrow circumstances, and finding that a writer of the most distinguished taste and judgment, Mr. Walpole [Horace Walpole, letter-writer, printer, and inventor of the Gothic novel], had pronounced the poems to be suspicious, in a fit of despair, arising from distress and disappointment, he destroyed all his papers, and poisoned himself. Some of the poems however, both transcripts and originals, he had previously sold, either to Mr. Catcott, a merchant of Bristol, or to Mr. Barrett, an eminent surgeon of the same place, and an ingenious antiquary, with whom they now remain.[1] But it appears, that among these there were but very few of parchment: most of the poems which they purchased were poems in his own hand. He was always averse to give any distinct or satisfactory account of what he possessed: but from time to time, as his necessities required, he produced copies of his originals, which were bought by these gentlemen. The originals, one or two only excepted, he chose to retain in his possession.

The chief of these poems are, the *Tragedy* of *Ella*, the *Execution* of Sir *Charles Bawdwin*, *Ode* to *Ella*, the *Battle* of *Hastings*, the *Tournament*, one or two *Dialogues* and a Description of *Cannynge's Feast*.

The *Tragedy of Ella* has six characters; one of which is a lady, named

---

[1] Mr. Barrett, to whom I am greatly obliged for his unreserved and liberal information on this subject, is now engaged in writing the *Antiquities of Bristol.*

Birtha. It has a chorus consisting of minstrels, whose songs are often introduced. Ella was governor of the castle of Bristol, and a puissant champion against the Danes, about the year 920. The story seems to be the poet's invention. The tragedy is opened with the following soliloquy.

Celmonde atte Brystowe.

Before yonne roddie sonne has droove hys wayne
Through half hys joornie, dyghte yn gites of gowlde,
Mee, hapless me, he wylle a wretch behowlde,
Myselfe, and alle thatts myne, bounde yn Myschaunche's chayne!
Ah Byrtha, whie dydde nature frame thee fayre,
Whie art thou alle that poyntelle[1] canne bewreene?
Whie art thou notte as coarse as odhers are?
Botte thenne thie soughle[2] woulde throwe this vysage sheene,
Yatte[3] shemres[4] onne thie comlie semlykeene[5],
Or scarlette with waylde lynnen clothe[6],
Lyke would thie sprite[7] [shine] upon thie vysage:
This daie brave Ella dothe thyne honde and harte
Clayme as hys owne to bee, whyche nee[8] from hys moste parte.
And cann I lynne to see herre with anere[9]?
Ytte cannotte, must notte, naie ytte shall notte bee!
Thys nyght I'lle putt strong poysonne yn the beere,
And hymme, herre, and myselfe attones[10] wylle slea.
Assyst, me helle, lette devylles rounde me tende,
To slea myselfe, my love, and eke my doughhtie friende!

The following beautiful descriptions of *Spring, Autumn,* and *Morning,* are supposed to be sung in the tragedy, by the chorus of minstrels.

Spring

The boddyng flowrettes bloshes at the lyhte,
The mees be springede[11] with the yellowe hue,
Yn daiseyed mantells ys the monntayne dyghte,
The neshe[12] younge cowslepe bendethe wythe the dewe;
The trees enleafede, into heaven straught[13],

---

[1] Pencil.
[2] Soul.
[3] That.
[4] Glimmers.
[5] Seemliness. Beauty.
[6] Perhaps we should read, Or scarlette vailed with a linnen clothe.
[7] Soul.
[8] Never.
[9] Another.
[10] At once.
[11] The meadows are sprinkled, &c.
[12] Tender.
[13] Stretching. Stretched.

Whanne gentle wyndes doe blowe, to whestlynge dynne ys[1] brought.
The evenynge commes, and brynges the dewe alonge,
The rodie welkynne sheeneth toe the eyne,
Arounde the alestake[2] mynstrelles synge the songe,
Yonge ivie rounde the doore-post doth entwyne;
I laie mee on the grasse: yette to mie wylle,
Albeytte alle ys fayre, theere lackethe sommethynge stylle.

Autumn

Whanne Autumne, blake, and sonne-brente doe appere,
Wythe hys goulde honde, guylteynge the falleynge lefe,
Bryngeynge oppe Wynterre to folfylle the yere,
Beereynge uponne hys backe the riped shefe;
Whanne alle the hylls wythe woddie seede is whyte,
Whanne levynne fyres, ande lemes, do mete fromme farr the syghte
Whanne the fayre apple, rudde as even skie,
Doe bende the tree untoe the fructyle grounde,
Whanne joicie peres, and berryes of blacke die,
Doe daunce ynne ayre, and calle the eyne arounde:
Thanne, bee the even fowle, or even fayre,
Meethynckes mie hartys joie ys steyned with somme care.

Morning

Bryghte sonne han ynne hys roddie robes byn dyghte,
Fro the redde easte hee flytted wythe hys trayne;
The howers drawe awaie the geete of nyghte,
Herre sable tapistrie was rente ynne twayne:
The dauncynge streakes bedeckedd heavenne's playne,
And onne the dewe dydd smyle wythe shemrynge[3] eie,
Lyche gottes[4] of blodde whyche doe blacke armoure steyne,
Sheenynge uponne the borne whyche stondethe bye:—
The souldyerrs stoode uponne the hyllis syde,
Lyche yonge enlefed trees whych ynne a forreste byde[5].

---

[1] i.e. Are.
[2] A sign-post before an alehouse. In Chaucer, the *Hoste* says,
   — Here at this *alehouse-stake*, I wol both drinke, and etin of a cake.
Wordes Host. v. 1835. Urr. p. 131. And in the *Ship of Fooles*, fol. 9,
a. edit. 1570. By the *ale-stake* knowe we the ale-house, And everie inne
is knowen by the signe.
[3] Glimmering.
[4] Drops.
[5] There is a description of morning in another part of the tragedy.
   The mornynge gynes alonge the east to sheene,
   Darkling the lyghte does on the waters plaie;
   The feynte rodde beam slowe creepethe over the leene,

But the following ode, belonging to the same tragedy, has much more
of the choral or lyric strain.

I. O! synge unto mie roundelaie, O! drop the bryny tear with me,
    Daunce ne moe atte hallie day,   Lyke a running river bee.
      My love is dedde,   Gone to his death bedde,
          Al under the willowe tree.

II. Blacke his cryne[1] as the wyntere night,
      Whyte his rode[2] as summer snowe,
Rodde his face as morning lyght,   Cold he lies in the grave below,
      My love is dedde, &c.

III. Swote his tounge as the throstle's note,
      Quycke in daunce as thought can be,
Deft his tabor, codgelle stote,   Oh! he lies by the willowe tree.
      My love is dedde, &c.

IV. Hark! the raven flaps his wynge,
      In the brier'd delle belowe;
      Hark! the dethe owl loud doth sing
      To the night mares as they go.
      My love is dedde, &c.

V. See the white moon sheenes on hie!
      Whyter is my true love's shrowde,
Whyter than the morning skie,   Whyter than the evening cloud.
      My love is dedde, &c.

VI. Here upon my true love's grave
      Shall the garen[3] fleurs be layde:
Ne one hallie saynte to save   Al the celness of a mayde
      My love is dedde, &c.

VII. With my hondes I'll dente[4] the brieres,

  To chase the morkynesse of nyghte awaie.
  Swift fleis the hower that will brynge oute the daie,
  The softe dewe falleth onne the greeynge grasse;
  The shepster mayden dyghtynge her arraie,
  Scante sees her vysage ynne the wavie glasse;
  By the fulle daylight wee scalle *Ella* see,
  Or *Bristowe's* walled towne. Damoyselle followe mee.

[1] Hair.
[2] Neck.
[3] Bright.
[4] Indent. Bend into the ground.

Round his hallie corse to gre[1],
Ouphante[2] faeries, light your fyres,   Here my bodie still shall bee.
My love is dedde, &c.

VIII. Come with acorne-cup, and thorne,
Drain mie harty's blodde awaie:
Lyfe and all its goodes I scorne,   Daunce by night, or feast by day,
My love is dedde, &c.

IX. Watere wytches crownde with reytes[3],
Bere me to your lethale tyde;
I die — I come — My true love waytes!
Thos the damselle spake, and dy'd.

According to the date assigned to this tragedy, it is the first drama extant in our language. In an Epistle prefixed to his patron Cannynge, the author thus censures the *Mysteries*, or religious interludes, which were the only plays then existing.

Plaies made from *Hallie*[4] *Tales* I hold unmete;
Let some *great story of a man* be songe;
Whanne, as a man, we Godde and Jesus trete,
Ynne mie poore mynde we doe the godhead wronge.

The *Ode to Ella* is said to have been sent to Rowlie in the year 1468, as a specimen of his poetical abilities, to his intimate friend and contemporary Lydgate, who had challenged him to write verses. The subject is a victory obtained by Ella over the Danes, at Watchett near Bristol.[5] I will give this piece at length.

---

[1] Grow.
[2] Ouphan. Elphin.
[3] Reeds.
[4] Holy.
[5] With this address to Lydgate prefixed.

Well thenne, good John, sythe ytt muste needes so be,
That thou, and I a bowtynge matche muste have;
Lett ytt ne breakynge of oulde friendshippe bee,
Thys ys the onelie allaboone I crave.
Remember Stowe, the Bryghstowe Carmalyte,
Who, when John Clackynge, one of myckle lore,
Dydd throwe hys gauntlette penne wythe hym to wryte,
He shewde smalle wytte, and shewde his weaknesse more.
Thys ys mie 'formance, whiche I now have wrytte,
The best performance of mie lyttel wytte.

Stowe should be *Stone*, a Carmelite friar of Bristol, educated at Cambridge, and a famous preacher. Lydgate's answer on receiving the ode, which certainly cannot be genuine, is beneath transcription. The writer, freely owning his inferiority, declares, that Rowlie rivals Chaucer

Songe to Aelle Lorde of the Castle of Bristowe
ynne daies of yore.

Oh! thou (orr whatt remaynes of thee)
Ealle the darlynge of futuritie!
Lette thys mie songe bolde as thie courage bee,
    As everlastynge to posteritie!
Whanne Dacya's sonnes, whose hayres of bloude redde hue,
Lyche kynge cuppes brastynge wythe the mornynge due,

    Arraung'd ynn dreare arraie,
    Uppone the lethale daie,
Spredde farr and wyde onn Watchett's shore:
    Thenn dyddst thou furyouse stonde,
    And bie thie brondeous honde
Beesprengedd all the mess with gore.

Drawne bie thyne anlace felle[1],   Downe to the depthe of helle,
Thousandes of Dacyanns wente;   Brystowannes menne of myghte,
Ydar'd the bloudie fyghte,   And actedd deedes full quente.

    Oh! thou, where'er (thie bones att reste)
    Thie spryte to haunt delyghteth beste,
Whytherr upponn the bloude-embrewedd pleyne,
    Orr whare thou kennst fromme farre
    The dysmalle crie of warre,
Orr seeste somme mountayne made of corse of sleyne:

    Orr seeste the harnessd steede,
    Yprauncynge o'er the meede,
And neighe to bee amonge the poynctedd speeres;*
    Orr ynn blacke armoure staulke arounde
    Embattell'd Brystowe, once thie grounde,
And glowe ardorous onn the castell steeres:

---

and Turgotus, who both lived in *Norman tymes*. The latter, indeed, may in some measure be said to have flourished in that era, for he died bishop of St. Andrews in 1015. But he is oddly coupled with Chaucer in another respect, for he wrote only some Latin chronicles. Besides, Lydgate must have been sufficiently acquainted with Chaucer's age; for he was living, and a young man, when Chaucer died. The writer also mentions Stone, the Carmelite, as living with Chaucer and Turgotus: whereas he was Lydgate's contemporary. These circumstances, added to that of the extreme and affected meanness of the composition, evidently prove this little piece a forgery.

[1] Sword.

*Cf. Job's warhorse, pp. 142 and 200. Ed.

> Orr fierie rounde the mysnter[1] glare:
> Lette Brystowe stylle bee made thie care,
> Guarde ytte fromme foemenne and consumynge fyre,
> Lyche Avone streme ensyrke ytt rounde;
> Ne lett a flame enharme the grounde,
> 'Tyll ynne one flame all the whole worlde expyres.

*

I am of opinion, that none of these pieces* are genuine, The *Execution* of *Sir Charles Bawdwin* is now allowed to be modern, even by those who maintain all the other poems to be ancient[2]. The *Ode to Ella*, and the *Epistle* to Lydgate, with his *Answer*, were written on one piece of parchment; and, as pretended, in Rowlie's own hand. This was shewn to

---

*I omit the others. Ed.

[1] The monastery. Now the cathedral.

[2] It contains 98 stanzas, and was printed at London in the year 1772, 4to. I am told, that in the above-mentioned chest, belonging to Redcliffe-church, an ancient Record was discovered, containing the expenses for Edward IV. to see the execution of Sir Charles Baldwin; with a description of a canopy under which the king sat at this execution. This Record seems to have given rise to the poem. A bond which Sir Charles Baldwin gave to Henry VI, I suppose about seizing the earl of Warwick, is said to have been mentioned in one of Rowlie's MSS., called the *Yellow Roll,* perhaps the same, found in Cannynge's chest, but now lost. Stowe's *Chron.* by Howes, edit. fol. 1615. p. 406, col. 2. And Speed's, p. 669, col. 2, edit. 1611. Stowe says, that Edward IV, was at Bristol, on a progress through England, in the *harvest season* of the year 1462. And that he was *most royally received.* Ibid. p. 416, col. 2. Cannynge was then mayor of Bristol. Sir Charles Baldwin is said to have been executed at Bristol, in the presence of Edward IV. in the year 1463. MSS. Wantn. Bibl. Bodl. ut supr. The same king was at Bristol, and lodged in St. Augustine's abbey, in 1472, when he received a large gratuity from the citizens for carrying on the war against France. Wantner, ibid. 'I have received some notices from the old registers of St. Ewin's church at Bristol, anciently called the *Minister,* which import, that the church pavement was *washed* against the coming of King Edward. But this does not at all prove or imply that the king *sat at the grete mynsterr windowe* to see the gallant Lancastrian Baldwin pass to the scaffold; a circumstance, and a very improbable one, mentioned in Rowlie's pretended poem on this subject. The notice at most will prove only, that the king assisted at mass in this church, when he came to Bristol. Nor is it improbable, that the other churches of Bristol were cleaned, or adorned, at the coming of a royal guest. Wantner, above quoted, is evidently wrong in the date 1463, which ought to be 1461, or 1462.

an ingenious critic and intelligent antiquary of my acquaintance; who assures me, that the writing was a gross and palpable forgery. It was not even skilfully counterfeited. The form of the letters, although artfully contrived to wear an antiquated appearance, differed very essentially from every one of our early alphabets. Nor were the characters uniform and consistent: part of the same manuscript exhibiting some letters shaped according to the present round hand, while others were traced in imitation of the ancient court and text hands. The parchment was old; and that it might look still older, was stained on the outside with ochre, which was easily rubbed off with a linen cloth. Care had also been evidently taken to tincture the ink with a yellow cast. To communicate a stronger stamp of rude antiquity, the *Ode* was written like prose: no distinction, or termination, being made between the several verses. Lydgate's *Answer*, which makes a part of this MSS., and is written by the same hand, I have already proved to be a manifest imposition. This parchment has since been unfortunately lost.[1] I have myself carefully examined the original MSS., as it is called, of the little piece entitled, *Accounte of W. Cannynge's Feast*. It is likewise on parchment and I am sorry to say, that the writing betrays all the suspicious signatures which are observed in that of the *Ode to Ella*. I have repeatedly and diligently compared it with three or four authentic MSS. of the time of Edward IV., to all which I have found it totally unlike. Among other smaller vestiges of forgery, which cannot be so easily described and explained here, at the bottom are added in ink two coats of arms, containing empalements of Cannynge and of his friends or relations, with family-names, apparently delineated by the same pen which wrote the verses. Even the style and the drawing of the armorial bearings discover the hand of a modern herald. This, I believe, is the only pretended original of the poetry of Rowlie, now remaining.

As to internal arguments, an unnatural affectation of ancient spelling and of obsolete words, not belonging to the period assigned to the poems, strikes us at first sight. On these old words combinations are frequently formed, which never yet existed in the unpolished state of the English language: and sometimes the antiquated diction is inartificially misapplied, by an improper contexture with the present modes of speech. The attentive reader will also discern, that our poet sometimes forgets his assumed character, and does not always act his part with consistency:

---

[1] At the same time, another MSS. on parchment, written, as pretended, by Rowlie, was shewn to this gentleman: which, tallying in every respect with the *Ode to Ella*, plainly appeared to be forged, in the same manner, and by the same modern hand. It was in prose; and contained an account of Saxon coins, and the rise of coining in England, with a list of coins, poems, ancient inscriptions, monuments, and other curiosities, in the cabinet of Cannynge abovementioned. This parchment is also lost; and, I believe, no copy remains.

for the chorus, or interlude, of the damsel who drowns herself, which I have cited at length from the *Tragedy of Ella*, is much more intelligible, and free from uncouth expressions, than the general phraseology of these compositions. In the *Battle of Hastings*, said to be translated from the Saxon, Stonehenge is called a Druidical temple. The battle of Hastings was fought in the year 1066. We will grant the Saxon original to have been written soon afterwards: about which time, no other notion prevailed concerning this miraculous monument, than the supposition which had been delivered down by long and constant tradition, that it was erected in memory of Hengist's massacre. This was the established and uniform opinion of the Welsh and Armorican bards, who most probably received it from the Saxon minstrels: and that this was the popular belief at the time of the battle of Hastings, appears from the evidence of Geoffrey of Monmouth, who wrote his history not more than eighty years after that memorable event. And in this doctrine Robert of Gloucester and all the monkish chroniclers agree. That the Druids constructed this stupendous pile for a place of worship, was a discovery reserved for the sagacity of a wiser age, and the laborious discussion of modern antiquaries. In the *Epistle* to Lydgate, prefixed to the *Tragedy*, our poet condemns the absurdity and impropriety of the religious dramas, and recommends *Some Great Story of Human Manners*, as most suitable for theatrical representation. But this idea is the result of that taste and discrimination, which could only belong to a more advanced period of society.*

But, above all, the craft of thought, the complexion of the sentiments, and the structure of the composition, evidently prove these pieces not ancient. The *Ode to Ella*, for instance, has exactly the air of modern poetry; such, I mean, as is written at this day, only disguised with antique spelling and phraseology. That Rowlie was an accomplished literary character, a scholar, an historian, and an antiquarian, if contended for, I will not deny. Nor is it impossible that he might write English poetry. But that he is the writer of the poems which I have here cited, and which have been so confidently ascribed to him, I am not yet convinced.

On the whole, I am inclined to believe, that these poems were composed by the son of the school-master before mentioned; who inherited the inestimable treasures of Cannynge's chest in Redcliffe-church, as I have already related at large. This youth, who died at eighteen, was a prodigy of genius: and would have proved the first of English poets, had he reached a maturer age. From his childhood, he was fond of reading and writing verses: and some of his early compositions, which he wrote without any design to deceive, have been judged to be most astonishing productions by the first critic of the present age.** From his situation

---

*I have omitted several footnotes here and below. Ed.

**'This is the most extraordinary young man that has encountered my

and connections, he became a skilful practitioner in various kinds of hand writing. Availing himself therefore of his poetical talent, and his facility in the graphic art, to a miscellany of obscure and neglected parchments, which were commodiously placed in his own possession, he was tempted to add others of a more interesting nature, and such as he was enabled to forge, under these circumstances, without the fear of detection. As to his knowledge of the old English literature, which is rarely the study of a young poet, a sufficient quantity of obsolete words and phrases were readily attainable from the glossary to Chaucer, and to Percy's Ballads. It is confessed, that this youth wrote the *Execution of Sir Charles Bawdwin*: and he who could forge that poem, might easily forge all the rest.

*

It is with regret that I find myself obliged to pronounce Rowlie's poems to be spurious. Ancient remains of English poetry, unexpectedly discovered, and fortunately rescued from a long oblivion, are contemplated with a degree of fond enthusiasm: exclusive of any real or intrinsic excellence, they afford those pleasures, arising from the idea of antiquity, which deeply interest the imagination. With these pleasures we are unwilling to part. But there is a more solid satisfaction, resulting from the detection of artifice and imposture.

What is here said of Rowlie, was not only written, but printed, almost two years before the correct and complete edition of his Poems appeared. Had I been apprised of that publication, I should have been much more sparing in my specimens of these forgeries, which had been communicated to me in MSS., and which I imagined I was imparting to my readers as curiosities. I had as yet seen only a few extracts of these poems; nor were those transcripts which I received, always exact. Circumstances which I mention here, to shew the inconveniences under which I laboured, both with regard to my citations and my criticisms. These scanty materials, however, contained sufficient evidence to convince me, that the pieces were not genuine.

The entire and accurate collection of Rowlie's now laid before the public, has been so little instrumental in inducing me to change my opinion, that it has served to exemplify and confirm every argument which I have produced in support of my suspicions of an imposition. It has likewise afforded some new proofs.

Those who have been conversant in the works even of the best of our old English poets, well know, that one of their leading characteristics is inequality. In these writers, splendid descriptions, ornamental comparisons, poetical images, and striking thoughts, occur but rarely: for

---

knowledge. It is wonderful how the whelp has written such things.'
Johnson, *Boswell's Life of Johnson* ed. G.B. Hill, rev. L.F. Powell (Oxford, 1934), vol. iii, 51. Ed.

many pages together, they are tedious, prosaic, and uninteresting. On the contrary, the poems before us are everywhere supported; they are throughout, poetical and animated. They have no imbecilities of style or sentiment. Our old English bards abound in unnatural conceptions, strange imaginations, and even the most ridiculous absurdities*. But Rowlie's poems present us with no incongruous combinations, no mixture of manners, institutions, customs, and characters. They appear to have been composed after ideas of discrimination had taken place; and when even common writers had begun to conceive, on most subjects, with precision and propriety. There are indeed, in the *Battle of Hastings*, some great anachronisms; and practices are mentioned which did not exist till afterwards. But these are such inconsistencies, as proceeded from fraud as well as ignorance: they are such as no old poet could have possibly fallen into, and which only betray an unskilful imitation of ancient manners. The verses of Lydgate and his immediate successors are often rugged and unmusical: but Rowlie's poetry sustains one uniform tone of harmony; and, if we brush away the asperities of the antiquated spelling, conveys its cultivated imagery in a polished and agreeable strain of versification. Chatterton seems to have thought, that the distinction of old from modern poetry consisted only in the use of old words. In counterfeiting the coins of a rude age, he did not forget the usual application of an artificial rust: but this disguise was not sufficient to conceal the elegance of the workmanship.**

Second Volume (1777)

---

*Warton here gives the accepted notion of the 'barbaric' or 'Gothic' 'first ages'. Cf. Blair, p. 264 and Hurd, p. 309. Ed.

**W.C. Hazlitt 'expunged altogether' this section from the *History of English Poetry* in 1871. Ed.

SAMUEL TAYLOR COLERIDGE (1772–1834)

If the mirror held up to Nature was the Popean ideal, the flowing stream of Gray and Blake which reflected and moved forward at the same moment was the ideal of Romantic writing. Without the aid of memory the mind mirrors its own processes in primitive poetry, Robert Lowth remarked (see p. 161). 'The philosophy of the east taught the first principles of human perception', Ezekiel instructed Blake in *The Marriage of Heaven and Hell* (see p. 296). The Neo-classical poetry of the Augustan era is an arena for debates on topics 'outside' itself, for example the *mores* of Lady Mary Wortley Montagu or Belinda. The poetry which succeeded it is epistemological. It is concerned with the process of cognition and extends to the reader the dissolving perspectives of the mind in action.

At the heart of English Romanticism may be discerned a central myth more artificial than any Neo-classical assumption. It is the image of the first men, the newly-created minds of Lowth and Wordsworth's *Excursion*, responding, some five thousand years before, to the 'sublime' objects of Nature in necessarily memory-less isolation in the 'New World' of God's Creation. As in the Bible or in Ossian these 'bards' composed irrational, frequently surreal lyrics in words which preceded intellection and abstraction, in which objects stood out in isolated iconography, avoiding the meanings which memory's categories gave to later poets of wit and judgment. Classical aesthetics had assumed that all art was textured with pastness, hence Mnemosyne or Memory was the mother of all the Muses. The new patron was Jubal, oriental inventor of musical instruments, notably the lyre. In sharing his triumph, Romantic poets 'sublimely' dissolved time's barriers and wrote, as it was assumed Adam had also, 'original' verse. Two streams converge in the rise of Romanticism. One is the confluence of psychology proper, cresting in Berkeley, Hume and Hartley, nurturing, though not exclusively, Shaftesbury, Addison, Young, Smart and Blake and later Wordsworth and Coleridge. The other is the tributary of primitivism, flowing partially from the oriental sources of the Bible and partially from the 'Gothic' or the Romance frequently located either in Scotland (*vide* Ossian, Burns and Scott) or – as in *Christabel* – in the Tarn Wathling area bordering on the Lakes.

In Coleridge these two flow into a broad sea. Coleridge's brilliance argues his originality, but little new ground is broken save perhaps in the explicitness of the union between literature, in his discussion of his own development and the art of Wordsworth, and his theories of cognition. At no other point, certainly in English literature has a major writer announced a particular view of the mechanism of the brain within, as it were, so belletristic a setting. It is only by special argument that we think of Coleridge's great work as a *Biographia Literaria* and not a *biographia epistemologica*.

The area of cognition which especially attracted the eighteenth century, as a perusal of the previous pages confirms, was the mind's relation to time. It is intriguing, therefore, that Coleridge's poetic achievement represented, for example, in *The Ancient Mariner, Christabel, Kubla Khan* and *Frost at Midnight* is concerned directly with the iconography of time. *The Ancient Mariner* is set in the Middle Ages and its central figure is a kind of Wandering Jew, *Christabel* is the closest approximation to an Arthurian romance that the Romantic movement produced, *Kubla Khan*, many of whose lines, especially 'ancestral voices prophesying war' read like echoes of Lowth, is derived from an account of an oriental despot in an Elizabethan traveller, *Frost at Midnight* contains a recollection, at the time mentioned in the title, of the poet's distant boyhood, and prophesies the form his infant's education will take.

A reading of the *Biographia* suggests that this interest in the relation between time and the creative imagination is not superficial. In effect in that work Coleridge isolates the occidental assumption that truth is related to the sequence of ideas and that if something, as we say, 'follows', it thereby makes a pattern of significance. Such a concern lies at the back of Coleridge's crucial assault on Pope's Homer. We have observed Homer's progress from Augustan divinity to original genius. It must have seemed inappropriate for example after the 'Romantic' translation by Coleridge's admired Cowper of the *Iliad* and the *Odyssey*, to discover Homer translated into terms that were not 'sublime'. It is not novel now to suggest that Pope's Homer is remarkably unfaithful in its form. Each verse paragraph in Pope embodies, as it were, the theme of his Augustan translation, the order of subordination. One may argue that each couplet is, as it were, a finished or finite event. Nothing lingers obscurely in the mind awaiting later completion. Nothing mysteriously accrues to a former image incomplete before. Like stepping stones each couplet serves its polished purpose during its short lifetime and then is done. A contrast is offered by the opening lines of, for example, *Kubla Khan*. What is going on precisely is not understood, but the obscurity beckons us. Coleridge concluded that Pope's Homer was a 'conjunction disjunctive'. Wherever there was an end there was a beginning. The poetry of reason, as opposed to imagination, carried us forward through a succession of temporal points. The reinforcement of finite temporality, we might conclude was the essential experience of the poem for the reader. 'Not so much . . . poetic thoughts as . . . thoughts *translated* into the language of poetry', Coleridge concluded (see p. 337).

'The act of consciousness is . . . identical with time considered in its essence,' Coleridge observed elsewhere (see p. 349), 'I mean time *per se*, as contra-distinguished from our notion of time; for this is always blended with the idea of space, which as the contrary of time is therefore its measure.' In this remark, in which lies a clue to perceptive theory stretching back a hundred years to the philosophy of Berkeley (see pp. 64-79), lies a key to the entire *Biographia Literaria*, itself an exercise in brilliant association. Since the Renaissance at least it had been the tradition in Western thought to suppose that given three simple ideas or single images, the central one, or the image in the middle, by and of its own nature 'associated' largely with the two on either side of it. Coleridge's comment on this assumption is that the way in which a moment, or an idea, links to others before and after it is not part of its nature as an event in time. Like the one red leaf in *Christabel*, the essence of time is within the static moment. A second, we might hazard, is a cosmic well, perhaps into futurity, rather than a link in a chain. *Before* and *after* are in effect spatial concepts related like our imaging of successions of centuries, to memories of ground covered. Time, as even John Locke had suggested, is perishing distance (see p. 41). In a sense we may see here not only a culmination of the 'oriental' movement of the eighteenth century, but also the final addition to the theory of 'the Sublime'. Infinity is not, Coleridge suggests, the alternative to time, but the effect of a true experience of temporality.

Discussing the nature of genius Coleridge observed (see p. 338) of Dryden's line 'Great wit to madness sure is near allied'

> a more than usual rapidity of association, a more than usual power of passing from thought to thought and image to image, is a component equally essential; and in the due modification of each by the other the genius itself consists.

One might observe the theory of association operating within one of Coleridge's perhaps most impressive poems, *Frost at Midnight*. The narrator of the poem sits in his cottage at midnight. Within the barred grating of the near dead fire flutters a blue flame (reminiscent of the dancing leaf of *Christabel*) which recalls for us the eternal light of Ezekiel's sapphire throne and 'the flaming bounds of place and time' in Gray (see p. 193). Known as 'a *stranger*' in country lore this flame within a flame recalls for him the similar phenomenon in the schoolroom grate of his boyhood and his restless wish, during lessons, for a 'real' stranger to appear (on the other side of the bars of his education) 'townsman, or aunt, or sister more beloved'. From this point his prophetic imagination moves from his boyhood to the future of his infant son (himself a potential stranger within the bars of time) now lying asleep. He shall 'wander like a breeze/By lakes and sandy shores . . . ' But what, one might enquire, of the 'frost' of the title? In a poem of seventy-five lines there is one mention of the 'secret ministry' of the frost in line 1, and then, *throughout the poem*, there is no other until the very end. The flame burns and consumes, eating away at time, the frost, absent but not forgotten, builds ice palaces. The reader himself associates these anomalous activities with each other, the bars of the grate with the education of cities, heat with freezing cold, the poet's restrictive education with the spontaneous freedom of his son's life, itself characteristically of the later Romantics the product of poetic creativity. Space and time are destroyed within the poem, dissimilar objects are associated in the poet's and reader's imaginations, and out of the new and unique associations appears a *prophecy* of timeless and paradisiacal humanity ('*all seasons* shall be sweet to thee!').

Coleridge's treatment of the pattern is sophisticated and self-aware. The poem, representative of the achievement of the English Romantics (and curiously similar to much of Wordsworth, for example *Guilt and Sorrow*), reveals that the Romantic creative imagination was one with the long tradition of prophetic poetry in the eighteenth century from Spence, Young and Gray on. It reveals also that in essentials the basic strategy of the poem of creative imagination had not changed since Collins (see pp. 186-188) and Gray (see pp. 189-194). The presence of the other ideas within the poem seems to hover around, even within any single one. This, we might hazard, is the source of the poem's sense of mystery and obscurity. The mind's subliminal associating power, in contradistinction to the linear progress of the poem, placing together concepts usually categorized far apart, is a major factor in the actual experience of the dismantling of time and space for the reader. Images associate as it were backwards out of their immediate groupings and against the apparent flow of time in the reading of the poem. Long past images like the frost re-awake; later ones are anticipated. The effect is of the destruction of memory in an experience curiously similar to the principle of the serpentine line (see pp. 280-281).

It is, of course, for such reasons of plastic and organic form that Coleridge attacks in the *Biographia Literaria* the associationism of Hartley (see pp. 219-248). Hartley's theory of growth was tied to the fortunes of two ideas which always recalled each other (see p. 228). Over a period of time, he had suggested one would encroach on the vibrant territory of the other, and little by little the second would be forgotten. Coleridge's observation, 'either every idea has its own nerve and corresponding oscillation, or this is not the case', is a brilliant illumination of an apparent absurdity. Timeless growth is not, perhaps we might paraphrase, inherent in time, but in the imagination's timeless affinities. We should be wary, however, of too narrow a view of Hartley. The essential revolutionary movement of the eighteenth century (see esp. pp. 4-9) is towards man's assumption of his place within the processes of Nature as subjective participant and Hartley has an important place in this movement. With this *caveat*, however, we might observe that Coleridge's famous definition of the imagination, 'the living power and prime agent of all human perception, . . . a repetition in the finite mind of the eternal act of creation in the infinite I AM', is the culmination of almost every 'pre-Romantic' text which we have examined in the preceding pages. For the poet, this definition is primarily important in its relation to the association of ideas. Logic, cause and effect and rationality, are all the cousins germane of memory. For the poet who creates Nature equally with God, the association of ideas is part and parcel of creation. The imagination builds and creates its structures of newness simultaneously as it perceives.

BIOGRAPHIA LITERARIA (1817)

from Chapter I

Among those with whom I conversed, there were, of course, very many who had formed their taste, and their notions of poetry, from the writings of Mr. Pope and his followers: or to speak more generally, in that school of French poetry, condensed and invigorated by English under- standing, which had predominated from the last century. I was not blind to the merits of this school, yet as from inexperience of the world, and consequent want of sympathy with the general subjects of these poems, they gave me little pleasure, I doubtless undervalued the *kind*, and with the presumption of youth withheld from its masters the legitimate name of poets. I saw that the excellence of this kind consisted in just and acute observations on men and manners in an artificial state of society, as its matter and substance: and in the logic of wit, conveyed in smooth and strong epigrammatic couplets, as its *form*. Even when the subject was addressed to the fancy, or the intellect, as in the *Rape of the Lock*, or the *Essay on Man*; nay, when it was a consecutive narration, as in that aston- ishing produce of matchless talent and ingenuity, Pope's translation of the *Iliad*; still a *point* was looked for at the end of each second line, and the whole was as it were a sorites,* or, if I may exchange a logical for a grammatical metaphor, a *conjunction disjunctive*, of epigrams. Meantime the matter and diction seemed to me characterized not so much by poetic thoughts, as by thoughts *translated* into the language of poetry.

*

Sensibility indeed, both quick and deep, is not only a characteristic feature, but may be deemed a component part, of genius. But it is not an essential mark of true genius, that its sensibility is excited by any other cause more powerfully than by its own personal interests; for this plain reason, that the man of genius lives most in the ideal world, in which the present is still constituted by the future or the past; and because his feelings have been habitually associated with thoughts and images, to the number, clearness, and vivacity of which the sensation of *self* is always in an inverse proportion. And yet, should he perchance have occasion to repel some false charge, or to rectify some erroneous censure, nothing is more common than for the many to mistake the general liveliness of his manner and language, *whatever* is the subject, for the effects of peculiar irritation from its accidental relation to himself.**

---

*Roughly, a series of syllogisms that predicate each other. Ed.

**This is one instance among many of deception, by the telling the half of a fact, and omitting the other half, when it is from their mutual counteraction and neutralization, that the *whole* truth arises, as a

For myself, if from my own feelings, or from the less suspicious test of the observations of others, I had been made aware of any literary testiness or jealousy; I trust, that I should have been, however, neither silly nor arrogant enough to have burthened the imperfection on *Genius*. But an experience (and I should not need documents in abundance to prove my words, if I added) a tried experience of twenty years, has taught me, that the original sin of my character consists in a careless indifference to public opinion, and to the attacks of those who influence it; that praise and admiration have become yearly less and less desirable, except as marks of sympathy; nay that it is difficult and distressing to me, to think with any interest even about the sale and profit of my works, important as, in my present circumstances, such considerations must needs be. Yet it never occurred to me to believe or fancy, that the quantum of intellectual power bestowed on me by nature or education was in any way connected with this habit of my feelings; or that it needed any other parents or fosterers than constitutional indolence, aggravated into languor by ill-health; the accumulating embarrassments of procrastination; the mental cowardice, which is the inseparable companion of procrastination, and which makes us anxious to think and converse on any thing rather than on what concerns ourselves; in fine, all those close vexations, whether chargeable on my faults or my fortunes, which leave me but little grief to spare for evils comparatively distant and alien.

*

from Chapter IV

This excellence, which in all Mr. Wordsworth's writings is more or less predominant, and which constitutes the character of his mind, I no sooner felt, than I sought to understand. Repeated meditations led me first to suspect, (and a more intimate analysis of the human faculties, their appropriate marks, functions, and effects matured my conjecture into full conviction,) that fancy and imagination were two distinct and

---

tertium aliquid different from either. Thus in Dryden's famous line, 'Great wit' (which here means genius) 'to madness sure is near allied.' Now as far as the profound sensibility, which is doubtless *one* of the components of genius, were alone considered, single and unbalanced, it might be fairly described as exposing the individual to a greater chance of mental derangement; but then a more than usual rapidity of association, a more than usual power of passing from thought to thought, and image to image, is a component equally essential; and in the due modification of each by the other the *Genius* itself consists; so that it would be just as fair to describe the earth, as in imminent danger of exorbitating, or of falling into the sun, according as the assertor of the absurdity *confined* his attention either to the projectile or to the attractive force exclusively.

widely different faculties, instead of being, according to the general belief, either two names with one meaning, or, at furthest, the lower and higher degree of one and the same power. It is not, I own, easy to conceive a more opposite translation of the Greek *Phantasia* than the Latin *Imaginatio*; but it is equally true that in all societies there exists an instinct of growth, a certain collective, unconscious good sense working progressively to desynonymize those words originally of the same meaning, which the conflux of dialects had supplied to the more homogeneous languages, as the Greek and German: and which the same cause, joined with accidents of translation from original works of different countries, occasion in mixed languages like our own. The first and most important point to be proved is, that two conceptions perfectly distinct are confused under one and the same word, and (this done) to appropriate that word exclusively to one meaning, and the synonyme (should there be one) to the other. But if (as will be often the case in the arts and sciences) no synonyme exists, we must either invent or borrow a word. In the present instance the appropriation has already begun, and been legitimated in the derivative adjective: Milton had a highly *imaginative*, Cowley a very *fanciful* mind. If therefore I should succeed in establishing the actual existences of two faculties generally different, the nomenclature would be at once determined. To the faculty by which I had characterized Milton, we should confine the term *imagination*; while the other would be contra-distinguished as *fancy*. Now were it once fully ascertained, that this division is no less grounded in nature, than that of delirium from mania, or Otway's

> Lutes, lobsters [laurels. Ed.] , seas of milk, and ships of amber,
>> [Cf. *Venice Preserved*, V.i. 369]

from Shakespear's

> What! have his daughters brought him to this pass?
>> [*King Lear*, III. iv. 63]

or from the preceding apostrophe to the elements; the theory of the fine arts, and of poetry in particular, could not, I thought, but derive some additional and important light. It would in its immediate effects furnish a torch of guidance to the philosophical critic; and ultimately to the poet himself. In energetic minds, truth soon changes by domestication into power; and from directing in the discrimination and appraisal of the product, becomes influencive in the production. To admire on principle, is the only way to imitate without loss of originality.

*

from Chapter V 'On the Law of Association — Its History traced from Aristotle to Hartley'*

In our perceptions we seem to ourselves merely passive to an external

---

*For Hartley, see pp. 219-248. Ed.

power, whether as a mirror reflecting the landscape, or as a blank canvas on which some unknown hand paints it. For it is worthy of notice, that the latter, or the system of idealism may be traced to sources equally remote with the former, or materialism; and Berkeley can boast an ancestry at least as venerable as Gassendi or Hobbs. These conjectures, however, concerning the mode in which our perceptions originated, could not alter the natural difference of *things* and *thoughts*. In the former, the cause appeared wholly external, while in the latter, sometimes our will interfered as the producing or determining cause, and sometimes our nature seemed to act by a mechanism of its own, without any conscious effort of the will, or even against it. Our inward experiences were thus arranged in three separate classes, the passive sense, or what the school-men call the merely receptive quality of the mind; the voluntary; and the spontaneous, which holds the middle place between both. But it is not in human nature to meditate on any mode of action, without enquiring after the law that governs it; and in the explanation of the spontaneous movements of our being, the metaphysician took the lead of the anatomist and natural philosopher. In Egypt, Palestine, Greece, and India the analysis of the mind had reached its noon and manhood, while experimental research was still in its dawn and infancy. For many, very many centuries, it has been difficult to advance a new truth, or even a new error, in the philosophy of the intellect or morals. With regard, however, to the laws that direct the spontaneous movements of thought and the principle of their intellectual mechanism there exists, it has been asserted, an important exception most honorable to the moderns, and in the merit of which our own country claims the largest share. Sir James Mackintosh,* (who amid the variety of his talents and attainments is not of less repute for the depth and accuracy of his philosophical enquiries than for the eloquence with which he is said to render their most difficult results perspicuous, and the driest attractive,) affirmed in the lectures delivered by him in Lincoln's Inn Hall, that the law of association as established in the contemporaneity of the original impressions [see Introduction, p. 12], formed the basis of all true psychology; and any ontological or metaphysical science, not contained in such (i.e. empirical) psychology, was but a web of abstractions and generalizations. Of this prolific truth, of this great fundamental law, he declared Hobbs to have been the original *discoverer*, while its full application to the whole intellectual system we owed to David Hartley; who stood in the same relation to Hobbs as Newton to Kepler; the law of association being that to the mind, which gravitation is to matter.

Of the former clause in this assertion, as it respects the comparative merits of the ancient metaphysicians, including their commentators, the schoolmen, and of the modern French and British philosophers from

---

*Last of the Scottish School; opponent of the senses in morality and perception. Ed.

Hobbs to Hume, Hartley, and Condillac, this is not the place to speak. So wide indeed is the chasm between this gentleman's philosophical creed and mine, that so far from being able to join hands, we could scarcely make our voices intelligible to each other: and to *bridge* it over, would require more time, skill, and power than I believe myself to possess. But the latter clause involves for the greater part a mere question of fact and history, and the accuracy of the statement is to be tried by documents rather than reasoning.

First, then, I deny Hobbs's claim in toto: for he had been anticipated by Des Cartes, whose work 'De Methodo,' preceded Hobbs's 'De Natura Humana,' by more than a year. But what is of much more importance, Hobbs builds nothing on the principle which he had announced. He does not even announce it, as differing in any respect from the general laws of material motion and impact: nor was it, indeed, possible for him so to do, compatibly with his system, which was exclusively material and mechanical.

*

The *general law* of association, or, more accurately, the *common condition* under which all exciting causes act, and in which they may be generalized, according to Aristotle is this. Ideas by having been together acquire a power of recalling each other; or every partial representation awakes the total representation of which it had been a part. In the practical determination of this common principle to particular recollections, he admits five agents or occasioning causes: 1st, connection in time, whether simultaneous, preceding, or successive; 2nd, vicinity or connection in space; 3rd, interdependence or necessary connection; as cause and effect; 4th, likeness; and 5th, contrast. As an additional solution of the occasional seeming chasms in the continuity of reproduction he proves, that movements or ideas possessing one or the other of these five characters had passed through the mind as intermediate links, sufficiently clear to recall other parts of the same total impressions with which they had co-existed, though not vivid enough to excite that degree of attention which is requisite for distinct recollection, or as we may aptly express it, *after-consciousness*. In association then consists the whole mechanism of the reproduction of impressions, in the Aristotelian Psychology. It is the universal law of the *passive* fancy and *mechanical* memory; that which supplies to all other faculties their objects, to all thought the elements of its materials.

In consulting the excellent commentary of St. Thomas Aquinas on the *Parva Naturalia* of Aristotle, I was struck at once with its close resemblance to Hume's *Essay* on association. The main thoughts were the same in both, the *order* of the thoughts was the same, and even the illustrations differed only by Hume's occasional substitution of more modern examples. I mentioned the circumstance to several of my literary acquaintances, who admitted the closeness of the resemblance, and that it seemed too great to be explained by mere coincidence; but they thought it improbable that Hume should have held the pages of the angelic Doctor worth turning over. But some time after Mr. Payne, of the King's mews, shewed Sir James Mackintosh some odd volumes of St. Thomas Acquinas, partly perhaps from having heard that Sir James (then Mr.) Mackintosh had in his lectures passed a high encomium on this canonized philosopher, but chiefly from the fact, that the volumes had belonged to Mr. Hume, and had here and there marginal marks and notes of reference in his own hand writing. Among these volumes was that which contains the *Parva Naturalia*, in the old Latin version, swathed and swaddled in the commentary afore mentioned!

It remains then for me, first to state wherein Hartley differs from Aristotle; then, to exhibit the grounds of my conviction, that he differed only to err; and next as the result, to shew, by what influences of the choice and judgement the associative power becomes either memory or fancy; and, in conclusion, to appropriate the remaining offices of the mind to the reason, and the imagination. With my best efforts to be as perspicuous as the nature of language will permit on such a subject, I earnestly solicit the good wishes and friendly patience of my readers, while I thus go 'sounding on my dim and perilous way'.

from Chapter VI 'That Hartley's system, as far as it differs from that of Aristotle, is neither tenable in theory, nor founded in facts'
Of Hartley's hypothetical vibrations in his hypothetical oscillating either of the nerves, which is the first and most obvious distinction between his system and that of Aristotle, I shall say little. This, with all other similar attempts to render *that* an object of the sight which has no relation to sight, has been already sufficiently exposed by the younger Reimarus, Maasse [contemporary German philosophers], &c., as outraging the very axioms of mechanics in a scheme, the merit of which consists in its being mechanical. Whether any other philosophy be possible, but the mechanical; and again, whether the mechanical system can have any claim to be called philosophy; are questions for another place. It is, however, certain, that as long as we deny the former, and affirm the latter, we must bewilder ourselves, whenever we would pierce into the *adyta* of causation; and all that laborious conjecture can do, is to fill up the gaps of fancy. Under that despotism of the eye (the emancipation from which Pythagoras by his *numeral*, and Plato by his *musical* symbols, and both by geometric discipline, aimed at, as the first *propaideutikon* [introductory discipline] of the mind) — under this strong ·sensuous influence, we are restless because invisible things are not the objects of vision; and metaphysical systems, for the most part, become popular, not for their truth, but in proportion as they attribute to causes a susceptibility of being *seen*, if only our visual organs were sufficiently powerful.

From a hundred possible confutations let one suffice. According to this system the idea of vibration *a* from the external object A becomes associable with the idea or vibration *m* from the external object M, because the oscillation *a* propagated itself so as to re-produce the oscillation *m*. But the original impression from M was essentially different from the impression A: unless therefore different causes may produce the same effect, the vibration *a* could never produce the vibration *m*: and this therefore could never be the means, by which *a* and *m* are associated. [See esp. p. 228.] To understand this, the attentive reader need only be reminded, that the ideas are themselves, in Hartley's system, nothing more than their appropriate configurative vibrations. It is a mere delusion of the fancy to conceive the pre-existence of the ideas, in any chain of association, as so many differently coloured billiard-balls in contact, so that when an object, the billiard-stick, strikes the first or white ball, the same motion propagates itself through the red, green, blue, and black, and sets the whole in motion. No! we must suppose the very same force, which *constitutes* the white ball, to *constitute* the red or black; or the idea of a circle to *constitute* the idea of a triangle; which is impossible.

But it may be said, that by the sensations from the objects A and M, the nerves have acquired a disposition to the vibrations *a* and *m*, and therefore *a* need only be repeated in order to re-produce *m*. Now we will grant, for a moment, the possibility of such a disposition in a material nerve, which yet seems scarcely less absurd than to say, that a weather-cock had acquired a *habit* of turning to the east, from the wind having been so long in that quarter: for if it be replied, that we must take in the circumstance of life, what then becomes of the mechanical philosophy? And what is the *nerve*, but the flint which the wag placed in the pot as the first ingredient of his stone-broth, requiring only salt, turnips, and mutton, for the remainder! But if we waive this, and presuppose the actual existence of such a disposition; two cases are possible. Either, every idea has its own nerve and correspondent oscillation, or this is not the case. If the latter be the truth, we should gain nothing by these dispositions, when the motion of any other nerve is propagated into it, there will be no ground or cause present, why exactly the oscillation *m* should arise, rather than any other to which it was equally pre-disposed. But if we take the former, and let every idea have a nerve of its own, then every nerve must be capable of propagating its motion into many other nerves; and again, there is no reason *assignable*, why the vibration *m* should arise, rather than any other *ad libitum*. [At one's pleasure.]

It is fashionable to smile at Hartley's vibrations and vibratiuncles; and his work has been re-edited by Priestley, with the omission of the *material* hypothesis. But Hartley was too great a man, too coherent a thinker, for this to have been done, either consistently or to any wise purpose. For all other parts of his system, as far as they are peculiar to that system, once removed from their mechanical basis, not only lose their main support, but the very motive which led to their adoption. Thus the principle of *contemporaneity*, which Aristotle had made the common condition of all the laws of association, Hartley was constrained to represent as being itself the sole *law*.* For to what law can the action of *material* atoms be subject, but that of proximity in *place*? And to what law can their *motions* be subjected, but that of *time*? Again, from this results inevitably, that the will, the reason, the judgement, and the understanding, instead of being the determining causes of association, must needs be represented as its *creatures*, and among its mechanical *effects*. Conceive, for instance, a broad stream, winding through a mountainous country with an indefinite number of currents, varying and running into each other according as the gusts chance to blow from the opening of the mountains. The temporary union of several currents in one, so as to form the main current of the moment, would present an accurate image of Hartley's theory of the will.

Had this been really the case, the consequence would have been, that our whole life would be divided between the despotism of outward impressions, and that of senseless and passive memory.** Take his law in its highest abstraction and most philosophical form, viz. that every partial representation recalls the total representation of which it was a part; and the law becomes nugatory, were it only for its universality. In practice it would indeed be mere lawlessness. Consider, how immense must be the sphere of a total impression from the top of St. Paul's church; and how rapid and continuous the series of such total impressions. If therefore we suppose the absence of all interference of the will, reason, and judgement, one or other of two consequences must result. Either the ideas, (or relics of such impression,) will exactly imitate the order of the impression itself, which would be absolute *delirium*: or any one part of that impression might recall any other part, and (as from the law of continuity, there must exist in every total impression, some one or more parts, which are components of some other following total impression, and so on *ad infinitum*) *any* part of *any* impression might recall *any* part of any *other*, without a cause present to determine *what* it should be. For to bring in the will, or reason, as causes of their own cause, that is, as at once causes and effects, can satisfy those only who, in their pretended evidences of a God, having first demanded organization, as the sole cause and ground of intellect, will then coolly demand the pre-existence of intellect, as the cause and ground-work of organization. There is in truth but one state to which this theory applies at all, namely, that of complete lightheadedness; and even to this it applies but partially, because the will and reason are perhaps never wholly suspended.

---

*Coleridge's account of Hartley is somewhat one-sided here, but it is of interest that his attack, like English philosophy and poetry for a hundred years, denies the cognitive importance of time and place. Ed.

**It is possible to see in Hartley's theory creative not merely 'passive' memory. See p. 220. Ed.

*

Chapter VII 'Of the necessary consequences of the Hartleian theory – Of the original mistake of equivocation which procured admission for the theory – Memoria Technica'

We will pass by the utter incompatibility of such a law (if law it may be called, which would itself be the slave of chances) with even that *appearance* of rationality forced upon us by the outward phaenomena of human conduct, abstracted from our own consciousness. We will agree to forget this for the moment, in order to fix our attention on that subordination of final to efficient causes in the human being, which flows of necessity from the assumption, that the will and, with the will, all acts of thought and attention are parts and products of this blind mechanism, instead of being distinct powers, whose function it is to control, determine, and modify the phantasmal chaos of association. The soul becomes a mere *ens logicum*;* for, as a real separable being, it would be more worthless and ludicrous than the Grimalkins in the Catharpsichord, described in the Spectator. [No. *361*.] For these did form a part of the process; but, in Hartley's scheme, the soul is present only to be pinched or stroked, while the very squeals or purring are produced by an agency wholly independent and alien. It involves all the difficulties, all the incomprehensibility (if it be not indeed, [as it appears to me], the absurdity), of intercommunion between substances that have no one property in common, without any of the convenient consequences that bribed the judgement to the admission of the *dualistic* hypothesis. Accordingly, this *caput mortuum*** of the Hartleian process has been rejected by his followers, and the consciousness considered as a *result*, as a *tune*, the common product of the breeze and the harp: though this again is the mere remotion of one absurdity to make way for another, equally preposterous. For what is harmony but a mode of relation, the very *esse* of which is *percipi*? An *ens rationale*,* which presupposes the power, that by perceiving creates it? The razor's edge becomes a saw to the armed vision; and the delicious melodies of Purcell or Cimarosa might be disjointed stammerings to a hearer, whose partition of time should be a thousand times subtler than ours. But this obstacle too let us imagine ourselves to have surmounted, and 'at one bound high overleap all bound!' Yet according to this hypothesis the disquisition, to which I am at present soliciting the reader's attention, may be as truly said to be written by Saint Paul's church, as by me: for it is the mere motion of my muscles and nerves; and these again are set in motion from external causes equally passive, which external causes stand themselves in interdependent connection with every thing that exists or has existed. Thus the whole

---

ens: (fr. L. *esse*, to be) a conceptual being. In alchemy an extract embodying *all* the virtues from before extraction. Ed.

**In alchemy, the residuum after distillation. Worthless dross. Ed.

universe co-operates to produce the minutest stroke of every letter, save only that I myself, and I alone, have nothing to do with it, but merely the causeless and *effectless* beholding of it when it is done. Yet scarcely can it be called a beholding; for it is neither an act nor an effect; but an impossible creation of a *something-nothing* out of its very contrary! It is the mere quicksilver plating behind a looking-glass; and in this alone consists the poor worthless I! The sum total of my moral and intellectual intercourse, dissolved into its elements, is reduced to *extension, motion, degrees of velocity*, and those diminished *copies* of configurative motion, which form what we call notions, and notions of notions. Of such philosophy well might Butler [Samuel Butler (1613–80)] say –

The metaphysic's but a puppet motion
That goes with screws, the notion of a notion;
The copy of a copy and lame draught
Unnaturally taken from a thought:
That counterfeits all pantomimic tricks,
And turns the eyes, like an old crucifix;
That counterchanges whatso'er it calls
B' another name, and makes it true or false;
Turns truth to falsehood, falsehood into truth,
By virtue of the Babylonian's tooth.

Miscellaneous Thoughts.

The inventor of the watch, if this doctrine be true, did not in reality invent it; he only looked on, while the blind causes, the only true artists, were unfolding themselves. So must it have been too with my friend Allston [Washington Allston (1779-1843), American historical painter], when he sketched his picture of the dead man revived by the bones of the prophet Elijah. So must it have been with Mr. *Southey* and *Lord Byron*, when the one *fancied* himself composing his *Roderick*, and the other his *Childe Harold*. The same must hold good of all systems of philosophy; of all arts, governments,wars by sea and by land; in short, of all things that ever have been or that ever will be produced. For, according to this system, it is not the affections and passions that are at work, in so far as they are *sensations* or *thoughts*. We only *fancy*, that we act from rational resolves, or prudent motives, or from impulses of anger, love, or generosity. In all these cases the real agent is a *something-nothing-every-thing*, which does all of which we know, and knows nothing of all that itself does.

The existence of an infinite spirit, of an intelligent and holy will, must, on this system, be mere articulated motions of the air. For as the function of the human understanding is no other than merely (to appear to itself) to combine and to apply the phaenomena of the association; and as these derive all their reality from the primary sensations; and the sensations again all *their* reality from the impressions *ab extra*;* a God not visible,

---

*'From the external world'. Again, Coleridge is unwilling to accept *some*

audible, or tangible, can exist only in the sounds and letters that form his name and attributes. If in *ourselves* there be no such faculties as those of the will, and the scientific reason, we must either have an *innate* idea of them, which would overthrow the whole system; or we can have no idea at all. The process, by which Hume degraded the notion of cause and effect into a blind product of delusion and habit, into the mere sensation of *proceeding* life (*nisus vitalis*) [a vital pressure] associated with the images of the memory; this same process must be repeated to the equal degradation of every *fundamental* idea in ethics or theology.

Far, very far am I from burthening with the odium of these consequences the moral characters of those who first formed, or have since adopted the system! It is most noticeable of the excellent and pious Hartley, that, in the proofs of the existence and attributes of God, with which his second volume commences, he makes no reference to the principle or results of the first. Nay, he assumes, as his foundations, ideas which, if we embrace the doctrines of his first volume, can exist no where but in the vibrations of the ethereal medium common to the nerves and to the atmosphere. Indeed the whole of the second volume is, with the fewest possible exceptions, independent of his peculiar system. So true is it, that the faith, which saves and sanctifies, is a collective energy, a total act of the whole moral being; that its living sensorium is in the *heart*; and that no errors of the understanding can be morally arraigned unless they have proceeded from the heart. – But whether they be such, no man can be certain in the case of another, scarcely perhaps even in his own. Hence it follows by inevitable consequence, that man may perchance determine *what* is an heresy; but God only can know, *who* is a heretic. It does not, however, by any means follow that opinions fundamentally false are harmless. An hundred causes may coexist to form one complex antidote. Yet the sting of the adder remains venomous, though there are many who have taken up the evil thing; and it hurted them not! Some indeed there seem to have been, in an unfortunate neighbour-nation at least [France, at the Revolution], who have embraced this system with a full view of all its moral and religious consequences; some –

– who deem themselves most free,
When they within this gross and visible sphere
Chain down the winged thought, scoffing ascent,
Proud in their meanness; and themselves they cheat
With noisy emptiness of learned phrase,
Their subtle fluids, impacts, essences,
Self-working tools, uncaus'd effects, and all
Those blind omniscients, those Almighty slaves,
Untenanting Creation of its God!

[Coleridge, The Destiny of Nations, 26–34]

Such men need discipline, not argument; they must be made better men,

---

timeless creativity in Hartley's vibrations. Ed.

before they can become wiser.

The attention will be more profitably employed in attempting to discover and expose the paralogisms, by the magic of which such a faith could find admission into minds framed for a nobler creed. These, it appears to me, may be all reduced to one sophism as their common genius; the mistaking the *conditions* of a thing for its *causes* and *essence;* and the process, by which we arrive at the knowledge of a faculty, for the faculty itself. The air I breathe is the *condition* of my life, not its cause. We could never have learnt that we had eyes but by the process of seeing; yet having seen we know that the eyes must have pre-existed in order to render the process of sight possible. Let us cross-examine Hartley's scheme under the guidance of this distinction; and we shall discover, that contemporaneity, (Leibnitz's *Lex Continui,*) is the *limit and condition* of the laws of mind, itself being rather a law of matter, at least of phaenomena considered as material. At the utmost, it is to *thought* the same, as the law of gravitation is to loco-motion. In every voluntary movement we first counteract gravitation, in order to avail ourselves of it. It must exist, that there may be a something to be counteracted, and which, by its re-action, may aid the force that is exerted to resist it. Let us consider what we do when we leap. We first resist the gravitating power by an act purely voluntary, and then by another act, voluntary in part, we yield to it in order to light on the spot, which we had previously proposed to ourselves. Now let a man watch his mind while he is composing; or, to take a still more common case, while he is trying to recollect a name; and he will find the process completely analogous. Most of my readers will have observed a small water-insect on the surface of rivulets, which throws a cinque-spotted shadow fringed with prismatic colours on the sunny bottom of the brook; and will have noticed, how the little animal *wins* its way up against the stream, by alternate pulses of active and passive motion, now resisting the current, and now yielding to it in order to gather strength and a momentary *fulcrum* for a further propulsion.* This is no unapt emblem of the mind's self-experience in the act of thinking. There are evidently two powers at work, which relatively to each other are active and passive; and this is not possible without an intermediate faculty, which is at once both active and passive. (In philosophical language, we must denominate this intermediate faculty in all its degrees and determinations, the *Imagination*. But, in common language, and especially on the subject of poetry, we appropriate the name to a superior degree of the faculty, joined to a superior voluntary controul over it.)

Contemporaneity, then, being the common condition of all the laws of association, and a component element in all the materia subjecta, the parts of which are to be associated, must needs be co-present with all. Nothing,

---

*Perhaps the 'water boatman' which 'rows' backwards against the current. Ed.

therefore, can be more easy than to pass off on an incautious mind this constant companion of each, for the essential substance of all. But if we appeal to our own consciousness, we shall find that even time itself, as the *cause* of a *particular* act of association, is distinct from contemporaneity, as the condition of all association. [See introduction p. 12.] Seeing a mackerel, it may happen, that I immediately think of gooseberries, because I at the same time ate mackerel with gooseberries as the sauce. The first syllable of the latter word, being that which had co-existed with the image of the bird so called, I may then think of a goose. In the next moment the image of a swan may arise before me, though I had never seen the two birds together. In the two former instances, I am conscious that their co-existence in *time* was the circumstance, that enabled me to recollect them; and equally conscious am I that the latter was recalled to me by the joint operation of likeness and contrast. So it is with *cause* and *effect*; so too with *order*. So I am able to distinguish whether it was proximity in time, or continuity in space, that occasioned me to recall B. on the mention of A. They cannot be indeed *separated* from contemporaneity; for that would be to separate them from the mind itself. The act of consciousness is indeed identical with *time* considered in its essence. (I mean *time* per se, as contra-distinguished from our *notion* of time; for this is always blended with the idea of space, which, as the *contrary* of time, is therefore its *measure*.) Nevertheless the accident of seeing two objects at the same moment acts as a distinguishable cause from that of having seen them at the same place: and the true practical general law of association is this; that whatever makes certain parts of a total impression more vivid or distinct than the rest, will determine the mind to recall these in preference to others equally linked together by the common condition of contemporaneity, or (what I deem a more appropriate and philosophical term) of *continuity*. But the will itself by confining and intensifying the attention may arbitrarily give vividness or distinctness to any object whatsoever; and from hence we may deduce the uselessness, if not the absurdity, of certain recent schemes which *promise* an artificial *memory*, but which in reality can only produce a confusion and debasement of the *fancy*. Sound logic, as the habitual subordination of the individual to the species, and of the species to the genus; philosophical knowledge of facts under the relation of cause and effect; a cheerful and communicative temper disposing us to notice the similarities and contrasts of things, that we may be able to illustrate the one by the other; a quiet conscience; a condition free from anxieties; sound health, and above all (as far as relates to passive remembrance) a healthy digestion; *these* are the best, these are the only *Arts of Memory*.

*

from Chapter XIII 'Of the Imagination or Esemplastic Power'
The *Imagination* then, I consider either as primary, or secondary. The

primary *Imagination* I hold to be the living Power and prime Agent of all human Perception, and as a repetition in the finite mind of the eternal act of creation in the infinite I AM. The secondary Imagination I consider as an echo of the former, co-existing with the conscious will, yet still as identical with the primary in the *kind* of its agency, and differing only in *degree*, and in the mode of its operation. It dissolves, diffuses, dissipates, in order to recreate; or where this process is rendered impossible, yet still at all events it struggles to idealize and to unify. It is essentially *vital*, even as all objects (*as* objects) are essentially fixed and dead.

Fancy, on the contrary, has no other counters to play with, but fixities and definites. The Fancy is indeed no other than a mode of Memory emancipated from the order of time and space; while it is blended with, and modified by that empirical phenomenon of the will, which we express by the word *Choice*. But equally with the ordinary memory the Fancy must receive all its materials ready made from the law of association.

Whatever more than this, I shall think it fit to declare concerning the powers and privileges of the imagination in the present work, will be found in the critical essay* on the uses of the Supernatural in poetry, and the principles that regulate its introduction: which the reader will find pre-fixed to the poem of *The Ancient Mariner*.

---

*This essay was not written. Ed.

WILLIAM WORDSWORTH (1770–1850)

Of special interest to the historian of ideas is the passage in *Night Thoughts* beginning with line 409 of 'Night VI' (see p. 143). The poet-prophet asks his friend, Lorenzo, where his true treasure lies. In terms similar to those of Stevens's *Sunday Morning* the poet remarks that he comes from a race 'sky-born, sky-guided, sky-returning' (Stevens uses the phrase 'returning to the sky'). 'The senses', the bard observes further, not only 'inherit earth and heavens' passively enjoying 'the various riches Nature yields'. They give 'taste to fruits', create the 'harmony' of 'groves' and bestow light on gold and on the sun. Summing up, Young concluded, the senses *'half-create* the wondrous world they see' (present writer's italics).

In *Lines Written a Few Miles Above Tintern Abbey*, which appears in *Lyrical Ballads* (1798), Wordsworth recorded the 'blessed mood' 'mid the din/Of towns and cities' he had experienced as a result of the scene before him not visited for five years, and prophesied 'life and food/For future years' in this return. He is still, Wordsworth concluded

> A lover of the meadows and the woods
> And mountains; and of all that we behold
> From this green earth; of all the mighty world
> Of eye and ear, both what they *half-create*,
> And what perceive . . .   (*Tintern Abbey*, 103–7)

At this point in *Tintern Abbey* recent editors of *Lyrical Ballads* R.L. Brett and A.R. Jones (1963) have observed a movement beyond the association-ism of David Hartley (see pp. 219-248) towards a concept of active creative perception closer to Berkeley (see pp. 62-79) and to Coleridge's theory of creative imagination (see pp. 349-350). In Wordsworth's own note to the term 'half-create' he admitted a 'close resemblance to an admirable line of Young . . . the exact impression of which' he could not recollect. The admission is unconsciously misleading, for it diminishes the apparent importance of what he did recollect. A key term, perhaps the key concept, in *Tintern Abbey*, came from Wordsworth's memory of Young's 'sublime' poem of 1742–45. Berkeleyan epistemology, we might conclude, first appeared significantly in Wordsworth's thinking through the agency of a poem of the mid-eighteenth century.

If *Tintern Abbey* is significant in Wordsworth's early verse, *The Excursion*, a poem whose title suggests the creative and heuristic journey of the creative imagination, is representative of his maturest thinking. In the crucial third book of this poem appears the haunting line, 'Lost in un-searchable identity' (*The Excursion*, iii. 112). Again in his own note, which runs to more than a page, Wordsworth observed that he had taken the image from Thomas Burnet's *Theory of the Earth* (see pp. 21-31). Enthusiastically quoting several paragraphs of the thoughts of Addison's mentor, who had died in 1715, he noted that he shared with Burnet 'corresponding sentiments, excited by objects of a similar nature'.

Wordsworth inherited from the eighteenth century the twin, indeed interdependent, concepts of the creative imagination, the fruit of the philosophy of the eighteenth century, and secondly, the concept of the poet as prophet, the product of the parallel line of investigation into the nature of primitive poetry. In the *Lectures on the Sacred Poetry of the Hebrews*, whilst detailing the separate characteristics of the individual prophets, Robert Lowth had observed that Ezekiel (see pp. 183-185) was the most sublime of all the prophets (see p. 165). One recalls that Joseph Spence had noted in the *Essay on Pope's Odyssey* (see p. 102) a technique intriguingly similar in Homer and in Ezekiel, in which a confusion or extinction of light in the heavens foretold revolution on earth. It need hardly be stressed that the most glorious example of Spence's '*an orientalism*' is Keats's *Hyperion: A Fragment*, a 'prophecy' of creative imagination which images the downfall of the Titan of the sun, who stalks through an oriental palace in the zenith remarkably suggestive of Ezekiel's splendour. The point need not be laboured that Ezekiel's vision supplies the central scheme of Young's *Night Thoughts*, the major image of Collins's *Ode on the Poetical Character* (see pp. 187-188), of Gray's *Progress of Poesy* (see pp. 191-194), and the most succinct account of primitive, original poetry in Blake (see pp. 296-297).

Perhaps the most significant moment in Wordsworth's *Excursion* occurs in Book II (see pp. 353-355). Cynical since his disappointment in the French Revolution, the lapsed minister known as 'the Solitary' tells of his search for a feeble-minded old man lost in the peaks of the Lake District during a storm. Curled up like a sleeping child he is finally found high in the 'urn-like' valley in which the poet now walks. By means of this simple and anti-rational agency, which offers a rich instance of the poet's use of 'associationism', the Solitary experiences a magnificent vision. It is like an oriental city. Among the mists he sees all the jewelled particulars of Burnet's 'sublime' world and, in the midst 'an object like a throne/ Under a shining canopy of state'. Of course, the line from Burnet, to Spence, to Young, Collins, Gray, Blake, and finally, perhaps to Keats, needs to be examined in minute detail. Nevertheless, we observe that Wordsworth's prophetic vision after the manner, and using the terms, of Ezekiel, places him in a firm tradition springing from the most central concerns of eighteenth-century thinking about the poetic process.

In the scholarly segmentation which we impose on the past the Romantic 'period' appears to begin somewhere in the third quarter of the eighteenth century and to be distinct from the eighteenth century 'proper' which we tend to view as the domain of Pope, Swift and Johnson. Somewhere in between, perhaps, appear Collins, Cowper, Gray, Smart, Young and the Wartons, the *soi-disant* 'pre-Romantics' seen as it were as writers who had a glimpse of the Holy Grail, but were not able, as were the inhabitants of the nineteenth century, to capture the castle. In this compartmentalized world of literary history, although following the steps of Thomas Warton, we place the philosophers, clear sources of later perceptive theories into a special compartment, not allowing them even the designation 'writer'.

It is clear that the 'pre-Romantic' writer should, in fact, be afforded the term 'Romantic'. In their essentials, the above-mentioned poets achieved, though perhaps with less subtle intellectualism, the major positions later elaborated upon by the 'great' Romantics. The nature of past time, human and national, and its relation to timeless creation was the concern of the eighteenth century, as it was of Wordsworth. The newly created mind of original man, whose experience is repeated in our own, is the focus of Lowth, as it is of Wordsworth.

In Wordsworth, perhaps more than anyone, the traditional lowly images of everyday life (see pp. 159-160) produced the most sublime poetry; his concept of 'the language of men' is heir to a century of linguistic awareness in Berkeley, Smart and Blake, for example, whom he follows most closely in the suggestion of a pre-intellectual language which, as in *We are Seven*, posits a Blakean dichotomy between referential meaning and imaginative 'becomingness'. The Lake District of the Lake Poets is, clearly, the heir to the eighteenth century's image of 'primitivism', in particular perhaps, to the Scotland of Ossian. One need not stress the importance of the Carlisle area in the Arthurian romances, and the closeness of the Lakes to this region. Wordsworth's 'spots of time', so significant in *The Prelude*, are the direct descendants of Spence's 'particulars' and Blake's 'minute particulars'. Wordsworth's and Coleridge's *Lyrical Ballads* stem directly from the mediaeval and Renaissance interests of Hurd, Warton, Percy and other antiquarians. Perhaps one might observe that the eighteenth century had, especially, moved toward a new theory of myth-making. Whereas Pope, and Johnson, had been concerned with allusion to the golden myths of Ancient Greece, the new writers of the early Romantic era concentrated on the subjective creation of contemporary myth, an ever-continuing process in which man combined harmony, thought, and the creation of an anthropomorphic Nature, as if, partner in God's creation, he were the original inhabitant of an ever-new earth. *The Excursion* is both the summation of a movement which is continuous in English literature from the early eighteenth century and, though flawed by its length, is the most mature statement of Romantic poetic principle.

THE EXCURSION

from Book II

                    ' . . . soon as help
Had been collected from the neighbouring vale,
With morning we renewed our quest: the wind
Was fallen, the rain abated, but the hills
Lay shrouded in impenetrable mist;
And long and hopelessly we sought in vain: 810

Till, chancing on that lofty ridge to pass
A heap of ruin — almost without walls
And wholly without roof (the bleached remains
Of a small chapel, where, in ancient time,
The peasants of these lonely valleys used
To meet for worship on that central height) —
We there espied the object of our search,
Lying full three parts buried among tufts
Of heath-plant, under and above him strewn,
To baffle, as he might, the watery storm: 820
And there we found him breathing peaceably,
Snug as a child that hides itself in sport
'Mid a green hay-cock in a sunny field.
We spake — he made reply, but would not stir
At our entreaty; less from want of power
Than apprehension and bewildering thoughts.'

   'So was he lifted gently from the ground,
And with their freight homeward the shepherds moved
Through the dull mist, I following — when a step,
A single step, that freed me from the skirts   830
Of the blind vapour, opened to my view
Glory beyond all glory ever seen
By waking sense or by the dreaming soul!
The appearance, instantaneously disclosed,
Was of a mighty city — boldly say
A wilderness of building, sinking far
And self-withdrawn into a boundless depth,
Far sinking into splendor — without end!
Fabric it seemed of diamond and of gold,
With alabaster domes, and silver spires,   840
And blazing terrace upon terrace, high
Uplifted; here, serene pavilions bright,
In avenues disposed; there, towers begirt
With battlements that on their restless fronts
Bore stars — illumination of all gems!
By earthly nature had the effect been wrought
Upon the dark materials of the storm
Now pacified; on them, and on the coves
And mountain-steeps and summits, whereunto
The vapours had receded, taking there   850
Their station under a cerulean sky.
Oh, 'twas an unimaginable sight!
Clouds, mists, streams, watery rocks and emerald turf,
Clouds of all tincture, rocks and sapphire sky,*

---

*Cf. Burnet, p. 35; Spence, p. 102; Lowth, p. 165; Ezekiel, p. 185; Collins,

Confused, commingled, mutually inflamed,
Molten together, and composing thus,
Each lost in each, that marvellous array
Of temple, palace, citadel, and huge
Fantastic pomp of structure without name,
In fleecy folds voluminous, enwrapped.   860
Right in the midst, where interspace appeared
Of open court, an object like a throne
Under a shining canopy of state
Stood fixed; and fixed resemblances were seen
To implements of ordinary use,
But vast in size,* in substance glorified;
Such as by Hebrew Prophets were beheld
In vision — forms uncouth of mightiest power
For admiration and mysterious awe.
This little Vale, a dwelling-place of Man,   870
Lay low beneath my feet; 'twas visible —
I saw not, but I felt that it was there.
That which I *saw* was the revealed abode
Of Spirits in beatitude: my heart
Swelled in my breast. — 'I have been dead,' I cried,
'And now I live! Oh! wherefore *do* I live?'
And with that pang I prayed to be no more! —
— But I forget our Charge, as utterly
I then forgot him: — there I stood and gazed:
The apparition faded not away,
And I descended.   880

*

from Book IV
        'Upon the breast of new-created earth**
Man walked; and when and wheresoe'er he moved,
Alone or mated, solitude was not.
He heard, borne on the wind, the articulate voice
Of God; and angels to his sight appeared
Crowning the glorious hills of paradise;
Or through the groves gliding like morning mist
Enkindled by the sun. He sat — and talked
With winged messengers; who daily brought
To his small island in the ethereal deep   640
Tidings of joy and love. — From those pure heights

p. 187; Gray, p. 193. Ed.
*Where time and space are absent objects have infinite 'extension'. Ed.
**Cf. Lowth, p. 152. Ed.

(Whether of actual vision, sensible
To sight and feeling, or that in this sort
Have condescendingly been shadowed forth
Communications spiritually maintained,
And intuitions moral and divine)
Fell human-kind — to banishment condemned
That flowing years repealed not: and distress
And grief spread wide; but Man escaped the doom
Of destitution; — solitude was not.   650
— Jehovah — shapeless power above all powers,
Single and one, the omnipresent God,
By vocal utterance, or blaze of light,
Or cloud of darkness, localised in heaven;
On earth, enshrined within the wandering ark;
Or, out of Sion, thundering from his throne
Between the cherubim — on the chosen race
Showered miracles, and ceased not to dispense
Judgments, that filled the land from age to age
With hope, and love, and gratitude, and fear;   660
And with amazement smote; — thereby to assert
His scorned, or unacknowledged, sovereignty.
And when the One, ineffable of name,
Of nature indivisible, withdrew
From mortal adoration or regard,
Not then was Deity engulfed; nor Man,
The rational creature, left, to feel the weight
Of his own reason, without sense or thought
Of higher reason and a purer will,
To benefit and bless, through mightier power: —   670
Whether the Persian — zealous to reject
Altar and image, and the inclusive walls
And roofs of temples built by human hands —
To loftiest heights ascending, from their tops,
With myrtle-wreathed tiara on his brow,
Presented sacrifice to moon and stars,
And to the winds and mother elements,
And the whole circle of the heavens, for him
A sensitive existence, and a God,
With lifted hands invoked, and songs of praise: 680
Or, less reluctantly to bonds of sense
Yielding his soul, the Babylonian framed
For influence undefined a personal shape;
And, from the plain, with toil immense, upreared
Tower eight times planted on the top of tower,
That Belus, nightly to his splendid couch
Descending, there might rest; upon that height

Pure and serene, diffused — to overlook
Winding Euphrates, and the city vast
Of his devoted worshippers, far-stretched,   690
With grove and field and garden interspersed;
Their town, and foodful region for support
Against the pressure of beleaguering war.

'Chaldean Shepherds, ranging trackless fields,
Beneath the concave of unclouded skies
Spread like a sea, in boundless solitude,
Looked on the polar star, as on a guide
And guardian of their course, that never closed
His steadfast eye. The planetary Five
With a submissive reverence they beheld;   700
Watched, from the centre of their sleeping flocks,
Those radiant Mercuries, that seemed to move
Carrying through ether, in perpetual round,
Decrees and resolutions of the Gods;
And, by their aspects, signifying works
Of dim futurity, to Man revealed.
— The imaginative faculty was lord
Of observations natural; and, thus
Led on, those shepherds made report of stars
In set rotation passing to and fro,   710
Between the orbs of our apparent sphere
And its invisible counterpart, adorned
With answering constellations, under earth,
Removed from all approach of living sight
But present to the dead; who, so they deemed,
Like those celestial messengers beheld
All accidents, and judges were of all.

'The lively Grecian, in a land of hills,
Rivers and fertile plains, and sounding shores, —
Under a cope of sky more variable,   720
Could find commodious place for every god,
Promptly received, as prodigally brought,
From the surrounding countries, at the choice
Of all adventurers. With unrivalled skill,
As nicest observation furnished hints
For studious fancy, his quick hand bestowed
On fluent operations a fixed shape;
Metal or stone, idolatrously served.
And yet — triumphant o'er this pompous show
Of art, this palpable array of sense,   730
On every side encountered; in despite

Of the gross fictions chanted in the streets
By wandering rhapsodists; and in contempt
Of doubt and bold denial hourly urged
Amid the wrangling schools — a *Spirit* hung,
Beautiful region! o'er thy towns and farms,
Statues and temples, and memorial tombs;
And emanations were perceived; and acts
Of immortality, in Nature's course,
Exemplified by mysteries, that were felt   740
As bonds, on grave philosopher imposed
And armed warrior; and in every grove
A gay or pensive tenderness prevailed,
When piety more awful had relaxed.
— 'Take, running river, take these locks of mine' —
Thus would the votary say — 'this severed hair,
My vow fulfilling, do I here present,
Thankful for my beloved child's return.
Thy banks, Cephisus, he again hath trod,
Thy murmurs heard; and drunk the crystal lymph   750
With which thou dost refresh the thirsty lip,
And, all day long, moisten these flowery fields!'
And, doubtless, sometimes, when the hair was shed
Upon the flowing stream, a thought arose
Of life continuous, being unimpaired;
That hath been, is, and where it was and is
There shall endure, — existence unexposed
To the blind walk of mortal accident;
From diminution safe and weakening age;
While man grows old, and dwindles, and decays;   760
And countless generations of mankind
Depart; and leave no vestige where they trod.'

*

'— The Shepherd-lad,* that in the sunshine carves,   800
On the green turf, a dial — to divide
The silent hours; and who to that report
Can portion out his pleasures, and adapt,
Throughout a long and lonely summer's day
His round of pastoral duties, is not left
With less intelligence for *moral* things
Of gravest import. Early he perceives,
Within himself, a measure and a rule,

---

*Cf. Keats's myth-making in his poem about the 'shepherd-lad', *Endymion*.
Ed.

Which to the sun of truth he can apply,
That shines for him, and shines for all mankind.   810
Experience daily fixing his regards
On Nature's wants, he knows how few they are,
And where they lie, how answered and appeased.
This knowledge ample recompense affords
For manifold privations; he refers
His notions to this standard; on this rock
Rests his desires; and hence, in after life,
Soul-strengthening patience, and sublime content.
Imagination – not permitted here
To waste her powers, as in the worldling's mind,   820
On fickle pleasures, and superfluous cares,
And trivial ostentation – is left free
And puissant to range the solemn walks
Of time and nature, girded by a zone
That, while it binds, invigorates and supports.
Acknowledge, then, that whether by the side
Of his poor hut, or on the mountain-top,
Or in the cultured field, a Man so bred
(Take from him what you will upon the score
Of ignorance or illusion) lives and breathes   830
For noble purposes of mind: his heart
Beats to the heroic song of ancient days;
His eye distinguishes, his soul creates.
And those illusions, which excite the scorn
Or move the pity of unthinking minds,
Are they not mainly outward ministers
Of inward conscience? with whose service charged
They came and go, appeared and disappear,
Diverting evil purposes, remorse
Awakening, chastening an intemperate grief   840
Or pride of heart abating: and, whene'er
For less important ends those phantoms move,
Who would forbid them, if their presence serve,
On thinly-peopled mountains and wild heaths,
Filling a space, else vacant, to exalt
The forms of Nature, and enlarge her powers?

'Once more to distant ages of the world*
Let us revert, and place before our thoughts
The face which rural solitude might wear

---

*Like 800ff these lines – also significant for Keats – reveal the heart of
Romantic theory: poetry *is* the imaginative fusion of natural and human
forms in a continuing prophetic originality. Ed.

To the unenlightened swains of pagan Greece.   850
— In that fair clime, the lonely herdsman, stretched
On the soft grass through half a summer's day,
With music lulled his indolent repose:
And, in some fit of weariness, if he,
When his own breath was silent, chanced to hear
A distant strain, far sweeter than the sounds
Which his poor skill could make, his fancy fetched,
Even from the blazing chariot of the sun,
A beardless youth, who touched a golden lute,
And filled the illumined groves with ravishment.   860
The nightly hunter, lifting a bright eye
Up towards the crescent moon, with grateful heart
Called on the lovely wanderer who bestowed
That timely light, to share his joyous sport:
And hence, a beaming Goddess with her Nymphs,
Across the lawn and through the darksome grove,
Not unaccompanied with tuneful notes
By echo multiplied from rock or cave,
Swept in the storm of chase; as moon and stars
Glance rapidly along the clouded heaven,   870
When winds are blowing strong. The traveller slaked
His thirst from rill or gushing fount, and thanked
The Naiad. Sunbeams, upon distant hills
Gliding apace, with shadows in their train,
Might, with small help from fancy, be transformed
Into fleet Oreads sporting visibly.
The Zephyrs fanning, as they passed, their wings,
Lacked not, for love, fair objects whom they wooed
With gentle whisper. Withered boughs grotesque,
Stripped of their leaves and twigs by hoary age,   880
From depth of shaggy covert peeping forth
In the low vale, or on steep mountain-side;
And, sometimes, intermixed with stirring horns
Of the live deer, or goat's depending beard, —
These were the lurking Satyrs, a wild brood
Of gamesome Deities; or Pan himself,
The simple shepherd's awe-inspiring God!'

*

                        'As men from men
Do, in the constitution of their souls,
Differ, by mystery not to be explained;
And as we fall by various ways, and sink
One deeper than another, self-condemned   1110

Through manifold degrees of guilt and shame;
So manifold and various are the ways
Of restoration, fashioned to the steps
Of all infirmity, and tending all
To the same point, attainable by all —
Peace in ourselves, and union with our God.
For you,* assuredly, a hopeful road
Lies open: we have heard from you a voice
At every moment softened in its course
By tenderness of heart; have seen your eye,   1120
Even like an altar lit by fire from heaven,
Kindle before us. — Your discourse this day,
That, like the fabled Lethe, wished to flow
In creeping sadness, through oblivious shades
Of death and night, has caught at every turn
The colours of the sun. Access for you
Is yet preserved to principles of truth,
Which the imaginative will upholds
In seats of wisdom, not to be approached
By the inferior faculty that moulds,   1130
With her minute and speculative pains,
Opinion, every changing!

                 I have seen
A curious child, who dwelt upon a tract
Of inland ground, applying to his ear
The convolutions of a smooth-lipped shell;
To which, in silence hushed, his very soul
Listened intensely; and his countenance soon
Brightened with joy; for from within were heard
Murmurings, whereby the monitor expressed
Mysterious union with its native sea.   1140
Even such a shell the universe itself
Is to the ear of faith; and there are times,
I doubt not, when to you it doth impart
Authentic tidings of invisible things;
Of ebb and flow, and ever-during power;
And central peace, subsisting at the heart
Of endless agitation. Here you stand,
Adore, and worship, when you know it not;
Pious beyond the intention of your thought;
Devout above the meaning of your will.   1150
— Yes, you have felt, and may not cease to feel.
The estate of man would be indeed forlorn

---

*'The Wanderer' speaks to 'the Solitary'. Ed.

If false conclusions of the reasoning power
Made the eye blind, and closed the passages
Through which the ear converses with the heart.
Has not the soul, the being of your life,
Received a shock of awful consciousness,
In some calm season, when these lofty rocks
At night's approach bring down the unclouded sky,
To rest upon their circumambient walls;   1160
A temple framing of dimensions vast,
And yet not too enormous for the sound
Of human anthems, — choral song, or burst
Sublime of instrumental harmony,
To glorify the Eternal! What if these
Did never break the stillness that prevails
Here, — if the solemn nightingale be mute,
And the soft woodlark here did never chant
Her vespers, — Nature fails not to provide
Impulse and utterance. The whispering air   1170
Sends inspiration from the shadowy heights,
And blind recesses of the caverned rocks;
The little rills, and waters numberless,
Inaudible by daylight, blend their notes
With the loud streams; and often, at the hour
When issue forth the first pale stars, is heard,
Within the circuit of this fabric huge,
One voice — the solitary raven, flying
Athwart the concave of the dark blue dome,
Unseen, perchance above all power of sight —   1180
An iron knell! with echoes from afar
Faint — and still fainter — as the cry, with which
The wanderer accompanies her flight
Through the calm region, fades upon the ear,
Diminishing by distance till it seemed
To expire; yet from the abyss is caught again,
And yet again recovered!
                    But descending
From these imaginative heights, that yield
Far-stretching views into eternity,
Acknowledge that to Nature's humbler power   1190
Your cherished sullenness is forced to bend
Even here, where her amenities are sown
With sparing hand. Then trust yourself abroad
To range her blooming bowers, and spacious fields,
Where on the labours of the happy throng
She smiles, including in her wide embrace
City, and town, and tower, — and sea with ships

Sprinkled; – be our Companion while we track
Her rivers populous with gliding life;
While, free as air, o'er printless sands we march,   1200
Or pierce the gloom of her majestic woods;
Roaming, or resting under grateful shade
In peace and meditative cheerfulness;
Where living things, and things inanimate,
Do speak, at Heaven's command, to eye and ear,
And speak to social reason's inner sense,
With inarticulate language.

For, the Man –
Who, in this spirit, communes with the Forms
Of Nature, who with understanding heart   1210
Both knows and loves such objects as excite
No morbid passions, no disquietude,
No vengeance, and no hatred – needs must feel
The joy of that pure principle of love
So deeply, that, unsatisfied with aught
Less pure and exquisite, he cannot choose
But seek for objects of a kindred love
In fellow-natures and a kindred joy.
Accordingly he by degrees perceives
His feelings of aversion softened down;   1220
A holy tenderness pervade his frame.
His sanity of reason not impaired,
Say rather, all his thoughts now flowing clear,
From a clear fountain flowing, he looks round
And seeks for good; and finds the good he seeks:
Until abhorrence and contempt are things
He only knows by name; and, if he hear,
From other mouths, the language which they speak,
He is compassionate; and has no thought,
No feeling, which can overcome his love.*   1230
From the edition of 1850

---

*The Wanderer's invitation to make one's life and the world an extension
of creative imagination, *an excursion*, recalls eighteenth-century ideas of
motion, and suggests the source in theories of imagination of Romantic
cosmic socialism. Ed.

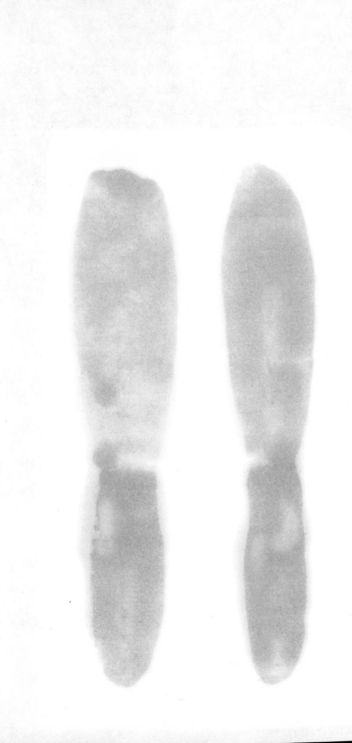